GOOSE GREEN

By the same author:

Bring Me the Arse of Saddam
Fighting for Queen and Country
No Fear
Gun for Hire
Terminal Velocity

Nigel 'Spud' Ely served in 2 Para as a private soldier and was later one of the youngest to pass Selection into 22 SAS. During the Falklands War he was on the first landing craft to hit the beach at San Carlos and was point man for the battle for Goose Green. He went on to fight in 2 Para's second major engagement, the battle for Wireless Ridge (2 Para was the only unit to fight two battles in the Falklands campaign) and as the firing died down, he and his comrades found themselves rapidly advancing into Port Stanley. So 2 Para became the first unit of the Task Force into the islands' capital, where they took the unofficial Argentine surrender. After leaving the British Army he worked as a military adviser for the British Government and a war photojournalist, and became a bestselling author.

GOOSE GREEN

The decisive battle of the Falklands War
– by the British troops who fought it

NIGEL ELY

JB

First published in the UK by John Blake Publishing
an imprint of Bonnier Books UK
4th Floor, Victoria House
Bloomsbury Square
London WC1B 4DA
England

Owned by Bonnier Books
Sveavägen 56, Stockholm, Sweden

www.facebook.com/johnblakebooks
twitter.com/jblakebooks

First published in hardback and trade paperback in 2022

Hardback ISBN: 978-1-78946-559-4
Paperback ISBN: 978-1-78946-554-9
Trade paperback: 978-1-78946-544-0
Ebook ISBN: 978-1-78946-560-0
Audiobook ISBN: 978-1-78946-545-7

British Library Cataloguing-in-Publication Data:

A CIP catalogue record for this book is available from the British Library.

Design by www.envydesign.co.uk
Map artwork by Envy Design Ltd

Printed and bound in Great Britain by Clays Ltd, Elcograf S.p.A

1 3 5 7 9 10 8 6 4 2

FSC MIX
Paper from
responsible sources
FSC® C018072
www.fsc.org

John Blake Publishing is an imprint of Bonnier Books UK
www.bonnierbooks.co.uk

This book is dedicated to my late brother Clive, without whose persistent encouragement to memorialise Goose Green, the following voices may never have left the field of battle. His spirit, his awe-inspiring courage through life, and his ability to think only of the positive, is truly embodied in this book.

1957–2017

CONTENTS

AUTHOR'S NOTE

Freedom is not free. It has to be paid for, and our freedom depends on our ability to defend it. In the case of the 119 civilians held hostage by the vicious Argentine junta in such inhumane squalor in one single room at the settlement of Goose Green during the Falklands War of 1982, the task fell on the shoulders of the 2nd Battalion the Parachute Regiment to take back their freedom, and to do it with force if necessary.

There was a time when we did extraordinary things. This book has not been easy to write. It has opened old wounds, as I knew it would. At times, it has drained me of all emotion. It has exposed me to the fragilities of war. It has put me in front of my mentors, baby-faced, eighteen-year-old boys, now old warriors and brothers-in-arms from across the Armed Forces and Merchant Navy, many of whom I left on the battlefields of Goose Green and Wireless Ridge back in the spring and summer of 1982. A lifetime later, I contacted them to ask if I could awaken a part of their memory that they would probably like to keep tightly shut, and could I share those memories with the world? A big ask, I can tell you!

I started off with the friends with whom I had kept in touch, and then as their stories opened up, my journey took me across our great nation to so many others that I had never met, or knew of back then, and theirs are some of the most powerful yet untold experiences I have ever heard. Some shocked me, some had me in tears of laughter, and others filled me with such sadness and fear. Those looking for the blood and guts of a war story across these pages will not find it, for that you need to look to my earlier book *Fighting for Queen and Country*, but if there is ever such a thing as a beautiful war story from the battlefield, I think I discovered one or two for this book.

My old SAS training officer, Major Paddy Baker, once said, 'Gentlemen, be aware of journalists, they are an anathema to soldiers.' He was of course referring to the regular sighting of journalists lurking around the pubs of Hereford, home to the SAS, ears and eyes wide open in the vain hope of gathering a secret or two from the drunken warfighter, which in my experience never happened. I mention this, because in my lifetime, I too have been a war journalist, but I have also been a Para and an SAS man, and was point man for the battle for Goose Green. This rare sequence of career choice, luck and timing, probably qualifies me as well as any to compile such a book. The well-respected historian – and my dear friend – the late Max Arthur (RIP May 2019), said to me upon my writing the screenplay for a film titled *Goose Green*, and what is now this book, 'Spud, old darling, I may now just consider you a military historian.' But I fear it takes more than sharing a few beers with some old warriors to warrant such a title.

The military theorist and historian Sir Basil Liddell Hart wrote in 1930:

The historian's rightful task is to distil experience for future generations, not to distil it like a drug. Having fulfilled his task to the best of his ability, and honesty, he has fulfilled his purpose. He would be a rash optimist if he believed that the next generations would trouble to absorb the warning. History at least teaches the historian a lesson.

In creating this book I have interviewed 114 veterans, which include 14 crew of the MV *Norland* and Falkland Islanders all between June 2017 and January 2022. Among the soldiers, I have only interviewed from the rank of captain down. This is deliberate, my choice, because this is generally where the up-front and personal stuff takes place; the rifle company commanders, the majors, have had their stories told many times before, and quite rightly so,. The one exception to my rule is Major Chris Keeble, who so gallantly took over command of 2 Para after Colonel H Jones was killed. This book would not be complete without his contribution and his quite brazen yet brave Argentine surrender document, which he drafted during a lull in the battle on the night of the May 28.

Of the 114 interviews, 104 were recorded face to face and 6 via telephone because of COVID; only 4 were written testimonials, those of Steve Tuffen, Paul Bishop, Ken Raynor and Bill Bentley. The latter wrote his in 1997 for personal reasons, and I have spoken to all four face to face for clarification.

The book runs in chronological order, and as I was transcribing, I retained certain contributors' vernacular because it truly adds to the grittiness of their story, so please do not expect a polished effort of academia; I've never been an armchair soldier, but I was certainly impressed to find that the expletives were kept to a minimum. Maybe age has mellowed us all.

Equally, it became apparent that many of the soldiers who fought at Goose Green had no idea of what their mates were doing, although they were no more than a few metres away from each other. Yet for the most part, I have been able to corroborate these similar stories, to my admiration of the contributors, and only a handful are *edited* verbatim accounts – some Scots and Geordie accents are particularly hard to translate, and of course, profanity has always been part of a soldier's vocab.

Lastly, I hope that you, the reader, can take something from these experiences, while for my part they could be taken from any modern battle; only the names change. And, as a soldier and veteran, I believe they need to be passed on and never forgotten.

Utrinque Paratus.

ROLL OF HONOUR

Officers and men of the 2nd Battalion, the Parachute Regiment killed in action on the Falkland Islands:

Lieutenant-Colonel H. Jones OBE	Commanding Officer
Captain C. Dent	2IC A Company
Captain D. Wood	Adjutant
Lieutenant J. A. Barry	D Company
Colour Sergeant G. P. M. Findlay	A Company
Corporal D. Hardman	A Company
Corporal S. R Prior	A Company
Corporal P. S. Sullivan	D Company
Lance Corporal G. D. Bingley	D Company
Lance Corporal A. Cork	D Company
Lance Corporal N. R. Smith	D Company
Private S. J. Dixon	D Company
Private M. W. Fletcher	D Company
Private M. H. Holman-Smith	C Company
Private S. Illingsworth	B Company

GOOSE GREEN

Private T. Mechan	D Company
Private D. A. Parr	D Company
Private P. Slough	D Company

Attached arms

Lieutenant R. J. Nunn RM	3 Commando Brigade Air Squadron
Corporal D. Melia	Royal Engineers

INTRODUCTION

David Norris, general news reporter, Daily Mail, *attached 2 Para. (This copy was written on the day of the surrender at Goose Green and has not been published until now.)*

It began when we waded in darkness the one hundred yards to a hostile shore – an eerie background of yelping dogs breaking the total silence – and ended a lifetime of twenty-four days later in the still-smouldering outskirts of Port Stanley.

I 'tabbed' it from one end of East Falkland to the other with the men I am now proud to call my friends – the magnificent Paras, whose kindness and generosity I will never forget: whose courage I will never cease to admire: whose special brand of humour lightened some of the hardest moments of my life. If I sound partisan and totally devoid of journalistic impartiality, then let me declare my interest now.

In the mud and the icy cold of the dangerous Falklands Campaign, where many of my friends lost their lives, the Second Battalion, The

Parachute Regiment became like a family to me. And I claimed my share of the fierce, protective loyalty which touches everyone, from the humble Tom to the Commanding Officer: from the highly trained, superbly fit and efficient to the militarily inept civilian reporter, struggling with his kit through clinging peat bog and across rainswept mountain.

Throughout the day Colonel 'H' Jones – I do know his name but he preferred to be called H – an extrovert Old Etonian who was to die, submachine gun blazing, on that same terrible hill of gorse – waited impatiently for the signal to go. 'I'm going to phone Maggie, that's what I'll do. I'll tell her the Paras are ready to – she'll understand.'

He knew his beloved 2 Para were set to lead the land assault and he paced about, not understanding why the green light had not been given. As it turned out, the Royal Navy, for some reason or other, held up for seven hours the signal telling us that Operation Corporate was to go ahead. That night HMS *Broadsword* came alongside to give us the message, just as the brash Colonel H was queuing with his men at the self-service cafeteria.

As the MV *Norland* turned left at Point Oscar to creep cautiously towards the San Carlos inlet, we were mustering, each complete with two 24-hour ration packs. In the Continental Lounge assault station, backs bent under heavy packs, sweltering in our steel helmets, combat smocks and layers of clothing.

From the brightly lit lounge, dense with the smoke of last-minute cigarettes, we filed into the darkness of the car decks, each man holding on to the one in front, dim red lights flickering, the hum of ship's engines providing a background to the echoing tape of 'The Ride of the Valkyries'.

They are etched on my mind forever – those terrible photographic images of war: the silver and gold cascade of triple-A shells exploding around us before the dawn of Goose Green – the smell of it will always be with me, an officer said – and the stretcher bearers silhouetted in the dusk against the billowing smoke and flames: a soon-to-be-killed colonel sharing with me the hard floor of a remote house and talking of the battle to come: shivering prisoners lined up on a beach, whimpering and crossing themselves: lines of stiff Argentine corpses, entrails spilling from shattered stomachs and a Para sergeant muttering, 'Why doesn't someone take them away. For God's sake, take them away.'

Those are the images which will stay on my mind. It is more difficult to document the hard facts of the campaign in military fashion – for much of it has blurred into a crazy kaleidoscope of cold days and nights, boredom and blinding fear. But, as far as I can remember, this is how it was: this is my Falklands lifetime.

On the morning of D-Day, we awoke to the tannoyed strains of 'The Ride of the Valkyries', the Paras' regimental march. We were still in the incongruous surroundings of the North Sea car ferry *Norland*, with its nightclubs and wall advertisements for tours of the Flanders battlefields.

It is, the voice of reason will say, most unfair. But to me there will always now be two completely separate military entities – the Paras and the 'hats', those less fortunate people who make up the rest of the British Army.

I have felt their pride in their battles won. Their sadness at comrades lost: shared their food, cigarettes, life-giving hot brews – their dreams of bacon-and-egg breakfasts and evenings of draught Guinness. We kept each other going with jokes, brews and cigarettes through the deathly cold nights in the open without sleeping bags, and revelled in the occasional luxury of a night under cover in a wool shed or remote building.

When you are huddled together for warmth in a two-foot shell scrape, listening to the awful whistle and crash of mortar shells falling around you, there are only friends and enemies: only those who will help keep you alive and those who want to kill you. There is a terrible beauty in the simplicity of it all. Polite London conversations over the rights and wrongs of Argentina's claim to the Malvinas are ghosts from a remote past. 'Let's waste the bastards,' someone says – and when it really happens, when you see poor teenage conscripts run screaming and on fire from their shattered trenches – there is, forgive me for saying it, a sense of almost brutal satisfaction. The horror that should be in your mind is not there. Instead there is first a sense of relief that it is them not you, and secondly, a sense of sweet revenge. I can only be honest with myself. That is what I felt.

Four days on Mount Sussex and the first cases of trench foot and frostbite were appearing. 'We've got to get going,' says Colonel H, impatient for action. 'It's another Anzio,' an officer complained. 'The road to Rome is open and we are still on the beachhead.'

Colonel H got his wish. We were about to move on Goose Green. We left the smoking devastation of San Carlos inlet, the graveyard of so many of Her Majesty's ships, and headed off under cover of darkness in the now familiar 'Para snake', a single file of men walking in silence across the treacherous tufts of grass and hidden crevasses.

Camilla Creek House, six miles away, was our staging post – an isolated wooden building, filled with debris left behind by Argentine soldiers – prayer sheets in Spanish littered the bare floors. Three forlorn prisoners were brought in, hands on head, caught by our recce platoon, their officer was clutching a tub of Kraft margarine, apparently their only rations.

'Have you heard the BBC?' shouted Colonel H. 'John Nott has given away our position. If any of my boys die, I will take him to court for manslaughter.' We moved from the house into a nearby gully to shelter from the expected Argentinian air attack – driven away from our dry refuge by the British defence secretary.

'Does Maggie Thatcher know what she has done to us?' asked one incredulous officer. 'Surely not. Surely she could not have known.'

Just before dusk we crouched in a gully as the Colonel held his 'O' group, his briefing for the battle. Officers scribbled down map references for the minefield, the gorse ridge that would lead us to the Argentinian positions, and the start-line – the place where the shooting would begin.

Then they gave their own reports, on ammunition and manpower. 'A Company has forty rounds of illume [illumination rounds], but no smoke'; 'D Company needs more tracer'.

Captain Steve Hughes, twenty-five and new to the armed forces, had been boning up on battle injuries. A civilian doctor, he was soon to mastermind, briskly and efficiently, the evacuation and treatment of casualties. 'We need casevac helicopters available, here, here, and here,' he told the Colonel.

H summed up in his own inimitable fashion. 'That's the plan. If anyone has a better idea and decides to change it, then for God's sake let me know first. Don't be frightened of brassing [killing] any Argie patrols you come across on the way. They will probably think it is just another small SAS operation. If you see them – brass them.'

We crept back after darkness and slept fitfully. 'By God, if we pull it off, we can whistle up a few landing craft and take off to Stanley,' a sleepless and tireless H told me.

Just before we formed up in the early hours of the morning to move off in our Para snake for the six-mile walk to Goose Green, he told me and a fellow reporter, 'Go with the battalion main. You will be just behind the forward companies and you will see everything, but with any luck you won't get killed.' It was the last I saw of him.

Pebble
Island

Port Howard

**WEST
FALKLAND**

King George
Bay

Swan
Island

Fox Bay

Falkland Sound

N

Speedwell
Island

Eagle Passage

George Island

SCALE OF MILES

0   10   20

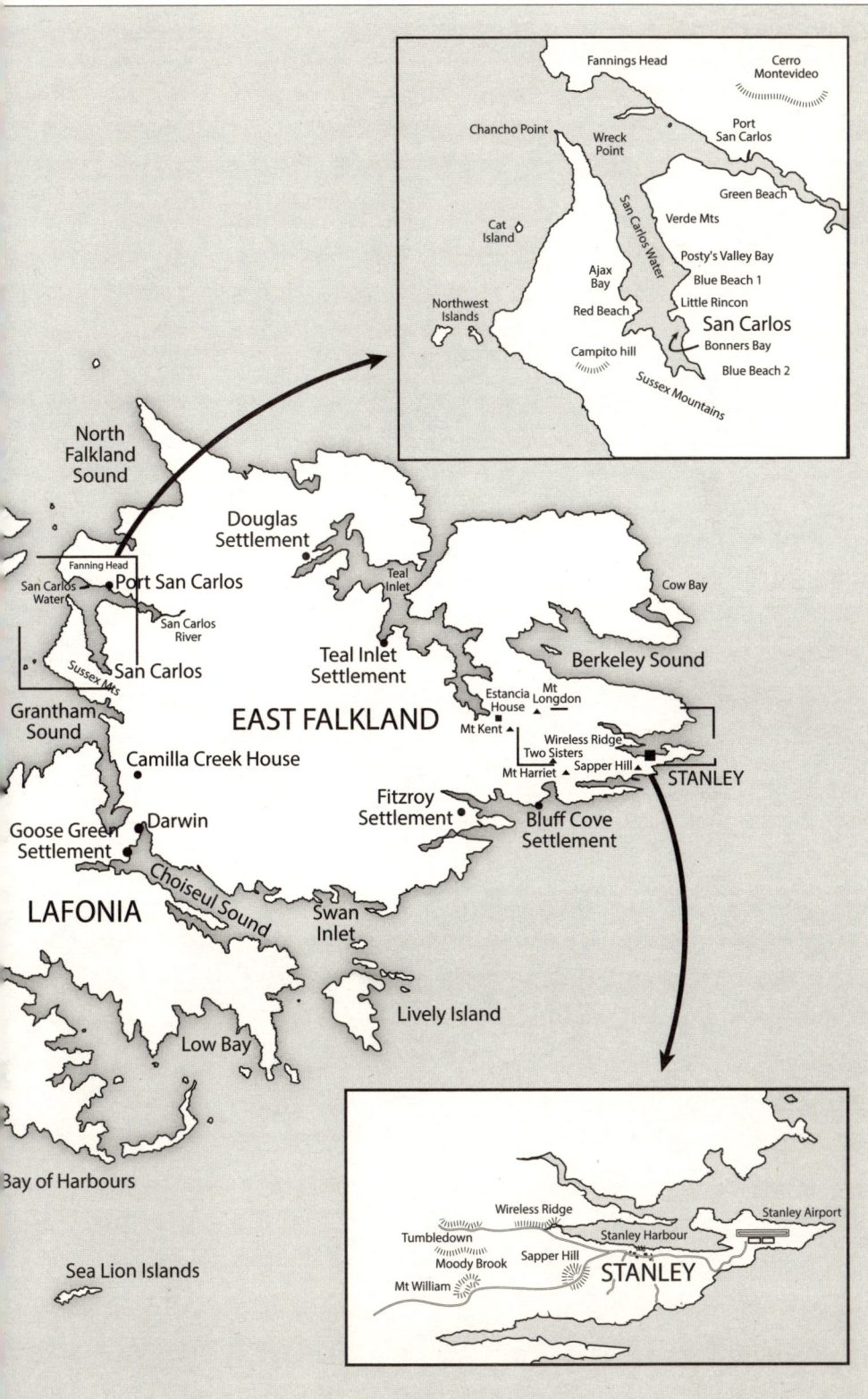

Fannings Head
Cerro Montevideo
Chancho Point
Wreck Point
Port San Carlos
San Carlos Water
Green Beach
Cat Island
Verde Mts
Posty's Valley Bay
Ajax Bay
Blue Beach 1
Little Rincon
Northwest Islands
Red Beach
San Carlos
Bonners Bay
Campito hill
Blue Beach 2
Sussex Mountains

North Falkland Sound
Douglas Settlement
Teal Inlet
Cow Bay
Fanning Head
Port San Carlos
San Carlos Water
San Carlos River
Berkeley Sound
Teal Inlet Settlement
San Carlos
Sussex Mts
Estancia House
Mt Longdon
EAST FALKLAND
Mt Kent
Grantham Sound
Wireless Ridge
Two Sisters
Sapper Hill
Camilla Creek House
Mt Harriet
STANLEY
Goose Green Settlement
Darwin
Fitzroy Settlement
Bluff Cove Settlement
LAFONIA
Choiseul Sound
Swan Inlet
Lively Island
Low Bay
Bay of Harbours
Sea Lion Islands

Wireless Ridge
Tumbledown
Stanley Airport
Stanley Harbour
Moody Brook
Sapper Hill
Mt William
STANLEY

PROLOGUE

30 April 1982
Brian Lavender, radio officer, MV Norland

Brian wrote in his log: Just off Madeira. Pretty normal day, getting warmer so move into greys [uniform]. Derek Begg [3rd Engineer] reckons he can get out of engine room now in 40 seconds! Went sunbathing in afternoon. Shooting practice for troops off the stern. Helicopter visit from [HMS] *Intrepid* at 10:00, landed on new flight deck fwd [forward] of funnel. Quiet evening, turned in around midnight.

Nigel Ely: Some time later on the same day at dark o'clock, on board HMS *Hermes* somewhere inside the Falkland Islands 200-mile Exclusion Zone, the very first SAS patrols were getting ready to be inserted around Goose Green.

GOOSE GREEN

30 April 1982
A 22 SAS call sign

Eventually we get the nod to go. We grab our kit and start to make our way up to the flight deck where a Sea King was waiting. We had so much kit it was fuckin' awkward, and heavy too, so we were told to use this big lift. It looked like the biggest lift in the world, a square platform designed to take aircraft up and down from the flight deck. It was huge, so as we were going up, and I didn't realise this incident until after the war, there was a Harrier with the pilot, I presumed, because he was standing by the said Harrier in full pilot gear sporting a big shitty grin and pointing to a big hole in the tail fin. He was surrounded by a load of media types with cameras and all the rest of it, clicking away.

The Harrier had attacked Stanley airfield and got twatted, and now this pilot was telling his story to a very attentive audience. Yet, while they were fixated by the pilot's daring tale, they missed their chance to see the first bunch of SAS men to be deployed behind enemy lines for a generation, because they all had their backs to the lift. If just one had turned around, they would have seen this motley crew of long-haired, Fu Manchu moustaches, carrying an array of strange-looking weapons and bombs, ha-ha! I often think about that moment, as it was really funny at the time, and still is. Great memories.

So, the lift kept going up and up until we arrived into the fresh night air. There was a Sea King sitting silently, engines off with only its rotors flapping in the wind. One at a time we offered our bergens up to the loadie, who looked like he'd have a hernia if he picked another one up, they were that heavy, so we gave him a hand to stash them. They were stashed in sequence, as not all of us were getting off at the same drop-off point.

We were initially told we'd be out on the ground for fourteen days, but we couldn't have carried fourteen days' rations, not even Mr Schwarzenegger could have picked that lot up, so we carried about five days, along with all the ops kit, even chicken wire, but strangely, no claymores! We all opted to carry more ammo, less food.

The deck lights were on but it was relatively dark about the chopper, and as I got in on the port side, whatever lights were on, went out, so it was now pitch black apart from the internal red tactical lights of the Sea King. I went immediately right and moved down the aircraft, but was a bit surprised to see four blokes already in the chopper up front. I thought, *what the fuck are they doing?* The loadie went around checking stuff and it was then I saw the face of one of these blokes! It was an SBS guy I knew from another operation two years back, and I wished I'd never seen his face, because of OPSEC [operational security – need to know].

Let's be clear, we were told that the Argies at that time had excellent DF and EW kit [direction-finding, electronic warfare equipment], and all this latest DF kit from Germany was very good. And don't forget they [the junta] were carrying out a counter-terrorist war against their own people back in Argentina too, so they were really into it. Ipso facto, I just didn't wanna know this guy, and I certainly wasn't going to acknowledge him. It's a Regiment thing, even on the ship we never discussed with any other patrols their task or our operations. 'Oh, where you going?' and stuff like that, it was plain basic SOP [Standard Operating Procedure]. You take the piss out of each other's patrols, sure, but never discuss a task or shit like that.

So, the chopper starts its engine and we're about to take off when the boss man comes in and gives it the 'Okay, boys,' has a word, then gets off. The loadie gives us the thumbs up, and flashes his light to make sure all of us got his message about take-off. We look away from the four faces up front, because there was a good chance we may get captured. The Argies had 16,000-odd troops deployed on the islands and the Int was telling us they were reinforcing daily, so if, God forbid, we got captured and they started twisting your testicles and giving you some 240 volts, you're gonna tell 'em stuff, and I didn't want tell 'em jack. There are very few people who don't tell. Like the White Rabbit, 'Tommy' Yeo-Thomas GC, the Second World War SOE [Special Operations Executive] captured and imprisoned by the Gestapo. They beat his bollocks flat with a truncheon, yet he had his faith to keep him silent, and I'm not sure the Argies would be that gentle; we knew they hadn't in the recent past, because there were those shocking stories coming out about the 'disappeared', the thousands and thousands of Argentinians who had gone missing, taken by the junta, which were now just filtering down to us troops. But, of course, our Government via the Foreign Office knew all about this shit well before the Argies started their invasion.

1 May 1982
Brian Lavender, radio officer MV Norland

Quite a lot of helicopter activity this morning. Captain Ellerby [Captain of MV *Norland*] did a transfer in a Wessex [helicopter] to HMS *Intrepid*. In the evening we were invited for drinks with the Para officers in the Snug Bar.

1 May 1982
A 22 SAS call sign

It seemed we were on the chopper for hours. It must have been carrying a large fuel bladder, but I don't recall seeing it. When we eventually got over land, the pilot started to make dummy drops, landing and taking off again in case the Argies were in that particular area. So, we did several of these drops and eventually it was my time for drop-off. All four of us got out and started to tab off away from the actual direction we wanted to go, put a loop in and observed our back track to see if any Argies had spotted us. We lay there for about thirty-odd minutes; no one was following, so we headed off in roughly the direction we wanted to go. A sort of reciprocal course you know, just off line.

Then we picked a place to have a kip. It was up quite high and away from the water table, rocky, by a few gorse bushes, so we snuggled in there and got our heads down. Then, the following night we pushed off; the ground was difficult, it made the going so hard you couldn't imagine. The wind and the rain was a shocker, an absolute ball-breaker, but we carried on towards our first task, which would eventually take us to Goose Green.

1

WHO ARE THE PARAS?

Para this and Para that, and Para go away.
Special rights for Paras when the bullets want to play.
GRAFFITI ON THE TOILET WALL OF THE
GLOBETROTTER PUB, ALDERSHOT, MARCH 1982[1]

Nigel Ely: Yes, it is fair to say the Paras aren't much liked by the rest of the British Army. In fact, I'd go so far as to say, in my day, we were hated as much as the enemy revered us. Yes, we are a cocky lot, loud, sometimes punchy and as a journalist once said, 'Paras come with a huge propensity for violence.' A bit strong, I thought, so I would like to add an edit – insert *controlled* after *for* – and this is born out of an esprit de corps forged by a level of physical fitness and infantry skills unattained by any other unit in the British Army, all bar the SAS perhaps.

Field Marshal Viscount Montgomery of Alamein, Colonel Commandant, The Parachute Regiment

What manner of men are these who wear the maroon berets? They are firstly all volunteers, and are then toughened by physical training. As a result, they have that infectious optimism and that offensive

---

1 A parody of Kipling's poem 'Tommy' (1890).

eagerness which comes from well-being. They have 'jumped' from the air and by doing so have conquered fear. Their duty lies in the van of the battle; they are proud of this honour; and have never failed in any task. They have the highest standards in all things, whether it be skill in battle or smartness in the execution of all peace-time duties. They have shown themselves to be as tenacious and determined in defence as they are courageous in attack. They are, in fact, men apart – every man an emperor.

Private Nigel Ely, Recce Platoon 2 Para

I was born into a white, working-class family from London's East End, and if one wanted to categorise me into a social class, you can call me working class. I call myself working class. I joined the Parachute Regiment as a Tom, Para slang for a private soldier. I was posted to 4 Platoon B Company 2 Para in Berlin.

After Berlin the battalion was posted to Northern Ireland [NI] for a two-year tour, where I served in 4 Platoon, then a stint in the battalion Intelligence Cell, which gave me a completely different and much fuller perspective of that war. After NI in 1981, the battalion returned back to its UK barracks in Aldershot, Hampshire. I then applied for, and passed, the selection course into Colonel H Jones's newly re-formed Pathfinders, C (Bruneval) Company; the Parachute Regiment's SAS equivalent.

I served with many Toms from all different backgrounds and persuasions. For example, during my time in the Paras I served with a ballet dancer, a Ugandan refugee,[2] an axe murderer (but he got kicked out), a classically trained musician, and a public-school boy who joined as a Tom and stayed a Tom and who had gone to school with Prince Andrew. But predominately, us Toms were

---

2 In 1972, Idi Amin, the President of Uganda, ordered the expulsion of his country's 60,000 Asian minority giving them 90 days to leave: 27,000 settled in the UK.

working class, mainly from up North, with a disproportionate number of warrior Celts.

I joined up at the same Army recruiting office as a lad called Irwin Eversley in Blackheath, London. Our dates of birth are identical, in fact, our joining up experiences are almost identical too, yet three years apart. I never met Irwin until I was in Battalion. Strangely, we both tried to join the Royal Marines first, only because of the Royal Marines' 'enticing' recruiting campaign posters! Both of us passed the entrance exam, both were turned down. We were also both about to get into serious criminal nonsense.

I had a police record, so the Marines said, 'No,' and time was not on Irwin's side; we both needed to get away from our environments. I asked the Royal Marine recruiting sergeant what my options were, and he said quite arrogantly, 'Go next door and join the Paras, they'll have you.' At that time, the Army and Royal Navy recruiting offices were next door together on Blackheath High Street. So, the Paras took us both.

Private Irwin Eversley, GPMG gunner, 2 Platoon A Company 2 Para

I was a black boy at an approved school for boys and I lived in Deptford, South London, so I could take all the shit the Paras wanted to throw. It was normal to me. They called me Chalky Eversley, but it didn't bother me. They called other non-white blokes the same, like Spick Arbino or Chalky White. I came to the UK in 1965 from Barbados and I hated it. You see, in the morning back home, I used to get up, find a chicken egg for breakfast, go in the sea a hundred yards, and that was my life as a kid.

The Royal Marine PR recruiting was so good, after reading all this crap in the books about them, I wanted to join the Marines, so off I went to the Royal Navy recruiting office in Blackheath. The recruiting sergeant says, 'Irwin, we're not taking on anyone for the next two months,' so I thought, *I have to get out of here*, because I was hanging around with the *boys*, all the white boys, and they were the villains and that. I used to knock about with that lot, but I knew it was not for me.

I'd done my time in an approved school, because I used to run away from home. Before I came here, I had the freedom of the world, used to go to the beach, fish, it was good, then I came here, and it was, you will do this and you will do that, and my old man was a bit of a bastard, you know, 'Come here,' shirt and belt off ready for a thrashing and all that, but it stopped when I got to about fifteen and started hanging around with the Peckham boys – I was too big.

Two months was a long time to wait as I had to get out of Deptford, so I went next door to the Army and joined the Paras. I wasn't quite sure about that, because I wanted to be a PTI [Physical Training Instructor] and I knew I was a good runner, good at 800 and 1500 metres and I was good at judo, I was a pretty good all-rounder even though I smoked a bit of blow. When it came to sign for the Paras, the recruiter, not a Para, says. 'You don't want to join the Paras, they're all thick.' I chuckled, and then he reaffirmed, 'Paras are thick, and you want to be a PTI!' I still signed to join the Paras.

When I was sent to do the basic three-day Army selection process up at Sutton Coldfield, I passed the BFT [battle fitness test] quite comfortably because of this fat PTI. I thought, *a PTI? Just look at you, you fat bastard!* Later on, we were all in an office with the instructors who all had their boots up on the desk, you know waffling to us, sort of big-timing it, when this bloke walks through the door and he had a maroon beret on, a Paratrooper. Suddenly the instructors all jumped up and flapped around in a total panic and that's what confirmed my choice. I wanted to be that bloke.

As a black guy, joining up in the 1980s was an experience.

Racism, name-calling stuff like that, but there was one horrible cunt. One day I was on the back of a wagon, we'd been out training or somewhere up in Brecon, but my first instructor/staff, a lovely guy, was Al Slater, who later got killed serving with the SAS. I got the *nigger* crack, or whatever it was, by this horrible cunt of an instructor and then Al stepped in and it never happened again.

Nigel Ely: Below is Paul Bishop's brilliant account of his experience while trying to get into the Paras, and he sums it all up quite neatly as to why the Parachute Regiment is, pound for pound, the best fighting force in the world.

Lance Corporal Paul Bishop, 6 Platoon B Company 2 Para

I'm a working-class lad from Stoke. Pre-Parachute Selection (P Company) is the selection process that every Parachute Regiment recruit and potential member of Airborne Forces must undertake. It was to be our biggest test. It is a series of physical tests over three days. I was very fit then and raring to go. I could not believe it when I was put on a twenty-four-hour guard duty the Sunday before the tests started, so I had very little sleep that night.

On the first day we embarked on the 10-mile march carrying full equipment, thirty-five pounds plus rifle. Easy for me, I was good at tabbing as it's called. Tabbing stands for Tactical Advance to Battle; it also stands for, march and run as fast as you can until your legs and lungs are burning and you just want to lie down and die![3]

The next test was one minute of milling. This is a form of fighting with boxing gloves, no head guard and no gum shield. The aim of milling is to show controlled aggression. I was paired up against Karl.

---

3 Some say the 10-miler came from when 2 Para jumped in at Arnhem. It was 10 miles from their DZ (drop zone) to their objective, the road bridge at Arnhem.

This fellow was the ex-junior Para champion boxer. I thought, *this one might hurt a bit.* Just before entering the ring, his corporal said to me, 'You're gonna get knocked out, Bishop,' and I thought, *he's probably right. I wonder if I could get away with kicking him in the balls!*

Ding, ding, time to punch, and straight *whack, whack,* Karl was all over me like a nasty rash. He was boxing me, I caught him with two or three, then I saw stars for the first time. He jabbed me in the guts. I crumpled to the mat, winded, on one knee. The instructor stopped the fight. He gave Karl a good telling off, then he told him to stop boxing and carry on milling. The fight continued. I went for it non-stop. We stood toe to toe for the rest of the bout. Lungs and arms burning, now my legs were like jelly and my head was spinning.

Ding, ding, ding, the bell tolled. Thank fuck for that. The referee held our arms and turned to the three officers who were the judges. *I hope I haven't let myself down*, I thought. I stood there shaking with the adrenalin screaming through my body, battered and bleeding.

'Excellent fight. That was good controlled aggression,' said the officer. A draw was announced. Easy, this P Company is, I whispered to myself.

I got through the remaining tests without too much trouble. When my name was called out at the final parade, 'Bishop! Pass!' I was ecstatic. This to me was the only difficult hurdle. All I had to do now was Advanced Wales, three weeks' advanced field training in Brecon, South Wales.

It was a freezing cold day in March 1978 as we boarded the 4-ton trucks in Aldershot. Four hours later we arrived at Dering Lines, the Infantry Battle School, at Brecon. I found advanced field training harder than I expected. I was still only seventeen and my body, although I felt super fit, was not fully developed. I passed Advanced Wales. Last phase, parachute training.

Holiday time now. We were all going on a spring parachuting holiday at RAF Brize Norton in Oxfordshire. We got to Brize some time in April 1978. Thank fuck the winter was over, as I've always been a bit of a summer soldier. One thing about operating in hot climates is that you can always find shade. In cold climates, it's hard to stay warm and find shelter. Brize Norton Number 1 Parachute Training School in Oxfordshire was a doddle. The PJIs [RAF parachute jump instructors] treated the platoon like human beings. They would actually talk to us. I could not believe it. We were so used to being shouted at from dawn till dusk by our corporals. HRH Prince Charles was attending Brize Norton doing his parachute training. He had recently been appointed Colonel-in-Chief of the Parachute Regiment, so fair play to him, he decided to earn his Para wings. Ten recruits were selected to train with him as part of this team.

In the corner of the parachute training hangar sat the RAF's rest room. Here the PJIs took their tea breaks during the day. During one tea break in the morning, one recruit from the team was asked by Prince Charles, 'Is there anything else you chaps want?'

'Some bacon sandwiches would go down well, sir,' came a cheeky reply.

Prince Charles turned to the regimental sergeant major and said, 'RSM, the men are hungry, can you oblige?'

One of the team told me the RSM went a purple colour and marched out, and later he looked really pissed off at having to serve up bacon butties to the blokes. After the feast, Prince Charles left the tea room, and the RSM then gave us all the biggest bollocking of our careers so far!

We continued on with the parachute ground training. We were jumping off high and low ramps, practising forward, side and backward landings. It was very tiring: you had to be fit to parachute. After two weeks of training, the big day arrived. We had to do our first parachute jump. It was a warm spring day in April 1978.

I hadn't slept much the night before, as I was very apprehensive yet strangely excited. Every time I thought about the jump, butterflies danced around my guts. We all jumped aboard the green RAF bus and sped out towards Weston on the Green DZ [Drop Zone]. As the bus neared the DZ, the mood on board turned into a serious one. I had never heard the lads so quiet. I made a quick joke, but nobody laughed.

The first jump, or to use the correct term, descent, was carried out from a tethered Second World War barrage balloon from a height of 800 feet. She wandered from side to side like a big grey sausage. I whispered to myself, 'I am going to do this. I'm not going to let my father and brother down.' I was shitting myself.

We all gingerly strolled towards the PJI. He gave us a briefing on the drills we needed to do in the balloon cage. He discussed the exit, descent, and landing – the landing is the hardest part of military parachuting. I don't recall much of what he said to us, as the adrenalin was already running through me. Knowledge Dispels Fear is the motto of the Number One Parachute Training School. I hoped that was going to be the case right now!

We'd had the parachuting drills hammered into us for the last two weeks and now we were ready to take the first step into becoming an Airborne Warrior. It was time to draw and fit the two parachutes we were going to wear. For this jump we had the new PX Mk 5 harnesses. This harness had two quick-release handles. One of these handles was to be pulled after landing, thus enabling the canopy of the parachute to deflate quickly.

The Mk 5 was a real bitch to fit. The parachute had to be fitted really high up on your back. Two back straps were then pulled down very tightly. This forced the jumper into a slightly crouched forward position. The second parachute, the reserve parachute, was attached on the front by two clips, high on chest, one either side on the harness.

I sat down amongst the platoon in the grass as a skylark chattered away up above us. It was really quiet. We were put into our groups of four men, or sticks, as they are termed – a line of paratroopers getting ready to jump. I lay back watching the lads leap out into the cool blue sky. You could hear a PJI shout, 'Go!' then the chute would deploy with a ripping sound. The canopy would breathe out like a jellyfish billowing in the sea. The RAF officer was talking the new Paras through their descent and landing by shouting through his loudhailer.

'Number one, steer away, assess your drift, pull down on your rear lift webs. Get into a good tight parachuting position now, lad.' Crash! The lad smacked into the ground. Now, you are taught to try and do a textbook parachute landing. The landing should go like this: feet, outer shins, outer thighs and then with a crouched back, roll your body into the ground. This only works occasionally. During a windy landing, it goes like this: feet, arse or knees then head, then get dragged 100 metres because you are half unconscious! Fucking hilarious!

It was my turn now. Our stick of four marched across the grass towards the sausage. Tied beneath the beast was a blue wooden cage with four compartments, one for each jumper. We all staggered in, gripping nervously on to anything we could. The PJI took our static line strops, then hooked them up to a strongpoint in the middle of the cage. I thought to myself, *well, son, there is no going back now unless you refuse*. But there was no chance of that after the ten months of the shit I had been put through.

The balloon was attached to a lorry with a winch. I looked across towards the winch operator: he was a fat RAF chap, who was sat on his large arse grinning.

'Up eight-hundred, four men jumping,' the PJI barked out to Fatty, who then repeated this command. I looked around at my three fellow recruits, they all had a 1000-metre stare. The winch kicked in with a whining noise, then the cage lurched forward under

15

the grey sausage and we started to ascend. All four of us snatched hold of the wooden frame; our knuckles went white, fearing to fall out. Falling out! Fuck me, we are going to be leaping out of it in a couple of minutes, into the unknown

As the balloon ascended to the jump height, the PJI was doing his best to keep us confident and was telling jokes. I don't remember any of the jokes. I was saying to myself, do not let the family down; you will jump, just don't look down. Suddenly, the whining from the winch motor stopped. The balloon lurched forward again. The knuckles got whiter. The PJI dispatcher looked down to the ground.

'There is a blue flag, lads, you are jumping.'

The blue flag denotes it's safe to jump and the wind was okay and the DZ clear and medics at the ready! The Number One was called forward. 'Hands across your reserve parachute,' the PJI dispatcher ordered politely, followed by a loud 'Go!' I looked over the side of the cage as he dropped like a stone. The khaki mushroom opened with a slight bang, he then drifted off down towards the lush green grass.

Now it was my turn to go. I heard those dreaded words, 'Come forward, Number Two.' I staggered forward, gripping every solid object I could find. I just remember the PJI dispatcher saying, 'GO!'

I stepped off into the unknown. I looked up, watching the rigging lines deploying from the pack. They rattled against my helmet. Within two to three seconds the parachute had deployed. I had dropped 200 feet. Yippee, that's it, easy, I've done it. I looked around at the field admiring the Oxfordshire countryside, then a PJI below started gobbing off at me, 'Number Two, have you forgotten everything? You are clear of the balloon, carry on. Assess your drift and pull down on your rear lift webs.'

This technique causes the canopy of the chute literally to spill air out of its front, so it should slow down your rate of drift across the sky. This meant that I was coming in for a backwards landing. Oh shit! I said to myself. Backward landings are awkward, because you can tend to look over your shoulder on impact with the ground. This can cause the parachutist to land in a very upright position, which could cause injury.

During the last thirty feet of any jump, the ground seems to rush up at you. I looked down with my chin on my chest. I was squeezing my whole body as tight as possible; trying desperately to keep my back rounded. Like a dickhead, at the very last moment, I looked over my shoulder. BANG! Feet, arse, shoulders – I crashed into Mother Earth. Immediately I pulled on one of the lower lift webs, and the canopy sagged and collapsed, but I knew straight away I had pulled something in my back. It hurt like hell. I didn't care. I had overcome one of my fears. The fear of heights. Nothing was going to stop me now. I was going to become a Paratrooper.

We were driven back to camp. The mood on the bus had completely turned around; everyone was joking and we were all telling each other how professional we had been. No fear! My arse! A lot of brave tales were told on that bus. A lot of bravado and testosterone filled the smoky air. This was just the first of eight jumps we had to do to earn our Para wings. A few days later, it was time for our first aircraft jump. We were to jump from a Lockheed C-130 Hercules. The Hercules was known as a Herc or Fat Albert. This was my first time ever in a plane, and I was going to jump out of it!

Your second jump was to be the scariest, or so we had been told by the seasoned Paras. I would say that is true: we were all quite nervous and apprehensive as we knew what to expect.

We boarded Fat Albert on a sunny Wednesday morning. Prince Charles was on a separate aircraft. His was to follow ours some minutes later. We were told that our aircraft would go first, so that if there was any turbulence or high winds, the second plane could be informed and then it could adjust its course. There was no way the RAF would want the future king injured. *Fair enough,* I thought, *the guinea pigs are us.*

'I suppose we're expendable then?' I said to one of the RAF chappies. He scowled and said with a snigger, 'Yes, you are.'

The C-130 screamed down the runway and was soon airborne, climbing at a steep angle. Within minutes the PJI barked out, 'Prepare for action!' I stood up nervously with butterflies in my stomach. I hooked up my static line onto a strop, which is attached to the wire cable above my head, and started to check my two parachutes.

'Check equipment,' came the next order. This was the call to check your own gear again and also the man's kit in front of you. Then the PJI came along the stick and checked us all again. My mouth was completely dry; sweat poured from my brow. Was Fat Albert about to break up and crash? It was scary. The strange noises – bangs, bumps, screeches, engines roaring – and the nervous tension all added to an overwhelming need to get out of this beast and into some fresh air, asap!

'Tell off for equipment check,' was the next order. Each man shouted his number and 'Okay' to the PJI. I was Number Three. With about three minutes to go before the green light, the jump doors were pulled up. What a relief I felt as the cool air rushed in. Some lads were airsick, so the smells were marvellous: vomit, sweat, aviation gas, and fumes. With about a minute to the green light, the order came from the rear: 'Action stations!'

Everyone in the stick then shuffled towards the fresh air. I looked out of the small porthole window and through the hazy exhaust fumes I could see the Oxfordshire countryside speeding by. I saw cars moving slowly along roads, a farmer was ploughing his field. I wished I was that farmer right then, sat on his tractor. We were now at our jumping height of 800 feet.

'Red on!' then the Number One in our stick placed his arms

across his reserve parachute and was ushered into the jump door. He was held back by the PJI. I looked at his grey face then down towards his shaking legs. Mine were probably doing the same, but I don't remember.

'Green on. GO! Two, three . . .' Quick as a flash, I was in the door and out into space. A great force, the slipstream forced me sideways away from the aircraft. This was some ride. In about two seconds it was all over; you don't get any sensation of falling due to the fact that the aircraft is flying at over 120 miles per hour.

'Thank fuck for that!' I shouted into the clear air. What do I do now? Oh yes, check my canopy; all-round observation then look up to my lift webs and steer away into some clear airspace. This is very important, so that you don't get entangled with any other parachutist. Your worst fear during a military descent is what's called an air steal. The best way to describe this is that when a parachutist drifts beneath you, his canopy will steal your column of air, and this will then cause your canopy to collapse. If that happens, you drop down and bounce off the lower canopy, then the parachutist drops below, and hopefully your chute re-inflates!

The problem is, you drop at least 60 feet if you don't try and steer away as quickly as possible. The two parachutists must try to separate themselves into their own airspace. If they cannot separate themselves, the unlucky guy could drop the last several feet into the ground in record speed. Ouch!

I was now merrily drifting down towards the ground. I guess I was at about 200 feet, concentrating on a good tight position and hoping that I would not further damage my injured back. I looked across to the vehicles. A PJI was gobbing off at me again through his loudhailer. I didn't pay too much attention to his orders. Bollocks! I was pulling down on the wrong lift webs. This meant that I was increasing instead of decreasing my lateral speed across the sky. I quickly changed lift webs as I descended towards the green grass.

BANG! This time it was feet, knees, then head as I piled in. *Easy-peasy this parachuting lark*, I thought, as I was being dragged across the earth.

After a short bollocking from the PJI, I ran across to the truck to hand in my chutes. We all sat around smoking, watching the Hercules circle around again and spew out more of its young cargo. The second aircraft was spotted approaching the DZ. We knew Prince Charles was on that one and knew him to be Number One, that's the first jumper out of the door, because there would be no chance of him colliding with any others in the air; also, there would be at least a five-second delay before the Number Two was despatched, ha–ha.

I looked up as it neared. Prince Charles jumped out. Well, it looked like he almost fell out with his legs apart, and this method of exiting the aircraft caused him to twist in the slipstream and thus began his rigging line twist.

'What a shite exit,' someone shouted, and we all laughed as we saw the future king kicking out in the air, trying to untwist his rigging lines. He landed like a bag of shite. We all started to clap and cheer; then we got another bollocking from the PJI.

Two jumps down, six to go, I said to myself, as I ran on to the little grey RAF bus.

We were presented our blue parachute wings at the hangar by another RAF officer. Most of us had already purchased five or six sets and had sewn a set on to our green pullovers. We were marched on to the bus and back to Depot Para, Aldershot. There were some good old airborne songs sung all the way back to our adopted home.

I passed out in May 1978, a fully trained Grade 3 private soldier in the Parachute Regiment, aged seventeen years and six months. The proudest day of my life so far. I was now a Paratrooper.

2

WHERE ARE THE FALKLAND ISLANDS?

Nigel Ely: The Falkland Islands lie 8000 miles (7000 nautical miles) away from Great Britain, and 300 miles off the east coast of South America. It is a collection of some 200 islands with a land mass similar to that of Wales. At the time, sheep were its only export, but now there is talk of massive oil reserves off its coast. It has two main islands, East Falkland and West Falkland. East Falkland is the largest island and has the capital, Stanley, and East Falkland is where the bulk of the fighting took place during the war of 1982.

Private Bob Morgan, Patrols Platoon 2 Para

Initially the rumours were that Argentina had invaded Scotland. I never knew where the Falkland Islands were. The first thing I heard about it was when we saw pictures on the television telling 3 Para to return to barracks. Nothing to do with us.

Lance Corporal 'Duke' Allen, Defence Platoon 2 Para

I knew where the Falkland Islands weren't. I'm a Scotsman and I knew they were not up in the land of my birth.

Corporal 'Ginge' Dawes, clothing storeman 2 Para

I was at home with my family in married quarters, Salamanca Park, Aldershot, and when it first came on the news, we were all saying, where the hell's the Falklands? Everybody thought they were up north of Scotland somewhere! Then 3 Para were on their way sailing south and a couple of weeks later I heard on the TV we might be going too. So I thought, *I'll take a walk into camp and see what's happening*, and that's when I bumped into the CO [commanding officer], Colonel Jones, and he just said to me, 'Open your stores and start packing.'

I looked at him and asked where, because I had already packed the battalion for Belize, as I was the clothing storeman at the time. So the CO said, 'We're heading south,' and he just walked off. He was very headstrong and abrupt, but I never took offence as we all knew that was his style.

I then went into the QM's [Quartermaster's] office, dialled nine – at that time that's what you had to do to get an outside line – then the girl in the exchange, the operator, asked me why did I want to make this call? I told her it was a 'Recall'.

'Okay, right, how many do you have?'

So I gave her the names of the QM's stores and she replied, 'I'll call them all for you and get back and confirm they've all been told.' The battalion was still on pre-Belize leave at the time. I recollect she had a very polite and helpful manner.

WHERE ARE THE FALKLAND ISLANDS?

Tony Smith, Falkland Islander

When the Argies invaded, I was living on a 250,000-acre sheep farm at Port Stephens on West Falkland. I was twenty. Very early on the morning of 2 April 1982, I was awakened by a friend shouting loudly, 'Turn the radio on, Argentine troops are landing in Stanley!', our small capital town some 100 miles from where I was living.

We listened to the live broadcast from our local radio station in Stanley, which was giving a detailed account of the events as they took place. Initially it was hard to digest the reality of what was going on, as back in those days nothing much ever happened in the Falklands, and although many people had a deep mistrust of Argentina, not many of my age believed they would go as far as carrying out a military invasion!

A little bit later that morning, Argentine troops burst into the radio station and demanded to read out some prepared statements. This was dreadful for us to hear, and at the end of the broadcast they played their national anthem, which made me suddenly realise, with a sinking heart, that this was not some horrible dream, it was a horrible reality!

For the next day or so we were all in a state of shock, and worried as to how Britain may respond; but when the news came a day or so later that a Naval task force was being assembled immediately to sail to the South Atlantic, I had the greatest belief that British Forces would do whatever had to be done to remove these Argentine invaders from our homeland. Then the mood changed to one of hope and determination that all was not lost, as some initially had feared.

Captain Paul Farrar, OC Patrols Platoon 2 Para

The only reason I knew where the Falklands were is because when I was at grammar school, my mate Ken B and I were studying South

America, and whilst looking at the geography on a map, there was the Falkland Islands. My mate says, 'Oh, look, the Falkland Islands, my dad was stationed there during the war, he was a Bren gun carrier driver there.' Now, back then in the mid–1960s everyone's dad had been in the war, and I thought, *ha-ha*, but all these bits of irrelevant information you log away, and even at that age I had an intention to join the Army. So when the Falklands was mentioned, I knew exactly where it was.

Bizarrely, when I was back there in 2016, I did ask one of the locals about the islands' Second World War experience and he said, 'Oh, yeah, we had the West Yorkshire Regiment here.' So, I thought, *there you go, all those years ago Ken was indeed right.*

Before the Falklands kicked off, I had only recently joined 2 Para. I was actually posted to 3 Para, where I'd asked to go. Before that I'd been Adjutant at the Depot [The Parachute Regiment Training Depot]. I had to do my Staff College exams, which were the second week of February, and then I was posted to 3 Para to be their OC Patrols Platoon. But in the interim, the sitting guy who was OC Patrols 3 Para was due to be posted but didn't go for whatever reason, so I was left sitting in this 'officer without a job' role.

So, I said to the CO, Hew Pike,[4] that whilst I was delighted to be with 3 Para, and was there at my own request, if another job came up elsewhere, could he please keep me in mind. Anyway, on a Friday night, I was at home and got a phone call from Hew Pike and he said, 'Paul, do you want to go to 2 Para?'

'Well, yeah,' I paused, 'to do what, sir?

'To become their OC of Patrols.'

Well, of course I said yes.

'But there's a snag,' he replied. '2 Para are leaving for Belize for seven months!'

---

4 Lieutenant Colonel (later Lieutenant General Sir) Hew Pike.

I said, 'Fine.' The one factor on my part being that I'd got married only four months earlier!

I believe the reason my name came up for 2 Para Patrols was because JC [Major John Crosland, OC, B Company, 2 Para] happened to know I was 'spare' in 3 Para and gave my name to H Jones the CO, because the then OC Patrols 2 Para, Captain Pete Adams, had a falling out with H over something. I wasn't quite sure what it was all about.

So the first time I met the guys in Patrols was when I came back from Belize and I was very much aware that the man I was taking over from was highly respected by all the men in C Company. This was Captain Pete Adams, whom I knew very well because we'd been in 1 Para together and in Depot too, and this is absolutely true, I always said to people back then, and still do to this day, that Pete Adams was probably the best platoon commander I had ever met in the Parachute Regiment – absolute fact!

Acting Sub Lieutenant Mark Stollery, HMS Fearless, *Royal Navy*

In 1982 I was an acting sub lieutenant, which is very nearly the lowest of the low in officer terms. I was what they call an Officer Under Training, so I'd finished my initial training at Dartmouth (Britannia Royal Naval College) and since late 1981 I'd been on board HMS *Fearless* for sea training; working in the different departments of the ship, completing task books and generally learning about life at sea. I also had a degree from Cambridge, which was partly in Spanish, and that became relevant later.

I first heard about the Falklands in March 1982 when we had just returned from an exercise in Norway with 3 Commando Brigade, practising opposed landings in a cold hostile territory, very handy in hindsight.

CODE WORD 'BRUNEVAL'

Nigel Ely: Operation Biting was one of the most important airborne raids of the Second World War and was carried out by C Company 2 Para against a German coastal radar installation at a place called Bruneval in occupied northern France, on the night of 27–8 February 1942. Its aim was to steal German radar equipment and bring it back to the UK, which C Company did, so you will see C (Bruneval) Company mentioned throughout this narrative.

It's funny that the British Government never declared war on Argentina, yet it still gave the campaign to retake the Falklands and South Georgia a codename: Operation Corporate.

Private David Minnock, GPMG gunner, 12 Platoon D Company 2 Para

I was home on pre-embarkation leave to Belize in Keighley, on the booze actually in Keighley town, and was watching 3 Para sailing off with the rest of the Task Force on the pub TV. Friends were asking if I was going and I said, 'No, we're going to Belize in Central America, all the kit's on its way and the advance party has already left, so we're going there.' Keighley is a smallish town in West Yorkshire, famous for its Timothy Taylor ale, and most knew that I wasn't going to the Falklands at that time. However, I came home one night with me curry, me takeaway, after a few beers, and I'm walking up and I see this Post Office van pull away from my house, that was on a housing estate where we lived. I walked in and the whole family were up and Mum's got this telegram in her hand, and on the telegram, all it said was, 'BRUNEVAL', because that was our code to get back to camp immediately.

So, me mum says, 'What you gonna do, son?' So, it's two in the morning and I'm doing nothing. I'm gonna eat me scoff, get my head down, and I'll sort it out in the morning. The next day I packed me stuff up and got on the train. You see, we didn't have a phone, that's why they sent the Post Office van, and I have no doubts whatsoever we weren't going until I came home that night and read the telegram.

When I got back to Aldershot, it was hustle and bustle, loads of activity, vehicles coming and going. Every night was our last night on the booze in Aldershot, because we thought we were going the next day. We had loads and loads of last nights: on the wagon, off the wagon, rumour control, a real big fuck-around, then eventually it was our last night and we did go. They put us on all these coaches, I can still remember what the firm were called, Alder Valley Coaches, and their livery was 'Continental Capers'. Yeah, no lie, that's what it said on the side of the coaches that took us to war.

I can confirm this was the case because I drive a bus for a living and, can you believe it, one of the drivers who drove us off to war, I actually work with now in Keighley! I always joke I ain't never getting on a bus with him again, ha-ha – he'll take you to war! We take the mickey out of each other all the time. Strange how a coach driver who took us to war ends up in my home town and now I work with him driving buses!

Corporal Marty Margerison, 6 Platoon B Company 2 Para

I'll always remember when the Argentinians invaded the Falklands, because my daughter was born on 2 April 1982, the day of the invasion.

Private Andy Hutchins, B Company 2 Para, posted to IDB Warminster UK

I was on a posting to the Infantry Demonstration Battalion Warminster [IDB] with elements of 1, 2 and 3 Para. We demonstrated military hardware for overseas clients. For example, battle tanks, weapons, stuff like that, and we'd get used as 'the enemy' on any exercises which were taking place around the training area.

I was nineteen at that time when I heard about the Falklands and the 'Bruneval' recall, and everyone wanted to get back to their battalions with the guys, so all of us put in to have an interview with the OC so we could state our case, as that was the procedure. But all of us were turned down, well, that was us younger ones. A couple of the older guys, who knew the score, just packed their kit and went. Not sure if they made it on to the ships, though. We had a job to do here, but even so, it was hard to take being left behind by my battalion as it headed off to war.

SHUTTLE DIPLOMACY

Nigel Ely: Back in 1982, shuttle diplomacy became as well known as the word Brexit is today. Shuttle diplomacy is the subtle art of an outsider to intervene between two disputed parties and try to seek a compromise. On Sunday 28 March 1982, the United States Secretary of State under President Reagan, Alexander 'Al' Haig received a letter via the British Ambassador to the United States, Nicholas Henderson, from Lord Carrington, the then British Foreign Secretary.

It stated that a party of Argentinians had landed nine days earlier on the island of South Georgia, then a Falklands Islands Dependency, now a British Overseas Territory, lying in the South Atlantic a few degrees above the Antarctic Circle and some 600 miles to the east of the Falkland Islands. The British Government then sent a message to the Argentine Government to remove their citizens. The Argentine Government refused. The letter to Al Haig from Lord Carrington requested, 'I should be grateful if you would consider taking up this matter with the Argentines . . .' On 2 April 1982, 10,000 Argentine troops invaded and occupied the Falkland Islands.

On 28 March 1982, 2 Para were designated the Jungle Battalion for the British Army. The 2 Para Advance Party had only recently arrived in the jungles of Belize, another British Crown Colony in Central America, formerly known as British Honduras, to begin a six-month tour. Belize had gained its independence from the UK only months earlier in September 1981.

Acting Sub Lieutenant Mark Stollery, HMS Fearless, *Royal Navy*

Fearless was designed as a headquarters ship for amphibious operations, so as part of our preparations we made plans to embark with 3 Commando Brigade. But at the time we didn't really think we'd be sailing, as the situation in South Georgia looked like just sabre-rattling, and we assumed it would probably be resolved by diplomatic talks.

Captain Paul Farrar, OC Patrols Platoon 2 Para

I flew to Belize with eighteen others from 2 Para, and the first time I heard of South Georgia and the scrap-metal merchants was when we were up in the trees in Belize with a troop of SAS doing some jungle training. I think it was the Mountain Troop, A Squadron, 22 SAS, and of course they said, it's okay lads, we'll be off now, thinking they would get called back to go down south, but it was us that went and A Squadron never took part in the Falklands at all!

So, I always remember sitting in the middle of the jungle with this troop of SAS telling us they'll be leaving us for the Falklands. It had been only about eighteen months since the Iranian Embassy Siege, which was still very much in everyone's minds, and dear old A Squadron that had quite a few ex-Para Reg guys in it, as you'd expect, stayed in the jungle.

I was trying to do the negotiation with the RAF to get us back

29

to the UK, but the big problem was getting capacity on the planes and we were always being bumped off. But I remember the day we did actually achieve it, and it was great, because the aircraft came in and a whole load of RAF wives who had been out on R&R were turfed off the plane so that some blokes from 2 Para could get on and go to war. So I left from Belize with nineteen other members of 2 Para environment.

Private Dave 'Charlie' Brown, HQ C (Bruneval) Company 2 Para

I was recently out of Depot and still a *crow* [a new recruit] when I was posted to C (Bruneval) Company. I knew the reputation that C Company had from the Northern Ireland tours and thinking, *oh my God*, as it was known to get into C Company, you had to do a cadre, like a mini SAS Selection. You had to have been in Battalion at least one year unless you were a specialist sniper, signaller or some skill they needed. I was ordered to call up to Baz Greenhalgh [Sergeant Major, C (Bruneval) Company, 2 Para, RIP], the sergeant major's office first, and then to the OC's, Major Roger Jenner, and it was then I started my life in C (Bruneval) Company 2 Para.

Corporal 'Ginge' Dawes, clothing storeman, 2 Para

As you can imagine, 2 Para was very short on cold-weather clothing since we had all been issued jungle kit, so I was ordered to take two 4-tonners and drive all the way to Moreton on Lugg, Herefordshire, close to the SAS camp, to pick up a battalion's worth of arctic clothing. A day or so later, I was then ordered to go up to RAOC [Royal Army Ordnance Corps] Marchington ammunition depot, somewhere up north, to pick up eight Milan wire-guided, anti-tank missiles, because that's all they had in stock, and crates of *Willy Peters* or *Warm Persons* depending on what you want to call them, which were in fact white phosphorus hand grenades. I took another two 4-tonners, and RAOC were waiting for me when I got there. I counted all the kit on board quickly, signed for it and disappeared back to the Shot [Aldershot].

For days I was going up and down in a 4-tonner towing a trailer from Aldershot to the MV *Norland* at Portsmouth, packing loads of extra clothing like denims, woolly pullies, the DMS [directly moulded sole] Army-issue boots – you know, the ones that fell apart – and other stuff! This was a good call by Captain Tom Goodwin, our Quartermaster, because weeks later he happened to be on the *Norland* when the Navy ships were being hit and sunk, so he handed out all this extra clothing to the Navy guys who'd lost their kit when their ships got bombed and sunk.

Private Dave 'Charlie' Brown, HQ C (Bruneval) Company 2 Para

Blokes running about, trucks and equipment going in and out of the stores. The daily briefing – we're going tomorrow, then no, stand-down – and hanging about waiting for the order to move; yet 3 Para were on the water, they were already sailing south towards the Falklands. For days we were still getting constant briefings, doing ten-milers, keeping fit. On the wagon, off the wagon. Every day was prepare to move, then it was stand-down, then prepare to move, then stand down again. Every night most of us went down the curry houses thinking it would be our Final Supper.

Private Bob Morgan, Patrols Platoon 2 Para

I distinctly recall Colonel Jones telling us, 'There will be no in-field promotions.' And I don't know why I remember this, because I had no intentions of getting promotion, and it was just plain stupid to say such a thing; well, in my opinion it was. I'm not sure where that came down from, the government or where, because what if a lance corporal got killed and a Tom took over the charge, then why shouldn't the *Tom* get a field promotion?

Lance Corporal Geoff 'Johnno' Johnson, HQ Company 2 Para, attached to D Company 2 Para

It wasn't until the entire Battalion mustered in the gymnasium for that Scale A where Jonesy [Colonel H Jones] had a map of the world pinned up, and you know those old exercises we used to go on around Imber on Salisbury Plain, where you had those mythical islands where the goodies and the baddies lived? They were named after something like a place in George Orwell's *1984*, and if you look at the Falkland Islands, well that's a Salisbury Plain fucking exercise – East and West Islands! And we're gonna land on here, this island, and we're going to be supporting this gang against that lot over on that island, sort of thing!

Jones said, 'Now, right, whoever is talking about these islands, well, I will show you exactly where they are.' He pointed at the top of the map of the world, at Europe, and then he slowly moved his pointer south, and kept moving it south almost to the bottom of the map. 'The Falkland Islands are down here.'

Everybody's eyes rolled up and followed his pointer right down to the tip of South America, and then some Welsh voice at the back says, 'Oh fuckin' hell, boyo, we're gonna have to do some waterproofing on those fuckin' Bedfords, isn't it!'

'Shut up!' bellowed an order from the front.

Regimental Sergeant Major Mal Simpson, 2 Para

I had the responsibility of telling the guys who were designated Battalion Rear Party. I explained to them all how sorry I was they were not coming with us. I got them all together, about twenty to twenty-five, a few of them were young chefs, some walking wounded who had been downgraded because of parachuting injuries, and to see those faces when they were told was particularly hard. The Rear Party's role was to look after the barracks whilst the battalion was away, and of course, we were still getting recruits coming up from Depot, so somebody had to be there to receive and process them.

It was the Families Officer, Captain Holborn, nicknamed Squeak, who was OC Rear Party and he didn't get the recognition he really should have. My wife Paula helped out enormously with the other wives and the kids too. They organised game days, taking them away to the London Palladium and all sorts. Although all the guys were frustrated they didn't go down; my wife, God bless her, was enamoured of all of them. There was nothing too much trouble.

Corporal Marty Margerison, 6 Platoon B Company 2 Para

Stevie Gerrard, RIP, was our colour man [CQMS – company quartermaster sergeant]. Steve could be very pedantic about everything, but funny with it too. God knows how many times we laid all our kit out due to the fact we were still training and using our kit! Me being me made sure all the lads clipped several more ammo pouches on their webbing and took those fucking kidney pouches off – you know, those two large rear utility ones designed to carry your fucking boot cleaning kit to war. We had an initial kit list put out and we'd laid our kit out several times, then more and more stuff started getting issued. But you know what? I don't remember any IWS [individual weapon sight, an infrared night sight] ever being issued.

*WOII Del Amos, Acting Technical Quartermaster Sergeant, B Echelon
2 Para*

I was responsible for the ammunition, working with other members of the QM's department, weapons and matters of resupply; logistics for the battalion. Well, my boss Captain Tom Godwin, 2 Para's QM, said, 'Off you go, Del, and take over the *Norland*,' so off I went with my merry gang and sure enough as I walked up the gangplank, I was first on board from 2 Para and proceeded to take over the ship.

There I was in command of this ship called the MV *Norland*, then within hours, scores and scores of military lorries started turning up and throwing off these massive cardboard cartons as big as fucking greenhouses and we had to stack them on the car deck. They just kept turning up, so I liaised with the ship's pursers, who were to all intents and purposes the quartermasters of the ship, and between them and my gang we managed to get these cartons sorted.

After that, and working in tandem with the RQMS [regimental quartermaster sergeant], we had to organise the blokes' accommodation; what company to billet on what deck and who to put in what bunk, it was quite a task! Then we set sail for Portsmouth to pick up the battalion and once we set sail south, it was my responsibility to sort out all these boxes. It was like that old school alphabet tablet, where you had to push an A here then a B there, shunting these boxes into some order ready for issuing their contents to the battalion.

Regimental Sergeant Major Mal Simpson, 2 Para

We could not allow anyone to get off the ship and go to war if they weren't eighteen. You could have sailed down with us, but as soon as you got off the ship and into that landing craft you had to be eighteen, and if you'd have been wacked at seventeen and eleven months, somebody would have been in deep doggy-do. I know there were guys who went down who were not eighteen, but they were when they got off the ship.

Captain John Greenhalgh DFC, Scout Flight 656 Squadron Army Air Corps

Aviation fuel. The duty officer at UKLF [United Kingdom Land Forces] said, 'How much do you want to take?'

'Well, how long are we going for?' I replied.

We then had this silly phone conversation where we got out a pocket calculator. 'Let's work on a thirty-day operation,' he suggested.

'Okay then. We'll be flying eight hours a day and we're taking six aircraft, which burn 500lbs an hour,' was my calculation. And then we converted that into 45-gallon drums of avtur, aviation turbine fuel. And the next day there was a train, a British Rail train, in the siding alongside the car ferry MV *Europic*, the ship that I was to sail south on, at Southampton docks. This train was carrying 600 drums of avtur transported from West Moors, the military fuel depot, overnight.

A next-day service, incredible! And that was done from Captain Greenhalgh to Captain Somebody-Somebody in UKLF with a pocket calculator, done on the *fly,* and we were the only people who took barrelled fuel on board, nobody else took any. They had to borrow from us or rely on Royal Navy ships.

Private Irwin Eversley, GPMG gunner, 2 Platoon A Company 2 Para

I joined 2 Platoon, A Company, 2 Para on the last night in Aldershot before we sailed off to war. I went to visit Steve Illingsworth, who was a real great mate of mine who got posted to B Company, and when I went into B Company lines, one of the full-screws [a two-stripe corporal] shouted out, 'Oh, the nigger's here to see his mate Illingsworth.'

Stevie, RIP, got it in Goose Green. Look, I don't think nothing of that racial bollocks.

Lance Corporal Pete 'Stubbo' Stubbs, MT Platoon 2 Para, attached to the Red Devils parachute display team

I had my car parked nearby and I was saying my goodbyes to you all and can still see it now as clear a day. When one of the guys on rear party shouted out a bit of banter, 'Oh, the Navy will sort it out before all you wankers get down there,' he got the finger in reply. We all thought the Navy would just blow the Argies all to pieces.

3

LET LOOSE THE *NORLAND*

NOTICE OF REQUISITION

The Secretary of State for Trade in exercising the powers conferred upon him by the Requisitioning of Ships Order 1982 hereby requisitions the MV *Norland* and requires you to place the said vessel at his disposal upon completion of discharge at Hull on Saturday 17 April.

DESIGNATION OF REQUISITIONING AUTHORITY

Nigel Ely: On 26 April we set sail to war from Portsmouth on board the MV *Norland*, a 27,000 tonne P&O flat-bottomed, roll-on/roll-off car ferry. Our send-off was no different to times gone by. Families and friends and well-wishers lined the quay, waving and crying, and the battalion band played on with a sense of purpose. I recall standing on the deck waving back at all the pomp and circumstance, but that's all. My parents couldn't make it to see me off. They were hard-working folk and the family just couldn't take a day off. Anyway, we had said our goodbyes over the phone.

The *Norland*, like the other car ferry *Europic*, was STUFT, the acronym for Ships Taken Up From Trade. In simple terms it was requisitioned. Its normal duty was to ferry 1,200 passengers, freight and vehicles on the Hull-to-Rotterdam and Zeebrugge route.

GOOSE GREEN

Corporal Marty Margerison, 6 Platoon B Company 2 Para

As we were leaving the docks, the missus and kids were crying and I shouted something stupid like, 'Tell the fucking milkman I'll pay him when I get home!' A nervous departure, and off we went.

Keith Thompson, Catering Officer, MV Norland

I was assigned to look after 2 Para and my orders was to make 2 Para fit and healthy from Hull to the landings at San Carlos – that is, if we ever got there. In short, we cooked and served up to 3000 meals a day for forty days, and I was to make sure none of the lads went to war with the shits! So that was my job, and I really enjoyed it.

Roy 'Wendy' Gibson, RIP, steward and ship's pianist, MV Norland

I'd been on sick leave for six weeks and just got a new apartment in the old town in Hull. I'd had an operation on my foot and it went all funny, so I was on the sick and I was bloody skint, and I had bought this new three-piece suite on HP [hire purchase] and it needed paying for.

The day I signed off sick leave was the day I signed back on the *Norland* to go down to the Falklands, and ended up signing a will! I said all the goodbyes to the family and whatever, then went to the ship, but before that, we all ended up in the Seaman's Mission, The Flying Angle down on the Hedon Road, Hull. Now, as the drinks flowed, I said to the padre there, 'Lend us your piano?'

So, he says to me, 'Well, I'm gonna tell ya something now, Wendy, you can borrow it, but you'll fetch it back.'

I wanted to take the piano on the *Norland*. I did have my grandma's piano on board, but I'd worn that one out, you see, so the padre lent us his piano to take to the Falklands just so I could entertain the crew.

Anyways, the Paras from the QMs helped us on board with it, they brought it on to the car deck, put it in the lift, then into the mess room. The word went round there was a piano singalong in the mess room, so then the lads [Paras] wanted me to go and play for them in the Continental Lounge, so I said, yes, I'll play for you, and I got permission from the captain, because you know what I mean, we were Merchant Navy and we had officers too, and you couldn't just take liberties.

So, I started playing for the lads. I was a bit nervous at first, because you were all big strapping lads as you know, and there's me, a Bloody Mary, but I weren't the only one, there were six of us on board at the time. I was apprehensive at first, you know what I mean, because I expected a bit of shit. Well, it's expected! It didn't bother me, I weren't frightened, but I didn't get no shit whatsoever. And I never got any hassle from the Paras whatsoever.

I was never insulted for being gay, as God's me judge, but when it was all over and we were sailing back with the 2 and 3 Para, and by chance, crossing the equator on Airborne Forces Day, all the Paras was fighting. It was like a massive bar brawl straight out of a Western movie, but I kept on playing, a bit like the *Titanic*; noses bitten, ears split, and flying blood!

Anyways, earlier I was playing and these 2 and 3 Para lads, they were dealing cards, poker I think, and one of the 3 Para lads says, 'What the fuck's this one on?' meaning me. So the lads from 2 Para says, 'That's our Wendy, so fucking leave him alone.' They were gonna nut him for sure!

Nigel Ely: For the trip home, the powers-that-be decided it would be prudent not to put the Paras and Marines on the same boat for fear of unit rivalry, so the powers-to-be, naively, in my opinion, allowed 2 and 3 Para to share the *Norland*, not really understanding the Paras' propensity for a good punch-up. The fight between 2 and 3 Para onboard the *Norland* on Airborne Forces Day 1982, which started in the Continental Bar and spread through the ship like a plague, when the armed guard were called out, is legendary.

Private John Bolland, Recce Platoon 2 Para

Soon after we set sail, we had to blanket every window with bin liners and masking tape, because once outside territorial waters we were fair game, and I remember Colonel H Jones got the whole battalion up and said, 'Forget all the peace talks. We have instructions from Mrs Thatcher to go in and take the Falklands back.'

Recce and Patrols Platoons C (Bruneval) Company was put below the car deck at the bottom of the *Norland* on G Deck, ten feet below the water line, and we had no windows to tape up. If you were claustrophobic, you were fucked.

Staff Sergeant Pete Harburn, Army Physical Training Corps, 2 Para's PTI

I was attached to the 2nd Battalion the Parachute Regiment as the PT Corps instructor [Army Physical Training Corps, now the Royal APTC]. There was one PT Corps instructor in every unit in the British Army and there were six of us down south, one per unit, and there was also one Special Forces PTI.

In war, the PT Corps duty is usually the CO's bodyguard – usually! – but this time Colonel Jones didn't want me; I don't think we got on, so I became the bodyguard for 2 Para's second-in-command, Major Chris Keeble. I looked after him along with my PT assistants, who were all badged Paras. That was on land, but on board ship, my job was fitness. To get all the companies fit and to keep them fit along with all the attached arms like the

Royal Artillery and Engineers alike. It was hard work for these two units, because once on shore, they had their missiles to carry around with them and they were very unfit, so I had them carrying dummy shells all about the ship to get their strength built up.

Reg Kemp, night steward, MV Norland

My job on board was to look after the galley night duties. When the day staff went off, my team came on. This was normal civilian procedure. If anything needed doing during the night, I or my crew would do it. For example, we had to prepare for breakfast, get all that ready during the night. If someone like an officer needed an early call, it was our job to sort that out too, and we looked after the boys who were guarding the ship. Kept the coffee coming, and the bar shut! We worked all through the night. You guys were well looked after with good food and lots of it. We made sure of that.

Private Steve Taylor, 3 Platoon A Company 2 Para

We were all sitting about resting and Sergeant Beatty would come across and always find us Toms something to do, even just for the sake of it, he was a real pest. So, one time we were having this briefing and he was talking down to the blokes, really not right, so Paul S turns to me and says, 'I'm gonna blow that cunt away when we're down there.'

Sergeant Beatty obviously heard this, because some time later he came back carrying a load of brews for us on a tray, and from that moment onwards he was as nice as pie – the best bloke ever! A bit of a wake-up call for him, I guess.

Mally Gelder, chef, MV Norland

There was some good news and some bad news. The good news, the reason we made such good speed was because the *Norland* was running on clean diesel, courtesy of the MOD. The bad news, the hook on the dough-making machine decided to break; it had snapped off its shank and if the word had got out, there would almost certainly be a mutiny onboard. *What! No bread!* Yes, no bread to eat certainly meant a hanging for someone! The ship's welder was asked to report to the kitchen and said he was too busy, but as soon as he was told of the crisis, he was on the hook in double-quick time and made a fantastic repair, so we were up making bread again. After that, the rumour was this trip was going to be a long one, so 2 Para had to post guards on the galley because we now had food rationing on board.

Private David Minnock, GPMG gunner, 12 Platoon D Company 2 Para

We cracked on with training, loads of weapon handling. We carried out gun practice off the back of the *Norland*. The crew would toss these black bin liners off into the sea and we'd shoot shit off of 'em with the GPMGs. We had to secure the legs of the gun by putting sand bags around them to stop the gun bouncing all about on the steel deck.

We did fitness and also did a lot of first-aid training from Dr Hughes, Captain Steven Hughes, Royal Army Medical Corps, 2 Para Doc, RIP. We basically went over all our soldiering skills to a real high level, and we learnt about vehicle recognition, you know, stuff like what vehicles the Argies had. We learnt a lot about them and in particular the LVTP-7 [a US-designed and built, tracked amphibious assault vehicle], so I knew that it could carry about eighteen marines and it had a crew of three.

This statistic stuck in my head and later as the war was in full fling, my platoon was tasked with going to investigate the sighting of two of these things at a place called Cantera House. We carried out our own little mission from the top of Sussex Mountains on to this house, and it was me who queried this mission, because there was only thirty of us and these things carried about the same, yet we had all been taught British Army tactics dictates that the attacking force must be three to one, but I was told to shut up!

Private Bob Morgan, Patrols Platoon 2 Para

Young Dave Grey, RIP, who we called Chopsy because he was always bumping his gums, joined us almost straight from Depot. Him and Pete Myers too; must have been hard for them to join the old sweats of the battalion. Anyway, as we're crossing the equator, Chopsy falls asleep on deck in the heli cargo nets that hung over the sides of the ship to catch anyone or thing which may get blown off the deck, and gets sunburned to fuck. He got charged for self-inflicted wounds and fined a month's wages. [*Queen's Regulations, Section 42: Conduct prejudicial to good order and military discipline did make yourself unfit for service.*]

So he fought in the Falklands War and didn't get any pay, and got his leg shot off by an Argy anti-aircraft gun at Goose Green too! I really liked Chopsy, he was a bit of a streetwise kid, and always chopsy, yet funny with it.

Corporal Marty Margerison, 6 Platoon B Company 2 Para

Are we actually going to war? We've got 8000 miles to go and the threat only became real when we crossed the equator, because we were closing within striking distance of the enemy. We were given two beer chits a day cut from a printed A4 size of paper, which

43

had about thirty chits on each page. One of the clerks had got hold of the printing 'skin' and just ran off loads of chits. So, we had all these black-market chits, and I think, up until H minus 4 days, the majority of the blokes were fucking leathered on the boat.

Regimental Sergeant Major Mal Simpson, 2 Para

Believe it or not I didn't have to jail anybody on board, but I had to put the provost staff [Royal Military Police] on guard at the shop because the boys were nicking all the stock. One day the purser for the *Norland*, John Crowther, RIP, comes up to me he says, 'RSM, we love the guys, they are the best, but they're going around in groups, there's about forty or fifty of 'em in there at any one time and we take a penny in the till, but there's fifty pounds worth of stuff missing, can you please do something?'

So I got hold of the company sergeant majors and asked them to tell the lads to stop stealing from the shop because they will close it down. And, of course, as soon as we got out of our territorial waters it was duty free and there was lots of good kit to buy in there, like watches and stuff, so every time the shop was open, the provost staff were on duty, but they were just as bad, ha-ha.

Our first stop on the *Norland* was at the port of Freetown, Sierra Leone, to pick up fresh rations, and that's when I got off the boat to make sure they weren't loading on board any shit.

Sergeant John 'Taff' Meredith DCM, 12 Platoon D Company 2 Para

To keep the boys busy, we had a spot of bayonet practice at the rear of the boat. We used those blue mattresses we were issued with, had them rolled up, and some of the crew came to watch, I guess because they hadn't seen it before. Anyway, the mattresses were so hard it was difficult for the boys to thrust their bayonets into them and I was wondering what the crew thought of it all, because it looked like the mattresses were winning.

Corporal Marty Margerison, 6 Platoon B Company 2 Para

In our four-man cabins you had these three- or four-inch-thick blue mattresses on metal beds, but some cabins had only two guys in, and if any water got spilt on these mattresses, well, it created a blue stain. You could instantly tell who had pissed the bed because you'd go to the communal shower, which was down the corridor, and you'd see blokes with this big blue stain all over their backs, so we called them the Smurfs. All their back was stained blue and it was a right twat to get off.

ASCENSION ISLAND

Nigel Ely: On 6 May we anchored at the volcanic island of Ascension just south of the equator. It lies 3,700 nautical miles from the UK and 3,300 nautical miles to target. It is very small, approximately seven miles wide by six miles long and apparently it has some excellent beaches, but we never got to see any because we never got off the boat. All ships headed for Ascension, and Ascension was where Colonel Jones joined us.

Lance Corporal Denzil Connick, Anti-Tank Platoon 3 Para

An operational jump. I was with the initial elements of the Task Force and we set sail on board the *Canberra*[5] from Southampton in the early April. Naturally we were kept informed about additions to the Task Force, and when we heard 2 Para were joining us, we were absolutely delighted, because we had been rather overwhelmed

---

5 The P&O liner SS *Canberra*, nicknamed 'The Great White Whale' during the campaign.

by the green beret [Royal Marines] up until then. We also heard about the other elements, the Guards and what have you; so, yeah, essentially it was 3 Commando Brigade and 5 Brigade. For the duration 3 Para stayed with 3 Commando Brigade while you, 2 Para, chopped and changed between 3 and 5 Brigade.

We waited at Ascension Island for 2 Para to catch up and it was while we were both on Ascension Island, I was wandering around *Canberra* and I'll never forget, I saw my CO, Colonel Hew Pike, walking alongside your CO, Colonel H Jones. They'd had a meeting on board *Canberra* and being the only two Para battalions that were there (our other battalion, 1 Para, was serving in Northern Ireland), one could only imagine what they had to talk about, and that would have been a lot!

And please don't forget, there were plans for us to carry out a parachute insertion into the Falklands from Ascension on C130s, refuelled inflight. They actually flew a load of the parachutes out from UK storage down to Ascension Island, so that if and when the plans got green lit, we'd be ready for Action Stations.

I know this was one of the options they were looking at. It was an outrageous option, but we Paras are always outrageous anyway! There were quite a few flat bits on the Falklands where we could have dropped on to, but, of course, one of the issues going against us was distance to the DZ. I had this funny feeling about what they wanted us to do, and it would have been a bit like Arnhem all over again, so I think that's why London decided not to do it.

Even if the Hercs could have got there, they probably wouldn't have been able to get back! We would have had to jump on to Stanley airfield and secure it, in order for them to land. This was one of the insertion options they were discussing, so it's no small wonder they pulled it.

N

Hull
London
Portsmouth

New York
Washington

5-6 April Falklands
Task Force sails
(2 Para sails 26 April)

Gibraltar

North Atlantic
Ocean

BRAZIL

ASCENSION ISLAND
Task Force Base

PARAGUAY

South Atlantic
Ocean

CHILE

URUGUAY

ARGENTINA

Falklands Island

ROUTE OF THE
TASK FORCE FROM
THE UK TO THE
FALKLANDS AND
SOUTH GEORGIA

Total Exclusion Zone

SOUTH
GEORGIA

SCALE OF MILES

0   500   1000   1500   2000

SOUTH
SANDWICH
ISLANDS

Chief Petty Officer Rich Edwards, Special Communications Unit (SCU) Royal Navy

I was a member of the Royal Navy's Special Communications Unit (SCU) and not long after returning from another seven-month tour in Diego Garcia (British Indian Ocean Territories), I was ordered to take some special equipment, provided by our friends in Cheltenham, to HMS *Fearless* at Ascension with a view to cross-deck to HMS *Hermes* later.

I arrived on Ascension Island in the dead of night courtesy of an RAF VC10 with my small team and my precious cargo of two equipment boxes. Because there was no accommodation available, and I forget how I got there, I found myself up in this crater on the edge of an ex-volcanic feature in amongst all this dust with a bunch of Royal Marines.

Anyway, we get a bonfire going, and I can't recall whether we'd got anything to eat or not, but we're all sat around talking, and it turned out these guys were *returning* Royal Marines. They were the ones who'd surrendered at Government House in Stanley, and they told me they were going back to reclaim their rifles, which had been taken off them by the Argentine Army! The following morning, I eventually got heloed on to *Fearless*, where I ended up staying for the duration of the war instead of playing with this kit on *Hermes* as planned.

Mally Gelder, chef, MV Norland

The crew were given the opportunity of getting off at Ascension, but no one did. It was a case of 'we took her [*Norland*] down, we're fetching her back'.

Captain Paul Farrar, OC Patrols Platoon 2 Para

As I mentioned earlier, I joined 2 Para at the rush immediately prior to the Falklands, and I hadn't actually met the commanding officer, Colonel Jones, until I came back from Belize, and of course having just left 3 Para, 3 Para were now on the high seas heading for the Falkland Islands.

I said rather lightheartedly to Colonel Jones, 'Bloody hell, I could have been with 3 Para now,' and he replied, 'Don't you worry, Paul, we'll catch them up.'

This stuck in my mind and it was only when he came on board the *Norland* at Ascension, because he flew down from the UK, that he said, 'I told you we'd catch them up, Paul.' And indeed, he was absolutely correct, because not only did we catch them up, we overtook them and landed first.

So, having been slightly frustrated at being left behind by 3 Para, I was actually most grateful to be landing at the vanguard of 2 Para. It's funny how small quirks in one's history can have unforeseen consequences – that's just what happens.

4

NORLAND SOUTH

Nigel Ely: The South Atlantic is no place for a small roll-on/roll-off ferry designed to cross the comparatively shallow North Sea on day-tripper tasks. The weather changed dramatically the further south we sailed. From blue skies and a Mediterranean sun, we moved into the dark dank depths of a most ferocious sea. Forty to sixty-foot swells of a thick, pea-green blanket covered the portholes and tossed our flat-bottomed boat around for fun. One time I recall sitting in the Continental Lounge playing cards, taking a brew, when from nowhere the lounge was plunged into dark as waves covered the portholes and threw us all about.

Most of the seating was fixed, but because the lounge was our only large area to meet up, extra tables and chairs had been brought in, so all this furniture came crashing down and I held on for dear life to the leg of a fixed table. South of Ascension was when we all started to switch on. The banter was still there, but an air of caution crept in that wasn't there when the sun was shining only a few days previously. Were we really going to fix bayonets, close with the Argies and kill them?

GOOSE GREEN

Private John Bolland, Recce Platoon 2 Para

Sailing down we had two Red Alerts – Argy subs or something – and on the second one they closed the watertight doors on us, which didn't impress any of us in C Company. So a couple of the blokes got hold of some PE4 [plastic explosive] and were going to blow the doors off if we had another Red Alert, and if that failed, we were gonna fire a 66 [a one-shot-only shoulder-fired rocket launcher] at 'em. All comms was cut off below the car deck, all doors were to be sealed watertight; what else are ye gonna do to escape?

All the officers were bunked up above the waterline, so I complained and one of 'em says, and I won't mention his fucking name, 'It's just as bad for us, we're above deck, we're subject to air attacks.'

I goes, 'Who's you kidding, are you taking the piss? You lot can jump overboard, we're down in the fucking rat trap below the dungeons.' So, soon after discovering what the blokes might have been up to, *they* allowed us to go on deck when the next Red Alert came. Honestly, we were forty feet below the fucking top deck, for Christ's sake, we don't have portholes – and put yer life jackets on and lie on yer bunks was the order! It really did come that close to C Company blowing the doors off with buckshee 66s. What a fucking insane situation.

Captain John Greenhalgh DFC, Scout Flight 656 Squadron Army Air Corps

Flying is a skill that perishes if you don't keep doing it. It's not like driving a car, you have to be flying regularly to keep the skill up. So I wanted to fly every day and there was always something useful we could be doing; we could be moving spare parts between ships, we could be moving the mail around and we could move people.

Later on, when Colonel Jones joined the Task Force, I'd generally get cryptic messages from him on board *Norland*, the ship next door – remember, I sailed down on the MV *Europic* – saying, 'Come and pick me up.' So, I'd fly across to the *Norland*, pick him up and take him over to *Fearless*; HMS *Fearless* was the command ship. I knew Colonel Jones from Kenya, because I flew him a lot on that Kenya exercise. I flew him down to the Masai Mara; we'd spent hours and hours together in helicopters so we knew each other rather well.

So, I'd get these cryptic messages saying, 'Come and pick me up.' Really? 'Where we going? We are in the middle of the Atlantic!' So, I would turn up at *Norland* and then *they* would all look at me, and I'd say, 'I've come to pick up Colonel Jones.' Then about five minutes later he'd appear on the flight deck looking all flustered, get in the aircraft, and I'd say, well, 'Where we going, sir?

'*Fearless*,' he'd reply. 'And where's *Fearless*?' I'd enquire. I'd then ask *Fearless*, because they had radar and they could see thirty miles, so I'd say, 'Where are you?' And they'd answer, 'Zero two zero at seventeen miles.' So, we would set off on a bearing of zero two zero for seventeen miles, and of course I'd recognise *Fearless* as soon as I saw her.

On one occasion when he was called to an 'O' group, I flew to *Fearless* but all the helicopter spots were full of aircraft and closed down. There was nowhere to land, so he said to me, 'You've got to get me onto *Fearless*, I've GOT to go to this O group.'

There's a flight deck officer, who's the senior naval guy who does all the stuff with the batons and wands, and he gave me the wave-off, indicating, 'You can't come on, we are full'. Now, who would you rather obey? H Jones, who says you've got to get me on there, or the flight deck officer telling me to go away!

So, I came in and just managed to put one skid on the side of the ship next to a Sea King as she sailed along at 15 knots with the sea foaming beneath, then Jones jumps out on to the deck and I flew away. Then the flight deck officer did a most extraordinary thing: he threw his batons on the floor in disgust.

I knew the Colonel very well and if you never let him down, there was never a problem. Colonel H Jones was not a man to disappoint.

After the wave-off incident and the fact I wanted to fly every day to keep the skills up, the senior naval officer on board the *Europic*, a chap called Charles, got very angry, because he said we weren't allowed to fly every day. I said to him, and remember, this is me, a captain, taking to the equivalent of a major, 'And what do you know about flying?' 'Nothing, but you can't fly every day.'

'We need to fly every day to keep up our skills,' I said.

'You can't, you'll wear the aircraft out before we get there,' he replied.

Stunned, I told him, 'That's why I bring a maintenance team with me.' Now, this is a young army captain talking to a salty and rather difficult old Royal Navy lieutenant commander.

We took enough parts with us. In the hold, we had boxes and boxes of spare engines, gearboxes, blades. We could service and repair the aircraft, and the boys were excellent, they really were phenomenal. So, we kept flying, and because I set sail first, I was given all the best Blue Beret REMEs [Royal Electrical Mechanical Engineers], who are specialists in aircraft maintenance and repair. They were a truly amazing team, there was nothing they couldn't do. Overnight they could rebuild the aircraft.

Acting Sub Lieutenant Mark Stollery, HMS Fearless, *Royal Navy*

I was aware about Goose Green from the very start of planning. At Ascension somebody realised I spoke Spanish, so I was taken off bridge watchkeeping duties and made an intelligence watchkeeper in 3 Commando Brigade's planning room, which was previously the captain's dining room and now had maps and charts plastered on the walls. My tasks were fairly mundane, but it was fascinating to be in the room where Brigadier Thompson[6] [OC, 3 Commando Brigade] and his key advisers planned the landings.

I was little more than a fly-on-the-wall observer – but what a wall! I remember being there when they were choosing which of the possible landing sites to go for, so I knew where we were landing even before the Commander-in-Chief or Prime Minister. It was no big deal, obviously, as I couldn't tell anyone.

The name of Goose Green was coming up more frequently as we approached the islands, but I didn't realise the significance of it, because I was trying to be invisible and blend into the wallpaper. At that stage it was just another name among many, as the planning staff looked at their various options. I now realise that taking Goose Green was a critical move politically, but at the time I didn't.

Lance Corporal Geoff 'Johnno' Johnson, HQ Company 2 Para, attached to D Company 2 Para

In the forward lounge there was this upright piano with three wheels and a block of wood underneath it, which was for Wendy. Anyway, on this particular occasion there was no playing of the piano, a film had just been shown when Padre David Cooper comes in, and he comes in with his specimen case and somebody was carrying a fold-up table too. As they were just pulling the screen down and packing up the projector, he said, 'Right, we are going in soon, so I'm having a service, and anyone who wants to stay can stay, and anybody that doesn't can fuck off.'

I will tell you now, it was squeezed shoulder to shoulder in there. Everything David said was straight to the point and that's why he's one of my heroes, good old Padre David Cooper.

6 Brigadier Julian Thompson RM (now Maj. Gen. Julian Thompson CB, OBE, RM).

Nigel Ely: As 2 Para steamed further south, we were continually prepping for war, yet unbeknown to us, the SAS *had* prepped for war and was getting ready for insertion behind enemy lines . . .

A 22 SAS call sign

We cross-decked from RFA *Resource* to the Fleet's flagship, HMS *Hermes*. Why? Well, all the helicopters, kit and equipment were on *Hermes* and the *Resource* was a small vessel, but it did carry a shitload of ammunition and just for that, was a big value target if the Argies knew about it. Probably a bigger value target than anyone realised. We cross-decked in the daytime.

When we landed on *Hermes*, we got downstairs and met up with the blokes from D Squadron and started asking questions like, 'Where's Willy? Where's Taff?' Your mates, you know, stuff like that. 'Ah, they're on HMS . . . ,' and so and so. We had the best OPSEC [operational security] ever. We didn't know what any of the other patrols were up to or where they would be operating, and we didn't want to know either.

So anyway, at last we get our heads down, then got woke up for scoff, or scran in naval vernacular. It was a long scoff queue but some naval officer says, 'Right, you boys, get straight to the front.' So, we go to the front and this chef says, 'What do you want to eat?', which was really unusual because one never gets asked that, you eat what's on offer, what's in the trays in front of you normally. The cooks had been given the nod we were going in!

'What do you want to eat?' this one cook says. 'You can have as much as you fucking want, mate.' We piled it fuckin' high! 'You want two steaks?' The cook didn't even wait for an answer. Bosh! Two big and juicy medium-rare landed on my tray. It was a fuckin' big feed, ha-ha! It was like going back to the old days when you carried two days' worth of marching scoff in your belly.

Just like the jungle days, get that scoff inside you, boy! So, we had our food and a little while later on 30 April we took off from *Hermes* in a Sea King with big bellies.

It was the first time the pilots had used NVGs [night vision goggles] on operations. We flew in, feet dry, and we did a nap-of-the-earth [very low altitude flight] like I've never experienced before, and I've had a few hairy chopper flights. We actually landed on May Day, May the first. The flight seemed to go on for ever, but it was only 80-odd nautical miles. Time of flight recorded as 1 hour 15 minutes. We were the first blokes on the ground before the war had even kicked off, and my flight was the very first SAS flight to be inserted.

Our task was to go into certain areas to see if it was suitable for this, that and the other. Go over there and look at this grid reference, is it suitable for our tracked vehicles? Any road or tracks? Lay of the land for possible parachute drops, stuff like that; then our main task was to OP [to observe, or observation post], the settlement of Goose Green. But you know what, we had not yet declared war on Argentina when we set foot on the ground.[7]

The ground and the terrain were so difficult, we had to cancel a couple of the tasks. It took us five days to get into a good OP to view Goose Green. We moved really slow and tactically during the night, sometimes covering only a couple of miles in one hour and sometimes dropping down to a few hundred metres in an hour across the rock runs. We'd pick what we thought would be a good place to observe, then the fog would come down, and then we were either too high or too low. It wasn't easy to find a place we could call home for a few days.

Yes, we could see Argies moving around, we could see and hear helicopters, we could see in which direction they were flying from

7 Neither Britain nor Argentina officially declared war, but both did declare the Falklands a war zone.

and where they were landing, and we made note of all of this. The big problem for us was that we were not in a close enough position to really count the Argy troops and their anti-aircraft guns as best we wanted, without compromising ourselves or the other SAS patrols.

On day six, I think it was, we got hit by this katabatic wind.[8] This wind keeps on coming across the ocean from the Antarctic and the first thing it would hit would have been the islands of South Georgia. We were the second thing it hit. This kind of wind brings with it a massive drop in temperature, rain and snow, and it also raises the water table.

So, we had found a good OP-cum-hide in a rock run and a couple of the guys were having a kip. We had got into a routine, and our routine was, two of us go walkies and if we see anything wrong like Argies, we walk away from the OP and see what they do. Then, if you have to, engage, but that would really be the last thing you'd want to do. I mean, that would be the shit option.

Then this wind hits us, soaking us all, the kit, our doss bags, fuckin' everything. I mean, we're not in survival mode just yet, but close to it. Being out there exposed in these harsh conditions with the Argies was hard enough and then to get smacked by a face full of Antarctic weather was real shit. The thing that saved my life was this North Face jacket. They'd only just come on to the market back in the UK and I was wearing it under my smock when the katabatic hit. It was desperate times, but we survived it.

ACTION STATIONS *BELGRANO*

Nigel Ely: The ARA *General Belgrano* was originally the US-built light cruiser USS *Phoenix* before America sold it to the Argentine Navy; a Second World War warship, she was equipped with modern

---

8 A downslope wind, common where there are extensive ice sheets, so found typically in Greenland as well as Antarctica.

Sea Cat air defence missiles. The *Belgrano* was sunk by HMS *Conqueror*, a nuclear-powered Royal Navy submarine on 2 May 1982, killing 323 men.

At the time we all cheered, but looking back at it today, I shudder at the foolish captain of the *Belgrano* and think about such great loss of life. Two days later on 4 May, Argentina got its revenge and struck the Type 42 guided missile destroyer HMS *Sheffield* with an Exocet at a cost of twenty-three dead. The ship sank six days later, while under tow.

Lance Corporal Geoff 'Johnno' Johnson, HQ Company 2 Para, attached to D Company 2 Para

When we sank the *Belgrano*, the *Sheffield* got hit two days later, then the attitude on board changed, just like that. Jonesy [Colonel Jones] turned around and said, 'If you haven't got your affairs in order, get 'em done now, because whether you like it or whether you don't, we *are* going to war. It's going to be a shooting war and there's no backing out of this now, because our boys have been killed.'

Everything then just snapped into place. It had been a holiday cruise up until then, we'd recently crossed the equator and we'd all got sun tans. Now we were sailing into colder weather and as usual, if it ain't cold and raining, it ain't training, and all that bollocks!

Roy 'Wendy' Gibson, steward and ship's pianist, MV Norland

I remember I used to get curry powder for the lads, then one day one of the head chefs said to me, 'Where's all the bastard curry powder going?' I was giving it away to the Paras because they wanted it to mix with their army rations when ashore. I learnt the Paras have curry powder with everything.

No one ever knew who was behind the missing curry powder

– well, that's until now, ha-ha. I looked at it this way, it was more important for the Paras to have curry powder than it was for us to have it kept in the store.

Private David Minnock, GPMG gunner, 12 Platoon D Company 2 Para

Immediately after the sinking, we carried out submarine drills. We became the target of Argy subs, or that's what we thought, so me being a machine gunner, you know the GPMG, the gimpy, I had to set it up on these oil drums at the back of the ship and look out for any periscopes and stuff. We were definitely switched on and shit hot when on periscope guard. A couple of days after the *Belgrano* getting sunk, we lost the *Sheffield* by a French Exocet missile and then our blood had been shed now, proper blood had been shed, so this was war. This outraged all of us. Then a few days later up on Sussex Mountains, we sat and watched helplessly as the Royal Navy got blown to pieces. The best navy in the world was getting a right pummelling.

Regimental Sergeant Major Mal Simpson, 2 Para

When the *Belgrano* got sunk, I knew deep down we were going to have to get off this boat and fight, and this was when Colonel Jones got quite frustrated. 'Right, RSM, we have got to change the outline of the *Norland*. The Argentinians by now will know us, so paint the funnel black.'

'Okay, sir, that's not a problem.' So, I go down and sees the QM, Tom Goodwin, and says, 'QM, you have any black paint?'

'Yes, I have loads of it. What do you want it for?'

'I'm gonna paint the funnel.' We both burst out laughing. Remember, we were sailing not far from the Great White Whale, the SS *Canberra*, and you could hear the disco at night and smell the steaks it was that close, so painting the *Norland*'s funnel wasn't going to help, but on orders, we start to paint the funnel with these little paint brushes. But how do we paint the top? So, I go and see one of the crew and ask, 'Do you have long poles?'

'Why?'

'Because we are painting the funnel black.'

'Oh why? That means we've gotta repaint it when we get back! Can't you leave it as it is?'

I tell him, 'No. It's going to be painted black.'

'Why black?'

I says, 'We're changing the whole configuration of the ship.'

He says, 'You've changed it anyway, you've got a massive helicopter deck on the back which has changed the outline of our vessel completely. You've ruined our *Norland*!' So, we get these bloody long poles and it's gotta be painted today, and the ship's going up and down, and the wind is blowing, and there's a Sea King on the midships helideck and the paint is being blown all over the chopper and across its windscreen, and everywhere. We then had to spend more time getting the paint off this Sea King. Years and years later, I'm at a do in London and I meet the pilot of this Sea King, and we both laughed and laughed.

We only painted two-thirds of the funnel as we couldn't reach the top, and if you ever get hold of an old photo of the *Norland*, you can see just that.

Roy 'Wendy' Gibson, steward and ship's pianist, MV Norland

We all had emergency stations to go to during an air raid or fire. 2 Para taught a few of the crew how to fire weapons, but not me as I didn't want to know, but there was a certain member of the crew who did have a go and he shot an albatross down, killed it dead he did. There was all hell on, because that's a bad omen for sailors.

I think he went in front of the Old Man, Captain Ellerby. Fancy shooting a beautiful bird like that down! Soldiers and sailors on their way to war, with the *Belgrano* and *Sheffield* sunk. Not good.

5

A PORT EXIT

Nigel Ely: My time had come. Our time had come. We had waited a lifetime for action, for combat, to close with the enemy and kill them. It was the end of the twentieth century and we were about to hit the beach in the conventional way. Hundreds of heavily armed paratroopers with live grenades hanging off webbing yokes crammed into the Continental Lounge, some with brews in their hands, others eating egg banjos through camouflaged expression, all standing.

Dulce et Decorum Est
Bent double, like old beggars under sacks,
Knock-kneed, coughing like hags, we cursed through sludge,
Till on the haunting flares we turned our backs,
And towards our distant rest began to trudge . . .
. . . The old Lie: *Dulce et decorum est*
Pro patria mori.

Wilfred Owen, KIA, November 1918

GOOSE GREEN

Corporal Marty Margerison, 6 Platoon B Company 2 Para

When we were getting battle prepped, I was given 2000 more link [a belt of 7.62 ammunition for the GPMG] to distribute between the men. Well, a belt of 200 link is twelve pounds; 2000 is 120lb, and that's a lot more weight to add to the bloke's ammunition scale, but still I had to distribute it. The plan was to give Frog French and Jim Meredith, the GPMG gunners, as much as they were able to carry and take some of their personal kit off 'em. That way I'd have all the ammo with the guns and didn't have to start passing link down the fucking line during a firefight when Frog and Jim needed a resup [resupply].

It seemed to have worked and as I weighed all the kit, the minimum was about 110lbs all in, bergens and webbing. The webbing was on average 50 or 60 pounds, and I had to get blokes to take stuff out of their webbing because these belts of 200 came in canvas bandoliers, and the metal clips that held the pouches to the 58-pattern webbing belt were starting to bend off the belts' canvas inserts. That was a lesson learnt.

Brian Lavender, radio officer, MV Norland

As we were getting closer to the Falklands, we used to go for meetings at night to find out what was going on. The naval party was in charge of these meetings, and the guy in overall charge was Commodore Esplin-Jones. However, he still had to answer to our captain; he couldn't override our captain, but they worked well together because they were all wondering what they were going to do. You see, as we were getting further and further south, the peace talks weren't working too well and the Paras were getting itchy to get ashore, and we were all beginning to think this was going to be the real McCoy.

So, we'd have these meetings in the Officers' Lounge where we would discuss what we thought was going to happen. Well, I mean, I thought the decision would be taken well beyond those Navy chaps on board. They were just going to follow orders, but they were saying what they thought might happen; what the plan would be.

The first plan somebody came up with was that they were going to do a frontal assault on Port Stanley! So they asked our captain, Don Ellerby, if he could go astern and run the ship up the beach at Port Stanley, drop the ramp, and then the Paras could all run off the back just like the Second World War movies you see! That was the first bright idea, but Ellerby said to them, 'No way, because by the time the ship runs aground and I drop the ramp, we'd be running into water and sink and I wouldn't be able to get that close to the beach anyway!' Later, when they knew we were going into San Carlos, the head-sheds sort of told us what was going to happen, and somebody stood up and said, 'We might be attacked by enemy aircraft.'

Then someone else, one of the *Norland* crew, said, 'Oh, nobody mentioned that when we were leaving Hull!' and all that sort of carry on was being talked about.

Another one asked, 'What happens if we get shelled really bad?'

'We'll drop one of the lifeboats, we'll all get in it and we'll go ashore, and we'll hide under the trees,' someone suggested.

Then some other bright spark stood up and said, 'There are no trees on the Falklands!' So we all forgot about that and we poured another drink each.

Captain Paul Farrar, OC Patrols Platoon 2 Para

The first time I discovered where we were going to land in the Falkland Islands was not from the CO or my company commander, it was from Lance Corporal Pete Carroll [HQ Company 2 Para] of the Int [Intelligence Section], whom I knew well from a previous NI tour, and later from our skydiving days. It was Pete Carroll who told me where the landing point would be, and what the initial plan was!

So, 2 Para had to go very quickly from, oh no, not another day on the ship, to, fuck, we land tomorrow morning! By some quirk of the system, and I don't know why, but 2 Para was definitely wrong-footed in the last twenty-four hours.

Corporal Marty Margerison, 6 Platoon B Company 2 Para

As we were disembarking ready to get into the landing craft there was Roy 'Wendy,' one of the crew, a gay man, and a good man as well (I never liked to call him Wendy). His boyfriend was sitting next to him and they linked arms and his boyfriend was fretting, 'Fuckin' hell, fuckin' hell.'

So I go up to Roy, because he always talked to the blokes and have a chat. Once at breakfast, I pointed out to him he had eye shadow on, and he says, 'Yes, I seen the lads work so hard last night, I thought I'd give them a little treat.'

Anyway, I goes up to Roy sitting with his boyfriend and looking at us all wary like, staring at live grenades hanging off our kit. I was standing, so I says, 'You alright, Roy?'

He replies, 'Yeah, if any of our boys get killed, I'm gonna get that piano [Roy, as you know, was the evening entertainment on the piano and played a big part in morale, in more ways than just singing!] up on deck by the pointy bit and play "God Save the Queen", then throw it over the fucking side.'

We all laughed, then he reached over and sticks one of those little sticky *Norland* lapel badges on me, you know, the ones crew stick on kids so as they don't get lost, and he sticks one on Straza

[Lance Corporal Jimmy Street B Company] too, all for good luck. The funny thing was, me and Jimmy both got wounded.

One of the blokes was going to run off and rob the ship's shop before we got on the landing craft, so another shouts, 'What if you get caught?'

'What are they going to do? Send us to war?' he replied, and everybody started laughing. Then the Padre started quietly singing the hymn 'For Those in Peril on the Sea' and some of the blokes sang, some hummed, some didn't, and some stood in silence, but we all puffed on our ciggies.

Private John Bolland, Recce Platoon 2 Para

Everyone was given a couple of mortar rounds to carry ashore, but I was given this big box for the Milan [anti-tank missile] and was told to dump it off on top of Sussex Mountains at the battalion RV. I was the LMG [light machine gun, the one with the banana shaped magazine] gunner and they give me this bloody thing to hump! Fifty pounds of webbing, me bergen, a hundred-plus, Christ knows how many LMG mags, my smock was bulging with magazines, and this fucking box and a fucking mountain to climb.

Roy 'Wendy' Gibson, steward and ship's pianist, MV Norland

The day you went ashore, it was a darkened ship and the lads was all rigged out, had your face blacked and whatever, you know what I mean, camouflage; and there was four of us on the buffet and I was frying up egg sandwiches and coffee. One of the Paras jokingly said to me, 'Come on, Wendy, get the piano in here.' You lot were all ready to go ashore and eating egg sandwiches.

GOOSE GREEN

Brian Lavender, radio officer, MV Norland

When we got the order to sail in, we were just on the 200-mile Exclusion Zone and it took us twelve hours to get into the area of Blue Beach where we were to offload the Paras. That day it was really bad visibility, low cloud, sleet and hail. It was ideal conditions, because it gave cover against any Argy attacks. We had the *Broadsword* [Type 22 frigate HMS *Broadsword*] alongside us and she was basically our air defence. She had the Sea Wolf missile system on board and she was providing cover – surface to air. *Canberra* had HMS *Brilliant*, which was the same class and was her escort.

When we got in sight of the islands, we were all blacked-out [on board no light no noise routine] and at the same time the Royal Navy were firing into Stanley to create a diversion, miles way over to the east as we went around the top of East Falkland. We were told there were Argy lookout posts all over, and we thought how could they not see us, as the weather was starting to clear by then, so no one was to show any light or make any noise.

Anyway, as we sailed silently past a point onshore called Fanning Head, the SBS [Special Boat Squadron] suddenly put in an attack on an Argy lookout post and destroyed it, which kind of gave the game away!

Captain Paul Farrar, OC Patrols Platoon 2 Para

I shared a cabin on the way down with Chris Dent [RIP], 2IC A Company 2 Para, and John Young, 2IC B Company 2 Para, and we spent our last night before the landing repairing Chris's extended boots. He'd been in 23 SAS[9] and he was what we might call a bit of a 'kit commando'. If you wanted a few detonators or an 'Igniter

---

9 With 21 SAS, one of the two TA (now Reserve) units of the SAS.

Safety Fuse Electric', you went to Chris – a super, super guy was Chris, and I knew his wife well, too. She'd been our medical officer in 1 Para several years earlier, and I'd served with Chris in both 1 Para and at the Depot.

Tragically, the next time I saw those boots, they were sticking out from under a poncho on Darwin Hill. I thought, *Fuck, they're Chris's boots*, but to be fair I knew he was dead by then. But it was very sobering to see his boots sticking out of this poncho in the immediate aftermath of that action on Darwin Hill.

Also, on the night before the landing, I'm in the cabin on my own and there's a knock on the door, so I open it and there's a bloke standing there, a Tom who I didn't really know at the time, but who I later knew to be 'Beast' Fuller. He was in A Company Headquarters, and he was always slightly lop-sided, like he'd been run over as a kid or something. Later, back in the UK he was on a Drill and Duties cadre I was inspecting, and he was stood to attention and I told him to straighten himself up, but of course he couldn't. He was permanently twisted! So, back to the cabin, he's at my door and says, 'Sir, I'm Private Fuller from A Company, is Captain Dent here?'

I say no he's not here, yet I sensed he was a bit agitated, so I said, 'I could give Captain Dent a message.'

So, he gave me this small parcel and said, 'Captain Dent said I could give him this watch I bought for my girlfriend, 'cos if I get fragged, the blokes will rifle my kit and nick it, and Captain Dent said he'd look after it for me.'

'Not a problem,' I said, and took the parcel to give to Chris. Strange how, in the Toms' minds, it's only Toms who die and officers don't! On seeing Chris's boots, strangely I thought, *what about that watch?* It was in a parcel addressed to Miss So-and-so and it's in Chris's kit and I thought it could cause confusion with his wife.

Later I tracked down David Cooper, 2 Para's padre, and asked him what happens about this sort of thing, and he says there's something called a Board of Adjustment, where a deceased soldier's kit is gone through by perhaps the Paymaster and Quartermaster, and anything that is thought to be potentially embarrassing or distasteful is taken out. I told David about the watch. I'll always remember that one, because it was the first time I'd come across the phrase, Board of Adjustment.

Private Bob Morgan, Patrols Platoon 2 Para

I remember the Padre, David Cooper, coming around just chatting to the blokes as padres should do. The funny thing was, he was the best shot in the battalion, a Bisley champion shot and he wasn't allowed to carry a weapon.

Private John Bolland, Recce Platoon 2 Para

One of the proudest moments of my life was some time before we were getting ready to load into the landing craft, when 'Ride of the Valkyries' came over the ship's tannoy. The whole battalion was wound up, proud as fuck – man, it brings tears to a glass eye! They can take everything else away from you, but they can't take that feeling I had then, and still have today. That's all mine!

THE LANDING CRAFT

Nigel Ely: It was 2 Para who hit the beach first, not the Royal Marines who the media kept showing on their TV footage every time there was a mention of the Falklands War; and you would have thought it was their bread and butter! After all, only two months previously, 3 Commando Brigade had conducted a FULL-ON beach assault in Norway, in these exact same landing crafts! Couldn't they do it for real? Couldn't manage it? Of course they could. Many felt there was something very sinister about the entire business of ordering an entire parachute battalion first into battle across an angry sea in transport none of us knew the first thing about.

2 Para had a very short practice, one attempt ONLY to get into a landing craft but not to experience exiting off the ramp end, when we were anchored off the Ascension Island. Ask any Royal Marine and they will tell you that getting off the ramp end is the most important part of a beach assault.

It was strange, because a lot of the Royal Marines were parachute trained, but no one in 2 Para was trained in landing craft or hitting the beach. In fact, I would say 99.99 per cent of us had never been anywhere near a landing craft, let alone in one, before Ascension. But I suspect the real reason why 2 Para went in first was because the Navy were prepared to sacrifice us; they were expecting an opposed landing, and they didn't want to bloody their 3500 Royal Marines. That was the back brief we all got – 650 men of 2 Para were thought to be quite expendable, of course, for the *greater cause*. There is really no other explanation for such a decision.

Gunner J. M. Love RA, 2 Para Group A Coy 2 Para, FOO [forward observation officer] party signaller, 29 Corunna Field Battery RA. (An extract of thoughts from his book, Poetry from a Fragile Mind *by James Love, independently published in 2019.)*

The inky blackness of the night's sky was slowly giving way to the deep blue of the dawn. The stars, spluttering like candles. Giving one last flicker, then once again lost in the depths of space. Behind him, the moon. Like some silvery white disc, suspended on invisible wires, giving shape and shadow, but no definitive colour

. . . Numbed, not only with cold, but with what was about to take place. He stood like the others, bent slightly forward. Head bowed, like some pagan ceremony, designed to appease the gods. However, it was not the burden of responsibility that caused this seemingly mass display of humbleness. It was the massive weight of their bergens, weapons, ammo. For this was the 21 of May 1982, 0200hrs Zulu. Their destination: BLUE BEACH TWO.

Sergeant Major Colin Price, A Company 2 Para

We were on Action Stations moving into Port San Carlos, and the battalion assembled to get off the boat. It was pitch black when we got to the landing craft, there was a Royal Marine there acting as the assist-to-board. The Marine helped me down and said, 'Go over there,' pointing to a place over towards the back, I said, 'No son, you go over there, this is *my* company,' and I helped every one of my men safely down into the landing craft – every man jack of 'em all bar one! Then you guys, C Company, came onboard with Jones, so then I was kicked out the way.

Nigel Ely: As A Company were loading, a young Tom, 'Nobby' Stiles, slipped in between the landing craft and the ship, and before the swell of the sea closed the gap, some lads on the *Norland* side managed to pull him back onboard, but not before the closing gap crushed his pelvis. He survived, yet some years later he was found sleeping rough on the streets of Dundee. A friend told me later that the drink eventually got hold of 'Nobby', probably because of his survivor's guilt at not being with his mates fighting their way up Darwin Hill. Sadly, another victim of PTSD [post-traumatic stress disorder]. RIP, Nobby.

A PORT EXIT

Captain John Greenhalgh DFC, F Flight 656 Squadron Army Air Corps

Dawn started to break with a clear sky as the *Europic* sailed round Fanning Head, following *Norland* into San Carlos Water. We were standing on the deck having just eaten our egg, bacon and beans breakfast, table covers and candelabras firmly stashed away, with a fully serviceable Scout [light helicopter] strapped down yet ready to take off to support 2 Para. As we rounded Fanning Head, we could see the SBS taking out an Argentinian lookout post on the side of the hill. It was surreal, with the ship's engines gently humming in the background, while watching the SBS pepper-potting forward and raking the hill with fire as they took out the Argentinian position.

Yes! the SBS doing a live attack right in front of us as we sailed past – look at these guys go! A ringside seat with small-arms fire, tracer, and grenades like I've never seen before, and all we could do was watch in awe. What a way to start a war, guys!

Normally my Scout is an anti-tank aircraft, but it was stripped down to increase our payload and a little bit later I got airborne with my gunner, John 'Gammo' Gammon, an ex-Para, and Rich Walker and Johns in a second Scout. We flew down the length of San Carlos Water as the light continued to grow, looking for 2 Para and Colonel Jones. I was told later that when 2 Para heard the approaching Scouts in the gloom there was a lot of cocking of weapons, which was a bit unfriendly, but those in 2 Para who had been in Kenya before Christmas were calling 'hold fire'. They knew that was the sound of a pair of trusty Scouts, which was always good news for the Toms, especially if they were wounded.

Colour Sergeant Pete Vale, HQ Company 2 Para

A crap-hat [same as a 'hat', a derogatory term for any soldier who does not wear the maroon beret; the SAS are termed 'hats

73

light'] signaller had an ND [negligent discharge] with an SMG [submachine gun] and shot one of our lads in the foot when loading into the landing craft. To get on it you had to do a sort of belly flop over the rail of the landing craft as it rose up on the swell, and then one of the Marine landing craft crew would grab you and pull you on board with all your bergen and kit on; if you missed the rail you'd be going in the water and have no chance. The funny thing was, the lad who was shot didn't realise he'd been shot until a day later. Probably because of all the adrenalin and the cold and that.

Private Steve Taylor, 3 Platoon A Company 2 Para

When we landed, most of us went up to our knees, even waists, in freezing cold water. We met up with the SAS and SBS blokes who, as briefed, were waiting on the shoreline for us. One of them said, 'There was no fuckin' reason why any of you lot should have got wet, they could have run you right up on the shoreline. We even recced and shored up a little bridge across the first stream to keep your feet dry.' *Well, that's gone out the window now*, I thought.

Corporal Ken Raynor, patrol commander, Recce Platoon 2 Para

When 2 Para landed on the Falklands Islands, most of the patrols from C Company were in the first landing craft, and one of the first missions was to lead the different elements of 2 Para off the beaches and up into the surrounding hills. As soon as the battalion established a foothold, most of the Recce and Patrols Platoons deployed forward, creating a blanket of observation posts towards Darwin and Goose Green.

A PORT EXIT

Corporal 'Ginge' Dawes, clothing storeman, 2 Para

I didn't get off the ship during the landings, I stayed on board sorting stores. On the morning of the landings, my main job was to lead you guys through the darkened ship down to the port side door where you boarded the landing craft, and to help you down all the stairs, because you guys were heavily laden up.

When you disappeared, I honestly felt lonely, because I knew what was going to happen; they would be coming to bomb us, and I'd rather have been on the beach than on the ship. The Navy guys in the ship kept saying, 'On air raid warning red, you've gotta get down to D deck out the way.' We said bollocks to that, we wanted to fire back – and we did. But I have to admire the Navy guys for their resilience. The Argies actually left us alone on the *Norland* and went for the Royal Navy instead, so I could see all that terrible carnage happening. One moment a ship would be slowly sailing past us, and then all of a sudden, its missile turrets would rapidly swing around, fire off a missile and you'd see it go after these low-flying Argies.

Corporal Marty Margerison, 6 Platoon B Company 2 Para

When we got on the landing craft, the driver of this thing, the Marine coxswain, was the spitting image of Sergeant Bilko, so we all started laughing, taking the piss out of him as we were facing death. When we saw all the other landing craft driving around in circles, just waiting like sitting ducks, we laughed again, but this time out of severe frustration.

You exit a landing craft from the side of the ramp so the waves don't lift the craft and squish you. So the coxswain ordered, 'Ramp down!' and the ramp started to move downward; we were expecting incoming fire, but nothing. He then shouted, 'Troops out!' The man at the front, Mick Conner [Cpl, B Company, 2 Para, RIP] a superb soldier and a funny guy too, said, 'Fuck! That there's water,' but the momentum of the rest forced all the front men out. The Company went onto the beach and formed all-round defence, whilst the boss, JC, talked to two guys from the Special Forces, who apparently weren't expecting us!

Sergeant Pilot Dick Kilinski, F Flight 656 Squadron Army Air Corps

A very good mate of mine, Andy Evans, a Royal Marine pilot, was flying a Gazelle at the time of the initial landings over San Carlos Water, and the Argies on the headland shot him down over the water by ground fire; rifles. Andy was wounded, but still managed to ditch the Gazelle in the water. Andy's crewman, Sergeant Eddy Candlish, had to drag Andy from the wreck; they managed to get out the aircraft, but as they were swimming ashore the Argies opened up and shot at them again, *in* the water.

They made it ashore, but sadly Andy died of his wounds shortly after. The Argies had killed him, unarmed, in the water, as they tried to struggle ashore! That was on the very first day.

Sergeant John 'Taff' Meredith DCM, 12 Platoon D Company 2 Para

There were two doors on the *Norland*'s car deck from which to exit onto the landing craft; port and starboard. The port was the lee side, which was the side Colonel Jones used, and starboard was the rough side, with swells of eight to ten feet; we got the starboard side, and of course it took much longer for us to load. As I was standing in the door of the *Norland* waiting my turn to step across, I saw one of the port-side landing craft circle round and then we all heard this voice shout, 'Hurry up, D Company, get a fucking move on, you're holding up the whole attack!'

It was Colonel Jones in his landing craft shouting, and of course one of the Toms replied back with, 'Yeah, you got off on the easy side, you wanna come and get off this side.'

'Shut up!' came the reply from Colonel Jones. Then all the Toms piled in and started chuntering. It was four o'clock in the morning, pitch black, and we were meant to be on silent routine, so Jones wouldn't have known who was answering him back.

On the front of our LCU [Landing Craft Utility] were two GPMGs, one on either side with belts of 800 link. I wanted my boys to have as much ammunition as possible, so we nicked it all and I shared it out, but we did leave the Marine gunner a belt of about twenty-five just in case he needed it. When he found out he wasn't happy, but what could he do about it, as we were roaring off to attack the beach!

We also had a shortage of HE grenades. There wasn't even enough for one per man, but we'd nicked a box of LMG mags from C Company, so every one of my men had an LMG mag of 30 as an initial *contact* mag, as opposed to the standard issue 20-round mag. So, all my blokes were carrying one 30-round mag, nine 20-round mags, a belt of 300 link and 200 ball, and that's a lot of weight, because nobody had explained to me how we were going to get resupplied.

6

THE BEACH LANDING

Standing at the front by the ramp, I felt no emotion at all;
no panic, just numb on the giants whose shoulders I was standing on.
This is just plain crazy.

Nigel Ely: We hit the beach in an LCU, all eighty of us, including Colonel Jones. We were packed in like sardines and for some unfortunate reason my patrol found ourselves right up at the front. Luckily, we were to be the second boat on the beach and not the first! This was the first time many of us in 2 Para had ever been in a landing craft of any sort. It seemed like an age we were bobbing about waiting for the rest of the battalion to get loaded – a couple of hours at least. Then we were on our way and crashing through the waves towards the shore. The Royal Navy was softening the beach with their big guns.

All I remember was I had water-sodden feet as I lay up by the ramp. There must have been a foot of water sloshing about. It shouldn't have pissed me off, because there were more serious things to worry about, but it did.

The first LCU got caught up in kelp, so we hit the beach first. Luckily it was an unopposed landing, but we didn't know that at the time and the thought still makes my teeth tingle with fear.

C (Bruneval) Company led the battalion on to the beach and up the mountain and into battle. Patrols Platoon led followed by Recce Platoon.

Lance Corporal 'Duke' Allen, Defence Platoon 2 Para

We were the first to land on the beach in front of the Marines, which is strange, because cabbage-heads, I mean, that's their game, isn't it! First to land, first victory, Goose Green, the only battalion to fight two battles and the first into Stanley; that was 2 Para.

I landed with the battalion during the early hours, when it was still dark, and I didn't get my feet wet. I listened to an old soldier telling us, 'Be last to get off if you can, because the more weight that leaves, the further it can go up the beach. Of course, my feet staying dry lasted for only about half an hour because of the dozy CO, or whoever it was, leading the battalion snake off the beach.

There was SAS guys guiding us away from the streams, who were telling us, 'Go this way. No go over there!' Whoever was leading this fucking snake ignored 'em, so the whole battalion ended up with wet feet before we had fucking started, and, of course, as you know, a lot of the blokes in the battalion went down with trench foot.

Captain Paul Farrar, OC Patrols Platoon 2 Para

We landed in the dark and Patrols were in the first chalk [a group of paratroopers in an aircraft] if you like, and to this day it still irritates the shit out of me when I see the pictures of the landings of the Falklands, and there's a *Royal* [Royal Marine] going in with his orange life preserver and his green beret in broad daylight. I remember getting into that landing craft, the LCU, and there wasn't enough room to put a life preserver on, let alone going in, yo-ho-ho as the Marines later did, and in broad daylight too!

The contrast of us and them in terms of yeah, fuck it, we'll just get on and do it. It was impossible, yet we were told, 'You will get on board, you will put on life preservers.' There were plenty on board the *Norland*, but we all went, bollocks to that. It was an unusual way to go to war, but thankfully the landing was unopposed. Had that landing been opposed, I shudder to think what would have happened. We'd have been absolutely slaughtered.

Once we'd landed, I was *not* met by the SAS or SBS as I should have been. This was important, as I was the point man for the battalion with Patrols, and they were meant to lead us to the track towards Sussex Mountains. They may have been there, but I never met them!

So, my task was to get the battalion off Blue Beach at San Carlos and lead the companies to the foot of Sussex Mountains and then they would basically go into assault formation and advance up Sussex Mountains. Patrols would then carry on up the re-entrant behind and head for Bodie Peak and Cantera Mountain.

You have a map, you have a couple of air photographs, and on the map, large bits say *Detail obscured by cloud*; and the maps themselves are twenty-seven years old. Okay, landforms don't change, but in the dead of night with pretty inadequate night vision equipment, the IWS image intensifier, in almost total darkness and with no ambient light, was practically useless. There was also the mental pressure of having 500 blokes landing behind you, and thinking, if I get this one wrong, and knowing H Jones's propensity for sacking people, I'll be in deep shit here. So, in terms of mental pressure, it was quite focusing!

We'd been on a ship for effectively four weeks and we definitely hadn't got our land legs, yes, we tabbed around the ship with bergens on, but the sheer weight – to this day, I know I've never carried as much weight as we carried ashore, never ever! I hear stories of blokes landing ashore with 350 lbs. No, you didn't! You probably had, 80, 90, 100 pounds.

The fact the Patrols were excused carrying mortar rounds ashore, which everyone else carried, was because we had to go in with four days rations rather than two. Every patrol also needed an HF and a VHF capability, so there would be a Clansman 352, and a 320, and a hand generator, and spares batteries, and as much ammunition and, and, and . . . all between four men. I could not have fitted anything else in. My bergen was at splitting point.

Lance Corporal Jimmy Goodall, Assault Engineers 2 Para

2 Para Assault Engineers was formed just before we went to the Falklands. Our job was to blow things up, but we never got around to do proper training before we sailed south. We were made up from lads from all over the battalion like the rifle companies, but I came from Headquarters Company. During the battle we were attached to the rifle companies. I seemed to be tagged on to C Company most of the time. We weren't tagged on as a platoon, but just small sections here, there and everywhere.

When I came ashore off the landing craft, I was carrying the radio, ten pounds of PE 4 [plastic explosive] in eight-ounce sticks, bandoliers across my chest, and a fuckin' Blowpipe missile strapped on my shoulders, like a giant green dildo. We were carrying them for the artillery and were supposed to drop 'em off at the bottom of Sussex Mountains, but they couldn't carry them up the mountains, so we had to. I think I was carrying about 160 pounds initially, what with all my personal kit too, which was about 50–odd pounds if my memory serves me correct. And, like everyone else I waded ashore and the water was a lot deeper than we thought, and yes, I was soaking from the first minute ashore.

Anyway, off the beach now, we were tabbing up towards Sussex Mountains and it was getting first light, and I could hear this helicopter coming in and I was shitting myself, because I didn't know if it were ours or theirs. I was stuck there out in the fucking open and I could hear it getting closer and closer, then all of a sudden, I just disappeared!

I'd fallen down this small yet fucking deep hole and it was only the Blowpipe that saved me, because it had wedged me solid. I couldn't feel the bottom of this hole, so I was dangling like a right twat. I called for help and young Karl L came over and pulled me out, as he was the only one who'd heard me. Those of us who were carrying the Blowpipe were eventually told to drop them off before we tabbed further up, and I'm sure none of those bastard Blowpipes worked properly, because they couldn't take the rough handling.

Private Phil Williams, Mortar Platoon 2 Para

When we got off the landing craft it was early morning, still pitch black, and the water went up to my ankles, then shins, then knees, then thighs, then waist and then right up to my chest, and when I eventually made it on to the beach it was fucking chaos, because the landing craft had been tactically loaded like you would in a C130 for a parachute jump.

So you had elements of all different companies on the one landing craft. Unlike when you jump on to a DZ, where you are in the aircraft, whether it's at the front, the middle or the rear, so your RV on the DZ is pretty much going to be in the front, middle or rear of the stick, and you know you're roughly in the right area. When we got off the landing craft, especially at night, we were all just a mishmash of the different elements of the battalion, and it was chaos. If it had been an opposed landing, then it could have all gone to rat shit very quickly!

That tab off the beach, well, that was the hardest tab I ever did in twenty-two years in Para Reg. Even when we did those fifty milers across the South Downs, and we did them regular, they weren't anywhere near as hard as that fucker, I'll tell you!

I was carrying a base plate weighing in at twenty-five pounds, a couple of bombs about ten pounds each, a third of the mortar tool bag weighing about twenty pounds, a C2 sight for the mortar of about five pounds. You're talking about upwards of seventy pounds even before you start weighing your personal kit like webbing: two days' worth of scoff, which was the Arctic ration packs, then all your water, your personal weapon and ammunition, your doss bag, radio batteries for the CP [command post] and all your creature comforts and other stuff. By the time you pick up your bergen and get it on your back, you're carrying the best part of one hundred pounds plus. That's why it was a hard tab off the beach and up Sussex Mountains.

A 22 SAS call sign

We hadn't seen any Argies up close and we didn't know if any of their air assets had spotted us and were preparing to mount an attack. We always had that threat hanging over us. The Argies had a mass of air assets; jets, lower flying Pucara aircraft, Huey gunships[10] and Chinooks, which could quickly dump a hundred troops really close and surround us. That would be our war over, unless the four of us decided we'd fight it out until the cavalry came, but we knew no cavalry would ever come; we were out here all on our own, alone and expendable, and it was up to our field craft and soldiering skills not to get compromised.

That was the long and short of it all. The trouble we had with setting up the Goose Green OP was that the settlement sat in a fairly low isthmus, and for the best part open surroundings, and the only unoccupied high ground was miles away.

---

10   Nickname for the American-built Bell HU-1 military utility helicopter, which first saw service during the Vietnam War.

THE BEACH LANDING

Sergeant Major Colin Price, A Company 2 Para

It was bloody cold, and there was at least an inch of frost covering, and our feet were wet through wading ashore. A Company never lost one casevac through trench foot throughout the war, and that is something as a sergeant major of a rifle company I'm still very proud of. When Monster [Cpl Steve Adams, A Company, 2 Para who was shot several times assaulting Darwin Hill] got casevaced to the hospital ship SS *Uganda* [the Red Cross P&O cruise ship], he told me there were more Royal Marines laid up suffering from trench foot than wounded Paras! And *they* were issued with all the proper boots and gaiters and all sorts of fluffy arctic warfare clothing!

Private Steve Taylor, 3 Platoon A Company 2 Para

Very early on in the war, I became 2 Para Land Casualty Number Two, with a stabbing pain to the eye; I'd accidentally walked into a radio antenna! A lad from my same company, who had been accidentally shot by someone else while on board the landing craft, was 2 Para Casualty Number One and we were flown off Sussex Mountains to the recently established (hours earlier) field hospital at Ajax Bay. There was an unfortunate bloke [Nobby Stiles], who lost his footing while boarding my landing craft and slipped between the *Norland*'s hull and the landing craft, only to be quickly saved by his mates grabbing him before he got more squashed. He could quite easily have been Number One, but his mishap was deemed to have occurred on the *Norland*, so it didn't count!

Even during the first two days, the rumour was that 2 Para were going to attack Goose Green, so me and the lad who'd got shot in the foot decided to do an escape from the field hospital. There

85

were these 59 [59 Independent Commando Squadron, Royal Engineers] guys, a totally different breed to the Marines, more akin to the Parachute Regiment than the Marines, who I knew from the rebuild of Forkhill location back in NI. One said his unit were going in with 2 Para as engineer support to do the mine and IED [improvised explosive device] clearing and said we could ride with them on their snowcats [small, truck-size tracked vehicles]. They don't go anywhere without 'em! As it turned out, I got released from the Doc and rejoined my company, who were still dug-in on Sussex Mountains.

Private Irwin Eversley, GPMG gunner, 2 Platoon A Company 2 Para

We were meant to be on the first landing craft but we got caught up in kelp, and when we did beach, I went straight up to my waist in water and thought, *Oh you bastard, you fucking cunts!* [Royal Marines]. I was soaked and fucking freezing and with all that weight we were carrying as well. I felt like a mule. When I got out of the water, I had a little breather, and I remember at one point we had to go to ground and with all that heavy weight it was almost impossible to get back up without help.

Well, it was pitch black on the beach and all quiet apart from a hundred Paras and the grunt of the landing craft engines, but I did know the mortars were over to my left as we started to climb Sussex Mountains. On a breather, Spanner [Lance Corporal Spencer, A Company, 2 Para] went over to see Cooney, his mate in the Mortars, to have a chat with him. He said to me, 'When you move off, come and get me,' then he disappeared, just like that, into the fucking darkness. With that, the sergeant said, 'Come on, let's move it.'

So, I thought, *well, I ain't gonna walk over there and get Spanner, especially being the only black geezer here* – like: 'Yeah, see you later, sergeant, I'm going to get Spanner and leave the platoon!' Like, that's near desertion. So, when Spanner eventually came back, he fucking chinned me for leaving him behind. I wanted to rip him a new arsehole, but I thought, *no*, because I knew what would happen, *they* would say, 'He cracked. The black boy couldn't hack it.' Spanner was mad because later the sergeant found out he'd left his blokes, so he got a right bollocking.

Sergeant John 'Taff' Meredith DCM, 12 Platoon D Company 2 Para

As the landing craft hit the beach, someone shouted, 'Troops!' Well, none of us moved, because what does 'troops' meant to us? Then another voice shouts, 'Get off!' so we all bundled off, and fair play to the Marine, he'd run us so far up the beach not one of us got our feet wet. I didn't stay dry for long, because we came across a stream with a bridge, which would have kept us dry, but no, we crossed a stream following the battalion snake towards Sussex Mountains, and I wasn't a happy chappy; I mean, I was really chuntering.

As we tabbed on up the mountain, we were passing some of the mortar blokes, who were on their knees because they were carrying so much weight, and the guys with the Brut bottles: Blowpipe operators, and their missiles that were carried in a green plastic container, which, to me, looked like a massive bottle of Brut aftershave.

We were supposed to be on the top by first light and there was A and B Company going up before us while we were still at the bottom of the hill. As we were moving up, the gun line for 4 Field [4th Field Regiment RA, 2 Para's artillery support] were setting up, and where our mortar line was going to be set up, we were thankful to drop off our greenies [two mortar rounds in a green, heavy-duty plastic case] because we all carried two greenies, before starting the climb.

As we were going up the mountain, you could hear choppers

and you can tell the sound of a particular chopper, then this idiot, an artillery officer screams, 'Enemy helicopters, take cover!' I was wet and still annoyed so I tells him, it's not, it's a Scout, but the blokes took cover anyway and then John Greenhalgh's Scout appears.

Captain John Greenhalgh DFC, Scout Flight 656 Squadron Army Air Corps

I still had no idea as to what it was I was going to do, except Jones had said, 'You come, I'll find you work to do.'

So, I called up, 'Hello, Zero, this is Delta November inbound,'

Of course, Jones would know it was me because we had this personal relationship, so he came up on the net, puffing, out of breath, no doubt weighed down by the weight of his bergen, 'This is Sunray, I want you to move my machine guns to the top of Sussex Mountains.'

At this point 2 Para are at the bottom of Sussex Mountains, so Rich Walker and I flew a series of GPMG teams to the top of the mountain. Our ship hadn't even anchored at this time, so we started doing racetrack loops up and down the mountain, and we moved some of the mortars, because they were overloaded with barrels and ammunition, and then we moved Steve Hughes, 2 Para doc, as well, and his RAP [regimental aid post], because they had huge bergens too. Everyone we flew up the mountain were utterly delighted. The mortar crews that we couldn't, weren't!

It wasn't long before we picked up our first casualty, and do you know what that was? Well, our first casualty ashore was heat exhaustion. I picked him up, and normally Gammo would be in the front with me, but this time I had him in the back working as a load master, so he'd make sure things got loaded. Sometimes I'd leave him behind on the ground, run up to the top of the mountain, drop people off and then come back down. He would have marshalled the right amount of weight, because obviously we had a weight limit, so he'd be organising people and kit.

Anyway, we landed to pick up this casualty, expecting a gunshot wound! We flew him to 2 Paras' B Echelon, which was still on the *Norland*, but by the time we got there, this guy with heatstroke looked normal and was smiling at us. The funny thing was, as soon as we got flying, Gammo on a helmet intercom says to me, 'There's fuck all wrong with this bloke.'

'We've started, so let's drop him off.' I replied. I sort of thought about going around and dropping him back off again with 2 Para. Can you imagine the look on his face if we had done that?

After that drop-off, we went back and carried on moving medical supplies, mortar rounds and the machine guns. Then, still on the first day, the 21st of May, I was sent to Port San Carlos to pick up a Royal Marine who had shot himself in the foot cleaning his rifle, then on to Ajax Bay, who were in the very early stages of setting up the casualty clearing station, the Field Hospital. How could he have shot himself in the foot? Well, he quite obviously didn't do his NSPs [Normal Safety Precautions]! He'd shot himself with an SLR [self-loading rifle, the standard British Armed Forces personal weapon at the time]. So, my first two casualties were heat exhaustion and a self-inflicted wound, but that was to change.

WOII Del Amos, acting technical quartermaster sergeant, B Echelon 2 Para

The first day the battalion landed, my job was to stay on ship and load up all your stores into underslung nets for the helicopters to lift. My team of blokes worked hard, and that morning we were making up a load when suddenly there was an air attack and one of the kids with me pointed to an Argy jet said, 'Oh, look. He's got his headlight on!'

'It's his fucking rocket!' I screams. So he scattered and I shouts after him, 'Get back here, you cowardly bastard!' such was my sense of humour, but we all scattered in truth.

Captain Paul Farrar, OC Patrols Platoon 2 Para

The big thing about our initial job was to mark the start-line for the battalion to cross and head up the mountain on an agreed bearing, and the patrols being the lead, we were going to secure the area and mark the start-line. We'd actually got rolls of mine tape, which is white and cut to length, so that we'd come up the axis and I'd say, right, this is the point. Then the guys in their call signs would fan out with their white tape so when each company arrived, they would see exactly what they'd been briefed to see and where to go.

When you do basic training and do an ambush or other set-pieces, you often do it on a football field first, so recruits can see what's going on and get an idea of scale; this is so everyone will know how it will work. I thought, *I'm going to do this the proper way*, so the guys fanned out and put white tape out at the bottom of Sussex Mountains and sat to one side, but when the battalion arrived, they tabbed straight through in an airborne snake straight up the mountain, with no pretence of going into assault formation as the orders dictated.

That big tab out from Blue Beach to our OPs was the hardest I've ever done. Forget the log races, forget the ten milers, it was the weight, the adrenalin, the fear, or whatever it was, the fact that we were now potentially in contact with the enemy.

Corporal 'Ginge' Dawes, clothing storeman, 2 Para

When I eventually got off the *Norland*, a Sea King came in and picked eight of us up from A Echelon [A Echelon was the forward-most stores unit of 2 Para; its job was to keep the battalion companies stored-up, while B Echelon, was further back and still on the *Norland*; their job was to pack and ferry stores to A Echelon]. We landed at the base of Sussex Mountains and I remember diving off this helicopter, going into all-round defence, and as I dived down, I landed in a pile of horse shit, but at least I had dry feet.

7

SUSSEX MOUNTAINS

Private David Minnock, GPMG gunner, 12 Platoon D Company 2 Para

The trudge up Sussex Mountains, well, that was just horrendous getting up there with the amount of kit we were all carrying, and we had other things to worry about too! We had to get up there before first light, but it was already first light and we were still only halfway up. We absolutely had no chance of getting up there before first light. We spent about four or five days up there. We dug trenches and sat there, and we had a grandstand view of San Carlos Water and the Navy, and the ships, and watched the attacks. It wasn't a nice thing to see, because at the end of the day the Navy had brought us here and they were looking after us, and they were being attacked and we felt impotent. We couldn't help 'em.

As you sat there as a soldier, in the morning the main thing is yer breakfast, yer rolled oats, and yer compo [one-man Arctic ration packs], and you're just sat there eating that, and then it's, oh God! At first we were complaining because we thought, lucky Navy, look at those fuckers in their nice warm ships watching

93

videos. But then when the Argy aircraft flew in, we all went, I'm happy to be in my hole in the ground here, freezing and wet with me rolled oats, rather than on one of those ships. I mean, they were being bombed to fuck.

Lance Corporal 'Duke' Allen, Defence Platoon 2 Para

Anyway, we headed it up Sussex Mountains and me being a switched-on soldier, really switched on, I wasn't given a G10 [official military issue] watch, and I was a section commander! So, how the fuck can you do this job without a watch. Anyway, on the *Norland* I bought a Sekonda, and because we were tactical, I thought I'd be clever and I put a bit of masking tape over the face, and of course, what happened? A couple of days later on top of Sussex Mountains, I pulled the maskers off to get the time and the fucking glass came off too, so then I didn't have a watch. You know? What a fucking disaster. No watch and two battles to fight through!

Corporal Ken Raynor, patrol commander, Recce Platoon 2 Para

There were five of us up in an Observation Post on Bodie Peak, which overlooked Camilla Creek House and the rolling hills towards Goose Green, some twenty-odd Ks away from the rest of the battalion. We had an extra guy, Steve Walters [Cpl 2 Para Mortars] our forward observation officer (FOO), who was attached to us, and who snored like a right bastard! Stevie brought a few fire missions down with the 105s from 29 CDO over a couple of days, and I always remember the first fire mission request took like two hours to be approved by Brigade Headquarters.

We were only aware of a small part of the big picture; however, we did come close on one occasion. We defo saw about three or four LVTP-7s, they were painted black and white; they were on the coastline just beyond Camilla Creek House and we dropped a load of indirect fire rounds down on them, but we never found out if we hit any of them. Due to the very rocky terrain and our close proximity to the enemy, who we believed were looking for us, we could only put limited shelter up during the hours of darkness. This was a pain prior to first light, getting out of your warm maggot and packing your kit away; this is called stand to, which we were all taught as recruits. The position also had a part to play in our normal routines like eating, drinking and taking a crap, especially as none of us were very regular due to eating nothing but arctic rations and the odd Pot Noodle.

There were other small points, like trying to position an HF antenna so it cannot be seen, but is in a good enough position to give you good comms. Mind you, all radios are dependent upon a good battery, and all we had were nicads that due to the cold did not hold a charge for long. It was not possible to exchange batteries through resupply, so we relied upon a hand crank generator, and approximately 500 hundred revolutions gave you about 20 seconds of transmit.

I remember late one afternoon, whilst Paul was having a rabbit poop crap, an Argentinian Huey helicopter hovered directly over our position no more than five metres above our heads; you could clearly see the tread of their American boots from around six soldiers sat in the chopper feet dangling over the sill. I must admit we did panic a little, but the noise allowed us to talk to each other over the noise of the chopper's engines. Our dilemma was: do we shoot it down and give away our position or do we let it go? The right decision was to let it go and that is what we did, but we all slept with one eye open that night.

GOOSE GREEN

David Norris, general news reporter Daily Mail, *attached 2 Para* (Unpublished copy, written during the war.)

San Carlos inlet turned into what Colonel H described, with refreshing and characteristic honesty, as a shambles. Loaded down with Blowpipe and Milan missiles, mortar bombs and other weaponry, some men carrying two hundred pounds in weight. People fell down exhausted to await the medics, working like fury in the darkness. 'Lie there and you will die there,' a voice in the darkness threatened. Instead of digging in before first light, we were still walking. The Blowpipes, which should have been protecting us from the wasp-like Pucaras that came with the unwelcome daylight, were scattered, higgledy-piggledy down the slopes of the mountain.

'I made a mistake,' Colonel H told me later. 'They were carrying too much weight.'

I dug my 'basha' or shallow trench in, as the icy sun gave way to freezing rain. 'Where are my bloody waterproofs – right at the bottom of my bloody pack,' I complained.

The Paras help them who help themselves. 'You'll learn,' said Lieutenant Alex Ward in the adjoining trench. 'You'll pick up tips.'

Sharing our 'scoff' – a welcome hot concoction of bacon burgers, chicken curry, rice, oatmeal biscuits and oxtail soup, heated up together in Alex's mess tin and devoured hungrily, one spoon between us, I picked up another tip. 'Carry a tin of curry powder, it peps up compo rations and warms you up,' said my companion.

'Where's my bloody tin hat?' I yelled, groping in the mud as Pucaras screamed towards us once again. 'Don't lose kit out here,' said a sergeant, handing me the lost helmet. 'It will cost you your life.'

When, for the first time in forty-eight hours, I settled down to sleep in my wet trench, they gathered around, vague shapes in the darkness: 'Have this extra sheet, it will keep you warm.' 'Are you dry enough?' 'Have some of my brew.' 'Do you have enough cigarettes?'

Private Tom Crusham, Signals Platoon, attached HQ Company 2 Para

The funny thing was, I really didn't have a job, I was like a dogsbody. I was detailed all over the place. Like, one time I had to go back to A Echelon to pick up some radio antennas. I had to cadge lifts anyway I could. Another time I jumped on the back of one of those snowcats the Marines used. Marines have a totally different mindset to Paras.

Corporal Marty Margerison, 6 Platoon B Company 2 Para

We shot a sheep, because we weren't getting our spare clothing and were running out of rations and freezing cold. I paired the lads off and made sure all had their spare socks under their armpits to dry out. I make sure the pairs regularly rubbed each other's feet to get feeling back into them, and every time they made a brew or cooked food, you made sure you'd warm those socks up. I don't sit in judgement of this at all, but I'd lost nobody up until I got shot, and then after I got shot, not just my section, but lots of others were going down with trench foot. Whether people were going, 'Oh fuck, I've had enough of this,' I just can't say.

The OC, JC, said to us, 'Now you can understand what it was like in the First World War in those trenches. We've only been here a few days and we are suffering now, and this is what we are fighting for, fighting on behalf of democracy and freedom.' So that gives you another kick up the arse.

We didn't get to skin the sheep. One of the blokes, Jim Moody, had been the battalion butcher so he was going to butcher it, but then we started getting our daily rations of Benson & Hedges cigarettes and Mars Bars for the non-smokers, and good luck with that, ha-ha. We didn't get our spare kit, though, and having been up to our waist in water when we landed and wet ever since, the elements were starting to affect us all. We didn't even get to eat the sheep.

I remember the Argy Vulcan flying over us, I'm convinced the fucking Argies had one, yes, they did! I'm fucking tellin' yer. I'll swear on my children and my grandchildren that, and it dropped a fucking bomb and I heard it whistle. It whistled and whistled and then an explosion. It was on the same day as the Royal Marines had a blue-on-blue [friendly forces accidentally attacking each other] with 42 Commando.

Chief Petty Officer Rich Edwards, Special Communications Unit (SCU) Royal Navy

On the way down I got talking to some RAF Regiment guys who were with two of the Rapier surface-to-air-missile batteries, and they would say, 'If it flies, it dies, blah de blah de blah!' What a shower they were, because they had left an important bit of test kit on the jetty back at Portsmouth, which meant they couldn't set the bloody batteries up. It took them a week to get the bloody things working!

One of our missile systems that did work well was the Sea Wolf. That was really effective. These were fitted to the Type 22 frigates. Now, *Fearless* had Sea Cat, which was hand directed; there's a little boy sitting on the upper deck on the end of a joystick in what they call the dustbin, driving this bloody thing. We fired off an entire year's allowance of Sea Cat missiles in the first few days while in San Carlos Water.

Fearless had 40/60 Bofor guns [40mm Bofors L60 anti-aircraft autocannon] and they really helped when the Argentine air force came over. The guns threw so much stuff in the air, I think some aircraft just flew into the stuff and probably fell out of the sky on their way back to Argentina. When there was an air attack, these aircraft would fly right overhead, and the Special Forces unit on board would run up the ladders to the upper deck and start firing from the hip! As soon as we sounded air raid warning red, *Fearless* would sound the siren to tell those in the surrounding area and especially those on the beach and mountain areas to jump into trenches, because when the 40/60s opened up almost horizontally, which was most of the time, they would pepper the surrounding hills with cannon shells and Sea Cat missiles.

Lance Corporal Graham Eve, 4 Platoon B Company 2 Para

On the very first night right on top of Sussex Mountains, the zip on my sleeping bag broke. In those extreme cold conditions, it would surely be a killer. You weren't often in your sleeping bag, but when you did get in it, it was like utter bliss. There really is no civvy equivalent to compare to this tragedy! Luckily for me, I was issued a new one a few days later.

Nigel Ely: It was those efforts by the QMs in war that make such a massive difference to the soldiers' wellbeing on the ground. Although some blokes never got the kit resupply they requested, Corporal Marty Margerison in point, many more did; so it proves the Army stores system does work even under constant enemy bombardment, ships sinking, and men dying.

Lance Corporal 'Duke' Allen, Defence Platoon 2 Para

I actually managed to dig in on top of Sussex Mountains and used a kip sheet topped off with peat for overhead protection and camouflage; I crawled into my little burrow. Big fucking mistake! Because the water table was so high and it didn't stop raining, of course the peat got really sodden and heavy. I got my head down for whatever it was, two hours, and fuck me I was nearly buried alive, because the weight of the peat slowly sank down, down and down, and I only barely made it out the fuckin' thing as the weight of the kip sheet came down on me – what a dick head! You know, most of the blokes built sangers, but I was in an area where there was no rock, can you believe it! I mean, the Falklands is one big rock! So that was another disaster.

Private Irwin Eversley, GPMG gunner, 2 Platoon A Company 2 Para

We made a slow ascent up the mountain side and as it was turning light, boy, was I glad when we were told to drop off the extra mortar rounds all of us were carrying. When I reached the beginning of the top, I was on one fucking knee, and I remember looking up and there was this major, I think he was just back from Belize or something, and he was carrying a little *baby* military rucksack with a radio in it, and that's all he had! I think he was marking the battalion route or something.

I was still down resting one knee gripping my gun tightly for a support and as I looked up at him, he said, 'Come on sunshine.' He had a big smile and I thought, *you cunt, all you have is a poxy little radio on your back, twat!* But just then, I remember looking to my left and saw this thing up in the sky, a little speck in the distance with smoke spilling out of the back of it. I thought, *fuckin' hell!* Then this speck seemed suddenly to shoot up real quick and BANG! – a big old explosion. I found out later it was an SAS patrol taking out an Argy jet with a Stinger [an American-built, shoulder-fired anti-aircraft missile].

Private Steve Taylor, 3 Platoon A Company 2 Para

Gibbo, who was one of the medics, was with part of Jones's Tac Group up on Sussex Mountains, and he told me this shortly after. Jones was with the Marines and he told them he was going to get off the mountain and do an attack on Goose Green, but the commander, Brigadier Thompson, Royal Marines, said no, because he evaluated the attack as a Marine Commando operation and not as a Parachute battalion one, and at that time he didn't take into account how different both units are. Maybe he didn't know back then, but fair play, General Thompson does now! He went on to write a very complimentary book about how the Paras operate.

Private David Minnock, GPMG gunner, 12 Platoon D Company 2 Para

Two days in on top of Sussex Mountains, we had lost three blokes out of the platoon through frostbite and stuff. When they were casevaced out, I don't think none of them ever came back! I believe the system was, when you got casevaced for whatever reason, you never came back. However, there was one guy from D Company who did get back, Dave Parr. He got hit by a bullet on his belt buckle later at Goose Green, and it then landed in his belly button. He never got casevaced proper, because the round only bruised him, but the next time he got hit, though, that was proper. [Private Dave Parr was killed in the second battle 2 Para fought on Wireless Ridge].

Private Phil Williams, Mortar Platoon 2 Para

In the mornings we watched the Sky Hawks and Mirages fly down the valley over us with the whole battalion opening fire at them. Not us, though, we had to take cover, because all those rounds have to down somewhere, and since we were at the rear of the mountains that's where a lot fell. It was entertaining – yeah! Some of those Argy pilots were pretty fucking brave, mate. Morning, noon and just before last light, they would come in and attack.

Private Andy Hutchins, 5 Platoon 2 Para, posted to IDB Warminster UK

When the firing started, all of us at IDB were transfixed to the TV, especially the footage about bomb alley, seeing all those dogfights with the Argies and the RAF.

Lance Corporal 'Radar', Defence Platoon 2 Para

It was about day two, and I was on guard at night on Sussex Mountains in a trench watching the boats burn down in San Carlos with Corporal JD, and there was a sound. The battalion was on one side and the mountains behind us, and HQ was behind us as well, so we was guarding for them; and there was this glacier, which millions of years ago had dropped all these rocks the size of footballs and bigger all over, we called them rock runs, and they were a bugger to tab over.

I could hear this rattling away in front on these rocks, it was pitch black, so I says, 'Fuck it! I can hear someone moving.' I aimed the night sight, scanned it across in front and I couldn't see anything, but we both agreed we could hear something. I couldn't get anything on the 351 [Clansman radio], so we sent a runner up to the Ops [Operations] trench to see if we had any patrols out: 'Tell 'em we got noise to our front, and tell 'em I'm gonna open fire.'

'No! No patrols out, definitely not,' came back the reply, so I put two bursts down towards the noise and then I heard someone call, 'Don't shoot, don't shoot, it's me, it's me!' It was one of our blokes, but I'm not gonna tell you who it was, ha-ha!

Private Phil Williams, Mortar Platoon 2 Para

For tactical reasons, our first mortar line was split into two lines of four barrels, as we didn't want them to be all in the same place. If we were supporting a rifle company, we'd have a section of mortars, which is two barrels. Like I said earlier, we went on the island with a full complement of eight barrels, which is the most you can really have as a Para Battalion. You have to have a big platoon to man eight, so that was pretty good.

When we got to the first mortar line, we got strung out, and there was this Argentinian Canberra bomber flying around above us, obviously doing a bit of a recce. We got to the first mortar position and got sorted out and set up the mortar line, but we didn't bed-in [secure the base plates] for a day or so, because we didn't have permission to open fire. When we did get the order, the force of the bomb firing off pushed the base plates through the peat crust.

So, you'd fire two rounds to bed-in, but the base plate would shoot down into the earth and the barrel would be sticking out of the ground only a couple of feet; the base plate would just crash straight through the crust and it would be down into the shitty, wet peat bog. So, every time we bedded-in, we dug it out again, and bedded-in again, and dug it out again and so on, and it was a right pain in the arse.

On that first couple of days, all we did was dig the fucking base plates out. The rifle companies had a similar problem as they couldn't dig trenches, so they built sangers out of rock and boulders.

A 22 SAS call sign

We moved our Goose Green OP further up the mountain and stayed there until we got orders to move again, because we had received a signal saying D Squadron were going to put in a diversionary attack into fooling the Argies our Task Force was NOT going to land on the beaches of San Carlos. As we started to tab off our hill, we hear some choppers away to our flank, which I later found out was D Squadron dropping off, and when they put their attack in, they shot the fuck out of everything, which then really poked the hornets' nest.

Now we had to stay another night, because the head sheds wouldn't risk a heli pick-up while all the Argies were still running around pissed off, so we made our way back up another rock run. We hid well out of the way, because the Argies put everything up in the air that flew and were out looking for D Squadron[11] and us, although we were just observers to the fireworks. D Squadron sorted the place where we had seen enemy movement at Burntside House where we'd seen the Argies moving big guns.

Captain Paul Farrar, OC Patrols Platoon 2 Para

Taken from the CO's O group at 14:00 hours on the 14th May, and my extraction thereof with regards to Friendly Forces, the words are: *Advance forces, D Squadron [SAS] Call Sign 6 on Battalion net or Company net, authenticate, Semper Fidelis.* So, the SAS had the same codes as we had and that was the password for them to enter 2 Para's position.

Lance Corporal 'Duke' Allen, Defence Platoon 2 Para

Gaz [Private Gaz Steele, Defence Platoon, 2 Para] was being woke up for stag on top of Sussex Mountains and he got up and just wandered off; he couldn't find the stag position, anyway we lost

---

11 Later on, D Squadron had to exfil by foot, so headed off towards 2 Para lines up on Sussex Mountains.

him. He didn't turn up till the next morning, when Ken Raynor [Corporal Recce Platoon, 2 Para] led him back into where our position was. Ken had found him. Gaz always wore these blue-tinted glasses for whatever reason, but one of his lenses had dropped out and I think he'd also lost his helmet, and as he came back in, he had this weird look on his face; funny as fuck it was. Just a nice little story in war.

Later on in the war, Gaz got fragged in the back on Wireless Ridge. I was on stag by the mortar line when the Wireless Ridge attack was going in, then suddenly this fucking rocket or whatever it was came flying over the top of this hill and exploded about twenty, thirty feet from us. A lot of the frag went into the poncho where Gaz and his buddy Spick Spiby was getting their heads down, and I went, fucking hell, there're dead.

So I ran over to their basha [a tented poncho] and screamed, 'Spick, Spick! Gaz, Gaz!' And I went, Oh no. I was dreading to lift the poncho up.

Anyway, I heard Gaz go, 'OOhhhhhahrrr, aahhhhhahrrr,' but he was alright. Yet it wasn't until later on when he was lifting ammo, he calmly stated, 'Fucking hell, me back's all wet!' and it was blood. He'd been fragged in the back. Spick was alright, not a scratch on him.

Funny really, we called the Argies 'Spicks', but we called him Spick well before the war . . . I don't know how he got his nickname. Like Joe Tilt, another Defence Platoon member, his name is Philip, Philip Tilt, but he's called Joe because of *Joe the Crow*. [Para vernacular for a new recruit.] Names like that just stick sometimes.

Lance Corporal 'Radar', Defence Platoon 2 Para

A day later, still in the same trench, we were told to stop shooting at the Argy aircraft, because we had 3 Para over on the next ridge. Anyway, it was dark o'clock, it was pitch black, no ambient light and blowing a fucking gale, and seriously bucketing down. Again, I could see moving shapes to my front, but I thought I was hallucinating. So I looked away then looked back, then took hold of the night sight and I could see a fucking extended line coming up the fucking hill towards me in my arch of fire!

The end of a little re-entrant was my right arch of fire, because that's where the battalion started, so they had come by that little re-entrant and were advancing across open ground towards me. Again, nothing on the 351, so a runner was sent again, back to the Ops trench and JD said, 'Well, shoot them!'

'You shoot 'em,' I said, 'you're the corporal.'

'No, you shoot 'em! I'm ordering you to fire.' And that's all I needed, and I was in!

We'd told the runner to say, 'We've got armed bodies to our front, ten plus, coming towards us in extended line and defo see weapons.'

So, I'm now thinking, who the hell could this be? I mean I really thought it was one of our patrols coming in, because their shapes were familiar. They just kept coming and coming, and this was, say, about six hundred, seven hundred metres away, and they kept coming.

When the runner came back, he says, 'There's no patrols out. Anything to your front is enemy.'

Okay, I thought, *this ain't right*. We were all issued these little pencil flares, red they were, so I thought, *this wind is blowing like fuck*, so I aimed it practically at three o'clock, fired it off, it just went *whooooff*, and it was gone in a second; no light, no nothing, just disappeared. I asked JD what are they doing now? He says they're still coming. I put another up, as it was the only lume [illumination] we had, and that didn't last in the wind either.

So, I'm gonna open up from right to left, because there was no cover on the left, and as I got another belt ready, they got closer and

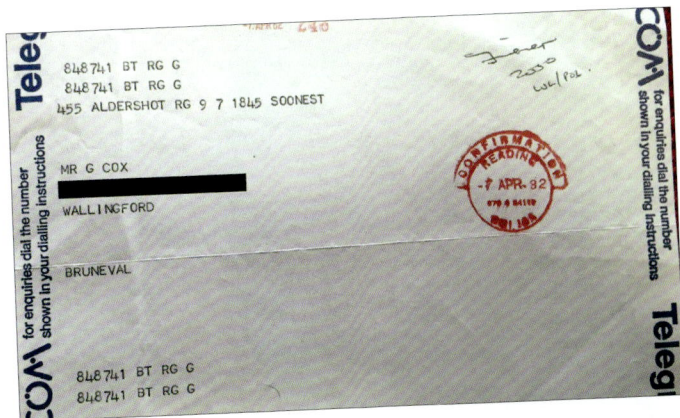

Left: The recall telegram sent to Private Greg Cox, Patrols Platoon 2 Para, using the code word 'Bruneval'.

(*Author's collection*)

Right: The author aboard MV *Norland* during the voyage south. (*Author's collection*)

Below: Ferry at war – *Norland* bracketed by Argentine bombs in San Carlos Water, 21 May 1982. At right is the amphibious warfare ship HMS *Intrepid*.

(© *Pete Holdgate/ Crown Copyright. Imperial War Museum via Getty Images*)

Right: Steward – and ship's pianist – Roy 'Wendy' Gibson (*centre*) with members of 2 Para aboard *Norland*.

(*All in the Same Boat*)

Left: Landing craft criss-crossing San Carlos Water on the day of the landings, 21 May 1982.

(© *Martin Cleaver/PA Archive/PA Images*)

Right: Lieutenant Colonel H Jones's Wessex hovering low in a re-entrant on Sussex Mountains to evade Argentine Skyhawks that were attacking 2 Para's positions. (*Author's collection*)

Right: The author and Corporal Ken Raynor in their OP overlooking Camilla Creek House.

(*Author's collection*)

Below: C Company going firm at Camilla Creek House, 27 May 1982.

(© *Airborne Assault museum archives*)

Right: Colonel Jones's second O group, Camilla Creek House, 27 May; the first was abandoned when it was found the that not all the officers could attend at the time.

(© *Airborne Assault museum archives*)

Left: Darwin Hill during the battle, shrouded in smoke from gorse set alight by white phosphorus grenades.

(© *Airborne Assault museum archives*)

Below right: Men of HQ Company 2 Para look on as the gorse burns on Darwin Hill.

(© *Airborne Assault museum archives*)

Below left: Lieutenant Colonel H Jones, VC, OBE, killed while assaulting an Argentine position on Darwin Hill, 28 May 1982. (© *Airborne Assault museum archives*)

Above: 'Sunray down!' – looking south from Darwin Hill. Today a memorial marks the spot where Colonel Jones fell.

(*Author's collection*)

Left: 2 Para on Darwin Hill. (*© Airborne Assault museum archives*)

Below: Argentine prisoners at the foot of Darwin Hill.

(*© Airborne Assault museum archives*)

Left: The 2 Para RAP on Darwin Hill after the Argentine surrender. The MO, Captain Steve Hughes, is fourth from right.

(*© Airborne Assault museum archives*)

Left: D Company 2 Para with Argentine prisoners near Boca House, 28 May; note the fixed bayonet.

(© *Airborne Assault museum archives*)

Right: C Company 2 Para waiting at Camilla Creek House before the attack on Goose Green; Scout helicopter in the background.

(*Author's collection*)

Left: C (Bruneval) Company 2 Para moving through the dead and wounded at A Company's position on Darwin Hill prior to assaulting Goose Green. (*Author's collection*)

Left: C Company
2 Para waiting for the
counterattack from
Goose Green that
never came.
(*Author's collection*)

Above: Private John Bolland of
the Recce Platoon taking cover
in an Argentine trench. Minutes
later he was hit by a rocket and
seriously wounded.
(*Author's collection*)

Left: Private Roy Charters, Recce
Platoon radio operator, taking
cover as the schoolhouse burns in
the background. (*Author's collection*)

Right: D Company 2 Para with captured Argentine troops near Boca House, west of Darwin Hill.

(© Airborne Assault museum archives)

Left: The ruins of the schoolhouse at Goose Green, set alight during the fierce fighting that followed the white flag incident.

(© Airborne Assault museum archives)

Right: 2 Para with Argentine prisoners, some wounded, after the battle.

(Author's collection)

closer. I knew somethin' was really wrong here, and that's when I heard this bod say, 'Are we fucking there yet?' I thought, *what the fuck's going down here?* It turned out to be a dozen or so SAS blokes, a couple who I knew from 2 Para. And I could have wiped them all out with a gimpy – a troop of SAS gone in a belt of two hundred.

Captain John Greenhalgh DFC, Scout Flight 656 Squadron Army Air Corps

One time I was flying up Sussex Mountains when I saw a group of long-haired blokes and one of them gave me the 'I am your marshaller' sign, so I thought, *who the fuck are these guys?* I flew back around, landed and one of them comes in and says, 'You couldn't give us a lift to HMS *Intrepid* (the alternative command ship), could you?' It was obvious who it was, because they all had long hair and most were carrying GPMGs and short-barrelled weapons or they had Stingers. They had all this kit and were very smelly and very sweaty from tabbing up the hill, and you know they were going to kiss us, they were so happy to get on to a ship where they could get cleaned up.

This SAS patrol had done a recce on Goose Green, then tabbed up Sussex Mountains through 2 Para lines, and if you ever want to stop a helicopter you adopt the army marshalling sign, both arms outstretched above head in a V shape, similar to the surrender stance. Well, it certainly worked for them.

Lance Corporal Graham Eve, GPMG commander, 4 Platoon B Company 2 Para

My patrol was sent down to find the remains of a Pucara, and if the pilot had ejected or whether he was dead. We did find the Pucara but the pilot wasn't there: he'd ejected and escaped, from what I can remember. The wreckage obviously wasn't complete, but I thought it didn't look too bad. It wasn't all smashed up as you might have expected. Everyone wanted a bit of a souvenir, so I broke off this wee yellow antenna thing on the front of the nose because it was small and light and would be easy to carry. On the top, it had like a wee dust cap thing, like you find protecting car tyre valves, and on it read, *Made in UK*.

I thought, *fuck me! I'm gonna go back to the UK with my wee thing here, which I took off a Pucara that was shot down by the SAS during the Falklands War and nobody's going to ever believe me.*

When we got back to our trenches on Sussex Mountains, JC came over to us and said, 'You lads were lucky. When you were away our own artillery fired a couple of air burst rounds by accident over *your* trenches and splattered them.' If we hadn't been on the Pucara mission we would have all been dead, or at the least seriously injured. Blue-on-Blue, they would tell Sandra.

Roy 'Wendy' Gibson, steward and ship's pianist, MV Norland

When you lads had gone ashore, I was helping move ammunition from the car deck to a landing craft through the lower port-side door in a chain-gang line, when one of the Paras gave me a quilted jacket because it was bloody cold. Then I got moved along this sort of chain gang and somehow ended up in a bloody landing craft with one of the lads from the Duty-Free shop; then the wind got up and the landing craft broke away full of ammunition in San Carlos Water heading towards Blue Beach!

The next thing, all of a sudden there was this bloody great big bang and all the magazines went up on the *Antelope* [HMS *Antelope*] that lit the entire sky up. We managed to get back to the *Norland*, but I was lucky. When I got back onto the ship, there was a real big tall lad with ginger hair wearing a green beret waiting for me, and he took me to the cleaners about accidentally boarding the landing craft. His language wasn't very nice, I think he was a Marine.

'Well, I can't bleeding help that,' I said and I carried on, 'Hey, don't you talk to me like that, I'm not under you, I've gotta captain who's my boss!' He apologised in the end.

Private Dave 'Charlie' Brown, HQ C (Bruneval) Company 2 Para

The whole thing was shit. We were losing the war stuck on Sussex Mountains, and for days we watched the bastard Navy get the shite kick out of them. It was depressing, real depressing, us Paras stuck on this mountain, what with the wind and the cold cutting through us. My glasses kept steaming up trying to write sitreps; paper was wet all the time, and I had no clean shit to wipe them on. I thought, *I'm going to die on this mountain; freeze to death or get bombed by the Argy pilots.* They were brave!

8

THE TAB TO
CAMILLA CREEK

Private Phil Williams, Mortar Platoon 2 Para

When we got the word to move off Sussex Mountains to Camilla Creek House, we took only two barrels with us as fire support. Two barrels, that was all it was! Why only two? Well, we was supposed to get a battery of guns, which then turned into half a battery of guns, the 105 howitzer light guns, and HMS *Arrow* as our guard ship with a 4.75-inch gun; but that jammed after only two rounds when we really needed it, as it was meant to fire in support of us when the battle for Goose Green kicked off.

The rest of the platoon carried as many bombs and charge eights as we could. At the time I thought two barrels was not enough, but given the amount of ammunition we had, if we'd had any more barrels firing the ammunition, we'd have used it up even quicker than what we actually did. So, I suppose two barrels was about right, paired with how much ammunition we had and how long it lasted.

WOII Del Amos, acting technical quartermaster sergeant, B Echelon 2 Para

As the battalion moved towards Camilla Creek House, I was ordered to go and liaise with the Marines on Red Beach, so this LCU comes alongside the *Norland* in the pitch black. I managed to get onboard and off it chugs and there's a really heavy swell and all the rest of it, and as always you know, this kid Marine says to me, 'Hey you, fucking get over to the starboard side of the craft.'

So, I said, 'Who the fuck do you think you're talking to? I presume you're a Marine?'

'Yeah,' he replies.

'Well,' I says, 'I'm a fucking warrant officer, so watch your fucking lip,' but I did go and stand on the starboard side.

My RV was the Red Beach jetty. So, I'm ready with all my kit and rifle and he smashed into the jetty, BANG! so he had to go around again. He obviously didn't like this mission in the pitch black. We goes round again and the same thing, BANG! So he says, 'Right. I'm gonna go round one more time and if you don't get off this time, I'm back to the *Hermes*.'

So, the jetty's coming up fast and he tells me, 'GO!' but I jump just as this Marine puts the craft into reverse and he's gone, leaving me clinging on desperately for dear life. I scramble up and start making my way along the jetty, then a voice pops up, 'Halt! And give us a password.'

'I haven't got a fucking clue,' I threw back. I was waiting to get slotted. 'My name's Del Amos, I'm the TQMS of 2 Para.' I thought, *if he's twitchy, I'm a goner!*

'Okay, come ahead,' the voice orders.

'I'm here to liaise with the QM.'

'Well,' the guard says, 'if you just go and wait in that trench.' And this was at 20:00 hours.

It was eight o'clock the next morning I got out of that trench and I still didn't get to see their QM. He'd just pissed off and left, obviously a change of plan. So, I was left in this trench for twelve hours getting bored to death by some Marine telling me how good he was.

Private David Minnock, GPMG gunner, 12 Platoon D Company 2 Para

We had this little escapade up at a place called Cantera House. Someone thought they had seen a couple of LVTP-7s up at this place come out of the water and onto ground. Potentially there were two of 'em and my platoon was sent to go and investigate. It was at night when we got choppered in, by a helicopter we'd never been in before. We see it land and we tried to get on it the normal way, but we couldn't for a brief second; sounds silly now, but it was a Sea King and we'd never been on a Sea King before, so we struggled with it at first.

We got on and they flew us there; we had two runs to get all of the platoon in. They dropped us off a fair way from the target, but before we got on board, we could hear more helicopters some way off to our front. They were Argy Hueys, as we didn't fly Hueys and if you've ever heard a Huey at night time, they make this real *wooker-wooker* noise. There must have been about five or six of 'em, and they were flying just ahead of us, *wooker-wooker, wooker-wooker*, and at night noise carries.

I thought, *how many blokes does a Huey hold, they must hold about seven or eight blokes and there were at least about five, six or seven and we were heading their way.* I mean, the loadie didn't say anything and we weren't briefed at all, really! We were told, 'Just go and check this place out and it will all get explained to you when you get there.'

So, we gets there, pitch-black night, a bit of a tab, and I was scared to death, because I knew if there were two LVTP-7s that had been seen, I knew how many blokes they could carry and I knew they had a crew of three, and it's got a heavy duty machine gun on it and a bloody cannon. I thought, *oh God, if there were two of these things floating about, and there's just my platoon of twenty-five blokes, it didn't bear well.* I voiced my opinion and was told to 'shut the fuck up'!

So, we enter the building, cleared it, and stayed in it for cover; no firing, just silent and clear. Come the morning, we stayed inside and we stayed there until dark, in case we were spotted. But years later, I read it in a book, we were seen and there was a report put in to do an assault on us. The strangest thing about this building was that it was on an estuary; it was said to be used by the Argy pilots who were attacking our ships as a turn point, because as they flew over us, they would make a turn.

It was obvious they were using it as a point of reference, so Taff Meredith [John Meredith DCM] my platoon sergeant passed this information on to whoever, with a possibility of setting up one of our Rapier air-defence missile systems there, but nothing ever came of it. We then had to tab all the way back, no choppers, but just in time to catch the rest of the battalion moving off Sussex Mountains towards Camilla Creek House, so we were pretty much knackered. We'd heard the enemy but not seen 'em, so we were more worried about that than being knackered.

Sergeant John 'Taff' Meredith DCM, 12 Platoon D Company 2 Para

Shortly before we moved off Sussex Mountains, I got an order for a Fighting Patrol to go to a place called Cantera House, and then it was cancelled and then suddenly it was back on again. We went across to where the LZ was, and we were supposed to have two Sea Kings to lift us but only one turned up, so the platoon was split into two lifts. I brought the second half in and I wasn't sure if they'd drop me at the same place as the first lift; and as usual, as we flew in, I couldn't see any of the others.

When we were offloading I waited by the door, as the loadie normally gives you the grid reference from the pilot where he's dropped you, but nothing was coming; so I had hold of the loadie as it was taking off and he nearly came with us! Luckily his belt was stronger than I was, so I let him go and the chopper few off, but luckily enough I could just make out the others. We then started to move off to find Cantera House, where we were told three LVTP-7s had been spotted. Now, I'm ex-anti-tanks, so I know what an LVTP-7 carries and what damage they can do, and I wasn't happy. Previously, I'd said to the OC, you can't send a platoon after them!

So, they gave us an 84 [84 Carl Gustaf. A two-man, anti-tank, shoulder-fired bazooka] plus two men and a FOO party, with a sergeant who was the FOO, to even up the odds! As we started to move off, I could hear somebody talking in front: English. *Who the hell's talking?* So I moved up and it was the FOO, so I says, 'What you doing?'

'I'm just telling the gun line what's going on,' he says.

So I says, 'I don't know what's going on, so how can you tell them what's going on, so just shut up!' The whole time he'd been on the net, the enemy may have had range-finding equipment and could have found us.

Then the rain came in again at a slant, but luckily, on our maps the fence lines were marked, and we'd come up to a fence line and stopped. I went up to my boss, Jim Barry, who thought we'd gone too far, but I said, 'Look on the map, Cantera House is right by the sea.'

He then says, 'The FOO agrees with me, we've gone too far.'

I didn't agree, so I said, 'It's already down as an X-ray, put a round on it. Get the FOO to do it, it's his job.' So we called it in and we're all looking in the direction they thought it would be as the rain was still lashing down. 'Shot over!' 'Shot out!' sort of thing came over the radio. Okay, twenty-one seconds [artillery round time-of-flight] and we should get a bang. Twenty-one seconds pass, then BOOM!

'There you go, it's over there,' Jim says.

'No, it's over there,' I replied, pointing a one-eighty.

'No, no, it's over there.'

'It can't be,' I pleaded. 'Look we got the fence here, a junction in the fence, yet the BOOM was about two klicks away over there,' exactly where I thought Cantera House should be. Then the weather started to lift and you could just make out a white blob where I thought the house was, and I was correct, as one of the outbuildings appeared. So off we went to do a side attack and luckily there were no LVTP-7s, otherwise we'd have got slaughtered, because they all carry a 50 cal [heavy machine gun], a 7.62 machine gun plus thirty men in each.

We went firm, and the next day we reported that Argy aircraft were using the buildings as a reference point, turning before they made their attacks, so we asked for a Blowpipe attachment, but that was denied. Then we were ordered to stay there for another twenty-four hours, which was a ball breaker, because we'd been told we'd be out for only twelve hours and were still in light order.

So then we moved to secure an RV for the rest of D Company, because they were coming to secure another location called Camilla Creek House. Once secured, I got through on the net and D Company said they were fifteen minutes out, then five minutes later, D Company were told to turn around and go back up Sussex Mountains and for us to return to Cantera House. I didn't want to go back, and orders like that just kill the men's morale. When we arrived on the outskirts of Cantera House, we had to assault it all over again, because we weren't to know if the Argies had moved in while we'd been away.

We were on our chin straps; the blokes were going down. I had two with trench foot, one bloke had a knee pop out. By this time, we were all starving, but luckily in the house was a tray of peas and tinned sausages, probably a shepherd's emergency rations. We had to get out of the elements and get warm, we also had a 360 defensive routine going, so the blokes didn't get much sleep.

We ordered more rations and a casevac to get the injured out. We had three so far out of a platoon of twenty-seven, with the FOO party over thirty blokes, but we were told the weather was too bad even to fly the casualties out. Yet we could see the choppers happily flying over Sussex Mountains, so why lie when *they* must have known we could see everything. So, they wouldn't come in for a casevac, but they said they were going to do a resupply, but the RV for the chopper to make the drop was three Ks away from us!

I said, 'That's no good, because that means I've gotta send most of the platoon three Ks to pick up a couple boxes of ration,' as although they could carry it, they'd still need protection. So I said it was pointless.

In the end they told us to return to Sussex Mountains, so we tabbed back up the mountain and got back into our original positions after last light, which we weren't happy about, because we weren't coming through our own position. While me and the rest of D Company had been away, *they'd* moved a company of Marines in, but we didn't know that until we got to our bergens, because they'd all been rifled: digging tools and personal kits had gone missing. We got a scoff and a hot brew on, and at the same time the three casualties were dealt with, but that night another bloke got casevaced with suspected appendicitis. He never came back, so I've now lost four blokes. Then thirty-six hours later, D Company led the battalion back down the mountain to Camilla Creek House.[12]

---

12 This rather odd decision must have been so morally and physically draining for D Company. My memory wandered back to Montgomery's line: 'What manner of men …'

Captain Paul Farrar, OC Patrols Platoon 2 Para

I led elements of D Company towards Camilla Creek House. We tabbed for a couple of hours but then were ordered back, so D Company and ourselves went back up to Sussex Mountains. This was intended to be an initial raid, but it was recalled. The following day H Jones came up with this idea that he wanted to cover his left flank.

I remember him saying, 'Right, Paul, what I want you to do is to take your platoon and I'm giving you a naval gunfire party and I need you somewhere here, so you can give us an early warning approach from that flank.' He was pointing on the map to a place called Flats Shanty, which is up in the area behind Bodie Peak towards Mount Usborne. He said, 'I want you to travel light. I want you to take food for two days, by which I mean, not two days' rations, just a couple of packets of biscuits.' These were his exact words, and he carried on, 'Don't take your helmets, as you're well out of artillery range.'

Although I'd only been with H Jones a short while, I had a good rapport with him, so I asked, 'Now sir, you're not going to send us anywhere else are you after this?'

'No, you'll be coming back to Sussex Mountains,' he replied.

So, off we went in light order to the ambush site. It was horribly cold and I wrote in my diary, *a desperate night*. And that is why 2 Para Patrols fought the battle for Goose Green with no helmets, because they were on still on Sussex Mountains. We fought in our maroon berets.

Come first light, we lifted the ambush and moved into the lower reverse ground of Bodie Peak, had a brew-up, and then we started getting radio messages asking, 'Can you move to grid so-and-so? What can you see from *this* grid? And can you see X from Y?' We were being pushed around this high ground all day, and of course, it later transpired that all this 'can you see this, can you see that' business was to try and look where the battalion checkpoint and RV was going to be beyond Camilla Creek House, ready for the assault, because by then, clearly the decision to go ahead with a proper attack on Darwin and Goose Green had been made.

Private Bob Morgan, Patrols Platoon 2 Para

We had been ordered to go out on a recce by a lake to find a spot for our mortars and gunners, so we were going to put some rounds into the lake to find a known point for them to aim off against potential enemy targets. We had been ordered to go in light order [no bergens, just belt order: weapon, ammo, water, and a little bit of scoff and emergency rations]. The only clothes we had were what we were wearing, and for warmth, the old army waterproofs. Jones [the CO] ordered us not to take sleeping bags either, so what the hell was going through his mind, because we almost froze to death that night, and then as things panned out, we attacked Goose Green in light order too with no helmets, because they were still at the bergen cache back on Sussex Mountains. Madness!

Sergeant Pilot Dick Kilinski, F Flight 656 Squadron Army Air Corps

We slept in our aircraft. We folded the back seats down to make more room. We cooked-up and ate our 24-hour ration packs in our aircraft and drank brews in our aircraft, but then we found out the Argies didn't have any night capability; they weren't flying at night because they wouldn't be able to get back to where they started from without seeing in the dark. They could attack us during the day, and at first light they would be there attacking the ships, but they couldn't do anything at night, so we'd shut down after last light and get a reasonable amount of sleep. But during the days, we had so much tasking on we started rotors just before dawn and most of the time we didn't stop rotors until after it got dark.

So, we were flying all day, hot refuelling, burning and turning on the ships, getting the fuel sucked off, and if you needed ablutions, you'd get out and be as quick as you could. My aircraft was my aircraft and I had all my webbing/belt kit and my SLR rifle by my side, no one else flew it, same for all of us. And for some reason every one of my rounds was tracer! I can't recall why I filled my SLR mags up all with tracer! NATO standard was one-in-five, five ball rounds to one tracer round.

Chief Petty Officer Rich Edwards, Special Communications Unit (SCU) Royal Navy

A lot of the MOD had been giving all our secrets away about how our bombs went off, too. The UK Government had supplied iron bombs to the Argentines Air Force, who were then dropping them on our ships, but they weren't going off as they should have been. The Argentine armourers, quite wrongly from their point, had set the bomb fuses so the bombs had to fly 250 metres or so before they were armed, and then to go WHOOSH BANG when it hit its target! That's why our boys were able to disarm a number of them early on in the war.

But these idiots from the MOD were gloatingly telling the entire world the Argy bombs weren't armed properly, and the Argentine pilots were flying so low one actually hit the top of HMS *Antelope*, and knocked a piece of the aerial off; but I'm not sure if the pilot later fell out of the sky, though. They flew past the bridge windows on *Fearless* too! So, when the Argentinians heard this over the world radio, they obviously corrected that immediately. I did hear of a rumour that some of these bombs were made in Margaret Thatcher's constituency!

Lance Corporal Geoff 'Johnno' Johnson, HQ Company 2 Para, attached to D Company 2 Para

Ah, another John bloody Nott broadcast! The BBC announced the Argentinians were hitting our ships, but their bombs weren't exploding. I've got two Labradors who could tell you the fuckin' fuses weren't right. The BBC were duplicitous bastards, like they are now!

Private Greg Cox, light machine gunner, Patrols Platoon 2 Para

We were all issued with a Hartmann's drip. Anyway, like any good soldier, I managed to secure additional ones just in case. The spares came in really handy when we were tabbing back from our OP and were about to tab out to Camilla Creek House and then on to Goose Green. Having used most of our water making hot brews to stay functional, I put one of the drips in my pocket and used the tube as a straw, drinking when I needed. It wasn't particularly pleasant, but it kept my throat wet for the remainder of that tab. I wish I had developed the idea further, perhaps I'd be a millionaire by now![13]

Captain John Greenhalgh DFC, Scout Flight 656 Squadron Army Air Corps

My engine started leaking oil badly as 2 Para moved off Sussex Mountains and I didn't want to stop flying just because it was leaking oil, but obviously if it ran out of oil, the engine would fail and you'd end up in a bit of a state. So I was cleared to fly for no more than

---

13 Personal hydration packs, a water bag with a straw, were first issued to the US Army in the first Gulf War. CamelBak, who make these packs, sold out for US $210 million in 2004. Greg was nine years ahead of his time.

forty-five minutes between oil checks. I took a gallon of oil with me, and every forty-five minutes I had to land, check the oil level and top it up myself. I was cleared to put the oil in myself too!

I had to do the paperwork to allow me to do this and tell them how much oil I was putting in, and the longer we went on, the worse the leak got and the more oil we were losing, so in the end we had to change the engine, which the fabulous REME team achieved overnight. It was dangerous to go on with such an oil leak, and all this maintenance was done in the open.

We had only one Land Rover command post with a tent on the back with all the radios. Being the only officer, I slept in the aircraft. My radio operators, Lance Corporal Angus, Air Troopers Beets and Coleman could wake me if they needed help. Private Beets became field promoted, Lance Corporal Beets (later becoming a WO1), and I am still in touch with them all today.

XT649 was my aircraft and my call sign was Delta November. I was initially in charge of three Scouts and then I went to six aircraft with fifty blokes, which was quite a responsibility for a young captain.

9

CAMILLA CREEK HOUSE

No one man makes a perfect plan.

Nigel Ely: The Camilla Creek House smallholding consisted of one main building, two barns and an outside toilet. It reminded me of *Little House on the Prairie*. All had their roofs still on, which was a bonus for some but not for me, as C Company never went anywhere near the place. We decided to lay off. For those tempted to move into these buildings, even just for some respite from the wind and rain, it was a personal choice, and I didn't blame them, because you either sorted yourself out and tried to get warm or froze to death.

You had to keep your head warm, and you had to keep that wind out, but C Company never went anywhere near them for fear the Argies had DF-ed the area [pre-marked the position for direct fire]. More worrying, it lay in a most exposed position.

Captain Paul Farrar, OC Patrols Platoon 2 Para

The main significance about Camilla Creek House was that it was where the CO's orders took place for the attack on Darwin/Goose

Green. As Patrols Platoon commander, I attended his orders along with Major Roger Jenner OC C Company and Lieutenant Colin Connor MC, OC, Recce Platoon, plus the company commanders. A guy called John Thurman gave the ground brief, because he knew the ground, having previously been a member of the Falklands Royal Marines detachment. He gave us a very detailed briefing on the settlement of Goose Green, which was quite handy because we couldn't see it at that time. The O group was fully attended, plus the Signals Officer, the Adjutant, the Intelligence Officer, the Ops Officer, and Mortars there too, so pretty much anyone who was anybody. It was in the open air in a peaty hollow with all of us sitting around. The weather was quite reasonable from what I do remember.

I think the O group was meant to be at 12:00 Zulu. At the time it got light at around eleven Zulu and was dark at around five Zulu, so it was first thing in the morning, which was really good because it gave us time to prepare. But, at around the same time, Peter Ketley, OC Anti-Tanks, 2 Para, captured an Argy Land Rover and took prisoners into OC A Company's area, so this delayed arrival of OC A Company and Pete Ketley at the O group.

Of course, H Jones was not a particularly patient man and used to get agitated about stuff, so he got really annoyed that OC A Company could not attend his O group, and I think his words were, 'Right, Farrar-Hockley's not here.[14] Bugger off the lot of you and come back at three o'clock,' or whatever he said. So, the O group was delayed three hours at the stroke of a pen.

H was a man always keen to use his assets, but he was not a man to take any shit. He would get very annoyed very quickly and so his O group, his defining moment as a commander, had just been delayed by OC A Company and others. So we scuttled away and went back three hours later when the O group reconvened, which went on and on and on. It was a long O group, and the problem

14 Major (now Major General) Dair Farrar-Hockley MC.

was, we C Company, knew we were going to be the first people to move.

It was a textbook set of orders by the way orders were delivered at that time; it was prescriptive: 'A Company, you are to . . . , B Company, you are to . . . , C Company, you are to . . . ,' and that's what we were trained for; there was nothing at all bad about the orders, because it was the way they were done at that time. And when we got to timings it was: 'Phase 1 – C Company when ready after last light. A Company to lead off at 0300 . . . Phase 2 – 0600, Phase 3 – 0700, etc.' So, every phase of this six-phase battle was going to start on the hour.

Well, of course, we had been out on the ground tabbing around, and we knew we couldn't cover these distances. I remember thinking at the time, these timescales are simply not going to work, there's just not enough time, and it's too prescriptive; so we were on a hiding to nothing, but orders are orders and C Company were to move at last light.

The plan was, A Company was going left flanking to attack the first known enemy at a place called Burntside House, and Recce were leading them on to their start-line, which in fairness was the harder task, I have to say. Patrols were to lead B Company and man the battalion checkpoint. The idea was, we'd move to a battalion RV then move to a checkpoint, which was a little pedestrian bridge across what's called Ceritos Arroyo, the last water feature before we got onto the Darwin/Goose Green isthmus.

It was almost impossible to judge how close we could get to the first known enemy positions and to say right, that's close enough, without alerting the enemy and then set the start-line. We'd already decided we weren't going to fuck around with white tape this time, but put the blokes down at five-metre intervals. The drill was, I'd pull back through the platoon sergeant then meet JC to lead him and his B Company up, and they could then spread out into their assault formation. It was only after a couple of hundred metres across the start-line they came into contact with the enemy; so we'd taken them pretty close.

The battle plan called for a series of sequential manoeuvres by A, B and D Companies, culminating with Phase 6 at 1030 Zulu, when the settlements of Darwin and Goose Green were to have been surrounded, critically whilst still under the cover of darkness! So, A and B Companies should have launched their first attacks at 0600 Zulu, and within four and a half hours, Phase 6 should have been complete, which would have been just cracking first light. That was not a lot of time to cover the ground and achieve what needed to be done. But, in actuality, it was broad daylight even by the time A Company secured Darwin Hill.

Now, and to be fair to H Jones, he did say the timings were a best guess, and they were flexible. Nowadays, you wouldn't give a set of full orders like that. You wouldn't be so prescriptive about the timescale. But the way orders were taught at the time, well, that was the way it was done.

So, the orders were good, they were clear, there was quite a bit of information about where the enemy were. I think some people say, *we weren't told this,* or *we weren't told that* on the orders! No! There was a lot of information given out to us. The most up-to-date intelligence came from some of the Recce call signs and Colin Connor – that was useful.

The SAS, as far as I'm concerned, provided no intelligence at any stage of the Falklands War, even though we bumped into D Squadron, 16 troop, as we were moving somewhere between Sussex Mountains and Bodie Peak, as they were coming back from their raid on Darwin on D-Day.

We knew they were coming and there was some slightly Mickey Mouse recognition signal; they would be wearing or showing pieces of white four-by-two [4-inch x 2-inch rifle barrel cleaning

Fanning Head

3 Para
42
Commando

GREEN BEACH
21 May

Port San Carlos
Settlement

N

SAN CARLOS WATER

Fleet anchorage
somewhere in San
Carlos Water

40 Commando

THE VERDE MTS

45 Commando

Ajax Bay

BLUE BEACH
2 Para
0715 hours
21 May

San Carlos
Settlement

SUSSEX

2 Para
Arrive dawn
21 May

2 PARA

22–6 May

Last light
26 May

Grantham Sound

Port Sussex Inlet

Port Sussex
House

Old Shanty Ridge

2 Para arrives 0700 hrs. 27
May Lies up throughout 27th

Camilla Creek House

Ceritos
House

C Company patrols
27 May

28 May

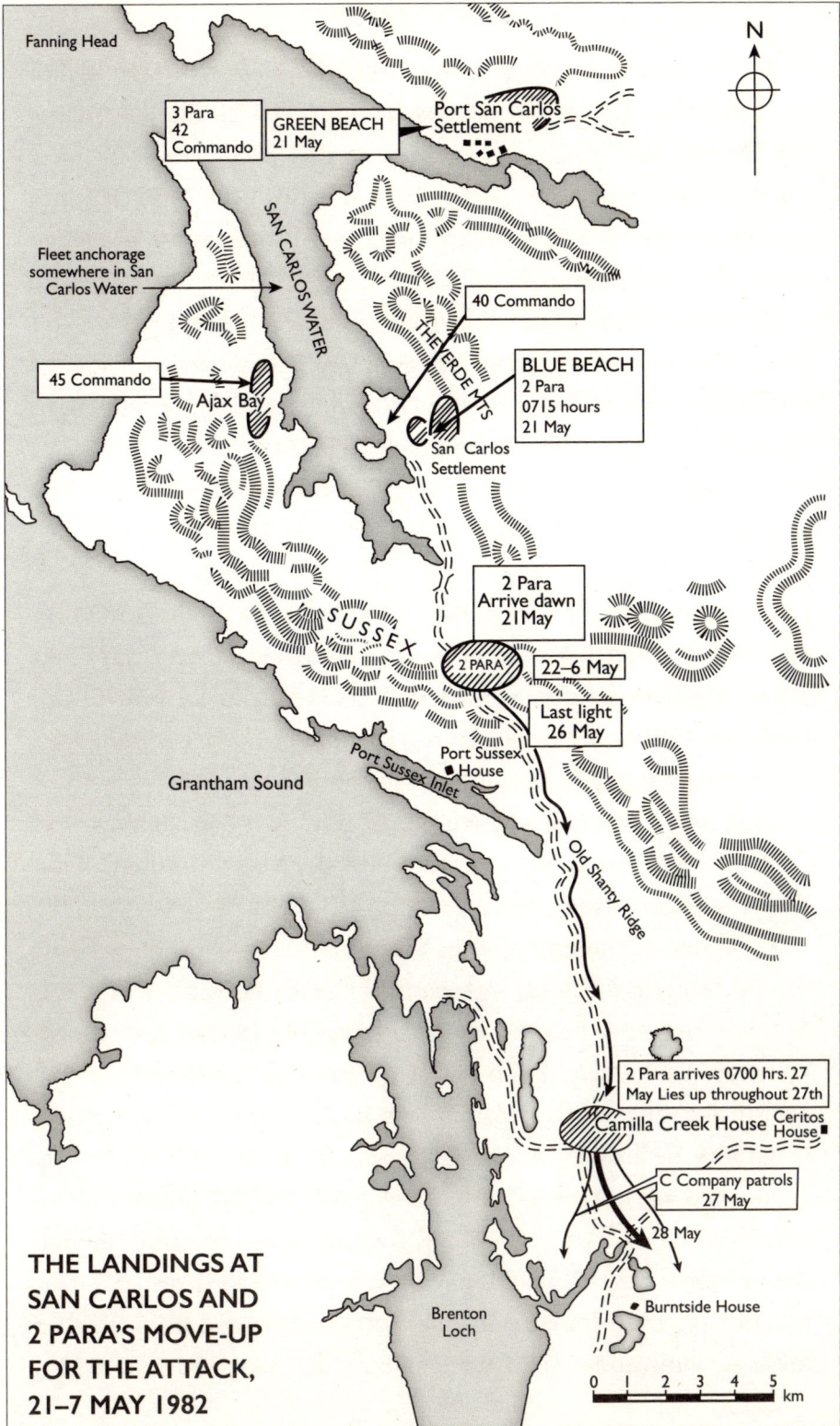

THE LANDINGS AT
SAN CARLOS AND
2 PARA'S MOVE-UP
FOR THE ATTACK,
21–7 MAY 1982

Brenton
Loch

Burntside House

0 1 2 3 4 5
km

cloth, white in colour with a thin red strip running through it] and the challenge was '*Semper Fidelis*' [Latin: 'ever faithful'], which is the Devon and Dorset's motto because OC D Squadron 22 SAS, Cedric Delves, was a Devon and Dorset at that time. Also, H Jones was also originally a Devon and Dorset, so I suppose the challenge had a degree of relevance.

We didn't speak to the SAS party a huge amount. I still reckon theirs was a stand-off attack; 2000 metres away at least; lots of GPMG fire, but of course, it was a diversionary attack, so I guess, in their defence, how close do you have to get?

Colour Sergeant Pete Vale, HQ Company 2 Para

I was at Colonel Jones's brief orders for the attack on Goose Green, and the only thing that worried me was when Jones sent the anti-tanks around the isthmus and not with the forward elements. Now, I had been with anti-tanks for ten years by then, but I never commanded the Milan [a portable, medium-range, anti-tank missile], yet I was waiting for an officer to say we should send two detachments with the forward elements, because that's how the Milan was used on the Kenya trip months previously.

I was one of the umpires out there and we brought the support fire in dangerously close, and that was Jones's decision, and it was the right decision, because we had recced the ground first. So we knew what it looked like and what we could get away with; for the realism side of live firing, you understand.

I think he had great foresight, because at the end of the day he was risking his career, and if somebody had been killed, there would be a Board of Inquiry and it would have all come out and the powers-that-be would have wanted a scapegoat, and that would have been Jones. But Jones was no fool, and if you fucked up as a commander, you were out of the battalion. The Milan targets in Kenya weren't tanks but bunkers, simulating tanks, and thank God for that, because they were eventually used like that against bunkers and trenches on Darwin Hill. Look at Afghanistan, the Javelin was an anti-tank weapon, but was used to great effect as a bunker buster too.

Now, the problem with Jones was, it didn't matter who was around, like Toms or a senior NCO, you should never bollock somebody like a senior rank in front of the Toms, but Jones would, and he did. Jones had bollocked this one officer in Kenya, stripped him down basically, quite severely in front of everybody, and I thought this was wrong. So, on the Goose Green orders, some officers did not say what they really should have said, like, 'I think you have got it slightly wrong, sir. We should send two Milans forward.'

Obviously, what broke the Argies up on Darwin Hill was a well-placed 66, but also, Milan was eventually forward by then and took out other bunkers and trenches.

I'm no great tactician and aren't we are all brilliant with hindsight, but maybe it was the mindset of our commanders at the time, because there was no perceived tank threat, Milan was forgotten! Or, maybe no one wanted to get the sack on the eve of their biggest chance to shine in all their careers!

Lance Corporal 'Duke' Allen, Defence Platoon 2 Para

It was the night before Goose Green when we heard that BBC John Nott radio broadcast. [Nott was the Secretary of State for Defence]. We were stood around the radio in a small gang along with the adjutant, Captain Wood, waiting for the latest BBC World Service broadcast, when we heard a voice out of the radio grassing us up, basically giving our position away. Captain Wood came straight across to us and he says to no one in particular, 'Gentlemen, the promotional prospects in this battalion tomorrow are gonna be fucking excellent.' He got killed a few hours later.

David Norris, general news reporter Daily Mail, *attached 2 Para*

While at Camilla Creek House, I watched H Jones come storming out of the bunkhouse in a rage, he'd just listened to that famous BBC broadcast. 'Nott has just give away our position! He's said 2 Para are ready to attack Goose Green. If any of my boys die, I will take him to court for manslaughter.' Jones was incandescent with Nott telling the Argies where we were. He went ballistic, and for a minute I thought he was going to blame me, but he didn't, and of course, he realised I had nothing to do with it.

Corporal Marty Margerison, 6 Platoon B Company 2 Para

It wasn't ideal, but I didn't want my blokes in those sheds or near the house, so I moved them out and I had a poncho, one of the old ones, the most crap piece of kit ever issued, a useless bit of fucking shite and heavy, but I had one! It had a hood on it, so what I done was, I got one of the blokes to sit in the middle of it with the hood on and he became the sentry, so he at least could see, because the BBC and John Nott let the Argies know we were within striking distance of Goose Green, and for sure we were expecting a counterattack.

I know this sounds so unprofessional, but he was covering the arcs of fire with the hood on looking out, and wearing a hood or any other item that covers the ears and screws with a soldier's hearing is a massive no-no in the Paras. Then I got my blokes to sit underneath this poncho, squeezed 'em all in with their feet facing the centre trying to create warmth, so effectively we had all-round defence. Most of my section were small young lads, eighten- , nineteen-year-olds, and I had to keep them warm. It was my responsibility to keep them fighting fit, to keep them alive.

Lance Corporal Graham Eve, GPMG commander, 4 Platoon
B Company 2 Para

We were told to get out of the weather in these tiny sheep sheds, so we did. We were crammed in there. It stunk of sheep shit, yet it was warm. Then we all started to cramp up and couldn't relax, because we were piled on top of one another. From my perspective, it was probably some of the worst hours of my life. It was horrible, because I was so uncomfortable and desperate, but we were dry and that was that. As paratroopers you just get on with it. The start of the battle couldn't come quickly enough. Come on, for fuck's sake, let's just get out of here and get on with it!

Private Phil Williams, Mortar Platoon 2 Para

I remember when Recce Platoon went out and captured that Land Rover with some Argies in it. I was walking past our commanding officer at the time, Colonel Jones, and he had that green puffer jacket on he always wore, and I went up to him.

'Excuse me, sir,' I said, pointing to one of the prisoners, 'can I take his boots, because they're better than mine?'

He just laughed at me and probably thought I was taking the piss, but I was really quite serious about it, because we were wearing the crappy DMS-issued boots, and fucking puttees! They went over the fucking top in World War One wearing the same kit. Puttees, for fuck's sake! That was the last time I saw Colonel Jones.

*Private David Minnock, GPMG gunner, 12 Platoon D Company
2 Para*

We all piled into the house and I lived under the stairs with about
three or four or five others. We all went into the house, but we
shouldn't have done. We did it to get out of the wind and the rain.
It was a real silly thing to do, but we were all in bits, it was a case of
survival. Once word got out about that BBC broadcast, though, we
all bombed out of there, but the whole of D Company was in there,
and I'm sure most of the battalion too before that.

*Gunner J. M. Love, 2 Para Group A Company 2 Para, FOO party
signaller 29 Corunna Field Battery RA*

During World War Two, everybody listened to the BBC. Forty
years later it was still the same. Except there were no French
resistance receiving coded messages to blow up railway lines. When
we got back, we were all going to go to Broadcasting House and
kick the crap out of as many of the staff as we could get hold of. It
was a thought that gave you a warm glow in your heart.

Lance Corporal Paul Bishop, 3 Platoon B Company 2 Para

B Company had been allocated what looked like a sheep-shearing
shed to sleep in for the night. Being part of 3 Section of 6 Platoon,
we were always last group to get administered. Guess what, no
fucking room in the Inn. Three of the section, Brummie, (who was
the section commander), Geoff and I lay down in the open. Geoff
was dispatched to look for some bedding. Our sleeping bags had
been left back at Sussex Mountains, as we could not carry too much
weight. He found a stinking fleece that still had a leg attached, it
smelled wonderful.

In the Falklands, body heat kept us alive, so the three of us lay down in close order in the spoon position. Young Geoff got a wee bit upset when Brummie, who was a big lad, got a hard on! Needless to say, Geoff moved out of the accommodation and proceeded to do push-ups, sit-ups, and running on the spot all night, to keep warm.

A 22 SAS call sign

At midnight we got our pick-up grid, but it was at least a six-hour tab away under all this Argy activity. Anyway, we got there in time, I mean, you always make a heli RV – always. The chopper lands to pick us up. Two pilots and a loadie. When we're all aboard, the loadie gives me the cans, the headphone set, to talk to the loadie and pilot. The loadie says, 'Sorry to hear about the cab [helicopter][15] that went in the other day.' Because I didn't know, well, none of us knew in the patrol; why would the boss tell us stuff that was irrelevant to our mission?

Anyway, the loadie goes on to say some of the guys are dead! 'Do you know Laurence?' he says. And, of course, the chopper is buffering all over the place, it's hot, a heat I haven't felt for weeks, and smelly and noisy, and we're flying over enemy territory with fast jets looking for us – and I'm trying to process all of what the loadie is telling me through the headset. I know he was trying to make small talk, but it was a hell of a shock to the system. He thought we all knew; but we didn't. Everyone in the Fleet knew apart from us.

'Yeah, I know Laurence,' I says. And I'm thinking, how many guys do I know in D, I knew at least half the squadron. Nineteen

---

15 On 19 May, Sea King HC4 ZA294 of 846 Naval Air Squadron crashed in the sea while cross-decking SAS troops from HMS *Hermes* to HMS *Intrepid*. Twenty-one souls lost, nine survivors. This was the worst single loss of life for the SAS on operations since the Second World War. Cause unknown, but suspected engine failure, possibly caused by a bird strike.

blokes from D Squadron all dead in a helicopter that piled in! Some fucking flight back to the *Hermes* that was.

We slammed down on the deck of *Intrepid*, otherwise known as the *Decrepit*, and not the *Hermes* as I thought. A cracking ship, but it was about to go and get made into razor blades in India. The Government had sold it just before the Falklands kicked off, but had held back on the deal for a few months.

We landed and one of the lads came out to meet us, Jacko, and the first thing I said to him was, 'What's the score with the helicopter crash?' The look on his face was like, shock, really shocked, I remember that. I had asked him the one question that he or any of the lads didn't want to be asked.

'I'm just here to get the kit, weapons and bergens. The OC will brief you up on that.' It was that sort of conversation – change the subject, like! I bet he was glad of the poor comms up on the heli deck because of a vicious cross wind and screaming engine noise.

Jacko was told only to go get the lads, get all the kit off 'em and show them the way downstairs to get cleaned up and debriefed. We go downstairs led by these sailors to get a shower and that. So, we make our way down to the shower rooms for our first scrub in almost a month. We still had our belt kit, our webbing on; Jacko didn't take that off us. So, this sailor starts fucking with my belt kit, so I says, 'Hang on, mate, I've got fuckin' ammunition and grenades and all that shite in there.'

'Don't worry about that, we know what we're doing,' he replies.

So, I says, 'Oi! that's my fuckin' kit!' Look, nobody fucks about with your belt kit, and I mean nobody! It carries all your ammo and all your personal stuff in it, and you know exactly what pouch has what in it; so if you had to, you could lay your hands on it in an instance for whatever. Unlike the Green Army, where you had to carry certain bits of kit like ammo and stuff in certain pouches, regimental like, but our system was different. Not even one of your own patrol goes near your belt kit, and if they did for whatever reason, you'd tell 'em, and watch 'em, and make sure to say, 'And mind you gives it back!' Robbing bastards, some of the lads could be, ha–ha.

Anyway, back down in the shower room, we were met by some more sailors, and remember, we're are all Boat Troop, we're all divers, we've been working with the Navy and we all know the Navy drill and we knew that Navy divers hate the Navy. There's always big bust-ups, because divers are generally scruffy critters and this and that, but asked, 'Can you get me a diver to get this bomb off?' say, then it's all nice and fluffy, then it's back to *fucking divers* once the bomb had been defused or the prop's been disentangled of crap. It's a sort of love-hate relationship, and like I said, we knew all this anyway, because we've been down to Portsmouth, been to Vernon, and we knew the Navy diving branch very well.

So, let me set the scene, we're in the heads, Navy for shower/toilets, a big room, say ten cubicles a side, twenty in all, a big shower room and a dhobi [laundry] for the Navy and Royal Marines to sort themselves out, and we are met by this fucking horrendous sight. I mean it was menacing – more sailors, who were standing there waiting for us and they've got rubber aprons on with these long, odd-looking rubber gloves way up their arms, and not only that, they've got the flash gear (anti-flash to stop burns from exploding missiles) on too, because the ship was at battle stations. They looked like extras out of *Battlestar Galactica*.

They tell us to take all our kit off and show us where to put it out of the way, so we are pissing ourselves laughing. We all thought these guys are taking the piss, this must be some wind-up by the OC or someone, and remember, we hadn't seen another human being apart from the four of us for weeks, and out on ops you don't talk at normal level, you communicate in whispers, forty decibels below. But this lot were here to take the rest of our kit off us, dhobi it, and make sure that we had a Dettol wash, basically to de-lice us; yet we were really taking the piss out of them.

We hadn't had a cup of tea, nothing to eat and we're fuckin' starvin'. We'd seen the D Squadron night show the night before and then had to crawl back up another hill and hide from the Argies for another day, and just heard about the lads' downed chopper. Trust me, we were in this euphoric state! So one goes back to this reserve position of taking the piss out of the people who are trying to get you to do something.

I says to one of them, 'Come on, mate, we know you fuckin' sailors, you'll be having us look for the golden rivet next. You're not stokers, are yer?' We were coming up with all this crap and these guys were getting very irate, saying stuff like, 'I am of this rank and I will get my boss and he will come and tell you what to do. You're onboard a Navy ship and you can't bring all these diseases back on ship and to the UK.'

'What diseases? I exclaimed.

'Well, there's all these sheep diseases on the island and if they get back to England, they'll kill all the sheep.'

For fuck's sake, we were thinking, but it did tell us a lot of things about how mad this war was turning out to be, and we thought, *ah, are we going back to England then?* It was so bloody surreal. It took our minds off the helicopter crash for a bit, though. So we stripped off bollock naked and got our bodies into a shower, still taking the piss out of the sailors. After the shower they handed out these survivors' kits with stuff in it like a nice big Guernsey oil wool jumper, and the old No. 8's Navy issue, the old ones made from cotton. If they'd had the Navy dressed in these old cotton No. 8's, there would have been a lot less burn injuries; no nylon crap burning through the skin like napalm!

Also in the box were these pumps, daps [early version of the trainer], and that was when I first started to get a bit of feeling back in my feet. Up until then it had been like walking, well, if you had filled my pump full of pins, it was like that. I hadn't realised I had trench foot and as my body started to warm up, I thought, *holy fuck*, yet I felt nothing in the field, not even a feeling of trench foot!

So then we were escorted up to one of the ship's mess dining rooms, the Petty Officers' Mess. First, we went through the *who the fuck are you?* stage. Obviously, this waiter chap wasn't expecting us, so we explained who we were and that we had been told to come in here and wait for a briefing. 'Oh well, um, what would you like to drink then?'

Two of the lads said, 'Oh, a nice cup of tea, please,' which must have blown the SAS myth about these guys eating a whole sheep for breakfast and drinking gallons of fucking rum, and shit like that.

'Oh,' said one of the two tea lads, 'and some toast, please.' The mess waiter repeated back, 'Two teas and toast!'

'Yes, please,' came the reply.

'All right then, if that's what you want,' really surprised, then he turns to me. 'What you havin'?' And as he's taking our order, he's tempting us with these small cans of beer and tots of rum. So me and me oppo couldn't let it go to waste, I mean, you can't put the rum back in the bottle, can you? So we swigged it all back. Then another voice says, 'Oi, what's happening here?' and the waiter says he's offering us a tot of rum. So this voice says, 'A tot of rum? Come here you!' to the waiter, and I thought, *that's it, five minutes on the ship and we're in the shit already*.

The voice turned out to be a PO, a petty officer, who fills four glasses to the rim and says, 'That's a tot, laddie.' Of course, me and my oppo had two helpings each, which was very, very nice and invigorating, then we had those four small cans of beer too and was offered more, but we opted for toast instead. Then this PO asks, 'Where have you been, lads?'

'You know that island, that's where we've been,' I says.

Soon after, a couple of the lads from D Squadron came down to use the dhobi and they heard a clonk, clonk, clonk coming out of one of the washing machines, then an irate officer appeared shouting, 'Grenade, grenade, there's a fucking grenade in the washing machine!' and ran off to hide with a couple more sailors, who had taken cover behind another washing machine. One of the D Squadron lads opened the washer, took out the grenade, brought it on deck and tossed it overboard. The lads reckoned it was my grenade.

After all that nonsense, we got debriefed, and they [Intel] said, 'Yeah, 2 Para is going over there to sort 'em out,' so I said, 'In that case, I'll go over to 2 Para's location and brief 'em up.'

'No, no, no, you don't have to do that,' they said. Funny that, yet our patrol's assessment was that the Argies could reinforce Goose Green easily as anything with the helicopter lift capability they had. They could put eight hundred men in Goose Green as fast as hell! Which they did during the battle. Not eight hundred, but they reinforced Goose Green with Special Forces by chopper. What you have to remember is, we didn't possess a Mystic Meg, and the crystal ball wasn't working very well, and that's your honest-to-goodness expert opinion we had brought back – Goose Green could be easily reinforced.

Corporal Ken Raynor, patrol commander Recce Platoon 2 Para

Camilla Creek House. The battle plan and orders were put together by the commanding officer Colonel Jones and his staff in the house at Camilla. The two thirds, one third theory – the ratio of planning and execution of orders – went out of the window, as there is a massive difference between the real thing and on an exercise, or a command course. There is no DS [Directing Staff] to step in and modify or adjust a plan. Each player or cog in this complex wheel has to know how and when to play its role, from commanding a rifle company, firing a mortar, being in charge of a stretcher party; whatever the task or job, someone has to plan it, someone then has to pass these orders down the chain.

The Battalion Headquarters are then responsible for ensuring higher command knows what the battalion are going to do and when, and this information is then passed to all flanking units. The preparation and delivery took longer than anticipated, and time during this phase is critical and very valuable, especially when most of the battalion were out in the cold with no kit, and mostly in the open and in the dark. Of course, light discipline was enforced, but saying that, you could smell Hexi [a pocket-size individual stove heated by hexamine solid-fuel blocks] and cigarettes.

The initial plan was for A and B to hold firm and for C and D to push through towards Goose Green. But this never happened, as both A and B companies, in the face of considerable opposition, got bogged down on several occasions, even though countless acts of bravery were witnessed on many fronts by individuals and groups of men.

Lance Corporal Paul Bishop, 3 Platoon B Company 2 Para

Before we moved out to the assembly area, the boss, Chippy [now retired Major General Clive 'Chip' Chapman CB] gave the platoon a full six-phase set of orders for the attack. The mood amongst the platoon changed to a serious one. One of the younger members vomited, due to nerves, I guess. I remember thinking, fuck me, this is the real deal and I hope I perform well as a junior non-commissioned officer. I must remember to use the ground well; fire and manoeuvre, use good fire control orders, and use good hard cover from fire. Also, I told my half section, personal infantry skills will keep us alive.

I had hoped the Argies had not pre-prepared their defensive mortar targets. We soon discovered they had. My fucking mind was going at 200 miles an hour. I thought of my parents and my girlfriend back home in Stoke; I can't die at twenty-one and let them down. I thought back to the *Norland* when I had attended the battalion church service, where Padre Cooper said, 'Some of you will die, most of you will pray.'

He was right, I was praying now.

10

THE START-LINE

We tabbed across such open ground. Could have died yesterday, could be dead tomorrow, but today, alive, so gloriously alive.

Nigel Ely: The start-line is where a unit forms up in file or extended line, and it is the last safe point before you advance towards the enemy, close with the enemy and kill them.

We were to advance due south across an isthmus of flat and horrendously exposed peat and gorse. The isthmus was only half a mile wide. We had water to our front, to our left and to our right. The battalion's aim was to attack the light force of about four hundred mainly air-force personnel, according to the SAS intelligence reports, securing the settlement at Goose Green, which lay at the end of the isthmus; and also to secure the 119 civilians being held hostage in the Goose Green community centre. Again, according to the SAS, a number of dug-in Argentine defence positions stood in our way. They included Burntside House, a smallholding, and Darwin, a collection of farms.

A Company was to attack Burntside House first, then move on to Darwin before clearing a small Argentine position at a place called Coronation Point.

B Company were to attack Boca House, an Argentine defence position over to the west, on our right, then move south-east behind the lightly defended Goose Green airfield, from where it was known the Argentine Air Force was launching the turboprop, ground-attack Pucaras to conduct strikes on the ground troops – 2 Para in particular!

C Company were to lay all the battalion start-lines. Recce Platoon to lead A Company to their Burntside House start-line. Patrols Platoon to lead B Company to theirs. D Company were reserve Company.

Plan A goes out the window when you get punched in the face. Picture the scene. It is dark, a drizzling rain covers a pitch-black background of nothingness. A bitter icy wind whips up and attacks your sodden mass, then disappears as soon as it has cut deep into your bones. It particularly enjoys the neck and legs, and makes an appearance every time you lift your head.

Ground: Exposed rolling plains of sodden tufty grass. Flat as a snooker table with the odd rolling fold of dead ground and nowhere to run to.

Situation Enemy Forces: The eve of the biggest, bloodiest battle the British Army has fought for generations. Everything to your front is the enemy.

Corporal Ken Raynor, patrol commander Recce Platoon 2 Para

So, less than twenty-four hours after meeting back with the battalion from our OP, we received a new set of orders to set off at last light to find and mark the start-line for A Company to attack their first designated target, called Burntside House. Now the real fun started. *Glad to be back with the lads*, I thought. *Hey, away we go; fix bayonets, last man to die is a cissy.*

THE START-LINE

Colour Sergeant Pete Vale, HQ Company 2 Para

Because I was the senior colour sergeant, it was my job to look after the ammunition and the other colourmen of the battalion; supply their requests. I'd set up just south of Camilla Creek House, a safe distance behind the start-line and the rifle companies, but close enough to get kit up quickly.

I had some very strong characters to deal with, so I got them all together and said, 'Right, there's no A Company, B Company, C Company, D Company. It's the battalion who you're gonna work for now. Whoever needs the aid; ammunition, rations, kit, that's where it goes. No company loyalties,' I impressed on them. I said this knowing every colour man wants to get the best kit for his company, and quite understandably so, but none of us had ever been in this situation where the battalion, as one, had gone forward into battle.

Stevie Gerrard, B Company's Colour, RIP, came up to me afterwards and said, 'I'm worried, I don't know what to do!' And I told him to think back to Salisbury Plain, which was the last big UK exercise the battalion had been on. 'All you do is what you did there, the only difference is, this is an exercise where the enemy are gonna fire back, so there will be upsets.' And he just walked away.

The battalion's bergens had been flown in from Sussex Mountains by now and I had them stacked into five piles. It was getting dark and I needed to sorted out the stag list and to get our heads down, that's if any of us could sleep.

Now the nearest pile of bergens to where we were, and just by chance, was B Company's, that was Stevie Gerrard's company, so I said, 'Right, take a bergen off that pile (because every bergen would have a sleeping bag in it). Get the doss bag out and get your heads down and we'll sort it out tomorrow.'

So Stevie says, 'They're mine.'

I said, 'No, they're not yours, they are the battalion's.' What I didn't want was for ten guys to dive into every pile, rooting through for their personal bergen. Stevie was a bit upset about it, but I assured him it would be all okay. Come the morning, I made sure every bergen was back in the same state, tied up and put back on the right pile.

Captain Paul Farrar, OC Patrols Platoon 2 Para

We had the orders, but it had been delayed, so there I am coming back to the guys from the first proper wartime O group in my life, Northern Ireland operations aside, thinking, I've got no time to give *my* orders here, because it's almost dark now and our orders were to move at last light. I remember saying to the blokes, the patrol commanders, 'Right, guys, this is the way it is. It's the normal drill, we're supporting B Company, Recce, A Company. The battalion will move to our battalion checkpoint, standard drills all round, they put in the attack, and I'll fill in the details when it gets light tomorrow.'

And that was my orders for the battle of Goose Green; there was no time to go into anything else. Then giving a proper set of orders, like ground, situation, enemy forces, friendly forces, mission, execution and so on, then Bob Morgan thrust a mess tin of hot food in my hand and that was it, we were off!

After I'd put John Crosland, OC B Company in position, and was moving back to the battalion checkpoint, I saw H Jones. He was on the track just on the enemy side of the checkpoint with his signallers and the battery commander and he had a brief chat with me.

'How's it going, Paul?'

'We're all good to go, sir,' was about the size of it.

'Okay, good, I'll see you tomorrow,' he said. That was the last time I spoke to or saw him, and off I went.

THE START-LINE

Corporal Ken Raynor, patrol commander, Recce Platoon 2 Para

In the pitch black of night, I quickly briefed my patrol; no time for anything else, and my four-man patrol headed off into the darkness – distance, not too far, maybe three or four Ks. I needed to find a decent safe route to a start-line and, of course, set up a start-line north of Burntside House, hopefully on a reverse slope out of sight of the enemy.

The route and ground was very difficult, rough and wet, Northern Ireland boots were not working that well! We stopped short of the small hill about 300 metres north and short of the enemy position, and I found what I thought would be a good position for the centre of the start-line. I left two guys there and took one guy about 100 metres left, briefed him, went back to the centre, picked up one guy, leaving one and took him about 100 metres to the right. I then went back to the centre and that is where I met back up with the last guy. We were supposed to use white mine tape on the ground to mark the centre, left and right flanks, no way! After a while, especially when the wind changed, you could hear the enemy to our front, and you could smell tobacco; it was very spooky and this is where things started to change for the worst. We were right out in the open and our own indirect fire support from the ships, artillery and mortar, started laying down supporting suppressive fire onto the enemy. This was pretty scary, as the shells were like massive earthquakes and not far away, and all we could do was lie flat and hope none got too close; we heard the pieces of shrapnel whizzing over our heads.

We had left our large HF radio in our bergens back at Camilla Creek House, so I had a small short-range Section 349 radio, but due to us all being on radio silence, I could not use it until we made contact with the enemy; this was a little frustrating as A Company were very fashionably late. There was only one option, so I crawled

145

back to a point on the designated route in, then I got up and started walking on the route we had taken in. I eventually met up with A Company and led them into the centre of the start-line, all of us on our knees. A platoon went left, another went right, Headquarters remained in the middle led by Major Farrar-Hockley, and the third platoon remained to the rear.

When everybody was in position, my patrol then moved to the rear of A Company's rear platoon. This was then the start. A Company fixed bayonets and advanced onto the enemy position, two up, one in reserve. They advanced over the crest of the hill in what can be described as advance to contact, then they went down a moderate slope, occasionally firing hand-held illumination rockets.

Of course, the majority of A Company are now in the bottom of the slope, we are still on our way down, and the enemy start firing their small-arms weapons, but they soon ceased fire as the full force of two platoons started to engage them as they proceeded up the hill. At the end of this short attack, my patrol's mission was to meet up with the rest of C Company, where we would form two platoons with Headquarters fighting company.

Sergeant Major Colin Price, A Company 2 Para

I can recall seeing something burning as we formed up to attack Burntside House. It certainly wasn't after the attack, because I thought, *what the fuck?* Other than that, it would have been a pitch-black night. It may have been some gorse alight after HMS *Arrow* fired its single salvo before its gun jammed. We had 2 Platoon on the right, 3 Platoon on the left, and 1 Platoon in reserve. I placed myself behind 2 Platoon along with 'The Beast', Private Fuller, the company clerk, who was with me at every stage. We hadn't taken 2-inch mortars, because the only ammunition we had for them was illum [illumination flares], as there was no HE [high explosive]. The

MOD had sold off the HE to the Indian Army before the Falklands War, so that's why A Company didn't take the 2-inch mortar.

I said, 'I'm not taking 2-inch mortars just to put light up, as they're too fucking heavy,' so we took Schermuly parachute flares instead, but they were rubbish, because as soon as the guys popped 'em off, that strong wind got hold of 'em and they were gone! So, when the assault started, 3 Platoon fired their Charlie G [84 Carl Gustaf] at the buildings, but they had a misfire! By this time 2 Platoon were advancing, and I don't know why, and it's probably something we all do in recruit training as DS, I was behind 2 Platoon urging them to push on.

'Come on, lads, let's move, let's move,' and 2 Platoon are doing good tactics, then suddenly we're getting tracer rounds coming towards us, so I got down on my knees, fired a quick twenty rounds off in the direction where it was coming from, then realised it was coming from the left, from 3 Platoon, who hadn't started their advance yet because of their Charlie G misfire. So, I stopped 2 Platoon advancing and shouted to 3 Platoon to stop firing, because they were hitting the building and their fire was coming back towards us. Then suddenly a Charlie G goes BOOM! and 3 Platoon get moving.

Then we found out there was no enemy in or around the building. They'd all bugged out, but you don't know that as you're assaulting and it's pissing down, and at night too.

Private Steve Taylor, 3 Platoon A Company 2 Para

When we attacked Burntside House, we lined up, we fired a couple hundred rounds into it, several grenades and 66s and still the occupants were alive. Several years later, when we [2 Para] went to lay the Colours, I met the people and they recalled that adventurous night. They said they all got on the floor and pulled a mattress over themselves. I didn't know this at the time, but when we stopped firing, Corporal John Camp, who could speak a little Spanish, called out in the darkness to the anyone to our front.

'*Manos arriba, manos arriba* [hands up]!' he shouted and some folk came out speaking Spanish. So we all shot above their heads and they screamed back in English, 'Why are you shooting at us, we're British!'

'Well, why are you speaking Spanish?' one of us shouted back.

'Because you are!' came the reply.

Literally a second after we got the order to cease fire, Baz K was about to throw a grenade. Obviously, he couldn't find the pin to put back in to make it safe, so he lobbed it over his shoulder and nearly took out the sergeant major.

Private Roy Charters, Recce Platoon 2 Para

We led A Company on to their start-line to attack the target of Burntside House. It was the first live start-line the battalion had crossed probably since Malaya, and I see this light, someone in A Company was lighting a fag up in the venturi [short tube] of an 84, when one of the blokes, and I can't remember who it was, sort of whispered, 'Put that fucking light out!' It was only then that you think, we've gotta take cover into relative safety, and A Company have gotta get up and advance towards the Argies and kill them. Looking back, whoever said, 'Put that light out,' still had their Brecon Head on [an exercise by the book attitude].

Corporal Marty Margerison, 6 Platoon B Company 2 Para

When we got to the start-line, my mission was to take out a machine-gun post. On my axis there was a machine gun and it was either a .3 or .50 Browning and this was why my SOPs to Eddy Carrol, my M79 [grenade launcher] man, were that if anything opened up, it was for Eddy to fire the M79, and I didn't give a fuck if he hit anything or not, it would have been a bonus if he did.

So, my orders were, 'On contact with the enemy, Eddy, you immediately fire rounds off,' and then we'd wait for the orders process to kick in. Right, I was ready to go now, but had a quick word with Big Bish, a C Company Patrols corporal [older brother of Lance Corporal Paul Bishop, B Company, 2 Para] and shared a nervous ciggy, not professional, but a required nerve agent!

Private Mark Sleap, Patrols Platoon 2 Para

My patrol set up the start-line for B Company. It was real quiet and the blokes filed in really quietly – no talking, no smoking – you know, just how we are taught and how it should be; then there was the click of the bayonets being snapped on and that noise broke the silence. But when we laid the start-line for D Company on Wireless Ridge, it was totally different, all the blokes were having fags and talking, seasoned veterans – it was a bit noisy.

HMS *Arrow* started to fire its big gun and dropped a round onto an Argy position and then the gun seized, and suddenly all these wild horses come running past us. We had marked the start-line with ourselves this time, and not marker tape and stuff, so all these horses came charging through us and disappeared into the night. Then another round dropped short and you could hear this thumping and they all came charging back through us again – twat!

Some time later I was told they weren't wild horses but they were from Goose Green, because back then Goose Green settlement was still non-mechanised, and they were using horses when the invasion came. Years later I met up with Colin Shepherd, a Falkland Islander who was a hostage child in the Goose Green community centre when we attacked, and he explained to me, 'The Argies just let 'em all go, so they were fending for themselves.'

Private Phil Williams, Mortar Platoon 2 Para

We moved to the start-line, crossed the start-line and started to advance forward and that's when it all went crazy. The Argies were using green tracer and we were using red.

Lance Corporal Paul Bishop, 6 Platoon B Company 2 Para

I could hear a strange rumbling noise. I thought a train was nearby, but fuck me, there they were, a pack of wild horses running through the battalion. What next, fucking Indians chasing them?

We crossed over a small footbridge. Then we passed by the Patrols Platoon, who were securing the start-line. I was looking out for my brother to wish him well, but didn't see him.

I recall seeing him the day before at Camilla Creek House; he looked a real tough soldier, straight out of a war film. He stood there with extra ammunition, high explosive grenades, and phosphorus grenades hanging off him. *Flash bastard*, I thought. I just prayed we were both in one piece in a few hours' time.

Corporal Tom Harley MM, section commander, 10 Platoon D Company 2 Para

We must have laid there a good hour when Glen Grace (HQ CMS) came marching up to the rear with a long line of stretcher bearers and asked if this was D Company. I said it was, and he was directly behind the point section, or penal section as it was to be known by the rest of 11 Platoon. 'Okay, we're here,' he told his men, and they settled in behind us.

As soon as the word [the stretcher bearers had arrived] got passed down the rest of the company, more and more tactical fags were being had. Neamesy (Major Neame, OC D Company) was among them. He never had fags on him and didn't smoke very often. He just bummed them off the lads. I think it was his way of keeping in touch.

As a section commander, I get my mission from the boss's orders and I normally have about half an hour to plan how I'm going to do it. I don't have time to make up models or maps and basically if I'm taking out, say, two trenches or whatever I've got to do, I have to be more flexible than the orders state; how am I going to use my guys? I also have to instil in them there's a good possibility they're going to die here, and I don't want anybody going down on their bellies either. If you go down, go on the knee only, and none of this ten paces stuff that you're taught; so the advance towards the enemy is going to be fractured, but as long as you have some semblance of control, you can accomplish stuff.

Eventually after about twenty fags, we were given the order to move. My biggest difficulty was trying to keep the guys separated. They had a tendency to bunch up. But they wanted to be closer together and I spent a lot of my time separating them. It wasn't so much a case of dying, nobody wanted to die alone; but if they had someone next to them, the dying part of it and the killing part of it was not so bad. That's the way I saw it and it makes sense to me.

D Company was reserve company at the start of the whole battle, but because B Company got bogged down, we just ended up at the front as point company. It was still night when we came across the Argy trenches and we were fighting through and had gone to ground, as there was this lull in the battle and the whole thing stopped. I could see my OC, Phil Neame [OC D Company], over to my right and that's how close we were. He was getting a sense of what was happening, because there was no rush.

I think half the trouble with the battle for Goose Green was that everybody thought there should be a big rush to get there. I mean there wasn't a rush, the Argies weren't going nowhere. They had water to the back of them, and water to their left and right, so we could have stayed there and starved them out! But there was always this push to keep going, when there was really no need to. That was probably our biggest mistake. I didn't know what the echelons were like, whether they were running short of ammunition and things needed to be pushed up a little bit, but I think it was more of the ego on Jones's part. This is my battle, sort of thing, and we'll do it my way.

I went firm and we were just about to prepare to move again. Someone from our side was putting light up and as that was happening, Gaz [Lance Corporal Gaz Bingley MM] says to me, 'Tom, I'm just going to go up there.' He was pointing to some high ground, because we needed to advance.

So, I says, 'Okay, Gaz.' And as soon as he and one other [Private Baz Grayling MM, D Company] got up there, they disappeared over the brow. The next thing I knew, and it was dark, I heard weapons being fired and screams which lasted for about ten seconds, that's how quick it was. I heard the words, 'My eye, my eye, my eye!' and by the time I got up there, Gaz was dead and Grayling was holding his leg, but there was no enemy there. B Company was over to our right at the time.

Then one of our guys puts light up again, 2-inch mortar flares, and I saw two guys running away, so I put rounds after 'em. The 2-inch flares were still hanging about, but nobody wanted the light. I found out later it was Goldsmith the company runner, who had about fifty of these 2-inch flares and I bet he thought, *I ain't carrying these bloody things any more*, and just fired 'em off.

Pete Lite, the platoon sergeant, came up and dragged Gaz's body out of the trench he'd fallen into and took him straight back to the RAP. Poor Gaz was shot in the eye and it took the back of his head off, and I don't know who said those words earlier, but it could only have been Gaz or Grayling! It was really weird, but I have my own theory.

Private David Minnock, GPMG gunner, 12 Platoon D Company
2 Para

At night, Patrols Platoon C Company led us to the start-line. They were waiting for us by a bridge that the engineers had cleared a few hours before, but we headed in a slightly different direction, it was a different route to the one we were supposed to have taken. So, we're in this dry riverbed and I heard the strangest thing ever, and I think it was only the machine gunners and the signallers that heard it. It was the blokes fixing bayonets, and it was like a quiet Mexican Wave. I had never heard anything like it before in my life and never heard anything like it since.

On a GPMG you don't fit a bayonet and all the signallers carried SMGs. The feeling was that everything had been like an exercise up till now, because we'd not met the enemy, nor seen the enemy, so everything up to this stage seemed unreal; until the fix bayonets bit, then you could hear it. It wasn't like you do when you're on the parade ground all at once, nice and regimental. No, it was like this Mexican wave sound, *clink, clink, clink, clink,* and it got louder and louder, and I thought, *oh my God! If they don't hear that!*

I just lay there and it passed me and it went on for a bit more, then quietened down. Then we got up and advanced to contact. The first thing I recall is the Argy artillery shells exploding all around. You could see the phosphorus exploding, but not near me. I saw the odd one and thought, *shit, go away, go away, keep away from me.* Then you're thinking, *that's your mates over there getting it,* so you're thinking, *please don't come near, but it's gonna go near somebody, right?* Your mates! It's a horrible feeling. The Argies had DF-ed the ground we were tabbing over.

My section ended up straying into Gaz Bingley's platoon. I came across two of our fellows dragging one of our blokes who'd been wounded, so we had strayed that far across to the right. We started having an argument, saying what the hell do you think you're doing? 'Pick him up and put him over your shoulder,' I told one of them. Someone replied, 'You try picking him up.' I tried, but I couldn't either. Another bloke says, 'He's got a pulse, he's alive,' but he was dead weight, you know what I mean.

So, it took four of us to carry him and then Sergeant Lite came along in the end and he carried our weapons for us. He carried my gun too. We were directed through 10 Platoon to HQ then to the RAP. Del Delaney [2 Para medic] met us. We were that knackered, we were actually laying on this bloke. Del then asked if we'd checked him for wounds. Well, we had, from the boots to the head, but someone says, 'He's all right, Del, he's just concussed!' Del turns his torch on and shines it onto the wounded bloke's head, and says, 'He's dead.'

'But he had a pulse, he can't be dead!' someone else replied. But he was dead.

I later found out this was Gaz Bingley. Gaz's gunner, Baz Grayling, had also been shot, but we didn't know where Baz was. He wasn't where we found Gaz, but he was laying out there wounded somewhere, we found out later. But at the time we didn't see him, or we'd have dragged him back too.

From where we found Gaz to the medics, it wasn't that far, but Taff Meredith DCM came over and led us to 12 Platoon. I don't know if someone got on the radio and told 12 Platoon there's two of your blokes back here or what, but Taff thought he'd lost us. Not sure what he meant by that, but everything in battle isn't that straightforward, I mean, no plan survives contact with the enemy and this was actual proof!

It was still night time, yet it was probably no more than about fifty or so metres from the front line where we left Gaz, and the battle was still raging. Rounds and tracer still going off and all that, so me and Budge got back on my gun and rejoined 12 Platoon. Like I say, it was still dark as we moved forward, still advancing to contact, still clearing trenches, and the platoon behind was making doubly sure they were clear of *all* Argies. I was thinking, what you doing, we've already cleared those bastards! But they were following up and obviously clearing them as they advanced behind us.

Apparently, we hadn't cleared 'em right good, because they were still finding Argies in 'em; we'd missed some, as a few live ones were cowering in their trenches. I mean, it was dark, and so much confusion going all about; but now they were cleared. It wasn't my job as a gunner to do that, that was the job of the riflemen. I had to cover the flanks. Clearing bastard trenches of enemy with a GPMG is for Hollywood or daylight.

Corporal Marty Margerison, 6 Platoon B Company 2 Para

B Company advanced to contact early hours in the dark towards a place called Boca House. We were the right side of the battalion's advance and I was on the far left of B Company, and right of A Company, who were a few hundred metres over to our left. The what–ifs, well, they are enormous, because no matter how hard you train or how well-practised you and your men are, there's no such thing as a perfect attack, and I was more concerned about enemy machine guns opening up.

We were at night moving across undulating open ground. We moved up a slight incline, I had Company HQ to my right and the reserve section behind me. So as we're advancing in extended line, there was none of this slow down, speed up nonsense, or anything like that, but as we got halfway up this slight incline – and it was that black, I could only see my blokes' shapes, who were only about ten feet away – in my peripheral vison I caught this shape to my front left at about ten o'clock. Then one of my blokes whispered, 'Stop, stop, enemy left.'

We all got down on our knees, so the conversation goes something like, 'Scouse, Scouse, there's somebody there!'

And I'm whispering, 'Shut up, shut up.' I then said, '*Manos arriba*,' which is 'put your hands up' in Spanish.

'*Por favor?*' came the reply. I repeated it again, and he said, '*Por favor*,' again.

Then someone says, 'Shoot him, Scouse.'

'Just fucking shut up,' I says.

Then another voice shouts, 'Kill him!'

My head is telling me, and this has taken seconds, if I shoot him now, a fucking machine gun is going to open up and decimate a whole load of us. So I says to Eddy, 'Eddy, keep looking forward.'

And this other voice keeps saying, 'Kill him, kill him!'

Then we both screamed, 'Fire!' as me, Jimmy Meredith and Frog let rip, and the flash from the GPMGs lit this fellow up and you could see the line of tracer going through him and beyond, because tracer doesn't light up until 110 metres. I said 'Fire!' because I saw this shape which I now recognised as a poncho slowly turning and raising a weapon. The Argentine sentry was now dead.

We immediately went to ground and there was no response, nothing, so now we're all thinking, fucking hell, we've got away with this, and where's this fucking gun position? Then we continued with the advance. We moved a further couple of hundred metres and stopped. Then we moved off again and came across this Argy position and did a left flanking move on it. At this time, I could see D Company had moved up over on my left, and further past us, A Company's fire was now about the eleven o'clock to me.

Private Jim Meredith, GPMG gunner 6 Platoon B Company 2 Para

I was the extreme left-hand man for my platoon under 2nd Lieutenant 'Chip' Chapman, now a retired general, and Corporal Marty 'Scouse' Margerison. I was Scouse's section machine gunner with the GPMG. We advanced forward then suddenly an Argentine jumped up wearing what looked like a poncho. Then Scouse shouts, 'Let him have it.' I don't know why Scouse didn't let him have it, but I fuckin' let him have it. The first ten rounds in me belt were tracer and the tracer lit up in the sky behind him. I'd rearranged my belt that way back at the start-line, normally it's one in five, one tracer to five ball, but my way of thinking was a bit psychological like, if I don't hit'em I'll make sure I'll let'em know we're here so to keep them heads down. Later I found out I'd shot the 'scarecrow' eight times, he had eight gunshot wounds in him, then after that first contact someone put up a Schmuley [Schermuly flare] just like the *book* says you do, which lit up the all the pitch-black sky – ours and theirs! And then I could then see a load of Argy positions in front so I engaged every position I could see. Later, I found out one was a dead horse but it just looked like a position. I fired at the horse that were dead which I didn't know it was dead at the time and brought covering fire down for the rest of the platoon. When I got up to the horse there were blood and guts and snot for miles behind it, because when 7.62 hits you it knocks big chunks out of you, and there were a lot of my 7.62 what had gone through it.

Private Ian Winnard, 4 Platoon B Company 2 Para

Although I was 4 Platoon, I didn't know about the scarecrow incident, but of course I knew we [B Company] had come into contact; I could see it all around me, but it wasn't until later on in the day, during a lull someone told me. I mean, I knew there was a contact, but I hadn't a clue what had happened, although it was only metres from me.

Lance Corporal Paul Bishop, 6 Platoon B Company 2 Para

Upon reaching the start-line, the company lay down on the soaking wet ground. I was shitting myself. Our bayonets had already been fixed earlier so we didn't make any noise, just as well, because later on we learned we were within 200 metres of the enemy. Someone lit up a cigarette. Now, to do this in training was a big no no, but then we all lit up, even some of the non-smokers did too – fuck this, it could be our last fag.

Still dark, it started to drizzle. Way over to our left, A Company's attack was going in and I thought, *yes, this is for real.* Time for a wee prayer. We received the hand signal to stand up and advance. Everyone was quiet, my section was in reserve. We moved forward slowly. The whispers started: 'Spread out.' 'Push right.' The whispers got louder and louder as we closed with the enemy; nerves, I guess. I looked around our platoon and everyone was walking in a crouched position.

I thought back briefly to a book I had read about the First World War. In it, an officer had described the men in his platoon after they had gone over the top of the trenches. He wrote: 'The men were advancing towards the Germans. They were all crouched forward.' That stuck in my mind. You crouch to make yourself a smaller target, but I wished I was invisible.

1 and 2 Sections were in front of my 3 Section and Platoon Headquarters were just slightly behind. I don't think it was cowardly, but I was quite happy being in the reserve section at this particular moment. The phrase 'self-preservation' springs to mind. We quickly dropped down on the soaking earth. Scouse the commander of 2 Section was to the front. Then I heard someone shout something

in Spanish. Next thing the two machine guns in his section opened up from point-blank range and cut this poor Argy soldier in two. I felt no remorse for this man. Fuck him! He was in the wrong place at the wrong time.

We were the best company in the battalion and we were going to succeed. It was them or us and that is the reality of the battlefield, and has been since man has fought against man as far as I am concerned. Let's get some killing done, so that we can all fuck off home out of this shit hole. After that first contact with the enemy, I felt only hatred for these Argies.

It's fucking real now, I thought. Scouse then went off to do an attack to the left, and after much shooting and shouting he came running back towards our position. We had occupied a trench he had destroyed minutes before. He was shouting 'Hands up!' or '*Manos arriba!*' to me and my gunner. 'Scouse, it's me, Bish, don't shoot!' Heart in my mouth time again. I saw my life flash briefly before me. Thank fuck he didn't open up. When am I going to get some killing done? No chance in the reserve section. But my time would come later in the day.

Corporal Marty Margerison, 6 Platoon B Company 2 Para

As we moved off up a gradual incline, A and D Company were in heavy engagement with the enemy; we could see all the firefights over to our left, as it was still dark. As we got up on this incline, we got fired on from the left and I shout, 'Enemy left!', so we spun round then assaulted through about eight enemy locations. The enemy trenches were in like a 'V' shape, so the section was starting to get split, then I stopped and Chippy started to take over from that point. We assaulted through, killing eight Argies, then Sergeant Bill McColloch came over and started bollocking us because we had taken the initiative!

Remember the lone sentry, or scarecrow as I called him, well he was just an individual, but here we were closing with trenches by throwing grenades then firing into them, clearing, then moving on to the next one, and by the time we had engaged them all, we had no grenades left. We now had only one HE and only two white phos per section, and it only becomes apparent a bit later we are running out of ammo too. That's not funny, not good for such a short engagement, yet we had gone through the correct procedure of keeping a count of rounds fired, and fire discipline was a lot tighter back then than nowadays.

Fire discipline was curtailed and now we knew the reason why. Bill bollocked us saying, 'Don't go off again without no protection.' Okay, it did get a bit confusing, you gotta be sharp, you gotta be aware of who's around you and keep your boundaries short. I think we'd probably reached our LOE [Limits of Exploitation] at that point. It would have been hard for me, certainly Chippy, to control it any further; but luckily, it all sort of stopped and fizzled out.

Then I watched Mick Connor [Cpl B Company, 2 Para, RIP] and his platoon, 5 Platoon, march some enemy prisoners through my position and off towards HQ, which was strange, because I thought our HQ was in a different direction. Orientation at night is difficult, you had to use your compass to get back on axis; back on bearings and all that.

Lance Corporal Bill 'Basha' Bentley MM, Combat Medical Team 2 Para

The battle moved forward ahead of us, but we remained in the dead ground where it was much more realistic to treat the casualties than on the battlefield itself. During quiet moments we tried to take a tactical nap, but the bitter cold made this almost impossible. As dawn broke, we went forward to search for our missing comrades.

Along with the Reverend David Cooper, our padre, I carried in our first dead body. The soldier, a friend of mine, had been shot through the head; the bullet had ripped the back of his head off and literally blown his brain out. While carrying his body back into the lines, in a poncho, his head kept banging against my knee and giving off a 'hollow echo', a sound that is not easy to forget!

11

ADVANCE TO CONTACT

Lance Corporal Paul Bishop, 6 Platoon B Company 2 Para

As it was getting light the company were advancing down a forward slope, 6 Platoon left, 4 Platoon right, and flunky 5 Platoon as we were nicknamed, in reserve. Through the early morning mist, we could see some figures, they had their hands in their pockets. They were kicking the ground trying to get warm. Some lads from our two platoons opened fire on them.

'Cease fire!' a corporal shouted, 'It's fucking A Company!'

'Fuck off,' was the reply back, 'they are fucking Argies.' The first corporal then shouted, 'Right, the next fucking bloke who opens fire will be put on a charge.' Then all those Argies with hands in their pockets opened up on us – the fog of war, ah!

Number 4 and 6 Platoons plus Company HQ, who had all those antennas on their radios, ran forward to the dead ground, a gully, and as we ran down, I noticed at least two large enemy bunkers about 500 to 700 metres away forward right, and also noted the location of the bunker half left 150 metres away. At some stage, the

163

two forward sections of our platoon were ordered to advance from the safety of the gully. I thought, *thank fuck we are still in reserve; I might live a bit longer.*

The battle continued 75 metres in front of where our section lay, but we couldn't see anything. Our section was then ordered to take out a bunker, which I believed had already been destroyed. Brummie briefed me to move forward to get into a fire support position. I moved my half section forward just out of view of the Argies to the right. Once in position, we started to give fire support.

Brummie's team assaulted the bunker; yes, I was right, there was nobody home. But shortly after they assaulted the bunker, I saw Brummie jump back. *Fuck me, he's been shot*, I thought, *OH FUCKING GOD, NO, I hope he's okay.* Then I quickly realised I was going to go up there and get him off the hill.

At this stage I could see Brummie lying on his back. He was pulling down his trousers and inspecting the family jewels. *Poor bastard*, I thought, *he's been shot in the bollocks!* I moved forward with my blokes towards Brummie's team. I noticed he'd fixed himself up. Fuck me, he'd been shot in the bollocks, now he'd patched himself up and was about to move back towards the rest of the company. He is one tough cookie. He later told me a bullet must have ricocheted off a rock and a rock splinter cut into his scrotum. He said that his first thought was, *bollocks, the wife is going to kill me!*

Corporal Ken Raynor, patrol commander Recce Platoon 2 Para

As A Company advanced towards Darwin, having worked their way through Burntside House, we tagged along, and then broke contact and went to a pre-arranged RV between A and B companies. The plan was for A and B to fight their way forward to the ridge line at the top of Darwin Hill, then go firm, and that would allow D to push through left of Boca House, then head south towards the airstrip.

As first light came in, I could see B Company over on the right flank and it was plain to see Battalion HQ trying to maintain the balance in keeping the two companies in line; unlike training it was not easy to give each other supporting fire, so there was a lot of smoke and straight up the middle, sort of thing. This was really the start of the battle for Darwin and Goose Green.

Private Dave 'Charlie' Brown, HQ C (Bruneval) Company 2 Para

As it got light, the whole company started to advance towards Darwin, while A Company went ahead again to clear Darwin Hill. We were then ordered to go support A Company and that's when we got mortared, caught out in the middle of open ground. And every time we started to move forward, we got it again. The Argies had spotters up on Darwin Hill and it was here we go again, and we just hugged the ground for dear life. Also, we were getting all the off-shoots from the Argies firing across at A Company pinging at us, and that was shitty too.

Lance Corporal 'Radar', Defence Platoon 2 Para

There was this track going up a slight incline and there were three of our guys [dead] laid out on the left of it. The padre, David Cooper, was up there as well by that time, so we put the three guys on ponchos and B Company came up behind us. I could see Argies up on the hill not far away, so I says to an officer, 'Are we gonna shoot them, or what?' So, this officer says, 'I'll have to double check.'

Later, when we got to the spot we saw the Argies earlier, we discovered they were Argy marines, because the conscripts were small and these were big fuckers. I saw one of our guys shoot this Argy five times in the chest! I had to go back with one of our guys who'd shot this Argy in a trench. He was still alive, but he was only alive because he'd fallen back, and he was on the spoils of the trench; if he'd been on his side, he would have died. So when I pulled him out of the trench to give first aid, he died; his lungs filled up.

Private Phil Williams, Mortar Platoon 2 Para

We got shelled and mortared quite a bit on the mortar line. The Argies definitely knew our position, because we got pinged by a Pucara. As it flew over us, he rocketed the mortar line, but we all scattered just before he came, because the Pucara makes a distinctive sound. Strangely, he didn't use his guns on us on that pass, but loosed off his rockets, missed, and as he banked and veered over me, I tell you what, he was so fucking low, it looked like you could have actually reached up and grabbed hold of his wing tip he came that low. It also looked like he was fucking laughing, as he was looking straight at me. I dunno if he was, but fuck me, he was looking my way wearing a big grimace.

Either side of his cockpit he had these 20mm cannons, but again decided to use his rockets and as he spun around to have another go at us, we all started digging in like crazy with our elbows. Then, just as he was lining back up, two of our Scout helicopters popped up over our hill, which had been taking back our wounded and bringing in more mortar rounds and GPMG link and stuff. Luckily, if that's the case, they were on an ammo resup not casevacing.

When the Pucara saw them, he forgot about us and went after the Scouts, and then I watched as he attacked them. He fired at one of them, which took a direct hit and it was shot down, but I didn't see it crash, and then it started to chase the second one. Later, the report we got was that some guy on the gun line back at Camilla Creek House shot down the Pucara with a Blowpipe missile. I never saw that happen; so not sure about that one!

Colour Sergeant Pete Vale, HQ Company 2 Para

Camilla Creek House, daylight. I watched the Pucara stalk Dick Nunn's helicopter and tried to get a radio net through to the helicopter to get him to fly over us, because we were set up with all the gimpys. We watched it shoot the chopper down, when suddenly it spotted us and swung around towards Camilla Creek, I guess that was his escape route out too. So, me and Doc Findlay, RIP [killed on 2 Para's second battle at Wireless Ridge] had rigged an air-mounted gimpy. We bodged it on a tall mound of peat and I gave Ken Lukowiak [Pte, HQ Company, 2 Para] an 84 and as this Pucara came in on its strafing run, I was watching our tracer when Lukowiak let rip.

There wasn't a cat in hell's chance of him hitting it, but Ken's missile shot up towards the Pucara, The pilot must have seen this 84 round and tracer heading his way, so banked sharply, and that was his fatal mistake, because we got a belly side-on view. He still had his reserve tanks on (but he wouldn't have got home if he had ejected them), then Doc hit one of the tanks and we watched as avgas spewed out. Unfortunately, it wasn't a tracer round or it would have exploded.

Five years later the wreckage of a Pucara was found crashed into the mountains. That was this Pucara. RIP.

Private Tom Crusham, Signals Platoon attached HQ Company 2 Para

I was still being used as a dogsbody and found myself flying along in this chopper for some reason that I forget now, and the next thing I saw two Pucaras come out of nowhere. They flew straight past us, and then they came round again, so we started dropping like we were contouring, just as we did in Northern Ireland along the border, sort of hedge-hopping but there were no hedges to hop this time.

We were keeping as low as possible, doing this evasive flying and heading for the mountains! The pilot slowed right down, then went into hover mode real close to the deck. We waited a few seconds, then off we went again, but this time creeping towards some high ground still keeping as low as possible. We didn't see Pucaras again, thank fuck! We were really lucky.

Sergeant Pilot Dick Kilinski, F Flight 656 Squadron Army Air Corps

We were constantly ferrying the wounded off Darwin Hill to any Navy ship who had aviation fuel, because the Scouts were very thirsty. So we always had to drop the casualties off, fuel up, go pick up supplies from Blue Beach, then back to the front line; drop off the supplies, pick up more casualties, then back to the ships.

As Scouts, we always worked in pairs, and we worked with the Navy pilots too. So, on one occasion John and Reg were working together and I was working with Dick Nunn [Lieutenant Richard 'Dick' James Nunn RM]. We had just picked up a load of ammunition from Blue Beach and supplies, and were flying back towards Darwin Hill down parallel valleys about half a mile apart, really down low to keep out of the way of any Argies. Suddenly, we got word a Pucara was chasing us and it was pure coincidence this Pucara locked on and thankfully not me, yet it could have been me, because we were still flying parallel. No, it had locked on to Dick and he just couldn't have avoided it. I dropped straight down and went to ground in the hover and watched what was going on with my air gunner. Sadly, the Pucara shot down Dick as he was trying to dodge it; he hit the ground and his air gunner was ejected out through the door. Sergeant Bill Belcher was his name, and as he hit the ground he was badly injured, but he lived, whilst Dick didn't. I carried on up to Darwin Hill, dropped off the much-needed ammunition, picked up more casualties and just got on with it.

ADVANCE TO CONTACT

Private Phil Williams, Mortar Platoon 2 Para

We had a decent position to put the mortars up, there was like a ready-made protective line in front of us that gave us a bit of protection from the direction of the Argy threat. The barrels lasted, and the base plates lasted pretty well too, although we were getting through all the ammunition that we had fairly quickly.

When it all kicked off, the fire missions came in thick and fast. The crews who weren't on the mortar line were used as outer cordon protection for the line. When all the fire missions came in, we started to run out of ammunition really quick. And this is something: everyone in the battalion was carrying two rounds, and I'm fairly sure Colonel Jones was carrying two rounds as well. They were dropped off at the original drop-off point at Sussex Mountains, then flown forward to Camilla Creek House and again moved slightly more forward of that.

So when we were running out of ammunition firing the blokes in, I remember Jack Reaper organising it: Jack, myself, and a gang of other crews ran backwards and forwards to the stockpile of ammo and we got as much of it as we could, dropping it off at the mortar line, running back and forward, back and forward from Darwin Hill to the ammo dump near Camilla Creek House. We covered miles and miles across all that open, grassy tufted bog. It was lung-splitting, but what drove us on was knowing our mates were in close-quarter combat with the enemy.

David Norris, general news reporter Daily Mail, *attached 2 Para*

Me and Foxy were well behind the advancing 2 Para, but we were close enough behind to keep getting mortared and then we came across a line of Argy prisoners. So I started talking to one of them who spoke English, he was a little lad but engaging, when this Para came across who was obviously guarding them, and I mean he was built like a brick shit house.

The Para said, 'You're not meant to be talking to the prisoners, it's against the Geneva Convention, so fuck off.' Well, I did bugger off and you know he was right, it was against the Geneva Convention, I later found out. Something else I found out when I met up with the brick-shit-house Para a bit later on in the war; he told me the prisoner I was trying to talk to was a medical student, who had been conscripted but was studying to become a doctor. It seemed that this Para had taken him under his wing, which I found very, very moving given the circumstances I found myself in.

Lance Corporal Bill 'Basha' Bentley MM, Combat Medical Team 2 Para

Ahead of us on the upward slope the battle was in full swing and casualties were being brought to us at the regimental aid post, which was no more than a group of medics and a doctor, all with rucksacks full of medical supplies. One young soldier had been shot in his water bottle, yes in his water bottle, which exploded, probably breaking his hip. Another, we could not identify his injury, so I persuaded the platoon sergeant to shine his torch onto the casualty and he was horrified at the thought of lighting up the darkness while the battle raged just ahead of us. Using his own body to screen the light from the direction of the battle, he did as requested.

We were then able to identify that this young man had also been shot in his webbing, the bullet had ripped through his equipment, travelled along the inside of his belt and had come to rest exactly in his navel. Clearly the lad was shocked and bruised, but as I could find no injury and there were obviously no broken bones, I wanted to send him back to his platoon. After all, they were in the heat of the battle. My boss Dr Steve Hughes, Captain, was more sympathetic and sent the lad back to Ajax Bay for a proper check-up. This young man rejoined us before the battle for Wireless Ridge, where he was then killed.

Lance Corporal 'Radar', Defence Platoon 2 Para

It was getting light back on the side of the track and we were told to dig a set of trenches. We're gonna go firm, for how long we didn't know. We were told, just go firm, so we started digging in and the trenches were as shallow as fuck and Ford [Captain Ford OC Defence Platoon] comes up to me and says, 'That looks big enough for two!' I said, 'If you're a pygmy like me, yeah,' and he went away in a huff. I thought I was gonna get a big bollocking after that, because he was a big lump of a man, but I didnae want him in my hole!

Anyway, a bit later as I'd just finished scraping out this trench, but really it was only a shell-scrape, we get this plop, plop, plop sound, and a couple of the young Toms says, 'What's that?'

'It's mortars,' I says, 'so get fucking down then.'

'How do you know it's mortars?'

'Look! Just take cover.' I mean, you could hear them and see them. Then suddenly fifteen metres away the ground rips up about three metres high.

And they say, 'Why aren't they exploding?'

'Because it's the peat that's absorbing the impact!' I screamed across at them. Honestly, it was like talking to a couple of schoolkids; but they were learning, and I was learning, we were all learning fast.

The Argies fired a dozen rounds at us and not one hit! I'm not the best soldier in the world but I'm not stupid either, yet I'm thinking, why aren't they carrying on mortaring us? We're stuck out here in the open, easy targets. But they stopped soon after. Maybe our lads had taken them out.

After the first barrage it was now light, so we were ordered to go collect the prisoners over at B Company's area, well, the ones who'd surrendered, but they were still in their fucking trenches! I couldn't believe it; they were still in their holes. We pulled them all out and took them back to HQ, and then the Padre says we need to go bring in their dead too. As we went back out again with some prisoners to get their dead, we gathered up even more prisoners, then all of a sudden two Pucaras came out of nowhere.

I shouts to the six of us to get in amongst the fifty prisoners we had, because the first one was lining up for a ground attack, and I thought, *we're all gonna get bounced here!* But he obviously sees the difference in uniforms, we're all in camouflage, the Argies all in olive green, so he pulls up, and I thought, *I didn't even have a chance to shit myself.* We were going to get seriously malleted for sure, and it was only a matter of time if this nonsense kept up.

Lance Corporal Bill 'Basha' Bentley MM, Combat Medical Team 2 Para

One of the medics indicated to me that another missing friend of mine was 'over there'. I found him alongside another body lying next to him. It was obvious that my friend had been injured first and that the youngster had gone to his aid. The shell dressing and the position of the bodies was unmistakable. They had then both taken a prolonged burst of machine-gun fire, which had made a real mess.

Out of respect for the youngster, I chose to carry him in first. Lying down next to him, I took his arms up over my shoulders and staggered to my feet, and as I did this the youngster rolled to the side and back to the ground. I was still holding one of his arms over my shoulder! Spreading my own poncho out on the ground, I rolled his body onto it and dragged him back towards the rest of the medics. Somebody came out to meet me and helped me drag the body the rest of the way. I desperately needed a rest; we had now been moving in extreme conditions for about fifty hours. I had to ask two other medics to go out and bring in my friend, while I had a brew and tried to take a nap.

During a heavy barrage I found myself sharing a previous shell crater with our Padre, what a guy! If anything put me off him it was the extra-long spade that he carried, just in case he had to 'dig a quick grave'. He always had a story or a quick joke, like 'not being fussy about who he has to bury and he would be proud to do me the favour'! Thanks, Padre.

12

EFFECTIVE ENEMY FIRE

Private Steve Taylor, 3 Platoon A Company 2 Para

After the Burntside House attack, we moved forward to a place called Coronation Point, giving fire support to the rest of A Company assaulting Darwin Hill, and one of the blokes had the 84 to lug around but with no more ammo, as we'd used that up on the Burntside House attack. Such was our front-line ammo scale; it was pretty small, we only carried two rounds for it! The first one was a misfire and you know, in training, you have to wait a bit, and then apply all the safety rules for a misfire, like get out of its way, and leave it on the range for the EOD [Explosive Ordnance Disposal] boys to come blow it up. Well, we just ejected the round and loaded another.

Corporal Marty Margerison, 6 Platoon B Company 2 Para

Once the scarecrow engagement was done, a bit later we started to move off again this time on the original bearing. So, to recap, we started off at Camilla Creek House waiting to get counterattacked by all of these Argies, then moved on to a start-line to advance on the enemy, killed their sentry and then engaged some trenches, so we knew that we were at the forward edge of enemy emplacements. It would transpire later they'd all fucked off, all done a runner and pulled back mainly to Goose Green, but obviously, we didn't know that at the time.

It was a bit of a long way to extract and I never knew what the scarecrow sentry was doing so far away from his mates all on his tod, because when we bumped into him, we came across no more enemy for at least a couple of hundred metres.

We got near to Boca House, which was initially our objective, so we went into all-round-defence and got reorganised. Then JC says, 'Right we're off.' It was beginning to get light now and we're off advancing again. We could see elements of D Company off to our left and at ten o'clock further on our left in the distance was Darwin Hill, where A Company was still engaging the enemy on higher ground. I mean, the ground would have been only about fifty foot higher, but viewing over 1000 metres it looked higher, and A Company's firefight was very intense.

Daylight came quick and as we made our way up another incline and then down the other side we got opened up on. Half the company's going down the hill and the other half is still on the top. Some of us ran forward towards a gorse line and into dead ground and took cover, the rest of the platoon made their way back up top to where the company had gone firm.

When we got into the gorse, I crawled forward and I could see these two Argies in their trench and being an Army shoot, I thought they were about 300 metres away, so I set my sights as such and fired and saw the strike. Then I heard Chippy go, 'Weapons tight, weapons tight.' Then I heard the Argies crack and thump as they returned fire, which gave me another indication they were firing from about 300 metres.

The problem being it was now broad daylight, our ammo was fucking minimal, we had no smoke to give covering fire, we've used up all the illume, we used the phos and run out of HE grenades. No 2-inch mortars, and all the 81mm mortars were now dedicated to A Company. Eddy Carrol was now back up the top of the hill with his M79 and HMS *Arrow* with its big 4.5-inch gun had gone fucking u/s. What a fucking position to find oneself in.

We remained in that gorse bush between four to five hours, because we had no method of extracting other than run like fuck. We were spread over about a hundred yards in this gorse watching A and D Companies continually fighting through, while every so often the Argies in the trench to my front would put a harassing burst into the gorse, because they didn't know where we were exactly. I was on my own and at about the four-and-a-half-hour point. Yes! Four and a half hours stuck there, while listening to the rest of the battalion carrying on their attack, it was so frustrating.

Then JC came over the radio, 'Stand by, there's a surprise coming.' What was the surprise? Was a B-52 gonna come over and carpet bomb the whole fucking Argy trench line, because these two Argies in a trench had held up a company of Paratroopers, because we had no support and we were desperately low on ammo and we couldn't realistically take them on? It was fucking embarrassing.

Weapons tight was the order, because the bigger picture was beyond our control. Ten or fifteen minutes later the surprise came, a single 2-inch smoke [mortar round] landed between the gorse bush and the top of the hill. A fucking 2-inch smoke and Chippy shouts, 'Prepare to move!' *For fuck's sake, here we go*, I thought. So, I shouted to the gunners and told them, 'When I say, give covering fire – fire, and listen for me to move.'

So, one guy shouts 'Go!' as he's up and running, so it's every man for himself sort of thing, and we all started to run back up this fucking hill. Jim and Frog started putting fire down while I ran halfway up, stopped, got down and shouted for them to come too. So as they turned, I gave covering fire and when they got level, I went to get up and felt this pain like I'd been hit by a shovel. Now, the problem with me was, a round had gone through my face and my arm and then I saw a round hit my rifle.

I knew something was wrong with my shoulder, but I didn't realise anything was wrong with my face until I started to speak. I was spitting blood and I was looking up the hill and I see one of the Toms and he was shouting, 'Scouse's been hit.' Then Baz Barsley MM, RIP, [L/Cpl B Company] and one other came down and pulled me back up to safety. Baz would often tell me I was shouting for my mama, but I was actually trying to say, 'My arm, my arm.' The fuckers were pulling on my shot-up arm.

When they bandaged my face up, I was still compos mentis, because I recall Mick Connor coming across with two Argy prisoners and he said, 'Hi, Scouse, these two have come to take you down to the RAP.' I told him, 'Not a fucking chance. Don't let them fuckers near me. I'll walk.' And I did walk; shot through the face, in the arm and fuck knows what had hit me below. But before I left the top of the hill, colour man Jed Petefield, Anti-Tanks, came over and took me to a Milan position, then told me to pull the trigger.

'There you go,' he said, 'you've just taken out that Argy trench.' One of the lads guided it, I think it was Brian Worrell, RIP. It decimated that trench and blew the Argies to pieces who'd shot me up.

Private Jim Meredith, GPMG gunner, 6 Platoon B Company 2 Para

Marty was two men away from me when he got shot. We were just advancing to contact again, and then as we were moving down this slope we came under contact, but the Argy rounds weren't landing that close, so we didn't have to take cover. Anyways, the next thing

I knew, Scouse had been shot through the shoulder and the face as well. I then took cover and that's when two of the guys went back to help him out. One took his weapon and his webbing off, and Baz Barsley MM, RIP, the other guy, just picked old Scouse up under fire and took him up and into a safe place. A bloody brave thing to do, considering.

The Argies had an SF position dug-in and were about a few hundred metres away and poured a massive amount of fire down on 'em. Scouse was covered in blood and snot and he looked bad, but luckily the round that entered his shoulder came out of his mouth; still, it took his bottom jaw out completely and it was just hanging on by the skin and resting on his chest. It did look bad, and at the time I found it very upsetting.

That Argy SF position kept us pinned down for the rest of the day. I was isolated and the plan was that the guys would give me all their spare bandoliers by throwing them over to me, so I could give them covering fire as they tried to leg it back into safety. I was left there with one other, but it didn't bother us being left, because we had plenty of link. I knew where the guys were and I knew the rest of the company had gone firm the other side of the hill, and that gave me comfort. Later, JC ordered up a Milan team, which took out that Argy position. The Milan blasted those Argies to shit.

Lance Corporal Paul Bishop, 6 Platoon B Company 2 Para

After Scouse [Marty] got hit, my platoon was ordered to advance. I thought this was a bit suicidal; after all, we had no fire support. Although 4 Platoon were covering us, Argy machine-gun fire still rained down on us. Then Chippy gave the order to move, 'Come on, let's get them for what they did to Scouse. Move!' as another burst of hornets came in. He stood up on his own, but everyone else stayed down, then Chippy got back down, and quite right too.

Those bastards in the other trenches would not budge, and at this stage of the battle we had one man killed (young Stephen Illingsworth, DCM. Steve was a good popular professional soldier in 5 Platoon), and we had about five or six wounded.

We were informed that a Milan anti-tank missile team was with 5 Platoon about 700 metres behind our two platoons. *Excellent,* I thought, *now we can get up to and kill those bastards and move off towards Goose Green.* I then heard a mortar or artillery round land amongst us, then some more of the blokes received shrapnel wounds. BANG! A Milan was fired off and as we looked towards the bunkers, nothing was seen! I looked over to my right and to my horror there was this high explosive missile zipping around between Company HQ and ourselves; it was a rogue Milan round. That's all I need now, a friendly fire death.

Luckily it just fizzed out, but a second Milan was fired off which hit the target smack on, dead centre, and that's when the white flags started to appear from the Argy trenches.

Lance Corporal Bill 'Basha' Bentley MM, Combat Medical Team 2 Para

I went out again, this time with Mark Polkey [Pte 2 Para medic] to search for our dead and wounded. Mark and I decided to split up, the area to cover was considerable and time was critical to the survival of our comrades. I soon became aware of someone sitting or crouching, about a hundred metres ahead of me. Looking for cover, I suddenly saw a trench ahead of me and ran to it and jumped in. In the bottom of the trench there was obviously someone hiding under a poncho; it was as if I had jumped onto a water bed with lumps in it. Instinctively I fired a long burst from my SMG, luckily past my own feet, into who or whatever was under the poncho. I guess shocked, I sprang back out and moved forward to another trench.

Here there was a severely wounded Argentinian soldier, who was unconscious. I became concerned that if I fired my weapon again, my own comrades might think that I was the enemy and open fire on me. I was also, I guess, afraid to leave this wounded man behind me and go forward. Time waits for no man and my comrades were out there somewhere. I finished this poor soul off with my bayonet. Again moving forward, towards the first person that I had seen, I realised that he was also an Argentinian soldier.

I moved quickly and cautiously towards him and as he had made no aggressive gestures, I was also not aggressive. In front of me was a youngster, he had been shot through the leg and was in deep shock. The better side of me, or my training, now took over. The youngster had no weapon at hand and so I hoisted him up over my shoulder in a classical fireman's lift and carried him into our own lines. Looking back this was quite a risk, as he would have been looking down onto my still bloody bayonet, with which I had just killed his comrade, and it would have been fairly easy for him to have drawn it and stabbed me in the back.

Sergeant John 'Taff' Meredith DCM, 12 Platoon D Company 2 Para

It was still dark when we cleared these trenches and then we had to go firm while the other companies were put back on line as per the battle plan phases, so B Company had to move up on our right, A Company had to move on the left towards Darwin, and as they were moving forward, we were getting all the splashback, the Argy overshoots; likewise when B Company came in contact, we were in the middle of it all.

It was light now and we realised we were on top of a grassy rolling ridge. Then the Engineer Section thought there was a minefield ahead, but while we were up there, I could see B Company had got caught on the forward slope of a similar ridge, half right to us. While up on this ridge, we could see all these Argies come walking along the beach to our right trying to get back into Goose Green, so I got my gunners to open up on them Then the OC Phil Neame came over and said, 'What are you doing?'

'We're just shooting at the Argies,' I replied.

'Well, they may have surrendered!'

'They haven't got their hands in the air!'

'They've got blankets over their heads.'

'Well, that's not my fault, and any way it's good practice for the gunners!' I replied back. Then I think you guys in C Company fired at them and, of course, there was still all this splashback coming in. We had to get out of it, so Phil Neame moved us forward into dead ground below the ridge where B Company were getting it. How long we were going to be there was down to the CO, who was running the battle over to our left at Darwin Hill, so we got a brew on.

Later, we moved behind B Company to the right of them and on to the beach (as they were still held up on their ridge), to attack B Company's original target of Boca House, and that's where B Company took most of their casualties; it's where Steve Illingsworth was killed [Pte, B Company 5 Platoon]. So, we came around B and headed for the beach and then walked into a minefield. What the Argies had done was they'd tied orange baling cord between the mines linking them all up, so at night you wouldn't see 'em, but during the day we did.

As we were moving through the minefield, I told the blokes to watch out for the baling cord and to make sure they kept their boots away from it, but as we were making our approach on to Boca House, all of a sudden there was a massive BOOM!, an explosion, and I'm eating grass. I'm on the deck thinking, what am I doing down here? I shook myself down and looked over to see if all my guys were okay, and there was Spencer, one of my Toms, sitting up by a massive hole from the mine he'd just triggered off.

He was shouting, 'It wasn't me! It wasn't me!' But there was a length of this orange baling cord wrapped around his foot, ha-ha. He'd detonated an anti-tank mine, not an AP [anti-personnel]! It was a huge explosion and that's what put me down, but luckily, we didn't take any casualties. Then Corporal Dick Barton comes across and says, 'Quick, let's get him up.'

'No leave him in there, he's the one who tripped it,' I ordered. From then on, Spencer was known as Boomer.

We took Boca House and started to clear the trenches, collecting all the Argy casualties, around about the time A Company took Darwin Hill. Then 10 Platoon was taken to look after the prisoners, of which we had about twelve non-seriously injured, and there were others who were still in their trenches badly injured, of around ten to fifteen. It was a platoon position. Then we were ordered to advance on to our next target, which was the Goose Green airfield.

Private David Minnock, GPMG gunner, 12 Platoon D Company 2 Para

Boca House was D Company's objective. It was a ruin, just the foundations of a former homestead on the shoreline. Before we captured it, we were moving to take the surrender of some Argies, but they had a taped-off area; a minefield. There was no way to go around it, so Taff guided us through; the mines were badly laid and we could see them all, we hoped! Then suddenly there was this massive explosion, and I thought, *shit, we're under attack again*, and all we heard was, 'It wasn't me, sergeant! It wasn't me!'

There was this bloke called Spencer, Boomer we nicknamed him after that, and he was running about the place pleading his case. We all looked round and Spanner had this mine tape wrapped around his boot, so Taff says, 'When I get you out of this minefield, I'm gonna kill you.' Taff was joking, of course, but the ludicrousness of the situation was mind-blowing, and funny too. Spanner wasn't injured, he was alright, but it was a massive explosion. He'd set off a tripwire as he walked across the tape, because there was a wire through it that pulled a pin on the mine, known as a booby-trap necklace.

It seemed all the Argy defences were to cover an assault from the sea, they didn't seem to be covering any attack from the land. So, it was all about an amphibious assault! I suppose they planned for our Marines to come in from the sea, not Paras across the friggin' land, coming out of nowhere!

Corporal Tom Harley MM, section commander, 10 Platoon D Company 2 Para

It was light now, and some order was beginning to take hold again. D Company had passed through A and B and taken up point, as they were getting bogged down in their own battles.

In the light of day, D Company found itself more than a tactical bound [a movement forward] in front of A and B. There was dead ground to our rear, but accurate sniper fire prevented A or B from closing up, although Recce and Patrols Platoons managed to move forward.

Neamesy could see we were losing the momentum, so he decided to take three sections and move around to the right along the shoreline, and roll them [the Argies] up from their flank. Mine, Wally McAuley's and Dick Barton's sections [Corporals, section commanders D Company] would be used. So off we went in snake formation. When we got to where we thought was roughly in line with their flank, Neamesy was acting like a section commander and was all for leading the attack himself. I pulled him back by his webbing and said, 'This is Toms' work,' and moved in front. I then scrambled up the bank and shook out to advance to contact.

We had only gone about a hundred metres when we could see the trenches. By the time we got there, most of the enemy had escaped, leaving their dead and wounded in situ. The Milan had done its job. After searching the trenches and patching up their wounded, we returned back to the company.

Captain Paul Farrar, OC Patrols Platoon 2 Para

It was getting light by now as we were following down the axis, which was our mission, and at some point we were slightly right of the axis, and of D Company. It was around then we stopped and waited, and we started getting mortared. We moved back around to the left, where we had this rather grandstand view of the end part of A Company's battle fighting up Darwin Hill, and then we moved directly across on to it.

Grenades were going off and mortar rounds landing and this is when Pete Kennedy came up with the offer of giving A Company fire support, because we had twelve LMGs in C Company, which was a lot of firepower, and we could have given a lot of suppressing fire. Pete actually spoke to H Jones on the radio, where Jones basically told him to keep his nose out of his battle, or words to that effect.

We knew B and D Companies were off over to our right in the direction of Boca House, and A Company's battle was the current main effort, but unbeknown to us, the CO's TAC group had moved up to A Company's position. This was the nature of H Jones, he would want to be where the action was, which is one side of leadership; others would say, well, that's a company commander's battle, the CO should be back behind and out of the way.

I'd seen this before on an exercise in Norfolk a few months earlier, when I was umpiring for D Company. I'd never been on exercise with H Jones at all, but I did see bits of him during this one. We got to a phase of the exercise where there was supposed to be a rescue of the hostages, and part of this phase called for a night bridging operation by 9 Squadron, Para Engineers, who'd have to put a bridge in at night. So the actual bridge, a Bailey bridge across this river, was all umpired off and had been 'demolished' with white tape.

The intention was that 2 Para would get to this water course and see the 'demolished' bridge and go, 'Oh shit! Sappers, we need a bridge!' and then 9 Squadron would come up to do their bit and build a bridge. But H Jones says, 'Well, I'm not having any of this.' He walked on to the 'demolished' bridge, ripped all the mine tape off and threw it in the river and went, 'Right, 2 Para follow me.' He completely threw the exercise plan out of the window. It was 9 Squadron's chance to do a night bridging operation, but he wasn't having that, because his battalion was being held up!

At the time I said to the other umpires, and this is absolutely genuine, 'Fuck me, if he ever goes to war, he's going to get himself killed.' That was his style of command. I had a huge amount of respect for Colonel H, he had enormous charisma and his guys were right behind him, but he had these tendencies to go into, like, overdrive if it wasn't going his way; incredibly frustrated, and I genuinely believe that he was in one of his red mists during the action on Darwin Hill.

Lance Corporal Neal Dance MID, 5 Platoon B Company 2 Para

We were pinned down on a forward slope just above the gorse line. Once we got out of that situation Jimmy Street Strāza [*sic*] had been shot in the leg. As normal, he was asking for a cigarette and being told to fuck off, ha–ha, and as guys were moving by him, they kept kicking him in that leg, and I swear it was an accident!

Corporal Marty Margerison, 6 Platoon B Company 2 Para

I'm in being looked after by Blackie Blackburn, the company clerk/ medic, and a variety of people came and tended to me also. I said to Blackie, 'Could I have cigarette?' and he gives me a ciggy. But I'm not actually smoking it, taking it down, as it's coming out the side of my face, because my lips was all split and I had only a couple of teeth left on the top, the two at the back. Then JC comes over and says, 'You alright, MaGee?' That's what he used to call me.

'Yes, sir, just having a ciggy.'

'Alright,' he says, 'just hang on in there and don't go to sleep, because you're in shock, and if you do, you won't wake up, mate.' (The company and battalion policy was, if you are injured, that's where you stayed until the firefight was won.) Later, I was walked over to the RAP by Mick Connor. At that point D Company had exploited as far as they could. A Company had taken Darwin Hill and gone firm, then C Company came through and advanced towards Goose Green.

When I was in the RAP there was a lad there, Terry Wood, Defence Platoon, his brother had been killed at Warrenpoint,[16] so I'm lying in this RAP and who's in with me? Well, it was Jimmy Street, the only two people given a *Norland* badge by Roy 'Wendy' Gibson. Jimmy had been shot through the leg.

To the right of Jimmy was Tam Mechan [Support Company, attached D Company] dead, so I rolled over to Tam, because Tam was one of my blokes before he went to Support Company, and I said words to the effect, 'You've always been a scruffy twat.' Then I zipped his smock up, sorted him out, cleaned him up a bit, then straightened his beret over his face and placed his arms together.

I got quite emotional about it. I carried on talking to him, 'It's

---

16 Warrenpoint, Northern Ireland. On 27 August 1979 the IRA detonated two IEDs and killed 18 men; 16 from 2 Para and 2 from the Queen's Own Highlanders.

alright, Tam, no more pain, you're out of here now,' and when I'd finished my words, this twat Wood is outside looking towards Darwin where the pond is and he's taking photos of this Pucara coming straight for us now, towards Goose Green! You could see the pilot!

I was deemed walking wounded, so later on a helicopter flies in, picks me up and takes me to Ajax Bay. The pilot was Dick Nunn and I was probably on his penultimate fight, because he got shot down and killed shortly after he'd dropped me off at Ajax Bay.

Ajax Bay was a cattle shed with a load of beds for the wounded and an unexploded bomb hanging through the roof. You know, the nose part was bearing down on us hung up on its tail fin. I was seen by Commander Jolly.[17] There were Marine medics and Paras from 23 PFA Para Field Ambulance; there were many different regiments and Navy in there, all working hard on us and the Argies.

Before they knocked me out, I recall having all my clothes cut off me, then sitting on the bed and Rick Jolly putting a pencil right through my shoulder, telling the doctors and medics, 'This is what you call a clean wound.' They all peered at it and my face, which was a real mess, and obviously I was then knocked out completely.

Private Ron Webster, D Company 2 Para

Let me say first off, I've never given interviews to anyone about my war experience but when you asked, it was a given.

It was light and there was a bit of a lull in the fighting. Me and Tam had taken cover with Company HQ. Then a bit later we got the order to move forward so I looked over to my right to see Tam, but he wasn't moving. So I jokingly shouts across to him, 'Wake up you fucker, get up, we're moving,' as we were really knackered and

---

17 Surgeon Commander Rick Jolly, OBE, RN (1946–2018), the only person from the Falklands conflict to be decorated by both sides, British and Argentine.

whatever else after our tab and into the fight. But he didn't move, so I went over to him and that's when I found him dead, that was a big shock. Tam had been shot dead and the fact he had been getting out of the Army but decided to stay on, made it even sadder.

At the same time I'd confirmed Tam was dead, we started to move forward so I took his ammo and handed it out to the guys who were short. Anyway, we started moving forward and when we went firm again further towards the airfield I was tasked to go back and find Tam, but I couldn't find him! A bit later I was tasked by the sergeant major to go look for Tam again then go to the RAP to help out there since I was combat medic trained, so that made sense. I spent an overnighter there with the RAP and we were getting fragged all over the place by Argy artillery, but unbelievably nothing hit the RAP though all around got smashed.

One of the most amazing things I saw at the RAP was John Greenhalgh's Scout helicopters just kept coming in taking our wounded out, they must have done three or four lifts and under all that heavy fire, if it wasn't for those pilots, a lot of blokes wouldn't be here now, as there was only so much treatment we could give them at the RAP. The guys at the RAP did an amazing job and with the help of the cold weather, helped many survive. The Scout crews had recently worked with us in Kenya, so they knew some of us.

During the battle for Wireless Ridge, I got injured and was casevaced out and ended up on the SS *Uganda*. And can you believe this? By chance I bumped into Tam's uncle, he was part of the Merchant Navy crew and over a few whiskies I'd been given, I built up the courage to tell him I was with Tam when he'd been killed. I mean, he didn't know and it was something completely out of the blue. He ended up giving me his ID card, I mean I wasn't going to refuse it now was I! I guess it was a sign of respect or something. I still have it to this day.

Private Steve Taylor, 3 Platoon A Company 2 Para

As we approached Darwin Hill, we started coming under fire, so 1 and 2 Platoon got down and my platoon ran off to the side. The 84 got dumped as it was a useless piece of kit by then, and later on Lieutenant Guy Wallis [OC 3 Platoon] ran back and got it, and we all joke that's what he got his MID for.

Inch by inch we took the ground, bayonets fixed. I found an enemy soldier left behind, a machine gunner with a belt of two hundred strapped on ready to go. Someone noticed it at the same time and shouted, 'Steve! Get him away from that gun!' but I moved towards him, rifle ready to take him out should he so much as breathe. I am covered in crap, red eyes from lack of sleep, cam cream on in my best war paint, and festooned with belts of ammunition.

He shrinks back from me as I approach. He's alive! I grab him under his armpit and lift him off the ground, surprisingly with one hand. He is weak, frightened and shivering; he has been wounded several times and patched up. All aggression leaves me and pity creeps in. I am freezing, wet, cold and hungry, yet still I have a sense of right and wrong.

13

SUNRAY DOWN

Nigel Ely: In the world of army radio communication before the era of secure comms, appointment titles were used, rather than saying a person's name in clear over the net. For example, if you needed to speak to the artillery representative, you'd ask for *Sheldrake*; someone from Intelligence, you would ask for *Acorn*; Royal Engineers, *Holdfast*; Signals, *Pronto*; and, *a* or *the* commander is *Sunray*. You get the idea?

Gunner J. M. Love, 2 Para Group A Company 2 Para, FOO party signaller 29 Corunna Field Battery RA

Darwin
His knee arched
While his temples throbbed
The left leg, asleep long ago.
The warmth that slowly spread
The overpowering sense of relief
As his bladder finally emptied.

He shivered; his throat ached for moisture
The cold was creeping back into his bones.
That momentary respite, replaced by wet trousers
Though the pain in his shoulder was gone.
Perhaps it was the morphine, perhaps he was dying.
The smoke covered his face as the gorse burned on.

THE BATTLE FOR DARWIN HILL

Private Irwin Eversley, GPMG gunner, 2 Platoon A Company 2 Para

Darwin Hill. 2 Platoon was centre. Initially, 1 Platoon, who were on the right, took all the shit and then we were in amongst the Argies before they knew it, so they opened up. That's when Ginge Shorrock [Pte, A Company] got done [wounded] and all them boys; he was the medic for all the rest of 'em and they were just behind him.

I got to the top or what I thought was the top, but it was only a half ridge of Darwin Hill. Spanner was next to me, yet we still weren't in a position to see the top, then as we crawled slowly up, these trenches came into view. I was the right-hand gunner with the GPMG, Pete G was my No. 2, so we engaged these trenches and took 'em out. Three forward trenches in all – that GPMG's a fearsome weapon. I sprayed the fuck out of 'em.

Dill [Private Dillip, A Company] was the right-hand gunner and I was the left, but the night before we swapped over; not sure of the reason why, we just did it. Manny [Private Andy Mansfield], Spanner and Davey 'Chuck' Hardman [RIP, Cpl A Company] went up to do a recce for the company attack. When they came back down, Chuck said the recce was positive and there were Argies up the top all dug-in, so we got organised, shook ourselves and went forward up to the top.

I never really got on with Chuck, but he was a hard soldier and I think of all the grief he used to get because he was small, so I guess he had to prove he was a hard man; and he did, and he was, he was naturally hard, and I know this much, that boy could tab.

Lance Corporal 'Duke' Allen, Defence Platoon 2 Para

I was around Darwin Hill behind A Company's attack, and as we made our approach up Darwin Hill, it all kicked off. Argy mortars exploding all over. I saw what looked like better cover by the beach as you look towards Darwin and Goose Green, a little beach, and me and Drew Shane [Pte, Defence Platoon] was hiding behind this bank of dunes a couple of feet high. So I says to Drew, 'Come on, let's go and have a fuckin' look.'

Luckily for me, Drew had a young daughter, a baby about a year old, so he says, 'Fuck off,' and I'm glad he did, because literally a second later, if he'd have said yes, we'd have been blown to fuckin' pieces, as a large shell landed on the lip of our dune. There but for the fuckin' grace of God, like!

Private Irwin Eversley, GPMG gunner, 2 Platoon A Company 2 Para

When we got almost to the top, Spanner was point. It was turning a bit light now, and he was only a few feet away from me when we both saw several figures in front, and Spanner says to me, 'They're B Company.' I thought, *no, it can't be*, like B Company were well over to the right by the sea and forward of us – no, it couldn't be, and they were all out of their trenches, like they had just got up, sort of thing. And with that, I thought, *what?* Then I heard BANG! and Spanner vanished, I didn't see him at all. I turned and looked at Dill on my left and then it all kicked off. Anything in front right I destroyed and Dill front left; we destroyed everything with our GPMGs.

Rob Paynes [Pte, A Company] joined with me, who now became my No. 2, and he was a little fucking bad boy, always in and out of the digger [Para jail]. He came out a couple of weeks before we sailed, he was a right mad little fucker, he was always in trouble. He was another little lad. Someone told me his dad parachuted into the jungle during the Malayan campaign.

At one point I threw a grenade into a trench and fired like fuck into it, mowing anything down and then the FUB [Fat Useless Bastard] as we all called him, a lance jack, no names, no pack drill, came rushing across and said, 'What you fucking do that for?'

I told him to fuck off, I was like fucking mad, and I asked, 'Where the fuck was you when it was all kicking off the past ten minutes?' But it wasn't ten minutes, it had been more like an hour!

When it kicked off, anything in front had to fucking go, and we mowed anything down. That's what you get taught in Depot, and if any enemy are on their backs, in order to clear them as dead or as a booby trap, one of yer gets down by the side of the Argy, pulls the Argy over, so your buddy, who's kept a bead on him, can see it they're holding a grenade or to confirm they're dead. Trouble is, you can't do that when the enemy are in the bottom of a trench!

Then I remember there was a ridge and there was a geezer, an Argy, on the right-hand side, who got shot to fuck by Brummie Hall and Rickards [Privates, A Company] and a GPMG. They were both seventeen-and-a-half and were with Monster [Lance Corporal Adams] and they dragged Monster back when he got hit. Then we were still having a go at more trenches and all the gorse was alight and smoke blowing all over the place and Chuck put me out on the left, in case there was a counterattack. Then the officer Lieutenant Coe came up and screamed, 'Get some fire down, get some fire down!'

'At what?' I screamed back.

'Give me the fuckin' gun,' he went, and took MY gun off me. I mean, he was the officer, and I thought, *what the fuck?* There was nothing we could see, so he went to rest it on the burnt gorse and started to fire it, but as he fired it off, he couldn't hold it and the gimpy went down through the gorse on the legs. It blew all the burnt gorse up everywhere and covered it in fucking ash; then he had jammed it up and it wouldn't fire.

I really wanted to deck him, knock him the fuck out, it was MY gun, MY responsibility, and he had fucked it. This was our section's fucking firepower, for fuck's sake, and this officer had just taken it out the game! I couldn't cock it and it cost time to clear it all. Then Chuck came along and said to the officer, 'Give us it here, now fuck off.' He put the gun down, stamped his boot hard down on the cocking handle and that cleared it.

A bit later, Jones [Colonel Jones RIP] came over and ordered, 'Evers, come with me,' and then he changed his mind, looked across at some others and said, 'No, Evers, you stay here, come on A Company, get your skirts on.' I remember thinking, *you cheeky cunt!* Then he turned to Stevie P [Corporal Prior, A Company] and Captain Dent, who had come over to see Colonel Jones, but before Captain Dent could say anything, he did about three paces over this little mound and that was the end of him! He was shot dead in an instant, then Stevie got it too about the same time.

Then Jones got pissed, grabbed some others, and decided to go over the top with Chuck. Chuck led Darwin Hill in my opinion, and got killed. He should have got the VC too. Yeah, no question he led the attack on Darwin Hill and paid for it with his life.

Soon after Brummie Hall or Rickards were about to fire our last 66, I shouted at them to get it off at a trench that I knew was the Argy main gun group and was causing us a shedload of problems. So one of them fired it and it went WHOOSH, right over the top of the trench. I shouted to no one really, 'Oh fuck, you bastards!'

GOOSE GREEN

Sergeant Major Colin Price, A Company 2 Para

When we were at Burntside House, Major Farrar-Hockley asked me to take the radio because Colonel Jones was a bit irate, so I went on the radio and Jones was ordering us to, 'Push on, push on, push on.' After Sergeant Ted Barrett's platoon had cleared a pond, we eventually moved on to Coronation Point, and, as we arrived at Coronation Point it was starting to become first light. At this point, Major Farrar-Hockley took the three platoon commanders away a little bit off to the left to have a navigation recce, and now the first light is turning to light and some of the guys were on a forward slope, so I went to move them back.

As I moved them back, Colonel Jones suddenly appeared and shouted across to me, 'What's going on, sergeant major? Why are A Company retreating?'

'We're not retreating, sir; I'm just pulling them back off the forward slope.' Then a bit later we advanced down that forward slope and all hell broke out as the Argentinians started firing at us with quite a few machine guns, hundreds of tracers coming at us. All we could do then was run for cover, and surprisingly we didn't lose anybody on the slope, because that's when they had the opportunity to make the difference, to make a mess of us, and it didn't happen.

So we all ran down to a bank of earth which was in dead ground at the base of Darwin Hill, where all the fire was coming from. Then Tom Camp [Cpl MM] says, 'There's a machine gun up there, sergeant major.' So, I says, 'Come on, Tom, let's take it out,' but as we started off, Farrar-Hockley says, 'It's not your job, sergeant major.' Which was true, so I pulled back and let it go, but I so wanted to go with the guys. I did go forward a bit, enough to throw a white phos in the direction of the gun, and that's what started the gorse bushes burning. Then I came back to my original position at the base of the hill.

Soon after, I was told the sad news that Corporal Mick Melia, attached to us from 59 Commando, had been killed. I wasn't sure how he got killed, because it was such a confusing situation at the time. I managed to find Mick's boss, a lieutenant, who was also attached and pulled him to one side and told him about Corporal Melia, and he said, 'Thank you, sergeant major, but I've just been told, but thank you.' Then I was told Stevie Prior [Cpl] had been killed, and then all of a sudden, this little Argentinian comes running down the hill from the direction of another machine gun position, so I rugby tackled him.

People have said why didn't I kill him, but there was so much stuff going off and he sort of fell towards me. We're in the middle of this battle and this little Argy drops on me, so I grabbed him, put him down and slapped him across the face, checked he had no weapons and said, 'Stay here, son!' And he was with me all the time, was this little Argentinian. We joked he'd be the platoon sergeant of 3 Platoon by the end of the fucking battle. He only looked about sixteen or seventeen. A Company had only eighteen-year-olds and above fighting with us.

There was this one lad who was seventeen before we left Aldershot, but really wanted to go with us, so I asked, 'When are you eighteen?'

'In three weeks' time.'

'Okay,' I says, 'you'll be eighteen before we get there, do you still want to go?'

'Yes, sir.'

'Get on the boat then.'

I respected this little Argy, this little kid who comes running down the hill, in uniform, the same as we are, in OUR uniform, so he's a soldier too. We're all soldiers, and let's be serious now, we're not fighting the IRA, hiding behind women's skirts like they do. No, the Argies are doing what they're ordered to, and they're doing it in uniform, and remember there weren't many of us on this battlefield who'd had the experience of fighting an enemy in uniform.

The battle started to become very slow. I had Ted Barrett and his gunner above me on a ledge with a GPMG firing initially towards the cemetery, where there were one or two Argies who I could see pulling back, and I think that's where Monster got wounded. I then see one Argy fall, but the tracer is still coming across our front and I'm shouting, 'Well-aimed shots, lads, well-aimed shots!' as we didn't know when we'd get an ammo resup.

Ted's machine gun was running low on ammunition, so me and several guys started making up link; they paired off, putting the link together for the gun, and at the same time got a brew on with the battle still raging. Also, a lot of guys weren't involved in the immediate action and at the moment we had only one machine gun firing. Then I heard Ted Barrett up above scream, 'More fags, more ammo, sergeant major, more ammo!' So I'm throwing up fags and link and that seemed to go on for some time.

'Major Farrar-Hockley, we need to do something,' I shouted across.

'I'm not losing any more men, sergeant major.'

Not long after I'd got the brews going, Monster came down and said, 'I've been hit, sergeant major,' and he's up above me, right.

'Get your arse down here and let's have a look at you,' I shouts back. So, Monster does a sort of belly slide down and lands almost on top of me. I took his belt order off, checked him and saw an entry point in his lower back, I then slit open his smock and shirt. He'd been hit by a 7.62, but instead of the pointy bit hitting him, it had hit him sideways on and you could actually see the shape of it; then blood started spewing out. A ricochet, no doubt about it. I treated him the best I could, laid him down and that was him for the next four hours.[18] He was conscious up until the end of that four-hour period, when he started fading, but he survived.

Things were working. I'd got the 7 RHA corporal [7 Para Royal Horse Artillery, a specialist unit of the Royal Artillery] making the brews, I've still got Ted screaming down, 'More fags, more ammo, sergeant major,' and we're still making up link. The Argy was still by me, behaving himself, but he nicked a packet of my hardtack biscuits, so I slapped him across the face again, the little bastard! He'd nicked 'em from my webbing.

We're still static in the same location, for what seemed to be at least an hour plus, when I see some movement from my right by that re-entrant, where the machine-gun fire was still coming from. I called across to Corporal Framington, 'Fram, come on, come with me!' So we move down there and I've got this tracer shooting across at me just above head height, and I could see some movement from some gorse bushes the other side of this little re-entrant.

'I'll cover you, sergeant major,' Fram says, and he puts his rifle around the corner, but not far enough to shoot at anybody, ha-ha.

'Fuck off, Fram, you don't think I'm going across there, do yer?' I shout to get some smoke over there. Someone throws smoke, I think it was red, and the wind just took it away, like it did with those Schmuleys.. So I shouts, 'Get some white phos down!' And this voice pops up somewhere behind, 'I know that, you fucking idiot.'

That was Colonel Jones, and they were the last words he ever said to me, 'I know that, you fucking idiot.'

I didn't know Jones had arrived at the base of the re-entrant, and I'm guessing he'd come up to try to get A Company to keep pushing forward. So he then moves across and outflanks me as I was

---

18 In fact, Monster had been hit several times, and some years later he had an ache under his armpit from which they pulled out another 7.62 bullet.

moving away from the re-entrant with Fram, and then I think what he did was, the Colonel moved up higher into the re-entrant with the Adjutant, Captain Dave Wood and Captain Chris Dent, my company's 2IC, to take out the Argy gun position, because the Argy machine gun was still firing, but wasn't hitting anything.

That got us going, then Davey 'Chuck' Hardman started an assault up the hill, going forward with his section. So, Davey's moving forward and I'm shouting, 'Push on, lads, push on lads, push on,' then suddenly Davey went down and somebody shouted, 'Get some 66s up here!' So I went to find a couple of 66s and offered one to Ted Barrett, who says, 'Fuck off, sergeant major, I ain't going up there!'

Then I moved forward with Pig Abols [Corporal Dave Abols, DCM]. I threw a 66 to Pig, then I saw a guy from Headquarters Company and asked where the position was and he pointed it out to me; but we hadn't seen this new position, and I didn't know Jones had gone forward either. So I famously fired the 66 for the first time in my life, and I missed. Pig fired his and hit the trenches, and then white flags started appearing. By this time Pig and I were quite forward with the rest of the company. So the Argies started coming out of their trenches, but they were coming out with their rifles in their hands!

Like in every war film you see, the enemy can speak English, can't they? And I'm ordering, screaming, 'Put your weapons down, put your weapons down!' By this time one of my machine-gun crews had come up to me, so I ordered them to put a burst over their heads, but all that did was make the Argies jump back in their trenches. So I did the thing with the rifle; I lay a rifle on the ground and put my hands up in the air, and then they started to get out with their hands in the air. Pig and I started running forward to take the surrender, when suddenly Pig says to me, 'Sergeant major, the Colonel!'

'What?' I said, then I see Jones, and he's in the sitting-up position, with entry wounds across his stomach, about seven or eight of 'em. So, I got to him and pulled him to me, and I slapped his face, because I could see his eyes were still clear. 'Stay with me, stay with me,' I was saying as his eyes started to glaze over, and then I knew he was on the way – he was dying – and every night, and still to this day, I have to see that image before I go to sleep.

Pig said, 'I'll take his belt order off.'

'No, fuckin' leave it, Pig,' I said, because I thought he'd fall apart if Pig was to release his belt order. He had front entry wounds and it was only his webbing belt that was keeping him together. Then when the Colonel had gone, I shouted, 'Sunray down!' Then I called Sergeant Norman over, the Colonel's bodyguard.

After that, I took my helmet off and put my maroon beret on. Pig says, 'What the fuck are you doing, sergeant major?'

'These bastards are gonna know who they are surrendering to,' I replied, and then we ran forward and we started to take them out of the trenches. I literally dragged one out, as the adrenalin was running like fuck by this time. I can remember leaning down to this guy, who's looking up at me terrified, and I just grabbed him by the fucking lapels and pulled him up out of the trench and I ain't no strong man.

Then from my memory, we got them in a long line, and then a Scout helicopter came in, so I went back to sort the casevacs out, and the first one I got out was Monster. We couldn't lift him properly, because he was so fucking big. I said, 'For fuck's sake, Monster, we can't lift you.' We'd managed to get him up onto the pod that was under the Scout, but he had to help himself too. 'Push up, Monster, push up, for fuck's sake!' It was a struggle.

The day was moving on by now and the admin kicked in. The gorse was alight and smoke was being blown all over. I got hold of one Argy and told him to get down, and this bastard was so arrogant. He turned out to be one of their Special Forces; you could tell he was more than just a soldier. He stood there and as I walked along, he gave me this contemptuous stare, so I goes up to him and ground his cigarette into his face! That made him sit down.

Accounting for my boys was paramount, and the casevac list. Like I said, Monster was the first one out, but Steve Tuffen was the last, as I thought he was going to die. He'd been shot in the head and you think, *this guy's gonna die*, so I pushed a lot less wounded out before I pushed Steve out, but that was part of my job. Then the RSM Malcolm Simpson comes over and says, 'Can I have your casualty report, sergeant major?' I told him I had Captain Dent dead, Davey Hardman dead, Corporal Mick Melia, and I also told him I knew Stevie Prior was dead, but we hadn't got his body yet. And he said, 'Alright, Colin, we'll have to put him down as missing believed dead.'

'Hang on a minute, sir, you're not getting my casualty report, nobody in my company's missing believed dead.' Then I called over to Ted and asked if he knew where Stevie Prior was, and he said, 'I think so.'

'Right,' I said, 'let's get a stretcher and go and get him.' Ted and I found Stevie, and this is where it gets me, always does – we gently lifted Stevie on the stretcher and brought him back to the company; Stevie was one of the recruits I took through Recruit Company. Me and Ted put Stevie with our dead and then went off for a fag and shed a tear.

Shortly after, and only then, I gave the RSM my casualty report. I just could not have one of my soldiers missing, and fair play to Mal Simpson, he fully understood me and my feelings.

Of course, Colonel Jones was dead, but he was not in my company so he didn't go down on my casualty report. Also, at that time, I knew Captain Wood was dead too. They were with

Jones the last time I saw them, but as sergeant major, I cannot tell you where they fell, because they had been recovered before I could account for them, and I was doing other jobs like casualty evacuation and a hundred other things.

As it got to last light the same day, Battalion Headquarters had moved up, as there was a gap of about five hours of daylight while the rest of the battalion moved forward with the attack on Goose Green. There was some heavy shit coming in, with anti-aircraft fire coming in at low level, I mean, that was some real shit for hours and hours. It was constant, it was awful, that stuff was; and under all that barrage of incoming, we had a load of prisoners to deal with, and as per the Geneva Convention we had to move them into a place of safety. So Malcolm Simpson took all the prisoners off me and marched them down to a safe place somewhere by the beach.

Nigel Ely: Colin couldn't see much of the continuing battle; all he could see were elements of B Company way over to his right, and that's because, generally, in battle, you are only concerned about yourself and your mates. Somebody ten feet away may have a totally different perspective of what is happening, or indeed not even see it or hear it, such is the madness of war messing with one's mind. In later years, and in particular while researching this book, I've been embarrassed, shocked even, to recall I didn't feel any empathy for what was happening around the corner from me on the battlefield.

My research also uncovered all the young men in A Company that I have met, who are so grateful for what you did in keeping them as safe as you could, Sergeant Major Colin Price, and at thirty-seven, you were a father to them.

Sergeant Barry Norman, Colonel Jones's bodyguard, 2 Para
(Extract from an interview.)

I was firing at the Argentinian positions and I looked over and saw Colonel H Jones actually pacing the trench I was firing at. He was checking his submachine gun to make sure his magazine was full; he then put the magazine on, cocked the weapon and started firing and charging up the hill. I continued firing to give him some fire support and then I realised quite quickly that the higher he was going up the hill to the trench he was attacking, he was coming into full view of an Argentinian trench position behind him.

I looked across again over the top of my weapon, and I could see the strike of the Argentinian rounds hitting the ground, so I shouted out, 'Watch your fucking back!' And he totally ignored me. Whether he heard me or not I don't know. Personally, I think he ignored me, and the higher he went up, the nearer he was to this fall of shot, then all of a sudden, his body and the fall of shot coincided. He was hit in the back and the momentum of the shot forced him forward and he fell within inches of the Argentinian trench he was going for.

Private Gaz Steele, Defence Platoon 2 Para

I was with Major Chris Keeble [2IC] and the RSM in Tac HQ2 when we got the message Sunray was down, and we started to move forward as the 2IC was needed up front. But as we started to move forward along this beach towards Darwin Hill, I could see a senior NCO from A Company screaming at us. I couldn't hear what he was saying, but I was tabbing next to the RSM so I felt safe from any bollocking. However, as we got closer, we could hear him a bit more clearly: 'Get off the fucking beach, it's fucking mined!' I suddenly felt a lot less safe stood next to the RSM. We all got off the beach pretty sharpish.

SUNRAY DOWN

Staff Sergeant Pete Harburn, PT Corps 2 Para's physical training instructor

Before Chris Keeble and I got called up to the front, everything seemed to be going as it should. Helicopters coming in with equipment, HQ and all the officers as they should. Chris Keeble was trying to stay awake, obviously, because he was constantly busy with things. I had to keep making his food, supplying him hot brews and sorting out his basha [makeshift shelter], and making sure he was alright. Along with that, I was on constant ammunition resupply detail too, but when we heard 'Sunray down' over the net, I went forward with Chris Keeble to Darwin Hill and to where A Company were.

As we closed up, I found this bunker, an Argy trench, and I noticed there were some prisoners just behind us. The next thing I knew, Captain Dave Wood comes crashing into this trench I'd taken cover in, and said, 'Hello, Staff, have you got any grenades?'

'I've got one or two.'

'Well, you won't need 'em,' he said. I gave him the grenades and he left and that was the last time I saw him alive, but I saw his body later.

He was the Adjutant, and he shouldn't have been up the front. Then I found out Captain Dent had been killed, too. But what really got me was Colonel Jones getting killed and his bodyguard, Sergeant 'Kraut' Norman survived, and I still think to this day, I should have been there and not Sergeant Norman. I'm not saying things would have worked out any differently, but it still sticks with me, if you know what I mean, because all the other battalions and the regiments had their PT Corps chaps as bodyguards for their respective colonels and their colonels' group.

I guess Colonel Jones didn't get on with me. That's what I think, and that's why I wasn't with him when he got killed.

GOOSE GREEN

Lance Corporal Bill 'Basha' Bentley MM, Combat Medical Team
2 Para

I became aware that one of the young platoon medics, with whom I had become very close during the training on the MV *Norland*, needed help. Paul had been shot some hours earlier and although he had been patched up by others, he was in danger of freezing to death when we found him. Gibbo ripped open his own shirt and placed the infusion bag against his naked body to try to give it warmth, while I placed the needle in Paul's arm. It was a desperate, full of emotion moment, which I can only compare with the delivery of my own two daughters into this world. We evacuated Paul on the next available helicopter, regardless of medical priorities!

Paul survived, as did, luckily, all other casualties who were alive when we reached them. Another young platoon medic, Steve, had been shot through the head. A squirt of his brain was visible on the back of his head like toothpaste that had been squeezed out of a tube. I did not consider that he could survive and told Phil Clegg [Pte 2 Para Combat Medical Team] to give him 'a lot of morphine', but Doc Hughes did think [*sic*] that he could 'have a chance', and with help from Phil and Mark Polkey [Pte 2 Para Combat Medical Team] he also survived. Thanks to all of them, Steve Tuffen is alive today, and a valued friend of mine.

Private Steve Tuffen, 2 Platoon A Company 2 Para

I was shot in the head while assaulting Darwin Hill and had to lay where I fell for hours. The guys couldn't get to me, as I was too exposed and in the killing zone. Eventually as we [A Company] took control of the battle the guys were able to get to me; they took my helmet off and some of my brain fell out through the hole in my skull. I had been shot in the head with 7.62 high velocity. I was casevaced off the battlefield to Ajax Bay field hospital some ELEVEN hours later.

Private Irwin Eversley, GPMG gunner, 2 Platoon A Company 2 Para

I remember looking at Steve Tuffen lying there shot in the head, thinking, oh God, why couldn't it have been me. He was crying in pain and my eyes welled up too; he was only seventeen and a half, and I was twenty-one. He was a nice lad, and when I saw him a couple of years later, he couldn't even recognise me. Then years after that he called out 'Evers' and that's when I went, great, his memory is coming back; and that's when I also cried my eyes out. Steve was left for hours before the medics could get to him.

Colour Sergeant Pete Vale, HQ Company 2 Para

Sunray down. It didn't register with me. I didn't have time to think about it. But afterwards, I felt more for Mark Holman-Smith [Pte C Company] and Stevie Prior and Chuck Hardman, because I'd served in A Company with them in Northern Ireland, and I thought, *what a waste*. They would have all made it in Battalion, they would have all been RSMs or QMs. Barry Norman [CO's bodyguard, Sergeant] didn't have a chance of doing his job! I also felt with Jones's death – what a waste, but it was his waste.

Later on in the war, when we were attacking Wireless Ridge, I tried to give the new CO, Colonel Chaundler, some valid advice about not going off axis and not going through a minefield, but he told me to 'fuck off'. So I guess that's why I ended up in 4 Para [Territorials] when we all got back, ha-ha.

If Jones had survived, my career would have panned out very differently. You see, I did two favours for Colonel Jones before we left for war. One, I sorted out the Officers' Mess for him, and two, I sorted HQ Company stores for him too, as it was a pile of shite. He promised me a rifle company and he also recommended me for RQMS [regimental quartermaster sergeant], which I would have achieved if Jones had survived. I would have taken over D Company and then would have become our RQMS, and it would have been up to me then, because my time was running out. I could have still got my RSM and an extension, but it all went wrong.

I don't look back with much regret, because I did five years as a Tom when I could have been a corporal. I was just a bit of a rebel when I was young. That's all it was.

Corporal 'Ginge' Dawes, clothing storeman, 2 Para

I knew the CO quite well, because back in Aldershot my office was just along from his. So I probably saw him every day, and sometimes he'd stick his head in and ask for a couple of pairs of socks, or something like that. He never called me Ginge and I never knew him as H, until after the war. That was something the media christened him. He seemed to be an impatient man, even before the Falklands; he wanted things to happen and wanted them to happen now, sort of thing, that's the impression I got. But what he did on Darwin Hill was real ballsy, and it was just a shame he got killed, and if he hadn't, he'd have got a DSO instead!

Captain Paul Farrar, OC Patrols Platoon 2 Para

We were the first formed body of men, C Company, Patrols, Recce and Company HQ, to arrive on Darwin Hill; D and B Companies were over to our right at places like Boca House. The battle had literally just ended in the last few minutes and that's when it all ground to a halt. Sunray was down by then and we all knew it had gone a bit tits-up, but at least A Company had secured Darwin Hill and the detail of that I'll leave for others. What I will say when I returned to Darwin Hill in 2016, is that I was amazed two platoons of A Company were fighting in such a tiny piece of land.

A Company's third platoon 3 Platoon, led by Lieutenant Guy Wallis, was back across the water from Darwin settlement, ready to support the investment of Darwin, so it was only two platoons and Company HQ and H Jones's command group and one or two others who were in the fight at Darwin Hill. And I'm standing in this small separate re-entrant, which was the one where H was moving up to and around before he got shot; H was trying to go slightly right flanking, and most of A Company were still in this slight hollow. Of course, when H died they hadn't yet taken the hill, but I remember thinking, this is an incredibly tight frontage.

So, back to the battle. When we arrived at Darwin Hill, I remember this vividly, because Roger and Pete Kennedy [Major, OC and Captain, 2IC C (Bruneval) Company 2 Para] were there too and OC A Company [Major Dair Farrar-Hockley], who'd obviously had a very difficult time.

I'll never forget this, as it's etched in my memory. As we arrived, he turned to Roger and said, 'Roger. Roger, thank goodness you've arrived. The commanding officer is dead. The adjutant is dead. My company second-in-command is dead.' He didn't say, H is dead, Dave is dead and Chris is dead. It was all incredibly formal, and I thought, *this is weird; we're in the middle of a battle, what a strange opening sally!*

I can see how some people may think, well, the CO, the Adjutant and the company 2IC are dead, and the commander whose battle it is, is still alive! But I think it's rather disingenuous for people to think like that. Although he was probably in a degree of shock, to the extent that the plan for A Company to take Darwin Hill – then swing left and go down to invest Darwin – certainly wasn't going to happen [because Darwin had not been taken at that time, as Darwin Hill was the immediate threat]. Initially this task was re-allocated to C Company, but then it changed again . . . !

Lance Corporal 'Duke' Allen, Defence Platoon 2 Para

A Company fought through and took Darwin Hill, and we followed to clear up the place. I recall coming across this young lad, an Argy; well, I didn't know how old he was, I was assuming, because somebody had emptied a full mag into his fucking face. It had swollen up to the size of a big pumpkin; you couldn't even recognise it as a face! That must have been one of our guys very upset about the lads being shot, that's what I thought anyway. His face was like a fuckin' pumpkin!

Gunner J. M. Love, 2 Para Group A Company 2 Para, FOO party signaller 29 Corunna Field Battery RA

The bodies lay in rows, at the bottom of the hill, to the left of the re-entry, near the RAP. I crawled back into the burning gorse, just to try and keep warm. The smoke and smell, which seeped into your clothes, and the total being of your body, would stay with you for ever. We sat in little groups, sombre to the fact the CO and the other officers and blokes had been killed that day. The wounded still lay where they had fallen, their wounds tended to by their comrades. They were now waiting quietly to be casevaced out, and away from the fighting that was still going on around us. Dinger had administered first aid to Monster Adams, using up all the available first field dressings we had at the time. Dinger was later to get a commendation for his treatment of the wounded under fire.

All our spare warm clothing had been given to the wounded, who were now dressed in a rag-tag affair of thermal quilted trousers, jackets, and waterproofs. Others lay in exposed inaccessible slopes, where they were overseen by the enemy trenches, making it impossible to retrieve them, or administer first aid. We had been taught that it was better to leave the wounded and fight on through, to capture the objective; returning later to check the casualties, and dress wounds where necessary. Unfortunately, we had progressed no further than where the injured had fallen, held up by the deep positions of the Argy trenches. It was shortly after Adjutant Captain Wood was killed, leading yet another assault on the enemy trenches, that we saw an Argentinian officer attempt to throw a grenade. It had only travelled a matter of inches from him and as it arced in the air it went off, covering his body with burning phosphorus, turning him into a human fireball.

The top of Darwin Hill was flat for a couple of hundred metres, then there was yet another row of gorse bushes, where it dropped down to the airfield and the settlement of Goose Green. The row of gorse obscured from view anyone on the top. But the forward slope down to the settlement, apart from a few gullies, was totally bare-arsed. The enemy anti-aircraft gunners had turned their guns onto the forward slope and the crest of the hill, where they merrily raked every exposed piece of ground from left to right, and back again. Their heavy .50 Cals. and 47mms would take a heavy toll on C Company.

All the enemy wounded were taken down the hill to the RAP to sort them out. The dead were laid out in rows, near our own.

It was still only day one of the battle for Darwin and Goose Green, and early at that!

Private John Bolland, Recce Platoon 2 Para

As we were called forward to move through A Company's position, I remember seeing Monster Adams injured, laid by the RAP, he'd been shot several times, and Ted Barrett MM, RIP, coming across and asking if we could help him.

'I'm missing one of me boys. I can't find him, I can't find him!'

As you know, there were stiffs all over the place, the gorse burning, a proper mess; yet there was one thing that stuck in my mind, this SLR poking out of the gorse, burnt down to the metal with the bayonet stuck into the ground. That's a marker, isn't it? One of the boys must have got hit or blown to fuck. There was fuck all left of him or that gorse line. Must have been one of Ted's boys.

American mercenaries. When on Darwin Hill, a lad from A Company told me during that battle, an Argy jumps up and screams, 'Soldier of fortune, I'm an American!' and he gets doubled-tapped [shot twice in quick succession]. Then his mucker jumps up and gets taken prisoner. This one gets taken off the islands within hours. Was the CIA working with the Argies? I had that story confirmed by a lad in HQ Company who dealt with such matters.

Lance Corporal Jimmy Goodall, Assault Engineers 2 Para

The Assault Engineers were following the battle and clearing trenches as part of the mopping-up process after A Company had gone through them as they fought for Darwin Hill. For some reason I was by myself at this stage, so I jumped down in this trench to check it out, when all of a sudden there was movement and then I saw the barrel of this weapon. So I fired and hit the Argy, I'd hit him in the thigh. I thought there was only one there at the time, but another Argy appeared, and luckily they both dropped their weapons and put their hands up, so I thought, *that's it, game over for them.*

I got them out the trench and searched them. I'd actually shot the one through his bayonet scabbard, who was in a bit of pain by now. Then some 2 Para lads came over, not sure who they were, but their blood had risen, and one of them wanted to shoot these two Argies. I said, 'No! They're my prisoners, they've given themselves up to me. NOBODY touches MY prisoners. Anyone who tries to kill them, I'll be the first one to shoot.'

At this moment RSM Mal Simpson turned up with his entourage, who then took them away and processed them properly.

Lance Corporal 'Radar', Defence Platoon 2 Para

I was at the aid post when I saw Ted Barrett MM, RIP, come in with the dead CO on a stretcher. They brought him straight to us over at the RAP and went straight back out to the fuckin' biz [to carry on fighting]. Ted was one brave fucker.

David Norris, general news reporter, Daily Mail, *attached 2 Para* (Unpublished copy, written during the war.)

A Tom called Soapy asked me in amazement, 'Don't you have a gun? I'll show you how mine works, then if I get wasted, you can use it.'

Some time during the night and day of horror, between the nerve-shattering screech and crack of shells, the pinging of shrapnel and the whine of sniper bullets, someone told me, 'H is dead, he got it with the Adjutant. They were leading a charge on a gun position.'

Lance Corporal Bill 'Basha' Bentley MM, Combat Medical Team 2 Para

Steadily, the row of our own bodies grew, and at some point my good friend Chuck's body was brought in, and I confess I broke down and cried. We were not getting any useful medical resupplies, we were all dead tired and hungry, even eating biscuits from the pockets of the dead, friend and foe alike, and the ammunition was running out. Their artillery had us pinpointed, the Colonel was dead along with a growing list of officers and men, and things were looking pretty desperate!

After the battle, OC A Company was going around telling people to 'Clean up the area,' as if he had been on an exercise.

Private Irwin Eversley, GPMG gunner, 2 Platoon A Company 2 Para

The firing had just stopped when I saw elements of C Company move through our position. There were a few blokes crying, there were fuckin' bodies everywhere. I remember little John Etheridge [Pte A Company, 2 Para] crying, and a few others too; they were just out of Depot really, months earlier they were still in Junior Para; they were in tears, it was the lull when it was quiet and the sun was coming up. I was in tears too at the re-org. There were dead Argy geezers in trenches and all over, and of course, our dead guys too.

It's pretty tough to grow up by eighteen.

14

TOP SLOPE, GOOSE GREEN

We must have been shrouded in the armour of God.

Private Irwin Eversley, GPMG gunner, 2 Platoon A Company 2 Para

After we secured the hill, C Company went firm on the south side overlooking Goose Green. It was so bizarre, because we saw all these Argies mingling around down in Goose Green and across at the airfield about a mile away, so I guess they thought we were Argies.

Private Dave 'Charlie' Brown, HQ C (Bruneval) Company 2 Para

C Company moved forward through the carnage, and it was carnage, dead Argies and wounded all over the hillside of A Company's position towards the reverse slope, and held that position. We sat there looking forward down at the Argies all strutting around the airfield as if nothing had happened, and all those trenches in front and to the left-hand side, thinking, they must think we are them! Why? It didn't seem logical, after all, we had just taken out their

215

forward position; it still puzzles me to this day. Maybe they thought they had repelled *us* off Darwin Hill!

We waited for an hour or so, got a brew on and had some scoff, then Sergeant Major Baz Greenhalgh mentioned something about two Pucaras looking for our mortar line. All of a sudden, Baz pushed me into a trench and I landed on top of about three dead Argies, well, bits of 'em. I thought Baz had done this as a joke, so I got out of that trench fuming, and there they were: I was looking straight up at two Pucaras ready to do a strafing run at our mortar line, who were still on the reverse side of Darwin Hill.

They flew very low right above my head. I fired a few rounds off and Baz Greenhalgh looked at me as if to say, what the fuck you doing, because I only had a SMG and you'd be lucky to hit a barn door at twenty paces with it! Very soon after, those who could fix bayonets, fixed bayonets.

Private John Bolland, Recce Platoon 2 Para

Looking down at Goose Green, the Argies were the size of ants, and you could make out they were looking at us; then I looked right across towards the airfield and saw those turboprop Pucaras parked up on the runway. There was no cover for us, we were out in the open and they could have outflanked us. It was like looking across a billiard table, and that's when all hell opened up on us and someone shouted 'Fix bayonets!'

I mumbled in disbelief, 'Gie's a break, you cunt, we ain't even gonna get that far. They'll get us before we get them.'

Captain Paul Farrar, OC Patrols Platoon 2 Para

So, we get Guy Wallace's 3 Platoon, who by now are attached to us, and a quick change of plan: Patrols to the left, Recce to the right, and Guy Wallace's platoon in reserve. Over the top we went, and began our advance down that lovely open, forward slope towards Goose Green.

Just prior to that, I was up and forward observing the ground to my front, and Roger and I could see blokes moving towards the airfield over to our right. Roger says to me, 'Are they ours or theirs?' We couldn't really make them out, but judging by the way they were moving, we both agreed it was D Company, because they were in a nice arrowhead formation.

So, we went over the top knowing D Company were over to our right and moving towards their objective, and we're off down the slope. We go a few hundred metres and all hell breaks loose. Company HQ gets hit and that's when the bulk of the casualties occur; Roger gets wounded, Private Mark Holman-Smith gets killed, and several others badly wounded. The A Company platoon quite rightly does a swift withdrawal and takes cover back behind a shallow wall and watches the whole thing pan out. Several of the guys run forward, some of us dart about and it all gets messy.

D Company are still advancing and eventually elements of Patrols end up merging with elements of D Company. I didn't see Recce and end up in the bottom of the re-entrant, out of sight of Goose Green. It's all very chaotic, and that's when Tony Tighe's hit and Chopsy's hit and has his leg blown off.

Corporal Douglas McCready, 1 Section commander, Machine Gun Platoon 2 Para

During the assault towards the dairy,[19] the boss, Lieutenant Hugo Lister, orders, 'One Section leading,' so I turns around to him and says, 'For fuck's sake, can ye not give one of the other fucking

---

19 The dairy was a single small, stone-built, roof-covered structure, which still had its electricity switched on.

sections a go?' So anyway, when he shouts, 'MOVE!' we got only about five metres and the fucking ground erupted in front of us like a ploughed field. That's when one of the lads, Coxhall [Pte, machine gunner 2 Para], got shot in the leg, so we dragged him back into the trench and stayed there. Hugo was only recently fresh out of Sandhurst, and I think was the most junior officer in 2 Para, but you know what? He did really well commanding us old sweats.

Lance Corporal 'Duke' Allen, Defence Platoon 2 Para

I was up on Darwin Hill when C Company advanced down that forward slope towards Goose Green, and I've never heard anything like it, even during the Battalion Concentrations we used to conduct on exercise – you know, when the Batt lets rip and does a firepower demonstration – I've never heard so much firepower in my life as there was at Goose Green.

The racket was just unbelievable and the only other time I heard it that loud was when 3 Para attacked Longdon.[20] When Twin Sisters and all that was going off [other battles during the push to Stanley], it was just pop, pop, pop, really, but when Goose Green and Longdon kicked off, fucking hell what a racket; it was continuous, it was deafening and it went on for hours.

Captain John Greenhalgh DFC, Scout Flight 656 Squadron Army Air Corps

We were coming up a finger valley to B Company, I think, and we'd already lost a Royal Marines Scout to aircraft fire, so we knew the Argies could do it – shoot us down. So, I'm up the finger

---

20 Mount Longdon, a key position overlooking Port Stanley, captured by 3 Para after a hard-fought battle, 11–12 June 1982. For his part in neutralising an Argentine position Sergeant Ian McKay of B Company 3 Para was posthumously awarded the Victoria Cross.

valley with Rich Walker behind me in a second Scout and I got as far up this finger valley as I dared; like driving a Land Rover up a mountain without cresting. I was constantly talking to the B Company radio operator, but I didn't want to break the crest, because obviously there were these anti-aircraft guns used in the direct-fire role [Argentinian Oerlikons] at Goose Green, and this stuff was coming over. The last thing I wanted to do was stick my nose over the top and find out some radar device could see me, and the next thing I'm getting it through the windscreen.

I got up as far as I could, but B Company were obviously quite busy now, as they were attacking and we were right in there with them. So, I kicked Gammo out and told him to go up to the crest and find out what the fuck was going on and where the casualties were, because the Paras were preoccupied on the radio with the attack. I didn't really want to talk casualties at that time, but we knew there were some.

Rich Walker's gunner Johno had also got out of his aircraft, so there were just the two aircraft and we were both empty apart from one casualty I had picked up at the bottom of this finger valley. I looked back over at him and he looked very alarmed, wondering why I was looking over at him; he had this look of 'please get me out of here!'

I saw Gammo and Johno tabbing off up the hill with their submachine guns, webbing and helmets, and as they got to the top, I got through on 2 Para's command net and heard, 'Air raid. Air raid, Pucaras from the south.' I looked over my shoulder and I saw a pair of Pucaras coming, the same type of aircraft that had shot down the Royal Marines Scout earlier. So, what do you do? Stay stationary on the ground like sitting ducks? They would surely see us; we're helicopters, we stand out like dogs' balls. So to protect yourself, the best thing to do is to get moving. It's so much more difficult to hit a moving target.

We turned around and we fucked off back down the finger valley. Gammo subsequently described looking down the valley after he'd heard the engine note change as the aircraft lifted, and he saw Rich and me take off. Gammo muttered, 'Fuck me, they're leaving us behind!'

So, the two gunners were left on the hill side while B Company put their attack in and we had buggered off. We flew back to Ajax Bay, weaving our way across the ground, turning and watching for the Pucaras coming from behind. We dropped the casualty off, got a suck of fuel, and bear in mind I'm solo in the aircraft, then we flew back. I found the same finger valley, hover taxied up it, and found Gammo and Johno.

When he got back in, Gammo said, 'I'm never ever getting out of this fucking aircraft, ever again. Don't you do that again!'

I was gone for about thirty minutes, long enough for Gammo and Johno to be made honorary members of B Company 2 Para.

Colour Sergeant Pete Vale, HQ Company 2 Para

Our QM, Tom Godwin, was located at Ajax Bay, and he would send forward my requests but there was a problem, because the *Atlantic Conveyor*,[21] which was carrying all our ammunition, helicopters, artillery rounds, batteries, cold weather kit, and every other piece of useful piece of kit to win a war, had the hell bombed out of it and sank. We still didn't have helicopter priority, as Brigade was moving stores all over. Then we suddenly started receiving urgent requests for more ammunition from the forward companies and quite out of the blue, a Marine snowcat arrived pulling a trailer with a load of

---

21 The SS *Atlantic Conveyor* was a British merchant navy ship hit by two Exocet missiles on 25 May 1982, killing twelve sailors, and it sank whilst under tow on 28 May 1982, the day we attacked Goose Green. With her were lost three of the five heavy-lift helicopters; only one Chinook and one Wessex managed to get off the burning ship.

ammunition, and all he wanted to do was to offload as quickly as possible to piss off back.

We did have some ammunition and the mortars were almost out, and we couldn't get a helicopter in because of the volume of enemy fire. So I said to Major Ryan [OC HQ Company], we can get the ammo forward using that civvy Land Rover we'd captured earlier, so we loaded it up all ready. Colour Frankie Pye was on my shoulder, because he knew I was going to drive it forward, so he started pleading, 'Take me with you, take me with you.' He wanted to be in the action.

'No problem, of course,' I says. I go back over to Major Ryan and let him know we we're ready to pull out. He'd already alerted the mortar line we were coming and he turns to me.

'You're not going.'

I asked him what he meant.

'You're in charge here. I want you here,' and that was that, but Frankie heard this exchange. So I went across to Frankie, because I was worried that he had to deliver this stack of ammunition to the rear elements of the attacking force, and he may just decide to stay in the action. I told Frankie I needed him back here and not to get involved; I ended with, 'I'll only send you, if you promise me you'll come straight back.' We shook hands on it.

I was gutted because I wanted to go forward, but in retrospect and in all reality, I too would have forgotten I was a colour sergeant and might have moved a bit further forward into the action. Frankie did eventually come back. But not until after several brave runs up to the front line.

Colour Sergeant Frank Pye, Support Company 2 Para

I think it was on my third run, me and Yank [Lance Corporal Thayer, Support Company 2 Para], who was my right-hand man.

Yank was driving and we'd arrived at where the first mortar line had been, but it had obviously been moved forward and they had left a load of rounds behind. So I thought, *fucking lazy, slack bastards, fancy leaving all these rounds behind, maybe they couldn't carry all the ones I'd been dropping off for them.*

So anyway, I drive towards battle and sees the new mortar line and goes up to Skelly [Sergeant Murdoch 'Skelly' Skelton, RIP, Mortar Platoon, 2 Para] and says, 'Oi! You wanker, leaving all these mortar rounds.'

'You dozy bastard, Frank, they're misfires.'

So, we had driven from the first mortar line to the second with a load of misfire rounds rolling around between our legs, and they could have gone off any time!

Later, on another run, again me and Yank were taking link up to A Company, who had just taken Darwin, but we obviously couldn't drive up the hill. So we went left onto a small pebbled beach, where we met Colin Price, Sergeant Major A Company. 'What you doing here, Frank, you're not our colour man?'

'Brought you some link,' I replied.

'Thanks, Frank,' and he calls across to a Tom and shouts, 'Put a brew on for the colour man, he's brought us some ammo.'

As we were brewing up, I was looking around at the battlefield and thinking this is an A grade re-org, you know, thinking my Brecon Instructor bit, because I'd recently spent two years up at Brecon as an instructor; wounded in one place, our dead put in another, prisoners being moved back and all the rest of it. Then OC A, Farrar-Hockley, calls across to Colin and says, 'Sergeant major, are the Argentinian wounded being looked after?'

Colin turned to me and says, 'I'm gonna kill him, Frank, I'm gonna kill him.'

'Calm down, mate,' I replied understandingly.

Private Dave 'Charlie' Brown, HQ C (Bruneval) Company 2 Para

C Company had twenty-four men in Patrols, twenty-four in Recce, and seven in Headquarters, we were fifty-five men strong. But once we got over that hill it seemed stupid, because as we moved forward, we didn't realise just how open it was; it was a good two kilometres to Goose Green and a klick [1000 metres] to the first Argy trenches, then suddenly I heard this massive volume of noise.

Up until this point we had become very familiar with the sound of incoming mortars and artillery, but we didn't know what the fuck was being fired at us now; we soon found out. Across to the left of the Goose Green isthmus, the Argies had four of the 35mm Oerlikons, which we didn't know they had at the time, and on the right-hand side at the airfield they had six twin-barrel 20mm. Now these things had previously chopped the Harriers to pieces out the sky, so as we advanced, we got caught in a head-height crossfire. No cover! And that shit was cutting straight across us.

Private Steve Taylor, 3 Platoon A Company 2 Para

We followed C Company through the gorse line and that's when the shit opened up.

Private Dave 'Charlie' Brown, HQ C (Bruneval) Company 2 Para

We were still getting cut down when the platoon from A Company realised what was happening and dashed back over the to the safe side. They realised, *fuck this*, and got back into the dead ground on Darwin Hill, so that's why we were left with just Recce and Patrols and the Company HQ out on that forward slope. So exposed, it was insane!

Private Steve Taylor, 3 Platoon A Company 2 Para

There were these two Argies over on the left by the sea, who popped up like rabbits and started running away under all our fire, and because they were the enemy, part of me wanted them to get it, then someone started shouting, 'Go on, go on, you can make it!' Hoping for them to get away, a bit like that bloke in the film *A Bridge Too Far*, when he runs to pick up what he hopes to be a container full of ammunition, but it turns out only to be full of maroon berets. Real bizarre!

Private Dave 'Charlie' Brown, HQ C (Bruneval) Company 2 Para

Everyone just went straight to ground. Company Headquarters consisted of the OC, Private Mark Holman-Smith sigs platoon detached, Private Charlie Holbrook sigs platoon detached, Sergeant Major Baz Greenhalgh, myself, and just behind us we had Corporal Stevie Walters and Tommy Collins, the MFCs [mortar fire controllers] attached from Support Company, who had been with us since the beachhead. The Argies must have seen our radio antennas and they just targeted us; bracketed us. The noise was deafening, like a swarm of giant hornets dive-bombing and crashing down all around us from all directions, that's what it seemed like.

We went to ground, couldn't move, not even dare to dig in. At that time, I didn't know who had got hit, because they were still zeroing in on us. It then went quiet for a few seconds, so I made my way further down the slope and into some dead ground. The Argies waited until we made progress further down the slope to a point where we couldn't get back up. It seemed we had all their 35 mils and the 20 mils in crossfire. We got the mortars and machine-gun attention too, even the Argy artillery was firing on all of C Company on that forward slope. It was unbelievable.

Next minute I heard the dreaded word, someone screaming out 'Medic! Medic!' I think the OC, Roger Jenner, shouted that and because I was the company medic I was literally across from Stevie, and then Metal Mickey,[22] who had the LMG, got took out by an air burst from whatever. How the entire Company Headquarters didn't get massacred, I don't know. I just heard someone shout for a medic, and about 200 metres further down I could see the OC, Roger Jenner, and he's crouched over a body.

He must have seen what had happened to Metal Mickey and rushed forward and was shouting 'Medic! Medic!' That's when I stood up and looked across at Charlie Holbrook, but couldn't see Mark Holman-Smith, who should have been by him, and only Charlie was sat there on my right sending a contact and casualty report. I broke cover and went flying down to help Roger, and it was at that point I could see the majority of Recce and Patrols had made it well down the slope. Then the giant wasps started up again. I got down there and saw Mark Holman-Smith with the boss Roger, who was crouched down working on Metal Mickey *and* Mark. I didn't know there were TWO casualties. Mark had run down to man Metal Mickey's LMG, when he got hit.

I immediately started looking for wounds on Mark, still under attack with constant airbursts. Metal Mickey's LMG had been fragged totally. Metal Mickey had been splintered by bits of his LMG, which had taken a full burst and fragmented up all over him. He was still conscious. He had shrapnel injuries to his neck, head, side, and an arm and one leg. In some respects, he was lucky; if they hadn't hit his LMG, the rounds would have gone right through his main arteries. He was actually talking – barely, that's why myself and Roger went to work on Mark, who was not talking.

---

22 Private Steve Russell, RIP, was nicknamed Metal Mickey almost immediately after he got wounded, such is the humour, because he carried tiny fragments of shrapnel in his body for the rest of his life.

I moved off Mark and started to check over Metal Mickey, you know, looking for any holes – exit wounds and stuff, then Mark suddenly looked across at me, and I said, 'You're alright, mate, you're alright, mate.' The look on his face was one of, *Oh dear God, please don't let me die*. I kept comforting him, 'You're alright, mate, you're alright, mate.' Then a mortar round exploded and shrapnel hit Roger on top of his shoulder, and I think bits of it hit Mark as well, and I reckon that's what finished Mark. It was fucking awful.

At the same time while all this shit was going on, Roger being the OC had his own radio, and out of the handset I could hear Charlie Holbrook sending more casualty reports, when all of a sudden he screams out, 'Ah! I'm hit. I'm hit – wait out!' He too gets it in the shoulders.

What the fuck do I do now? At first, I didn't know Roger had been hit because he didn't let on, he just carried on working on Mark; but I knew he must have been hit, how could he not have? So I asked him if he was alright, but he just looked at me and carried on. It was a desperate situation, no comms, still under heavy fire, in the open with three casualties, and then shortly after, Roger moved across to help me with Metal Mickey. He looked at me and said calmly, 'Mark's gone.' Poor Mark bled out.

I tried to keep Metal Mickey conscious, telling him he was okay, but really, his body was like a colander and I can still see one of his gloves I took off, which was shredded. Then Roger did a brave thing; injured, he made his way back up the slope to get help, so I was left to attend Metal Mickey with a poxy SMG, which looking back at it now, was such a fucking useless piece of kit. Then every time I tried to move, a sniper had his bead on me and Mickey, probably from the School House, because later I spoke to Taff Wilcox, 2 Para Snipers, who said he took a sniper out from the School House.

I spent my time comforting Metal Mickey. I just wanted to get him back over the hill into safety, but all our choppers had stopped flying near the forward slope because of the amount of incoming. I mean, you couldn't blame them. We had taken about twelve casualties in a fifteen-minute period and the blokes were suffering. Most through those Oerlikon anti-aircraft guns.

Corporal Ken Raynor, patrol commander Recce Platoon 2 Para

It was not long before our company commander, Major Roger Jenner, briefed both platoon commanders, and each platoon commander then gave a very short set of orders to their platoons. Patrols went left and Recce slightly right and forward, with Company Headquarters in the middle. Then on a command from the company commander, we advanced in extended line towards Goose Green. We increased the pace and started to zig-zag, just like at Brecon, dash down, crawl, roll, observe, sights, and fire. There was a massive amount of lead heading in our direction, mainly from the front and the left flank, but thankfully none of our guys were hit by small-arms fire or from the 105mm artillery shells.

Unfortunately for us, the enemy were also using a fully automatic 30mm twin-barrelled anti-aircraft gun in the ground role, and that's when a couple of 30mm shells exploded over on my left flank, right in the centre of Company Headquarters, killing a radio operator and injuring Roger Jenner, peppering his back with shrapnel. At the time I was stunned that no one else was hit [but of course there were more casualties], including Dave Wright [Cpl, Signals Platoon, 2 Para], who was on the OC's flank with a massive radio on his back, allowing the company commander to speak with the newly appointed commanding officer, Major Chris Keeble.

A combination of luck and our aggression sent a very positive message to the enemy, so they decided that a rearward move back towards Goose Green would be a wise move and that is what they did. In the meantime, having our Company Headquarters knocked out so quickly caused a little confusion; however, we all kept moving forward. I did manage to get several rounds of 40mm gold top [HE round] off from my M79 Thumper [we nicknamed the M79 grenade launcher 'Thumper', because it made a rather pleasant thumping noise as the round left the barrel].

One of the first positions we went through was the anti-aircraft guns position, now deserted; we did try to get it working and turn it on the enemy, but they had cut through the main power cable. We managed to fire a single individual round, which had to be hand fed, but decided to leave it alone and continue on.

It was at this stage that C Company broke off the attack and decided to carry on down the re-entrant towards Goose Green, using the slope to our left as cover, and we also met elements of D Company, who were the company to our right flank. Roger, the OC, did get up and continue, although his back was shredded, and that was the last we saw of him until Fitzroy. Any normal human would have been casevaced, but not Roger, he commanded until endex in Stanley, some twenty days later.

Lance Corporal 'Radar', Defence Platoon 2 Para

The prisoners kindly helped me carry ammunition up to our aid post, and some bloke – I can't recall who, but he had a bit of an overbite – well, he came up to us when we got to the RAP, and this happened every bloody time, and said, 'I need blokes, we've got another guy down . . .'

I mean, it was a right fucking distance we were carrying ammo from where it had been dropped off, then up to the RAP. We did it at least four times and we were taking prisoners back on the return run, but it was like, 'I'm Spartacus, no, I'm Spartacus,' because every fit guy and walking wounded at the aid post stood up, and although we were fucked, I mean utterly fucked, we volunteered.

Me and Pete Blackburn [Pte, Defence Platoon] were told to take more ammunition over the hill and down the forward slope, then pick up more wounded. Well, we had the ammo on a stretcher, but we always seemed to get to the wounded before we could drop off the ammo in a good spot to support C Company, so we dropped off the ammo and loaded the casualties.

15

BOTTOM SLOPE, GOOSE GREEN

Private Roy Charters, Recce Platoon 2 Para

We were running down the forward slope towards Goose Green when our own SF [sustained-fire role GPMG on a tripod] switched fire and it seemed to cut across us; I'm sure a couple of our own LMGs were firing at us too. Then Argy artillery started to throw everything they had at us, so I got down and took cover, as you do, then someone dived across to me and shouted, 'You alright, you alright?' Because he thought I'd been hit.

So I went, 'Yeah, of course.' I guess he didn't hear me through all the bombardment. Again, he said it, 'You alright?'

So again I screamed, 'Yes!'

And he screamed back, 'Well, don't fuckin' do that again!'

Then he just got up and carried on down the slope, but I saw him get hit by a round striking the top of his helmet, which knocked him clean off his feet, so I ran down to see if *he* was okay and asked, 'You alright, mate? You alright?'

All he did was get up and start shouting, 'Fucking hell, fucking hell!' Then he got up sharpish again and just carried on soldiering. That was really funny.

Private Dave 'Charlie' Brown, HQ C (Bruneval) Company 2 Para

At one point our Machine Gun Platoon couldn't get fire down to support us, not even on SF (2 Para's GPMGs, Machine Gun Platoon firing), so Geoff Hough,[L/Cpl, RIP] and Dougie McCready's [Cpl] teams did a real brave thing and broke cover along with Tony Cottrell [Pte] and moved rapidly down the hill to give the guys much needed fire support. Argy mortar shells were raining all around and one landed right beside this bloke, tossing him upside down. We thought he was gone, but he just picked himself up and carried on.

Private Bob Morgan, Patrols Platoon 2 Para

I remember running down that slope with hell all around when we came across this wire fence, which I now know to be an Argy minefield, and I think that's when Tony Tighe [L/Cpl Patrols Platoon] got shot up. I didn't see him get it, but I heard him moaning and knew Greg Cox [Private Cox, Patrols Platoon] was over there with him. I wasn't aware Chopsy [Private Dave Grey, Patrols, RIP] got it there too, because I was still moving forward.

Nigel Ely: When I revisited Goose Green at the back end of 2017 for the film recce, I met an old 9 Squadron pal, Jugsy, who was working for a civilian company contracted to clear those mined areas that could be cleared. He told me that the minefield myself and C Company assaulted through would be fully cleared by early 2018, some thirty-six years after the war; that was his task.

Lance Corporal Tony Tighe, Patrols Platoon 2 Para

We moved off Darwin Hill and advanced-to-contact all in a nice long line, when we got opened up on and there was no cover at all, nothing; we just lay on the ground getting shot at and returning fire. We tried to locate where the fire was coming from and put down as much fire as possible towards the Argies. In the end, someone just shouted, 'Let's go!' so everyone stood up and started advancing down the hill pretty sharpish at a good pace.

We were getting well down towards Goose Green and that's when I got blasted [fragged] and went straight down. The first person over to me was the LMG gunner, Greg, who shouted over to our patrol medic, Chopsy, 'Get over here and give Tony morphine!'

Chopsy was already on his way over. 'Where you hit, Tony?'

I said, 'My arm,' so he injected morphine into my leg. Every time he attempted to put a field dressing on my arm, it was agony; I felt the bones crunching. I was too much of a coward to look at the arm, I didn't want to go there. I couldn't move either.

Chopsy said, 'I'm gonna have to move you into cover.' There was cover ten metres away. 'Can I, hell,' I said. I was like a dead weight, and then all of a sudden a mortar landed very close, and I panicked. 'Yeah, I can move!'

I picked up my arm and moved ten paces forward, but as we were moving, Chopsy got hit by something that took half his leg off, though I didn't know that at the time. I could hear him moaning and groaning a bit, so I shouted across, 'You alright, Chopsy?'

'No, no, no!' he screamed out.

I knew we would get help, but I also knew it was going to be a long time, because of the amount of Argy firepower coming down on us. We lay there talking to each other, keeping each other going. Then I saw him holding up both our berets and waving them about, and we started to get mortared again, so I screamed to put his arm down and play dead, as it was the only way to stop the mortars coming down.

All the rest of the lads were continuing the assault and we just lay there on the battlefield, and I realised we might not get out of there. I thought we'd get a quick bullet to the head and that was gonna be it! Yet we kept each other going by talking about going for a beer together when we got home, and for some reason I kept on asking Chopsy what the time was. I guess it was just something to keep us both talking and not passing out.

When the stretcher bearers arrived, I didn't want to go. I was asked how I was, and I told them I could now feel my hand and my fingers. I knew my arm was hanging off, but I thought they'd be able to fix it on again and I could carry on; it wouldn't be much of a problem! They tried to put me on a stretcher and I didn't want to get on it, but Bill [Lance Corporal Bill Bentley MM] ordered, 'Tony, you're coming out with us.' So they took me off the battlefield and that was the end of the war for me, and by the time I arrived back in the UK, the Argies had surrendered. I wish I'd been there with the blokes, you know, after a victory like that.

Lance Corporal Bill 'Basha' Bentley MM, Combat Medical Team
2 Para

Bob Cole [L/Cpl, Recce Platoon] came staggering down from the crest of the hill towards us, his bayonet still fixed and he told Doc Hughes that yet another platoon medic, Dave 'Chopsy' Grey, and Tony Tighe, another friend, were injured on the other side of the hill. Doc looked at me and I heard myself volunteering.

Bob led me through our own front line, through a gap in a stone wall, where he suddenly opened fire on two enemy soldiers. I also breeched the gap and opened fire. By the time I came up level with Bob, he was thrusting his bayonet into the second soldier, the first was already most definitely dead! We moved on, down the forward slope to a small depression where Bob could point out the casualties to me. We were now about twenty-five metres from them; fully exposed to the enemy down in Goose Green. I told Bob to wait for the rescue party and to creep over to us on my signal.

I crept over to Dave and Tony. Tony told me to look after Dave first, who was in a bad way. Dave had gone back to rescue Tony, who had been shot through the arm, and in doing so got hit full on by a mortar bomb, which had shattered one leg, broken the other and he was full of fragmentation. I quickly decided it would not be possible to deal with all of this on the spot, so opted to amputate the shattered leg.

By now somebody had become aware of my presence and bullets were plopping into the soft ground around us. I placed a tourniquet on Dave's leg and severed the remains of his lower leg with my Swiss Army knife, so that I could place a stump bandage. Dave just cringed into the ground, which was already soaked with his own blood. The sweet sickly smell mixed with the cordite, burnt flesh and fresh earth is unforgettable!

Private Greg Cox, light machine gunner, Patrols Platoon 2 Para

In my patrol was Big Bish [older brother of Lance Corporal Paul Bishop, B Company] my patrol commander, and Tony Tighe who was the 2IC, then Chopsy, the patrol medic, and me on the LMG. Chopsy and I shared a bunk on the *Norland*.

We'd been following the battalion since leaving the start-line and had some interesting moments along the way. We'd helped with the clearing of various locations and had collected some souvenirs. Tony and I had been on a searching the enemy dead detail when one of the dead Argies moved, so, as cover man, I shot him just to confirm he was dead and not hiding a grenade or booby trap under him. That may cause assorted war-crime rumblings today, but it was our SOPs at Goose Green and the rest of the Army; a hard lesson learned from previous battles, and lessons that were drilled into us during training.

As we advanced over Darwin Hill and across the ridgeline with Paul Farrar's patrol, we immediately started taking fire and went to ground. We returned fire, but were still a fair distance from Goose Green. We obviously couldn't stay where we were, then Big Bish gave the order, 'Let's go!' and as I was folding the legs of the LMG, I watched him do the textbook break from cover; crawl back, spring up, and zig-zag forward down the slope and towards the enemy. But as Tony pushed himself up ready to do something similar, he was hit almost immediately and went back down; he did yell out, but it wasn't a scream or anything, just a yelp!

I crawled across to him and checked him over, and he confirmed that the wound was to his arm. I screamed at Chopsy to get across to Tony quickly and to 'Shoot him up with morphine, get him to the RAP and stay there.' I also left my Argy bag of souvenirs and asked him to look after them for me, then I legged it down the hill, and caught up with Big Bish and another patrol, who were firing at an Argentine anti-aircraft gun.

Lance Corporal 'Radar', Defence Platoon 2 Para

If we could, we'd take a load of ammunition forward when picking up the wounded. We got to this young lad Chopsy, who had his leg hanging off, taken out by one of those Oerlikons I guessed, but what surprised me was the little blood; it had all seeped into the ground. There was a medic, Bill Bentley, working on him like fuck. He had already put a tourniquet on; Chopsy's leg was shredded like fuck. Then Bill started to cut the skin off with a pair of scissors, but they wouldn't go through the shredded skin. He says, 'Hold it up, hold it up.' So I did, and then Bill got out his clasp knife, then someone else came running over to help with the bandaging. He had an SLR with a bayonet on and was waving it all over the fucking place, dangerous like.

'What's all this ammo doing here?' he demands, like it should all be neatly stacked up and back in the stores.

'Help yourself,' I says, thinking his comments were well bizarre, and at the same time I'm leaning over talking to Bill and covering Chopsy to stop him seeing what's going on. I mean he was still screaming his brains out, and I'm still trying to hold the leg up to keep it steady for Bill to cut it off, and that's when I saw a Pucara fly in, and I thought, *shit, get the fuck down*, as his cannons let rip and the ground erupted around the blokes. I was surprised anyone came out of that one.

We were now starting to draw more fire than normal. We had to move, so we started to make our way back up the hill. We had Chopsy and another casualty, a medic, and some others, so by this time we had four guys, one on each corner of the stretcher, and bullets were winging up everywhere as we were moving to the crest of the Darwin Hill towards cover and safety. Then Bill yells, 'Where's his leg? Where's his leg? We need the leg!'

I goes, 'Who gives a fuck, you've just cut it off!'

'We need the leg,' Bill goes on.

'You ain't gonna put it back on, are yer?' I shouts back. And that was the last time I saw Bill, because he ordered me to go back and get this fucking leg. I know it sounds absurd, and it was absurd, but I ran back down, found it, stuffed it in my smock with the boot hanging out and tabbed back up, and all done under fuckin' fire. They hadn't gone far, so I put the leg with boot attached on Chopsy's stretcher. He'd stopped bleeding out by that time and he didn't see his leg, as he was well out of it because of all the morphine. Bill had just vanished into thin air on the battlefield.

When I got back to safety, I questioned the leg decision, but there were other priorities. It was a fucking stupid time!

A bit later Pete [Private Pete Blackburn, Defence Platoon], one of the stretcher team, comes up to me and says, 'Give us a look at your rifle?' So he takes a quick look and hands it back, 'Yeah, that's yours.'

'I know it fucking is,' I says. 'Where the fuck's yours?'

'I don't know, it must have slipped off the stretcher when we're picking up Chopsy.' He then points towards the crest of the hill in the direction of Goose Green.

'I'm not fucking going back down there, no fucking way,' I says, so we went around the other guys who'd helped us on that stretcher run, and none of them had his rifle.

So he says, 'What the fuck am I gonna do? We're in a fucking war. I need a fucking rifle.' So I offered to go with him to see the RSM, Mal Simpson. When we get there, I says, 'Sir, we were just recovering a casualty over from the forward slope and I think his weapon's fell off.'

'Don't worry about it, lads, there's loads of 'em over there, take your pick.' He pointed over to a stack of SLRs, and Pete was so relieved.

Private John Bolland, Recce Platoon 2 Para

Why didn't they tell us about the minefield? I heard from various different sources that it was laid with anti-tank mines and thank fuck for that! Otherwise, if they'd have put a Dolly Mixture in [a mixture of anti-tank and anti-personnel], we'd have all been blown to fuck.

I saw this track on the right where all the boys were heading, because we were getting blasted and shot at by those anti-aircraft guns; it was a bridge and there were Argies all over and everyone was shooting at 'em. I turned left and all this green tracer – Argies used green, we used red – was heading my way and it hit all around. If the Argies were using the same mix as us, one in five, then there were four more fuckin' bullets for every tracer you saw coming your way! I rolled over, crawled back to cover, rolled over again and thought, *what the fuck?* I saw Argies in front, then they started running about at the back of us! What the fuck is the enemy doing behind us? Am I missing something here?

Then I saw this red tracer coming from behind, shooting at these Argies and me, so I got me beret out and stuck it on me bayonet and fucking waved it about to inform the newly fucking formed Machine Gun Platoon[23] to stop fucking firing at me. I knew it was them, because I saw their fire coming from the gorse line on the slope, and of course we used red tracer.

Lance Corporal 'Duke' Allen, Defence Platoon 2 Para

While loading up our bodies at Darwin, the Scouts would fly over, land, and drop off ammo and stuff like that in little piles all over the place, and that's when the RSM got some Argy prisoners to pick up this ammunition and start tabbing forward with it. As one of these Scouts landed, I could see he had an ammo load, so I shouted at him and you know, the noise of the blades was a fucker, and I just shouts, 'Look, you gotta keep going forward!' pointing to over the ridge of Darwin Hill towards Goose Green. I mean it was fuckin' useless dropping the stuff where I was.

Private David Minnock, GPMG gunner, 12 Platoon D Company 2 Para

I was in between C Company who were on my left, and B Company on my right. I was heading towards Goose Green airfield, which was to the right and forward of the Goose Green settlement. It was

---

23 Machine Gun Platoon 2 Para had been formed only recently, in early 1982.

daylight and we were now moving on to our second objective, the airfield at Goose Green. The company sergeant major came by and I asked him, 'Sir, who's them blokes way out on the flanks?'

He looks and says, 'That's the enemy, son.'

Because we'd punched a hole in their defences, the battle had bypassed them, and they didn't know what to do. So they were following us in from the flanks, but they weren't carrying their weapons at the ready, in fact some weren't carrying any at all; probably dumped them, which was a good thing for them. They just didn't know what to do. You could see them in the far distance from either side and I thought, *fuck, they're behind us as well, following like sheep!*

'But that's the enemy,' I says. 'Can we shoot 'em?'

'No, you can't fucking shoot them,' says the sergeant major. But they were coming in towards us in an arrowhead formation, and they were tactically spaced as well! Bloody crazy place it was, and we were still taking incoming from our front too.

Colour Sergeant Frank Pye, Support Company 2 Para

It was around about the time you and C Company assaulted down towards Goose Green when I was ordered to take a load of A Company prisoners back with an escort of our walking wounded. I remember the horrendous racket from the Argy fire concentration. Anyway, there was only me and Yank who were physically fit, so I said to Yank, 'You cover one side and I'll cover the other and if any of 'em decide to do a runner, just open up.'

So now I'm trying to explain this to the prisoners that if any of 'em run, we'll shoot them. I'm jumping up and down pretending to run, and I'm sure they thought I was telling them to run, so we could shoot 'em, ha-ha. Anyway, we hadn't started back that long before we met the RSM Mal Simpson on the track. 'What you doing with all those prisoners, Frank?'

'I'm taking them back to Camilla Creek House, sir.'

'No, leave them with me.'

Well, he's the RSM and you do what you're told, so I handed them over to Mal and I heard later that he used them as ammunition carriers.

Further on with only the wounded, we pass a few dead Argies still in their trenches and one of the wounded asked, 'Can we stop please, Colour, and look for goodies?' I couldn't see no reason, so we stopped and all the wounded, well, those that physically could, started searching trenches. I mean, I was thinking it was just one of those things that happens in war.

It took us some time to get back to Camilla Creek and then I was tasked to go back up to the mortar line and A Company with two snowcats pulling trailers full of ammo and rations. I think the drivers were Royal Marines, because they have snowcats. Anyway, I put Yank as lead.

'Why am I in the lead vehicle?' Yank appealed.

'Because, just in case there's any minefields ahead – lance corporal!' I replied.

We had just started off out of Camilla Creek and hadn't gone more than a hundred metres and my driver turned the bloody thing over, and I always thought he'd done it on purpose, because he flipped the trailer on its side on the track and all the mortar ammunition was strewn all over. I managed to get out through a side window, but my knee was bruised up badly and my SMG was bent. So I was hopping about, rubbing my knee, while all the time Yank was stood there laughing his head off. But I was bloody furious with the driver. Our guys needed this ammo, because the assault into Goose Green had now started, and there were now mounting casualties to be picked up.

The Doc wanted me to take one of our wounded back, Steve Tuffen, so I turned to Captain Doc Hughes MID, RIP, and said, 'Sir, he won't survive a trip back in the Land Rover. He'll be bouncing all over the place.' The thing was, several of the medics had written poor Steve off – Hank Hood, Bill Bentley MM, the Doc – and now I did. Years later, I was at a garden party at Doc Hughes's house and we took a group photograph of me, the Doc, Bill and young Steve, who we'd all written off!

THE ASSAULT AND FIGHT THROUGH

Sergeant Pilot Dick Kilinski, F Flight 656 Squadron Army Air Corps

One time Doc Hughes came up to me and asked, 'Would you take some Argentinian injured out, please?'

So I said, 'Only after all the 2 Para lads.'

He told me, 'You've taken the most needing.'

So I took the Argy wounded out. There was one dead Argentinian, who looked like he had half his head missing, and as the medic went to retrieve his dog tags from him, the dead soldier moved; he still had a pulse! Because it was so bloody cold, his body had shut down, which actually saved him. Anyway, I flew this lad out too.

Colour Sergeant Pete Vale, HQ Company 2 Para

Some guys had led eighty or so prisoners back to Camilla Creek House, so because all the ammunition had been dumped off all over the place, I found an Argy officer who spoke English and told him to move the ammunition, but he said, 'No, it is against the Geneva Convention.' Then I pointed to a pile of rations and asked him who they were for, and he enquired, 'My men's rations?'

'Yes,' I said, but they weren't, and I laughed, then I told him he'd have to earn his rations by shifting ammunition, and that's what happened; it was all very much a mutual, gentlemanly thing.

We just didn't have enough free men to move it ourselves. The prisoners formed a chain and shifted the ammunition into a re-entrant out the way.

At the early stage of the battle, logistics were an issue, because of the lack of helicopters. We didn't get what we should have, and those rations were the battalion's rations, not meant for prisoners, but you gotta be flexible, you have to balance stuff out. But seriously, as soon as we radioed back that we needed rations for the prisoners, they were flown in straight away. All of a sudden, 2 Para got priority!

Private Roy Charters, Recce Platoon 2 Para

We crawled up this track around Goose Green and I saw this bloke facing away from Goose Green. I was gonna fucking slot him, because I had a Suit sight on [L2A2 sight unit infantry Trilux – telescopic sight] and I could see he was wearing a pair of OGs [non-camouflage, olive-coloured trousers], but he was one of ours, and I was just about to shoot him dead. It was a bloke from D Company; the cock!

Corporal 'Ginge' Dawes, clothing storeman, 2 Para

I felt bloody helpless stuck way up on Sussex Mountains when the names of the casualties and our dead slowly filtered out from Tac HQ. I'd served in Northern Ireland with many of them, had scoff with them, drunk many a beer too with 'em. No, I felt bloody helpless, but my job was keeping the ammunition and rations moving to those who were doing the fighting.

Private Phil Williams, Mortar Platoon 2 Para

We had three of the 105 light guns firing in support of us at Goose Green. Well, they ran out of ammunition. On 2 Para mortar line, we fired everything we had, the whole shebang, there was nothing left, mate, we'd run out of ammunition. I would say we fired 800 mortars, minimum! Say we all carried two, and about 450 of us crossed the start-line towards Goose Green – maybe the best part of a 1000 mortars, what with the resups!

Staff Sergeant Pete Harburn, PT Corp 2 Para's Physical Training Instructor

I did prisoner handling when we got prisoners from Goose Green, and I had to march them back to Camilla Creek House, and then at some stage get them airlifted back on to the *Norland*, as that's where they were being held. There were a hundred-odd prisoners, and we had them all in Camilla Creek House.

Roy 'Wendy' Gibson, steward and ship's pianist, MV Norland

While you were still fighting, we had to take a load of prisoners back to Argentina. There was this one time I was feeding the prisoners down on the car decks, and this one prisoner reminded me of my brother, RIP, because my brother were a real big fella; he was six foot five, me twin, but I just made six foot and shrunk with age now.

Anyway, this lad, a Navy lad from the *Hermes*, like military police, sort of marshals, we had Marines and Navy onboard too, says, 'Don't be giving 'em too much.' So, I looked at him and I got the ladle and I threatened him with it. I told him to mind his own effing business.

'You'll wear this bastard if you start on me!' I told him. It was a big ladle. I always gave that prisoner an extra helping.

BOTTOM SLOPE, GOOSE GREEN

Private Roy Charters, Recce Platoon 2 Para

When I got down and crossed the bridge towards Goose Green, there were these Argies, so I started shooting, and so did the guys next to me, but I can't remember who they were. Anyway, then Sid Higginson, RIP [Sergeant, Recce Platoon], comes rushing over screaming, 'Who you shooting at? Why are you shooting?'

I just carried on firing, because he couldn't have seen the Argies; then he fucked off, and I didn't see him again until after the re-org.

Corporal Ken Raynor, patrol commander Recce Platoon 2 Para

Still we kept assaulting until we ended up once again in dead ground, and at this point the company sort of broke up into smaller groups, identifying individual targets and going for them, but all the time heading roughly south towards Goose Green. We worked our way south, following a track down the centre of a valley. We were running in single file about 10 metres between each man, with Spud [Nigel Ely] leading, then me then Paul then Jock, and once again there was a lot of lead flying through the air. I remember removing a spent 7.62 from the hood of my windproof and it was still hot.

At this point I lost Jock: he got a 7.62 or something to the middle of his chest. He fell to the deck like a sack of potatoes, and as I approached him he was lying on his back like a turtle, with a wheezing, sucking chest wound; it was already starting to froth, so I just stuck my finger in the hole.

Paul, who was our patrol medic, caught up and was on Jock like a vulture on a leper, then Spud and I legged it forward to the crest and put down some fire in the general direction of the enemy. With Jock stable and in the relative safety of the bottom of the slope, I decided to leave him and the three of us moved forwards again. The intention was to establish comms or link up with friendly forces, so we continued down the valley where we came across a small bridge and a tin hut that was no more than 5 metres by 5 metres, with a wriggly tin roof that was now like a sieve caused by enemy indirect fire.

The priority was to sort ourselves out and get reorganised, sort out our own casualties and enemy prisoners of war and, of course, our ammunition. We were lucky in that the enemy also used 7.62, which we were able to borrow. We had now been on the go for over eighteen hours, our supply of adrenalin had worn down, and of course we needed a brew and a fag.

Lance Corporal 'Duke' Allen, Defence Platoon 2 Para

Some of the blokes wanted to shoot the wounded, I mean, there was rabid anger about the place. Well, there was only one that we came across and he was in a right state, a very young bloke, and I said, 'Fuck off, don't shoot him, he's fucked,' as he was gargling and all that. But I tell you what, I did hear the odd shot, you know, *bang, bang* – a double tap! – which didn't impress me one bit. Mind you, having said that, if you've lost a mate, what are yer fucking to do?

Look, some of them Argies were still in their trenches, and the point is, when you clear a position, what you are supposed to do is this: if the enemy are lying on the ground playing dead, after a warning, you shoot 'em, then your buddy gets down in the spoon position, grabs hold of the Argy's shoulders and pulls them over to check for grenades and booby traps. We learnt all this shit from the Germans. As terrible it may seem to a civvy, these were hard-learnt experiences; we were taught the buddy-buddy system in Depot. You shoot first, one of you gets behind the body and slowly rolls it over to expose the front, while your buddy keeps a bead on it from a distance, just in case a grenade pops out or something.

Then the choppers started coming in for us to load up our dead. Me and Radar moved most of our dead; Captain Dent, he was a big heavy bloke, the CO, he was light, light as a feather, and others. It was a gut-wrenching task. We loaded them up into a Sea King, I think. You can get a lot of dead bodies in a Sea King. The only consoling point was, as Sergeant 'Dinger' Bell [Defence Platoon] says, 'They've gone now, that's just an empty husk you're picking up.' But it's not, is it, really? – because they are, well, still warm, if you know what I mean.

Lance Corporal Pete 'Stubbo' Stubbs, MT Platoon 2 Para, attached to the Red Devils Parachute Display Team

There was this news flash about 2 Paras going into Goose Green, so I thought, *where the fuck's Goose Green?* But what stuck in my mind was the phrase, 'casualties are light'.

16

THE WHITE FLAG INCIDENT

Sergeant John 'Taff' Meredith DCM, 12 Platoon D Company 2 Para

As we advanced towards the left-hand side of the airfield, my platoon was ordered to give covering fire to C Company, who were about to launch an attack on the schoolhouse at Goose Green, so I had two sections facing the schoolhouse and then my reserve section, which was Sully's [Corporal Paul Sullivan, RIP] section, was behind. Earlier in the day, Sully, who had been point since we'd set foot on the islands, had asked me if he could change, so I said, 'Yeah, I'll ask the platoon commander, Lieutenant Jim Barry.'

Sully was the most experienced full screw, because he'd done Senior Brecon and had been told he was to be picked up for his sergeant in June, so I said to Jim Barry, 'You need to ring the changes to give these blokes a break.'

Sully used to come past me every time we moved off and he'd shake his head and go, 'This is going to be the death of me.' So, anyway, we swapped Sully's section to reserve section, and I recall saying, 'Reserve section, Sully! You'll get thrown in when the crap really hits the fan!'

'Yeah, but it gives my blokes a rest for now,' he replied, relieved.

So, we had two sections looking over towards the schoolhouse with me controlling them, when Jim Barry said he saw something across a fence line 45 degrees to my right, and someone else said they saw an Argy waving a white flag up by this fence line. Then Jim Barry came up and said, 'Right, I'm going to go forward to take their surrender.'

'No! If they want to surrender, they can come to us,' I said, 'we don't need to go to them. We're in a good position here, we've got some cover,' because the ground was really like a billiard table.

'No, no! One of the last things the CO said in his orders was to allow the enemy every chance to surrender,' he insisted.

'Well, you are, but get them to come to us.'

But he said no and started to move forward to take their surrender. He took Jerry Godfrey [Private], the radio operator, with him.

There were quite a few Argies, easily a section [10–15 soldiers]. So as Jim got up to the fence line, a couple of the Argies came forward to the other side of the fence, and then Sully had his section start to move up to a flank. Then suddenly from my behind and left of me, around about where A Company were, a hell of a lot of fire came over the top of us and the Argies just started opening fire.

Did whoever fired from behind me know we were there? Did they see the Argies skylining? Who knows? When the Argies opened up, Jim Barry got hit, Geordie Knight [Private Knight] shot one of the Argies and the other fled, then Sully was killed, and Midge Smith [Lance Corporal Nigel Smith] was killed, and then Slough [Private] was hit. That section was pinned down, so I had to change our axis to get around them; I fired off a couple of mags to keep the Argy heads down so I could pull back, then took a GPMG off one of the sections, got into a position where I could see them, and started to take 'em out.

Then Boy Roach [Private] came crawling back and shouted, 'I've been hit, I've been hit!'

'You'll know if you'd been hit,' I said, because it didn't look like he had.

'I think I have,' he pleaded.

'No, no, you will know for sure,' I replied reassuringly, but the back of his trousers had been ripped, and then I thought, *ooops, he's right, that looks a bit nasty!* There was a little nick where a bullet had touched him, but he was alright. Then Geordie Shevill [Private] came crawling back and also said he'd been hit. I told him you'll know when you've been hit, and he had. He had one through the shoulder and at least one entry and exit wound. The medics started to give him first aid and then I looked over and Boomer was sort of lying with his head down, so I shouted, 'Return fire!'

'But they're shooting at us!'

'I'll shoot at you if you don't,' I screamed back. So he started to return fire.

Shortly after, we were told to leave our casualties in place because we had other things to deal with, but I did go up to see Jim Barry, because I had to get the maps and stuff from him. So I got up to Jim and obviously he was dead, and I was quietly saying to him, 'If you'd listened to what I said, we wouldn't be in this situation.' As I was saying this, I was taking his radio and getting his map, his ammunition and anything else we could use, because we didn't have enough of anything: compass, spare socks, food. He had an IWS, but that had been hit so it was u/s.

I carried on chatting, 'However, the boys are alright, we're all okay.' I noticed young Minnock had come up behind me. It was all very sad. Jim was in the upright position on the wire just as he was hit, so we lifted him off and gently placed him on the ground.

Private David Minnock, GPMG gunner, 12 Platoon D Company 2 Para

It was full daylight now as we neared the airfield and the Argies were still pumping out a constant volley of fire on us with the anti-aircraft cannons. We approached a position on a rise and I saw it. The biggest flag I'd ever seen flying, an Argentine flag, a massive one, and it's fluttering away! Then we got word that some company, which I thought was us, was going to put an attack in on the schoolhouse, because my 12 Platoon were D Company's left flank next to C Company, and we were to give them fire support. I didn't know it was C Company putting in the attack at that time; why should I? I didn't even know what the other platoons in D Company were doing. So the platoon commander Lieutenant Jim Barry says, 'Right, C Company's going to put an attack in, so you've gotta get across this track and cover the schoolhouse.'

I didn't know what the schoolhouse even was. It was the first time I'd ever heard it mentioned, but I was told it was over to my left a few hundred metres away by the sea. Anyhow, the track wasn't an actual track, it was mud ruts made by tractors driving along it and defined by a barbed-wire fence line.

'Get across that fence and give covering fire,' he continued. He gave that command to me and Budge, and I was thinking, I'm not going over there if there's enemy, but of course we did, as you do. As we were going across the ground towards where we thought was the schoolhouse, as we couldn't see it from where we were, we were still keeping our heads down. Then we popped up and I could see this flagpole again, up on my right, now less than a hundred metres away, and the Argies were just looking at us and waving! It was fucking weird, but we were too concentrated on what was to our front, like enemy trenches! So, I ignored them.

Look, the situation was really tense, you couldn't take your eyes away from what was to your front, and yes, those Argies up at the flagpole would have been easy to shoot, but I didn't know what to do. Do I shoot them or what? That's how much war can fuck up your decision-making. It was so surreal. And I remembered what the RSM Mal Simpson said to us on the *Norland*, 'Anyone shoots out of turn, you'll be in trouble with me.' So I assumed someone else would probably be dealing with them.

Now, these guys weren't looking to surrender, but for some reason it felt like they thought *we* were going to surrender, because we weren't firing at them! But, why would we surrender? We were the ones advancing and attacking THEM! Again, because I wasn't concentrating on them, they were being left out of it all, and I don't think they were happy about that, and this is where it gets bad, this is where it gets to me now.

[*At this point I had to turn the tape off.*]

[*Tape back on.*]

Jim Barry now comes with the reserve section, which was Sully's, and says, 'Right, you get across there,' pointing over to the flagpole; then Barry and Sully move up with the section towards the flagpole to communicate with the Argies. I don't know who was covering them, but it wasn't me, I was facing the wrong way. I was facing east, while Jim Barry and Sully were facing south of me, because I was about to cover the schoolhouse assault; as that was the important thing and it was about to go in.

This flagpole business with the waving Argies; well, it looked like they were waving their white underwear at us, you know, like the ones we were issued with, the Arctic drawers type, and it was just a side issue as far as we were concerned. So, Jim Barry and Sully moved up to deal with these Argies and that was the last time I saw them alive.

A few seconds later, that's when it all goes to rat shit, because they go up there and they are shot up. Jim Barry actually speaks to them, he has a bit of an argument, and then an Argy officer type comes up and tells Jim to get back down the hill. 'You son of a bitch,' or words to that effect, and then Sully's section is shot up.

You've got Jim Barry, the platoon commander, now shot in the back as he's climbing back over the barbed-wire fence; he falls down dead and is hanging over the fence. Sully's killed, Mino [Nigel Smith] killed, and the machine-gunner [Private Geordie Shevill, D Company], Sully's GPMG man, was shot three times, both shoulders and his buttock and the rest of 'em. Well, it was a fucked-up job!

At the same time as the shooting started, I immediately switched direction and crawled forward in support of Sully, then I had a problem with my GPMG. Thank fuck for the deep tractor ruts, because the Argies started firing at us too. Just being several inches deep in the ground, these ruts gave us protection to take on these Argies up at the flagpole – they saved many a life that day.

Because I didn't know what had happened, only that there were our blokes up there and there was a shitload of firing, it was bollocks to the schoolhouse. We were in real trouble now, because whatever happened up the hill with our section, I knew something had gone wrong by the amount of heavy fire coming our way. So, we were trying to get there with no guidance, trying to get forward, but the volume of fire coming down at us was horrendous; you couldn't get your head off the ruts to see.

It was either Budge or Corporal Steve Kitchener kept shouting, 'Get your fucking head and arse down, or you're gonna get shot!' But I had to move to a point where I could get the gun up to bear. So, we were all there now in position and the rest of the blokes were waiting for me to fire, so they can break cover and do the assault. This had never happened in training and has never happened since, but I'd just got the gun up on the bank, secured the legs and started blasting away at the Argies, when all of a sudden, I heard this, *click, click*. A stoppage! I thought, *shit, shit, shit.*

'STOPPAGE!' I scream. Again, 'STOPPAGE!' Right, think, think, think; safety catch on, top cover open, clear the top tray and try to pull the cocking lever, but no, it wouldn't budge, the gun had jammed completely. I put it down to all the mud and shit that had got into it. I'm pulling clean, fresh link from me pouches, not like some of the blokes did, and carried them around their bodies. But it wasn't dirty link. The gun had just jammed up! I'm now in a panic, and I shout back to Budge and tells him the gun's jammed, and Budge shouts out, 'SPW, get out your SPW' [spare parts wallet].

What the fuck? I'm thinking! So, what I did was, I actually got my fucking SPW out in the middle of a fucking battle and started to strip the fucking gun down with the tools of the fucking SPW. I started cleaning out the stoppage, but in the meantime, because the incoming fire was so intense and I couldn't bear the gun down to give the blokes covering fire as they tried to advance, they all had to back off. I was in such a panic and I'll hold my hand up and say I started crying, telling myself, 'I've fucked up here, I've really fucked up,' and through the tears calling myself a knobhead and stuff. I was only eighteen, for Christ's sake.

The enemy must have seen the blokes backing off, because I could hear the Argies shouting at me, something like, 'Get up, Punto!' or something. They wanted me to stand up so I could get it over and done with, and I'm saying to myself, 'No, no, no.' So, I'm doing my best clearing the gun, and in the meantime, and I didn't know this at the time, but Sergeant 'Taff' Meredith had come up from the rear, because he was controlling the rear of the attack, found out what had happened to Barry, and taken control.

Taff immediately sussed out what had happened, spotted the Argies who were giving us the grief from the side of the flagpole and fired an M79 round into one of the Argy trenches. Of course, our lads up front didn't know what it was that exploded, but whatever it was, it was a direct hit, and no Argies came out. So Taff fired three more M79 rounds at other targets. By now the Argies knew what was coming, so they all got out of their trenches and started to run back towards Goose Green, and as that happened, Taff picked up an abandoned GPMG from another one of our casualties and fired bursts into these Argies and cut them down dead.

By now, I'd got my gun working again and up on its legs, and I started riddling 'em too. Taff was shooting, I'm shooting, we're firing off like fuck; we weren't taking any prisoners after that, no, no, no! No fucking prisoners, but they weren't surrendering anyway! We weren't taking any more chances and as we advanced, clearing the area, I double-tapped the dead ones in the head, just to make sure.

I was so glad of Taff's action. You see, we'd had it all our own way up until we came out on those tractor ruts and the flagpole. We were advancing, taking ground, killing and taking prisoners and winning, then things went completely wrong and it just turned. We were attacking and then it went wrong, because we tried to do the right thing.

When I first saw them Argies up by the flag, I could have done away with 'em, turned the gun on them and wasted the lot of 'em – easy, and I should've have done, because when I go to Aldershot Military Cemetery to see my old mates, there's three graves there: Jim Barry, there's Paul Sullivan, and there's Mino Smith. There are three blokes together, and there's no need for them to be there, because we tried to do the right thing! I have to face that each time I go to that cemetery. You're damned if you do and damned if you don't.

I could hear the fierce battle still going on over by the schoolhouse, but on our part of the battlefield there was a welcome lull, so I moved up to see Taff, who'd gone up to Jim Barry, and Taff was there talking to Jim, saying, 'Now then boss, right, I've gotta take these of you, I'm sorry about this.' Taff was taking Jim's WOCS [War Office controlled stores] from him, you know, his binos, his compass and maps, and I thought, *is he still alive?*

That's when I turned around to see if anyone was about, but it was only me and Taff, and he continued, 'I'm sorry I've got to leave you like this boss, but I've got to look after the lads, you understand that, I'm taking the lads on and I won't forget you, and I'll make sure you get looked after, but I've got to leave you here like this and I'm really sorry.'

I'm covering Taff while he was saying all this. He has now got Jim's compass, binos and maps, and Jim's hanging over this wire fence.

Years later, I brought this subject up with Taff, and he said, 'It made me feel better talking to him.'

Nigel Ely: The Argy who shot Jim Barry in the back was an officer called Johanne Gormlos Centurion. He got the Argy equivalent of the Victoria Cross, because the Argies thought Gormlos had killed Colonel H Jones, but he didn't, he killed Jim.

THE SCHOOLHOUSE

Nigel Ely: As a few of us scoured around the dairy and beyond, we started to see some blokes from D Company who had made it across from the airfield. At the time, the schoolhouse was the biggest building on the Falkland Islands, yet it did not figure high up in the set of orders I received. Okay, the orders were given in a rush, at night, and with the threat of the BBC broadcast and counterattack hanging over us, yet I honestly do not recall hearing of its existence until someone mentioned Patrols were going to put an attack into it.

Then I saw it over on my left at about the seven o'clock and I was shocked I hadn't seen it before, as I was so concentrated on my own space, ground, and immediate threat around me. Spanish voices being one, and combat-clad bodies darting about in front, another!

THE BATTLE FOR DARWIN AND GOOSE GREEN, 28–9 May 1982

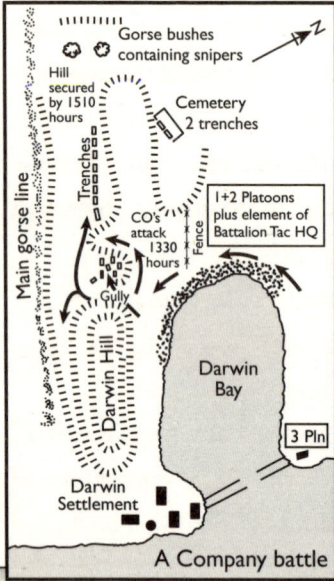

N

Camilla Creek House
'A' Echelon and gun line 2300 hours, 27 May

C Coy clears start-line, 2300 hours, 27 May

Support Coy

B Coy 0710 hrs

A Coy 0630 hrs 28 May

Support Coy

0740 hrs

Burntside Pond

Burntside House 0650 hours

Camilla Creek

D Coy

C Coy

Coronation Point

Support Coy

0900 hrs

Fire support from HMS *Arrow* till dawn 28 May

Boca House 1600 hours

1500 hrs

DARWIN

OP SAS

D Coy

B Coy

1640 hours

Minefields

Airstrip

Schoolhouse 1900 hours

ARGENTINES SURRENDER 1450 hours 29 May

Flagpole

GOOSE GREEN

1840 hrs

Harrier strike on Goose Green Point 1925 hours

Argentine reinforcements by helicopter 2000 hours

0 — 1 km

Inset: A Company battle

Gorse bushes containing snipers

Hill secured by 1510 hours

Cemetery 2 trenches

Trenches

Main gorse line

CO's attack 1330 hours

Fence

1+2 Platoons plus element of Battalion Tac HQ

Gully

Darwin Hill

Darwin Bay

3 Pln

Darwin Settlement

A Company battle

THE WHITE FLAG INCIDENT

Corporal Tom Harley MM, section commander, 10 Platoon D Company 2 Para

We were opened up on from the schoolhouse and an outbuilding 200 metres to our front. Wally McAuley collected two 66s and fired one off. Nothing happened, because they had been wrapped in wet sandbags – it misfired, and much to Wally's embarrassment, he missed with the second. Then he said, 'Are you ready?' as he was unclipping two grenades from his webbing. I nodded and did the same. We looked at each other for a second, then he shouted, 'NOW!' and we both ran towards the outbuilding. He was zigging, I was zagging, and threw the grenades in and around the building. No one came out.

Captain Paul Farrar, OC Patrols Platoon 2 Para

Meanwhile, at the schoolhouse I recall seeing Dave Trick and John G very close up by it and seeing this hole appear in it, which looked like a 106 recoilless firing out of the building, and it was at that time I was running across towards the smaller buildings on the left. There were a lot of rounds going into it and then I saw it burning – we had set it on fire – and as I was running along the flank of the buildings somebody, and I don't know who, fired off a 66 as I was passing; you know, it's all about the back blast with a 66, and I'm thinking, *this is insane!* And there were mortars landing continually all and around in the estuary.

We can't get anyone on the net, and after this initial rush of blood, everyone's back on the foreshore of the re-entrant, in dead ground. So, I decided to move stealthily up towards the schoolhouse again and we ended up near a kids' playground and took cover in two small shell holes. We spent what seemed to be about two hours there; I mean, we were there a long time thinking, well, what the hell is happening?

We could see what looked to be the main Argentine command post, so the CSM got on the net and called in a fire mission and it was given, but the gunners must have had a big box on the map saying *No Fire Into Goose Green*, and the rounds were falling short into the sea. We were all firing into the schoolhouse and there were Argies running away along the coastline. I engaged them, but can't say if I hit any.

Private Mark Sleap, Patrols Platoon 2 Para

We were on that forward slope by the schoolhouse looking down on it, and me and Bob Morgan couldn't get in any trench, because Steve Jones [Pte, Patrols Platoon] and a few others had already claimed them, and there was no space, so we just had to lay flat next to them. So anyway, the Argy artillery starts to bracket us, because we heard the first salvo being fired off, which made a sound exactly like 'BOMB, BOMB, BOMB, BOMB, BOMB, BOMB!'

Name That Tune in One? I looked across to Bob, and he went, 'Tell Laura I Love Her . . . ,' as he was obviously thinking the same song, and then those six shells came in. It was so fucked up, so strange. These rounds were dropping just across from us, and lying next to us was Steve Mac [L/Cpl, Patrols Platoon], who was Artillery before joining 2 Para, and knew about stuff like this. He went, 'Alright lads, they're bracketing us, but keep calm. The next one will be dead on target!'

Corporal Tom Harley MM, section commander, 10 Platoon D Company 2 Para

Just prior to C Company's left flanking by their sergeant major, Baz Greenhalgh, I grabbed hold of him and said I had four guns [GPMGs] and he said, 'Tom, give us fire support. We're gonna go down this way and we're gonna try and do a right flank on to the schoolhouse.'

I saw him go down the track and head off along the shoreline; there was nothing tactical about it, just cover from fire and they got fairly close to it. So I waited until he got about 300 metres from the schoolhouse and that's when I gave the order to the guns to lay down suppressing fire. Shortly after that, I remember seeing a whole contingent of C Company there.

You'd obviously done what you had in your four-man teams and then all got together again and, now as a patrol company again of about sixteen or twenty guys, did the business. Then someone made the sensible decision, 'Let's go back.' I saw them come back in line with the rest of D Company and that was that.

Corporal Ken Raynor, patrol commander, Recce Platoon 2 Para

We then as a group of C Company met up with the rest of Patrols, who were about to sort out the schoolhouse. The ground was pretty straightforward: there was a long, thin valley feature running towards the schoolhouse and on the flank was the Goose Green airstrip. The valley was only a couple of metres high; it was not wise to stick your head above the bank, as the enemy had several gun positions across the flat terrain that were able to put down suppressive fire.

I believe the Argies were probably a little surprised by how far we had advanced, and although they had by far the greater numbers, they did not have our aggression or eagerness to win. They also did not use their indirect fire weapons as well as they could have, and had an issue with their 105mm artillery shells not exploding on impact. Several artillery shells landed very close to us; you heard them flying through the air and then plop as they dug into the soft peat.

We made our way towards the end of the valley, where we met the rest of the Patrols Platoon; the scene was a little weird, six to eight guys lying on their bellies converting live rounds to empty cases. The fire from both directions was pretty heavy, and at this stage I had only a couple of gold top 40 mills left, so I fired them into the schoolhouse and assisted as part of the fire support group.

The assault was made a lot easier as the building started to burn, one reason being that 66 rockets were being fired on target; in fact, I can remember rolling a cigarette, having crawled out of fire but needing a fag; a lot of guys took up smoking. I had just about made my rolly when someone fired off another 66 and the back-blast stopped me smoking for a while, but the rest of the Patrols Platoon dealt with the schoolhouse.

Private Greg Cox, light machine gunner, Patrols Platoon 2 Para

After we got into the area around Goose Green, I stayed with Big Bish and we gave fire support for the Patrols assault on the schoolhouse. I and others laid down covering fire for the Patrol Platoon attack on the Goose Green schoolhouse. Watching the attack go in, I saw one of our guys get completely blown off his feet; he did a full somersault landing back on his feet and kept running as if nothing had happened!

Private Mark Sleap, Patrols Platoon 2 Para

There was this swing in the playground of the school and a round hit the back of Steve Jones's neck. It had ricocheted off the frame of a swing to which the Argies had rigged a multi-barrel rocket launcher, and landed in the neck of his windproof.

Private John Bolland, Recce Platoon 2 Para

I was close to the schoolhouse when somebody shouted, 'We're being outflanked!' so I thought, *I'd better get the fuck outta here*, and as I turned to run, I got hit, and the next thing I'm on the ground. I had been thrown up in the air and landed on my knees. I realised later the Argies had fixed a rocket pod, which was mounted to the kids' swings, and this fucking thing whooshed past me from right to left as I turned, and it took me out.

The fins on this bloody rocket took eleven inches out of me as it ploughed across my chest, smashing my ribs, and taking out the top of me lung with it. It then broke off and carried on and exploded in the estuary, where some of the lads were taking cover. Doc says if it had been just under a quarter-inch more, I'd have been a dead Jock.

That was the only time in my life I felt I had no worries, no more cares, because I knew I was dying. I remember quietly saying, 'Gie' us a break,' and watching all those mortars landing in the estuary a few feet from us. Then looking down and seeing my ribs sticking through my smock.

The thing was, I got the sucking wound to the chest injury, and we always kidded that a sucking wound to the chest is nature's way of saying you've fucked up! So, Mad Dog [Private Doug Warren, Patrols Platoon] slaps a few field dressings on me and you lot started nicking me kit. You nicked me baccy [cigarette rolling tobacco] and me ammo and shit, ye bastards.

Then I got moved onto some wriggly tin[24] and the boys slid me into what they called the dairy and that was like an Argy aiming mark, like they'd DF-ed it, which is a pre-marked position to bring fire down on at a later time. But that's where all the wounded were

---

24 The wriggly tin – also known as corrugated iron – came from the Goose Green pig farm, which we were fighting through, and during the Argy occupation, they had dug trenches all about and used the tin as overhead cover.

taken, and God forgive me, there was one boy, wounded next to me, who put his arm around me and cuddled me, so he did, and I felt and heard him go, 'Eeerrrr,' and that was that; he was gone.[25]

Private Bob Morgan, Patrols Platoon 2 Para

There was a bit of a lull in the battle, you know, getting towards twilight, and we were behind a six-foot sandbank that marked the estuary, and still getting mortared on that thin, pebbly beach; it hadn't stopped all afternoon. Well, a lot of us were laid up there, having a smoke and a good old chat and a laugh really, because we hadn't seen many of us from C Company since the forward slope.

Mad Dog the medic was sorting out the wounded, being very calm as the battle raged overhead, and the noise from the incoming was ear-deafening. Then he just turned around and screamed to us all, 'Can't you lot be quiet, can't you see there's men dying here!' Old Mad Dog was serious – he was a Bristol man, very simple, to the point, if you know what I mean!

Lance Corporal 'Duke' Allen, Defence Platoon 2 Para

As the wounded mounted up, so did our stretchers. We based ourselves by the RAP at Darwin Hill. That way we were on hand to be tasked. Some time later, we got another order to go down the forward slope to the front line, where C Company were reportedly pinned down on the left somewhere by the schoolhouse, to pick up their wounded. Captain Ford says, 'Right, I want some volunteers to go down and get the wounded.'

'Fuck me, sir, you can't say "volunteer", you're just asking for trouble,' I said back. I mean, it's like the old story, isn't it? The

25 This was quite probably an Argentinian soldier.

sergeant major asks, 'Who's interested in music?' and a couple of twats will put their hands up, and the sergeant major says, 'Right then, lift that fucking piano and take it up those stairs.'

So one has to think, because if you volunteer, you're bound to get shot. But having said that, enough of us stepped forward and then off we went. There must have been eight of us.

As we moved through and off the top of the hill, I got a lovely smile from Evers [Private Irwin Eversley, A Company], just a big broad smile holding a big mug of tea, and he was one of the last blokes I saw as I went over the top and into certain death.

Ford then dashed off down the slope, I really didn't know what he was up to, going off on his own; but he probably had a rough idea where the wounded were, and I had no idea. So, he goes hoofing off on a diagonal route down the hill, so we did the same and followed, but a short tad later. That probably helped us not get shot, because we weren't literally going straight down, nor did we do any of that zig-zagging you get taught to do, we moved in a straight diagonal line only; we sauntered, we didn't run or anything like that, and anyway some of us were carrying those fold-up issued stretchers, which made our descent very fucking awkward.

Then Captain Ford told us to wait, which I thought was a bit strange, and he just pointed over about twenty paces, and I thought, *what the fuck?* Then he hoofed it off again on his own. We got down in a rut, but there was no point because it was a tiny tractor-tyre type rut and was forward facing and, of course, it didn't stop the rounds coming in, which were exploding all over the exposed ground we'd taken cover on.

I saw Col's [Private Colin Stevenson, Defence Platoon] arse behind me stuck up in the air with a 66 strapped across it. It must have come loose when he took cover, and I thought *if that got hit, we'd all go up to see God.* I can't recall how long we stayed there, but we couldn't have stayed there that long otherwise we would have got hit, and that's when I looked behind me.

Shit, we couldn't even move back into the gap in the gorse as tempting as it was, and at least out of sight; no way, that would be construed as cowardice in the face of the enemy. So I just said to the boys, 'Fuck this for a game of soldiers,' and up we got and charged off down the forward slope towards Goose Green.

I still don't know to this day why he did it, and it was the same when he ordered me to dig into a fuckin' puddle a bit later on in the war at Fitzroy. When the *Sir Galahad* got hit, the battalion moved out and away from the sheep-shearing sheds and into open ground. B Company were on top of this mountain and Defence Platoon were at the bottom of it. Captain Ford then said to me, 'Get a trench in there,' and he was pointing right in the middle of a fucking puddle, I mean a huge fucking puddle. He was ordering me to dig in it!

Well, I couldn't believe it. I was so dumbfounded, and it was exactly as it was when he asked us to wait on that forward slope. So when he gave me that order, I thought, *what am I going to do?* There was no way I was going to dig a hole in a fuckin' puddle, so I asked Barry Norman.

'Look,' I said, 'I think Captain Ford's gone off his head and said dig a trench in there.' I pointed to this massive puddle. Barry went, 'Fucking hell, come with me,' and he took me off and sited the trench somewhere else.

Barry 'Kraut' Norman was part of Tac HQ, he was the CO's bodyguard and he did a great job there! Well, he did really, he said to the CO, 'Don't go there. Don't fuckin' go.' You know that Captain Dent and Stevie Prior were killed probably because of the CO. The CO went and got himself and at least two other blokes fuckin' killed. Captain Dent was such a smashing bloke, and Stevie Prior was something else, a beautiful man. Crazy! Fucking awful.

Captain Wood was a great bloke, too. Killed up on Darwin Hill – what a fucking waste.

Anyway, back on the forward slope at Goose Green, looking for our wounded. I was conscious of all this small-arms fire pinging around us, but not the mortars or artillery, and I guess that was funny, as I was so fixed on getting down the slope. I could see some of Recce and Patrols at the bottom, and of course, they were behind quite a decent looking embankment really, so that was it, we headed towards them.

We eventually got to see the wounded and loaded up one lad who'd taken a couple of rounds and was off his head on morphine, and Taff Evans, Corporal, Recce Platoon, seemed to be alright among this insanity, at least the big fat bastard was talking, but we had to take these two back up the hill in open ground whilst still under fire. It was a fair way back up, a good eight hundred metres easy, and I mean, Taff was a real heavy bastard, so it slowed our move back. I'm not saying we were complacent about the mortars dropping, but what to do? We had to get the injured back. It was a miracle none of us was hit.

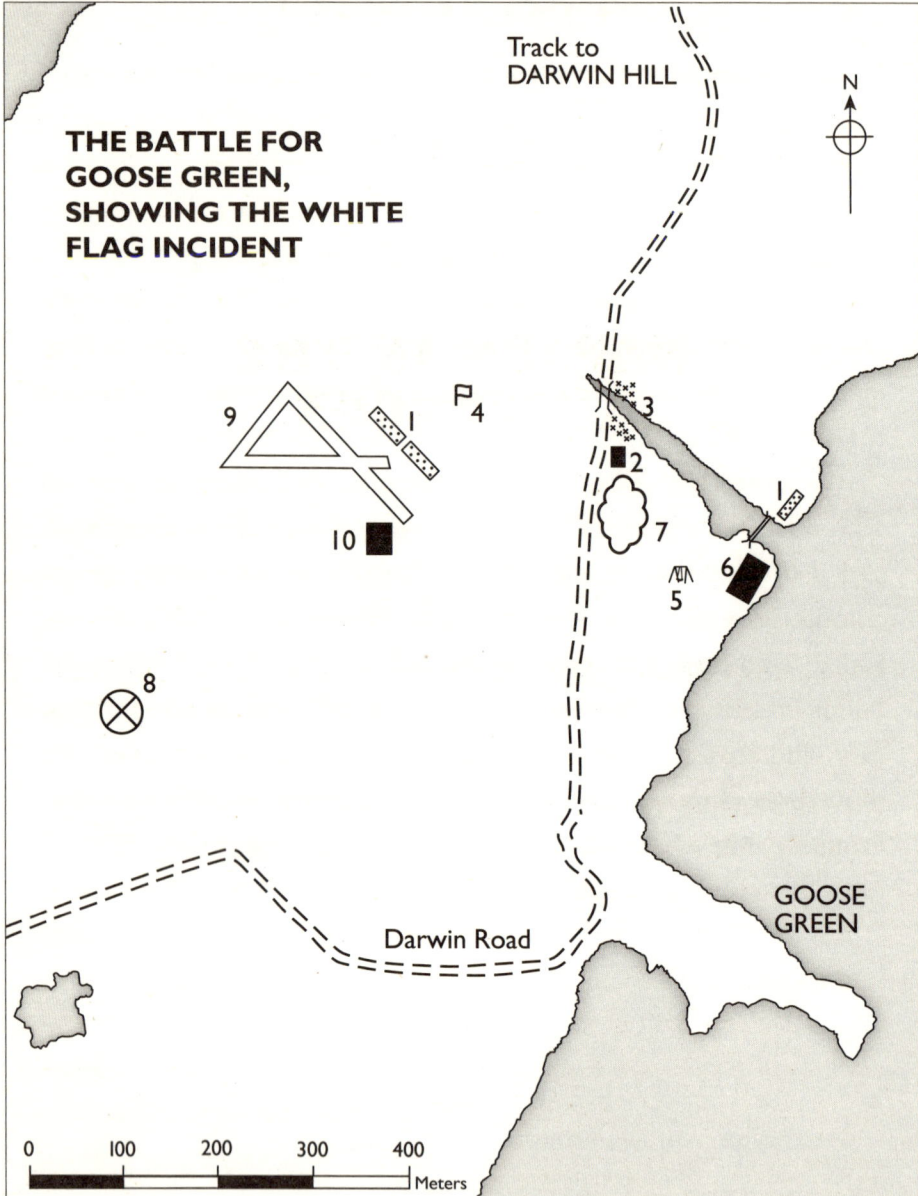

THE BATTLE FOR
GOOSE GREEN,
SHOWING THE WHITE
FLAG INCIDENT

Track to
DARWIN HILL

N

GOOSE
GREEN

Darwin Road

0   100   200   300   400
                         Meters

1	Minefields	6	The schoolhouse
2	The dairy	7	Napalm drop
3	Argentine prisoners	8	Pucara crash
4	White flag incident	9	Airfield
5	Rocket launcher on children's swing	10	Hut where surrender was negotiated

17

NAPALM IN THE AFTERNOON

Private David Minnock, GPMG gunner, 12 Platoon D Company 2 Para

After we pulled back from the white flag incident, the OC got a grip of us, and pulled us all back to a position he thought was safe. The company was lying up on the only track to Goose Green. He had us lined up either side, and said the RAF were coming in and going to sort this situation out. We were getting an air strike. But it wasn't the RAF who turned up, it was a couple of Argy Pucaras, or Aermacchis, or one of each. We got up to run, and you know rabbits caught in the headlights, they don't know which way to go: do you run left, do you run right – we were like that. I can remember the sparks; the pilot must have been as shocked as we were when he flew over the hill and saw a company size of Paras all lined up on both sides of this track.

Nobody fired at him because nobody saw him, he flew so fast and low, and he didn't fire back; it was real quick, but we were expecting RAF Harriers! We thought he'd come around again but he didn't, then a bit later they came back and this time flew in attack mode, but now we were well spread out. We were all firing at them; their plan was to kill us – and ours was to severely fuck the pair of them up. To be fair, we did pump a massive amount of fire into them. I had the GPMG butt on the ground and was just firing up at it, we all were.

Then one of the pilots ejected and came down under his canopy, so we all carried on firing, then the OC screamed, 'Stop firing at that man!' And he was right, the pilot was now only a bloke helplessly suspended under a parachute. But some were still firing, anger I guess, as you could see the tracer was going through his rigging lines and canopy. We just wanted to destroy him.

He landed right next to us, it were my section, and Corporal Steve Kitchin and Spanner went out to pick the pilot up, and because it were our section, we marched him through our position to drop all his kit that was hanging off him. It was like madness, because the boss was scared of one of us shooting him, so Spanner and Steve marched with him so close that you couldn't shoot him unless you hit one of our blokes too.

We were angry at him; we were all swearing at him and that. As he was marched past me, he was made to drop his kit off, so I thought, *great, we'll go rob his emergency rations.* You always get one bright spark, don't you? The thing that hangs off the back of his pack, like a bum thing whatever, well one bloke pulls down hard on it and a fucking big orange dinghy thing springs out and starts to inflate. So we had to deflate this thing quick and we were stabbing it with bayonets, as it was a massive aiming point being stuck up on this hill.

In the end we found only a couple of hardtack-type biscuits. What an embarrassment, but we were hungry, really hungry, because 2 Para had this thing whereby you had to carry a 24-hour ration pack on your belt kit or in your smock. We'd done away with that. All my belt kit pouches were filled with ammo, except for a water bottle, because you have to have water; you can get away without food, but you need water because you get dry.

I must have carried about 800 rounds, broken down into 100 rounds of link, also I had two or three of those 200-round canvas bandoliers slung around my body. I wasn't gonna have all my link in the shit other than what was on the gun and you can't help that sometimes, especially when you're crawling forward under heavy fire trying to keep your arse down and eyes open; like the time when my gun jammed as I've described before, left on my own when the rest of the blokes had backed off.

Luckily Taff was watching all this and he'd come up from the back and saved my neck. I've never thanked him for it, nor has the platoon to my knowledge, because we were all embarrassed. WE got ourselves in a bad position, the whole platoon – and one man, Sergeant Taff Meredith DCM, got us out if it.

Remember I said Geordie Shevill got shot up at the white flag incident? Well, he had two blokes looking after him, though he'd had it, so they gave him morphine to make his passing easier. Two or three syrettes they gave him! Then they shared half a syrette for themselves; a quarter each, like 'let's not waste it' sort of thing, and they were rolling about laughing when the napalm came in. So Geordie then came to life, got up, and before anyone could stop him, he was up and away, running like a crazy man carrying his drip, with his trousers half down. Then he leapfrogged over the barbed wire fence, shouting, 'You ain't shooting me again, you Argy bastards!'

Taff Meredith saw this and shouted across at the other two, 'Get up and get after him, because you're responsible for that,' pointing over at the running Geordie.

Sergeant John 'Taff' Meredith DCM, 12 Platoon D Company 2 Para

After I'd taken out most of the Argies, we went into a re-org and by this time Geordie Shevill was lying down with his kegs around his ankles and a drip stuck up his backside. Then during the re-org we were checking where everybody was and we got a radio message saying that there were two friendly aircraft coming from the north, but the next minute these two 'friendly' aircraft strafed our position! Lines of cannon fire chased up the track we'd taken cover on.

During the Argy strafing, Shevill was up and running, how he did it I do not know, but he jumped over the wire fence with his kegs around his ankles and with a drip hanging out of his arse, so I sent two blokes to catch him; it was like something out of *Monty Python*. We got him back, checked his dressings, and obviously because of his burst of adrenalin he turned and said, 'Can I have some more omnopon [morphine]?'

'No – no, you can't, you've used all yours up,' I told him.

Private Bob Morgan, Patrols Platoon 2 Para

I was with Kev Mortimer [Pte, Patrols Platoon]. He saw the Pucaras before me and just quietly and calmly said, 'Bob, we're gonna die,' and with that he hit the deck and pulled me on top of him into this Argy trench. For years I thought Kev pulled me on top of him to save himself, but I now know why he did it. He did it to save me, not himself, because I was so stunned, shocked, I wasn't moving, and he just had to get me down. He saved me rather than saved himself. I know that was a bit cheap of me saying that, but at the time you just think different.

Corporal Tom Harley MM, section commander, 10 Platoon D Company 2 Para

We were all laying on this track waiting for whatever's gonna happen next. There were a few mortar rounds landing, but not a great deal, and then this napalm mixture gets dropped by a Pucara that shot us up on his first pass. Yeah, he came around again and dropped napalm!

Corporal Ken Raynor, patrol commander Recce Platoon 2 Para

None of us had comms and it was all a little confusing. It was at this point we found out there had been several casualties on the route, including Jock, who we left on the track about 700 metres away. Paul and I decided to grab this wheelbarrow and we ran back until we met some of the casualties. We put the first in the barrow and proceeded to run back to the tin shed, all the time under a lot of fire from many directions. It was on our third run with the third casualty when the Pucara flew in and dropped the napalm on the track we were running along.

I can even remember the large, grey cylindrical bombs being released from the plane; when they impacted with the ground they both exploded, and the explosion burnt the oxygen out of the air for a few seconds. We put the casualty back in the barrow and carried on, and we did several casualty runs up and down that track. By the time we had finished, the tin shed was full of casualties and we had several lined up outside on the concrete; unfortunately we also had several dead, some our own guys and quite a few enemy, and in addition to this we had about thirty-plus prisoners of war all huddled together about 20 metres from the shed.

Once we had carried out a bit of reorganisation, we were about to put a brew on when over the top of the hill from our south appeared a small jet fighter firing a machine gun. Everyone in our area immediately opened fire, the aircraft was hit, and as the plane banked around back towards the south, the pilot baled out. A few of the guys rushed over to where he landed, and he then became a prisoner of war. He was brought back to the area of the shed and was searched; I removed his chrome-plated Colt .45 that I kept until endex [end of the exercise], but no one knows how he lost his Rolex. He spoke perfect English, but was clearly upset about being shot down.

Back to putting the brew on, Syd and I decided it was time to share a Pot Noodle. The water had just boiled and Syd was holding the plastic cup whilst I poured water into it until it reached the mark. You could start to smell the chow mein wafting around the bridge area, and the look on the prisoners' faces was one of sorrow. It was at this stage that another large explosion went off, this time from another enemy artillery shell. Syd went down like a sack of potatoes and received shrapnel to his back, but my reactions were absolutely perfect, as I caught the Pot Noodle in mid-air before it hit the ground, never spilling a drop. This meal now belonged to me – Syd no longer needed it.

Private Mark Sleap, Patrols Platoon 2 Para

We all shot up at this Pucara and amazingly the pilot parachuted out and drifted into our position. I remember seeing this pilot under the canopy and I fired off a few rounds; a few of us did, but it was wrong, especially us being Paras and all that. I still get nightmares about doing that.

Lance Corporal 'Radar', Defence Platoon 2 Para

I'm leaning over talking to the medic and covering this injured lad, trying to keep him calm as the medic worked on him. I mean this lad, I can't recall who it was, but he was still screaming his brains out, and that's when I saw the Pucara come in and watched in horror as a canister came flying off. 'Get down!' I screamed. The place erupted. Fucking napalm, the Argy bastards! It was dropped on what looked like our blokes, but I later found out it was near our blokes and a load of prisoners, which was lucky. The place erupted. I was surprised anyone came out of that one. Then I saw this parachute come slowly floating down in the middle of the fucking battle; it was surreal, it was madness. Then every swinging dick started firing at him.

Private John Bolland, Recce Platoon 2 Para

I'm in the dairy and still getting mortared, because I could see this light bulb hanging on a long piece of flex swinging every time a bomb landed; I knew that, at least, as I drifted in and out of consciousness. Then Sergeant Major Baz Greenhalgh and Dick Morell [Pte, Recce Platoon] came and got me out of there on another piece of wriggly tin to move me away.

I found out later that all the wounded were trying to get out of the dairy too, and I didn't know it at the time, but the Pucaras had come and strafed up our lads and were coming around for a second run, and it looked like they were using the dairy as their lining-up point. Anyway, I was being dragged away when the boys had to drop me, and I was lying there in the middle of the battle on a piece of wriggly tin.

I didn't know why they'd dropped me and I was fucking bleeding out. I've got field dressings on, and I'm lying on my side watching this cigar-shaped thing tumbling down, heading towards me, and I'm thinking, they're gonna napalm me, I'm gonna cook here. Then all the air was sucked out around me.

After that I got dragged into a hollow next to Smudge [Private Dave Smith, Recce Platoon], who'd got it in the stomach. The lads had put Smudge in this wheelbarrow, and fuck knows where that came from, and we were both bleeding out as you do. He was screaming all the time and the next thing I know, this hand comes from the wheelbarrow and grabs mine. I think, this boy is on the point of death. I've seen this shit [blood] dripping through the bottom of the wheelbarrow. He held my hand just like the other chap did in the dairy.

Private Ian Winnard. 4 Platoon B Company 2 Para

It was late in the day by now and we'd got pinned down by some Argies around the airfield, and our ammo was running low. Some of us kept hearing a strange noise coming from behind us, so we turned around to see what the fuck it was, then realised it was Argy mortars dropping but not exploding, just going, plop, plop, plop, as they bedded deep into the soft peat. We were lucky, I mean really lucky. We were lucky all throughout the war, then I was ordered to go back and pick up an ammo resup from Pete Richens, Sergeant Major, B Company, so I was just taking off when someone screamed, 'Enemy aircraft!'

I looked up and saw this Pucara turboprop ground–attack aircraft coming towards us, so I fired a couple rounds off at it then I realised it weren't actually coming towards us to attack, but was crashing towards us. There was me, Graham Eve, Spike Redwood, and Jim Bush, and the next thing we thought was, *we're all dead*. I think the pilot had baled out and as it was coming in really close, it started to do a cartwheel across the ground. It came right above us and I heard later that one of the wing tips clipped one of our guys' webbing and smock, possibly Kev D. It smashed up in front of us, and we all got covered in smoke and it felt like it was raining; it was, but it was aviation fuel.

Funny thing was it didn't explode, it hit the ground, sprayed fuel and dirt everywhere, then came to rest with crump in a cloud of smoke. Then we heard blokes screaming out, 'Medics, medics, medics!' When the shit cleared, we all just looked at each other, flabbergasted in amazement. It had crashed literally only a few feet from us and not one of us got hit. Jim Bush was so far up my arse it was frightening.

Lance Corporal Graham Eve, 4 Platoon B Company 2 Para

I was laid flat down praying, because all of a sudden I could see this Pucara come into view, very, very low and looking like it was going to crash right on our position. And it did crash. It crashed only metres away. It was something to see, slow motion, and it was like, fuck! And never mind the guys forward of me. Kev D had two belts of ammunition ripped out of his hand from the slipstream or aftershock, he was that close to it.

I mean, it was unbelievable, stuff that if you wrote it, people wouldn't believe it; they'd say you were a fucking Walt [Walter Mitty], a bullshitter, but it did happen. When Kev staggered over to me, he was smelling of and covered in avgas, and I could see one of his epaulets had also ripped too, probably by some flying wreckage; but he was okay, and like I said, he's a hard man is Kev. It didn't explode right away, but it did once the lads were clear.

As soon as darkness came, the artillery stopped and the firing stopped. It was like someone had hit a switch and had all gone to bed. We lay there for a while and then word came down to get back to the company, so we got up and we just walked back and rejoined the rest of the company. It happened literally like that. I felt a bit of joy, but really I was massively disappointed, because we were in a situation where we'd psyched ourselves up.

We were resigned to the fact that this was it and we were going to do the battalion proud and fight our way out, with all the adrenalin, and the fact we were so prepared for it; and then all of a sudden, the Argies just stopped firing. From thinking, I'm probably dying in battle, to walking away and absolutely nothing happening, was surreal. And, I remember, that night was the coldest night of my life, even though we all got in the spooning position and cuddled up to the bloke in front; that's how we got through that night.

Lance Corporal Pete 'Stubbo' Stubbs, MT Platoon 2 Para, attached to the Red Devils Parachute Display Team

I got a bluey [armed forces airmail, BFPO (British Forces Post Office), a freepost letter coloured blue] and it was just addressed: 'To the MT'. No names on it, so I opened it, and there were three white feathers in it, and I thought, *what a complete shit, who the fuck would send this?* I took it to mean a joke and I thought it was just the guys having a laugh. But when you flew back into Brize [RAF Brize Norton], I knew you were all coming back here and I was dreading it, because you'd all been to war and I had not. I never found out who sent the bluey, but I had a sneaky suspicion it was one of the pads [wives]!

Captain John Greenhalgh DFC, Scout Flight 656 Squadron Army Air Corps

One time earlier on in the battle during the daylight, RSM 2 Para Mal Simpson said to me, as I flew in to pick up more casualties and was bringing in even more 7.62 link ammunition, 'For fuck's sake don't bring any more link ammunition, bring us some food.'

Corporal 'Ginge' Dawes, clothing storeman, 2 Para

The light was just beginning to turn and I was desperately after a helicopter to get down to 3 Commando Brigade, Blue Beach, as the battalion was running out of rations. A chopper crew, Fleet Air Arm, had just landed with a water ration, so I pleaded, we need food rations, 2 Para are almost out. And the pilot says, 'Hop on, let's go find some.'

We flew down to Blue Beach, which was a mass of stores activity, as Blue Beach was where all the rations were bundled up ready to send out to the units. There was this Marine standing on a cargo net sling pallet, full of ration boxes, holding up a large piece of cardboard with a grid reference on it, which was the procedure back then. This Marine was thinking my helicopter was the one he was waiting for, but it wasn't, as we hadn't pre-ordered any rations; time just hadn't allowed. So this Marine gave my pilot the thumbs up, then our crewman skilfully marshalled the pilot just above the Marine, who discharged any chopper static with a big hook on a long pole, secured the cargo net full of rations, and off we went in a flash.

The crewman then turned to me and said, 'Here's your rations.' I smiled and thanked him very much. The rations were destined for some Royal Marine unit, but the Paras had them now! Those Fleet Air Arm boys are the best.

Private Bob Morgan, Patrols Platoon 2 Para

We had twenty or so prisoners all cowering down on the ground, because the battle was still raging, but me and Kev Mortimer were ordered to take these prisoners back up to Darwin Hill along with some of our walking wounded. Why the fuck us? I mean, it was fucking lunacy in open sight of the enemy.

When we eventually got them back up the hill, we put them in a ditch and waited for the RSM to take them off us. It was getting dark and the RSM still hadn't turned up and these Argies were looking a bit dodgy, so me and Kev slipped off our safety catches on our LMGs, just in case they made a rush on us. And I tell you what, I spoke to shrinks about this incident, and one of them said, 'You were too scared to shoot them.' Well, I wasn't! I was scared, but it was my discipline in not shooting them! Of course, if they had rushed me and Kev, we would have both opened up. Anyway, the RSM came with his prisoner detail and they took them off us. I still have very bad dreams about that incident.

Nigel Ely: I'm often drawn back to the movie *Breaker Morant* and that famous line when the prosecuting lawyer in a court-martial case asked, 'And what rule did you shoot them under?'

The defendant, Lieutenant Harry 'Breaker' Morant, played by the late great Edward Woodward, replied, 'We caught them and we shot them under rule three-o-three.'[26]

The images, the faces of those twenty or so prisoners all cowering under the heavy weight of fire, are etched so firmly in my mind, they quite often flash past me. The blokes did such a professional job at keeping them at bay in such violent circumstances, and one could have made a strong case for shooting the Argy officer, who still had hold of his sidearm at the time I looked, and seemed to be up for a fight.

When I hear of troops shooting prisoners, I can have some sympathy, but of course I do not condone it; some soldiers react differently.

Private Dave 'Charlie' Brown, HQ C (Bruneval) Company 2 Para

Still pinned down on the forward slope. Eventually, after a few hours with Mark, I had to leave him where he fell and move back up the slope and out of danger. I took Mark's signal codes on me too.

It was starting to turn dark when I made it back over the top and I found Roger sitting alone in the burning gorse. Nearby were Tommy and Stevie, who were still trying to give fire support to

---

26 At that date, during the Second Boer War of 1899–1902, the British Army's standard service rifle was the .303-inch Lee-Enfield.

C Company, and I looked at him and realised he was still carrying that wound, although he didn't show it. His eyes looked bloodshot and tired, like almost in tears.

He said, 'Charlie, we've lost the company, I've lost my company,' and even at this stage of the battle no one knew where the hell C Company was, because we had lost all comms to them. All we could see and hear was the dying embers of the fierce battle around the schoolhouse.

Major Chris Keeble came by for the second time and said, 'Go get patched up, Roger,' then Keeble sent a re-org signal to those who could make it, to get back up the slope. That's when I burnt all of Mark's signal codes. Then slowly a couple of C Company patrols came stumbling up the slope, then a couple more, then more and more arrived, until we had about thirty of the blokes back. You should have seen Roger's face, he even afforded a bit of a smile as he realised a lot of his men were still alive.

LAST LIGHT

Private Steve Taylor, 3 Platoon A Company 2 Para

Just before last light, we were told to stand by for a Harrier bombing run, so when it flew over and the bombs were gone, we saw it had completely missed the target of Goose Green. We all shouted, 'You've missed the target, you wankers!', but no one told us Toms that it was a firepower demonstration sending a message to the Argies, this is what we can do.

Corporal Ken Raynor, patrol commander Recce Platoon 2 Para

We were all exhausted, virtually out of ammunition, wet and cold; with the added effects of the adrenalin running out, and the overriding rumour that a counterattack was probably on the way. So we carried out a redistribution of ammo, as we all expected to continue the fight in the morning.

Captain John Greenhalgh DFC, Scout Flight 656 Squadron Army Air Corps

It was dark when I heard about another B Company casualty being found, but there was disagreement in the Brigade Air Squadron as to who would retrieve him. So I said, 'Right, I'm off,' and managed to locate and pick up the casualty in pitch-black darkness (this was before night vision goggles). B Company's 2IC, Captain John Young, had been missing on the battlefield for several hours, having been hit by a mortar round, and Rory Waggon (the other doctor) thought he would never survive his extensive injuries. As we transited back north with the casualty in the dark, we flew into heavy rain and then immediately into thick cloud at 200 feet above the ground; in mountainous terrain, that is criminal, because you can't see in front of you.

So I did an emergency climb on instruments up the hillside, the radar altimeter reading 30 feet, 50 feet, 70 feet, and went above the mountain top and also the freezing level, which is why the aircraft iced up. We then did our own procedural let down again using the radar altimeter, as there was no external radar, and let back down south towards Darwin, because that's the last place we knew where we could see the ground, and when we broke cloud in the dark, my log book shows we spent six minutes in cloud.

I turned around again and went back north across the mountain, but we got down very, very low, put the landing light on and all the other lights, because I thought, *fuck it, we've got to be able to see.* We hover taxied up through the rain and low cloud up the hillside over Sussex Mountains and down the other

Right: Major Chris Keeble (*left*) with RSM Mal
Simpson in front of a captured Argentine field
howitzer after the campaign. Major Keeble, 2
Para's 2IC, took over command of the battalion
when H Jones was killed, and engineered the
Argentine surrender at Goose Green.

Above: Argentine helmets abandoned on the battlefield of Goose Green.

Left: A Scout helicopter evacuating wounded Argentine POWs at Camilla Creek House.

(Author's collection)

Right: A wrecked Argentine Pucara ground-attack aircraft at Goose Green.

(© Airborne Assault museum archives)

Left: Goose Green playground with a multi-barrelled rocket launcher mounted on the children's slide; it was one of these rockets that wounded Private Bolland.

(Author's collection)

Above: A member of 2 Para with a captured Argentine 20mm anti-aircraft cannon at Goose Green, 29 May 1982. *(© Airborne Assault museum archives)*

Left: The author, Private Nigel 'Spud' Ely, C (Bruneval) Company 2 Para, with his SLR immediately after the battle; on his left hip is an old-fashioned sword bayonet taken from a dead Argentine. *(Author's collection)*

Below: The 1000-metre stare – the author after the action at Goose Green ended.

(Author's collection)

Above: The first interment at Ajax Bay of 2 Para Group's dead from Darwin and Goose Green.

(© Airborne Assault museum archives)

Right: The memorial to 2 Para Group's dead at Goose Green, erected by the islanders, with the settlement in the background. Author's photograph taken in December 2018.

(Author's collection)

Above: The community centre at Goose Green, where the hostages were held. Photographed in 2017, but very little changed since 1982.

(Author's collection)

Left: Lance Corporal Jimmy Goodall, 2 Para, with baby Matthew McMullen, Goose Green 29 May. The youngest hostage was kept safe under the floorboards of the community centre.

(Author's collection)

Right: Jimmy Goodall and Matthew McMullen reunited in the Falklands many years later. *(Author's collection)*

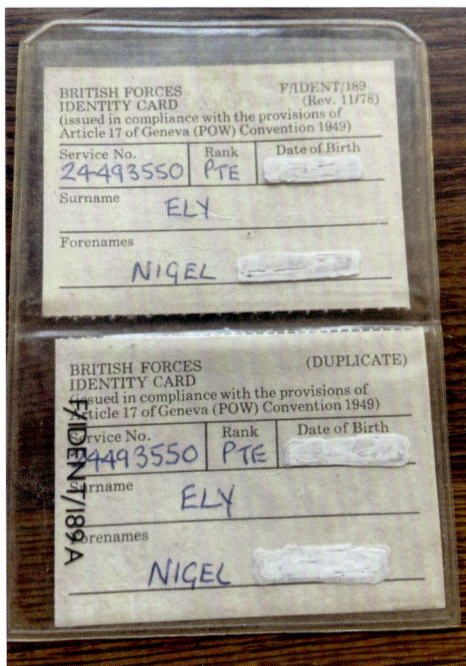

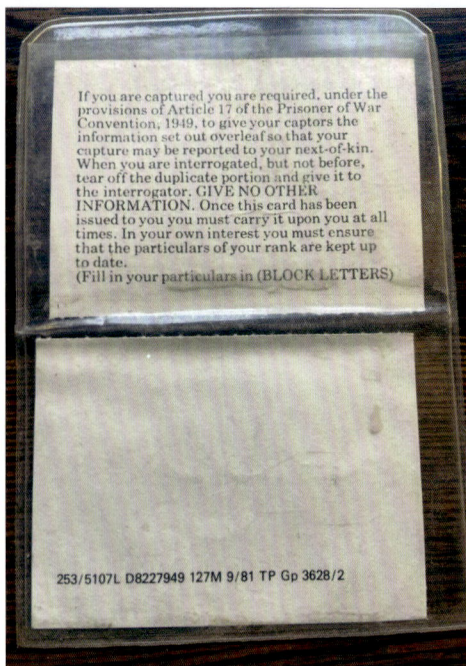

Above: The author's ID card for use in the event of capture, issued to all British servicemen in the Falklands campaign.

(Author's collection)

Right: Return to Goose Green – the author at the settlement in 2001.

(Author's collection)

Above: 'Bomb Alley' – San Carlos Water seen from Sussex Mountains in more peaceful times, December 2017. *(Author's collection)*

Below: Blue Beach, where 2 Para landed on 21 May 1982, photographed in December 2017. *(Author's collection)*

Right: 2 Para's view of Sussex Mountains from the battalion's landing point at Blue Beach.

(Author's collection)

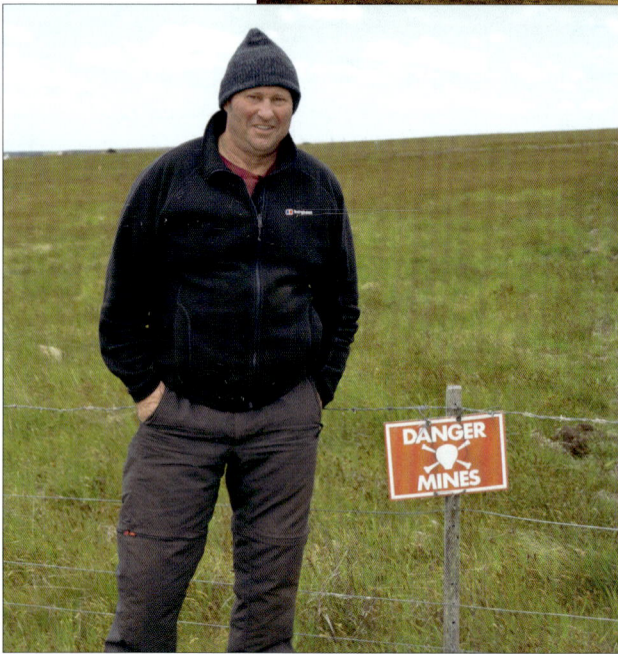

Left: The author outside one of the minefields at Goose Green, December 2017; the mines were finally lifted in 2018.

(Author's collection)

Right: C Company's view of Goose Green from Darwin Hill, before they assaulted down the slope, showing just how exposed the attacking Paras were. *(Author's collection)*

side, using the landing light. Then we flew towards the hospital at Ajax Bay, nearly flying into the sea, but Rich Walker saved us on that occasion.

We were having difficulty staying awake, because we were so knackered, and Peter Cameron, my Royal Marine boss [Major Peter Cameron MC, RM], was up because he was very worried about me, as everyone else had said, 'We're not going, we're too fucking tired.' By the time I got to the far side of Sussex Mountains, I called Zero, stating where I thought my rough location was: 'North side of feature, casualty on board. We are lost.'

We had just broken night IMC [instrument meteorological conditions – flying by instruments] and we were running out of fuel, plus it was very windy and turbulent. It was Peter Cameron who immediately called 'weapons tight' on the Royal Navy. The Royal Navy were about to shoot me down, thinking I was an Argentinian aircraft attacking the ships in San Carlos Water. Peter Cameron saved my life – saved all our lives that night.

Later, me and Rich Walker flew in the dark up to the back of the ridge at Darwin Hill, dropping off more supplies. There were still all sorts of things going on and I didn't want to come over the top of the ridge and get shot at in the dark, so I sat at the back of the ridge knowing we had spare capacity to help, but without night vision goggles it would be difficult to fly low level at night so close to the enemy.

We knew there were more wounded and I was desperate to help, having just come back from dropping John Young off at Ajax Bay. But it was pitch black and the sky was full of tracer. It would have been suicidal, but a lull in the firing came, so I tried to help, along with Rich Walker in another Scout.

I got this desperate radio call for casualty evacuation from a C Company 2 Para call sign, so I said, 'Send grid?'

He came back with, 'We don't know where we are.'

It was pitch black, after all! It was a Tom on the radio, I could tell that, so I took off and I said, 'Can you hear us?'

'Roger,' he confirmed.

'Give us directions,' I replied. So we set off and I completely forgot Rich was behind me, because we were working no lights. We came forward and the radio op says, 'Keep coming, come left, come right, come left.'

'You've gone past, you've gone past us!' said the agitated radio op, so I had a near mad panic, because we were flying over Argentinian positions or close to.

'Don't go home, Delta November,' he pleaded, 'we've got casualties here.' He sounded very distressed and because they were C Company, they had comms back to the Brigade net as well as us.

Still the Para talked me in, 'Come left, go right. You've gone past us again!' The voice was harsh now.

I pedal turned the aircraft and started turning and, all of a sudden, I was looking at Rich's Scout windscreen head on, and I thought, *oh God!* So, in these circumstances everyone goes right, and I went right and he went right and I thought our blades would hit. Then Rich said on the radio, 'You fucking bastard, tell me if you're going to turn around!' I had forgotten he was even behind me, because he'd kept quiet and we were all very tired, not having slept.

Then Gammo was standing on the skids as we hover taxied forward, and out of the darkness and despair came a big group of men. I was worried he was seeing Argentinians, but then I recognised the Para helmets, so we landed in and amongst them and kicked off all the remaining ammo.

Once the ammo was out, the Paras loaded a shitload of casualties into the external stretcher pods and inside too, so much so, we couldn't get off the ground. Arms and legs everywhere. We were too heavy to take off. The aircraft would not climb. So, you guys all got a grip of the skids and lifted and heaved the aircraft up, until

I managed to get some lift and I transited away forward. Then the aircraft started sinking and I hit the ground in the dark, and I was full power and more. I actually smacked the ground and bumped along with all the casualties in the back.

Later after the battle, I went back to look at the ground and I spotted fence lines near the schoolhouse, and can you imagine if I had caught a fence with one of the skids? The aircraft would have rolled and everybody would have been killed. Casualties, me and Gammo, everyone would have been a goner. So, we were very, very lucky.

We took the Para casualties back to Ajax Bay and I also found out it was Lance Corporal Paul 'Geordie' Grundy, Recce Platoon [RIP] I was talking to over the radio and it was your camera flash I came in on, and just about landed without the rotors hitting the bank.

Private Mark Sleap, Patrols Platoon 2 Para

When that casevac Scout came in, we were behind this little hillock and then someone fired one of those mini flares, a red one, and you know, what with all the rounds still being fired off it was a really pathetic attempt, especially when we were using red tracer too!

Private John Bolland, Recce Platoon 2 Para

I think it was dark when a chopper came in and I was put in this pod, which was bolted to one of the skids. I can remember it so vividly, on top of this pod was written: *THIS IS NOT A COFFIN.* So, I'm stripped fuckin' naked, all my kit's been robbed, my weapons and personal kit, and some cunt's taken me baccy – I've got fuck all. Then the lid was closed and someone screwed down the butterfly clips.

I was never claustrophobic in my life until that time. A wee Perspex window to look through was all I had, with *THIS IS NOT A COFFIN* staring me in the face!

Lance Corporal Bill 'Basha' Bentley MM, Combat Medical Team 2 Para

I was exhausted and moved into the gorse for a little cover and a brew. Doc Hughes still teases me today, because he claims that my making the brew started the gorse burning. I had not even finished the brew when Doc said, 'A helicopter is on its way, there are more casualties to pick up.' Being the only one there, as the other medics were working flat out while I was having a well-earned brew, I had to say yes. Doc gave me a scrap of paper with a grid reference on it, 'Give that to the pilot and go with them.'

The helicopter landed, I hopped in and gave the scrap of paper to the pilot, who turned to me and said it was wrong. 'Check it with HQ,' I replied, which he did. He looked at the co-pilot, then at me, and they tightened their seat belts. We're going into Goose Green!

It was almost dark as we flew over the hill, and scouring the land for signs of our lads, I suddenly realised we were under accurate and effective enemy fire, which was ripping through the cabin. Neither the pilot nor the co-pilot seemed to have been aware that we were 'taking in fire', so I got up, hit one of them on the back, and pointed towards the gun flashes. It was as if we had been hit by a tornado, the helicopter lurched to the left then right, dived then climbed, followed by a crazy zig-zag course back over the hill.

By now we were in total darkness and with no board lights whatsoever. It seemed like ages to me, scouring back and forth, and staring into the darkness, then all of a sudden there were our lads guiding us in on what seemed like a pinpoint torch light. Everything went very quickly triage, ha! The wounded were piled by their mates into the helicopter, three across the back seat (which,

I think, was designed for two), and one in each of the two pods on the outside.

The pilot wanted to take off, but Smudge Smith, who had been 'belly shot', was sitting in a pinched wheelbarrow and was squealing like a stuck pig. I don't know if the pilot could hear him or how he became aware of the situation, it was completely dark. Then the pilot on the left-hand side of the helicopter got out and gave up his seat for Smith. The said pilot then straddled the pod on the outside and gave the other pilot the sign to take off, but it became immediately obvious that the helicopter was way overloaded and it just would not fly!

Realising the problem, at first several of us, then every available man started to lift the helicopter. *Heave ho, heave ho!* The helicopter at full revs, burning fuel, shuddered and shuddered. *Heave ho, heave ho!* Then slowly she started to carry her own weight . . . and ever so slowly, she started to climb, up, up and away.

The idea had been that I should fly in, pick up a couple of guys with a few scratches, and fly home with them. Thanks, Doc! I was now with the platoon that had attacked the schoolhouse. Three of their dead were back down the hill, including their officer. If I'm not mistaken, six wounded were evacuated in the helicopter. I've never spoken to anybody about these events since they happened, it's not exactly a coffee-time chatting subject. Anyway, I'm standing there with what was probably the ugliest bunch of thugs on the planet at that time [Recce and Patrols Platoons, C (Bruneval) Company, 2 Para].

I now became aware that there were more injured to be taken care of and we needed to get the hell out of there as quickly as possible. There were also, I'm guessing, about a dozen prisoners of war. The prisoners were politely requested, at gunpoint, to carry our remaining wounded, and a stretcher appeared from God knows where, so we set off, back up over the hill to our own lines.

I can't really remember much of the march, how long it took or how far it was. I was knackered, but I do have a memory of what looked like a medieval funeral procession, a stretcher being carried at the shoulder by the enemy prisoners, who were being escorted by soldiers, some with bloody bandages and who were at times using their weapons as walking sticks. I don't know who was in charge of this platoon at this stage, I could easily look it up but I have never read a single book about what happened in the Falklands; the books are on my bookshelf, but I doubt that any could ever be a scratch on my own experiences! Anyway, bless you, whoever you were, for your presence of mind at a time when I was no longer able.

Ahead of us was the crest of the hill, an orange glow against the clouds from the fires, through the smoke the eerie silhouettes of those in front of me, then we were back. I guess somebody must have guided me like a lamb, because I have no recollection of how I got back to the other medics. I was woken up; even the cold had not prevented me from sleeping this time. I don't know how long I had been asleep, the devil could have abused my body and I would not have felt a thing, perhaps he did. Somebody was shaking me, telling me it was my turn to guard the prisoners.

I recall being with Gibbo, one side of us scalding hot, the other numb, freezing cold, standing in the burning embers of the gorse. The prisoners loosely assembled in groups, also trying not to freeze to death. We became aware of one prisoner who was much too close to the fire, his comrades had moved away from him. We went to have a closer look and saw that he was bandaged up and the bandages had started to burn.

We needed to move him away from the fire to see what we could do for him, so Gibbo took his feet, and I, his arms. As we increased the pull to lift him, one of his arms just came off at the shoulder socket; he appeared to be cooked through! We dragged his body as best we could off to the side, where there was a ditch, and we placed him in it. It seemed ironic from 'hell fire' into a freezing cold, wet ditch. Somebody came to relieve us and this time I was awake enough to find a spot to sleep.

Corporal Tom Harley MM, section commander, 10 Platoon D Company 2 Para

Come last light, D Company took over some Argy trenches by the airfield and some of us tried to dig shell scrapes in with our eating spoons, because we never had our bergens and no shovels or anything like that. Actually, myself and Wally found a big Argy scrim net and used that and a dead cow, but it wasn't rotting, so we wrapped ourselves in this scrim net and couched up right next to the dead cow. The lads jacked with the spoons because the shell-scrapes were filling up with water, so they had to lay on the ground trying to get some sort of shut-eye.

Private Greg Cox, light machine gunner, Patrols Platoon 2 Para

It wasn't until later that evening that I heard what had happened to Tony and Chopsy. We withdrew to the gorse line back up at Darwin Hill and I went across to the RAP, sorted through the various items of discarded kit and retrieved some ammo, some chocolate bars and Tony's beret. I kept the ammo, but no one wanted to share the chocolate when they heard where it came from. Weeks later, I returned Tony's beret to him when I visited him back in England, having carried it with me throughout the remainder of the conflict. He was shocked, yet so pleased I'd kept it safe.

Private David Minnock, GPMG gunner, 12 Platoon D Company 2 Para

I never did give covering fire to C Company for their attack on the schoolhouse. All I remember is, it was bloody cold that night, and

I'll tell yer how bad it were. I've never experienced hypothermia until that night, and you know, I thought, *if I go to sleep now, I'm not going to wake up in the morning.* We were laid against this small water tower thing; we had a gun position there where the Argies had had one a couple of hours earlier, but they'd all been killed, so we moved their shit out the way and set ours up.

It wasn't my time for stag, but I crawled to the bloke who was on guard and I says to him, 'I'll take over.'

'You're not due on for four hours!' he said, thinking what I said was a joke.

'I can't sleep and I've survived this far, and I'm gonna die if I fall asleep, so fuck off.'

Private Steve Taylor, 3 Platoon A Company 2 Para

As night time came in, it was surreal: burning gorse, silhouettes of the blokes walking about, whispering names of our mates and confirming who had been killed and who was missing. It was then I heard Sergeant Beatty had been fragged in the shins and his wounds had started going manky. He tried to hide it, as he wanted to stay with the platoon. He had kept it quiet until the medics spotted him, so he was casevaced out and he never came back.

Private Mark Sleap, Patrols Platoon 2 Para

We were out of ammo, so we had to de-link any Argy 7.62 we came across; prepared and waited for a counterattack to come at first light. If the Argies had been using 5.56, we would have been well fucked.

18

THE SURRENDER

Victory begets victory. It's almost impossible to overstate the victory at Goose Green, and we never lost our humanity.

Major Chris Keeble, acting commanding officer, 2 Para

After the tragic death of Colonel H, I assumed command and directed the main effort of the battalion assault onto the right flank. Through the brilliant collaboration between B, D, and Support Companies, we broke through the Argentine defence, outflanked their key terrain of Darwin Hill (captured by A Company), and encircled Goose Green, bravely supported by C (Patrol) Company.

From my command post on top of Darwin Hill, co-located with the firebase of Support Company, I called in close air support from three Harriers, who were tasked to drop cluster bombs close to the settlement, to destabilise the Argentine defence and further weaken their will to fight.

By the end of the day, 2 Para was exhausted, short of ammunition and suffering from the shock of combat. After last light, I returned to the RAP and A Company on the reverse slope of Darwin Hill, with the prospect of facing a counterattack, and the added burden of not having achieved the battalion's mission of capturing the Argentine garrison in Goose Green; an essential task for the next day.

The wind chill had dropped to minus ten degrees, one in six of the battalion was either killed or wounded, the cohesion of our assault was fractured and disbursed, ammunition was almost depleted (with no mortar and artillery ammunition), the radio batteries used up, and most combat soldiers were cold, hungry, and exhausted. I also realised that to secure the mission it would require a bitter house-to-house battle, which would put at risk the 125 settlers known to be inside Goose Green.

I knelt in the gorse line and prayed a 'prayer of abandonment to God'; 'Thy will be done'. In a moment, I was crystal clear about what was needed. I would have to change the original battalion's mission ordered by 3 Commando Brigade, to one of 'securing the safety of the settlers' and concluded that offering the enemy the opportunity to negotiate was a better moral choice than continuing the violence.

To that end I used the settlers' CB radio network to advise the Settlement Manager of my intentions, acquired the reinforcement of a Royal Marine company and ammunition resupply, and released two Argentine prisoners with an ultimatum (see below) offering the Argentine garrison the opportunity to surrender. I also arranged an on-call artillery firepower demonstration on some waste ground, should my negotiation appeal be unconvincing.

We met the Argentine army, navy, and air force officers in a small hut on the Goose Green grass airstrip, who eventually accepted my offer and agreed to surrender all their forces. Allowing them to concede with dignity and without the media filming their humiliation, they became our responsibility to care for them as POWs.

The Argentine garrison formed up in hollow squares, said their prayers and sang their patriotic songs, and laid down their weapons.

It was over. We entered Goose Green and freed all the settlers. 2 Para had won an outstanding victory.

During 2 Para's repair and regrouping at Goose Green and Darwin, General Moore[27] visited the battalion to hear first-hand of our victory. I explained we had shattered the enemy's will, and that the best course of action would be to negotiate with the Argentine command in Stanley, for the surrender of all forces on the islands. He was unable to get agreement from the UK and so the fighting was to continue.

2 Para was 'chopped' to 5 Infantry Brigade, and its commander, Brigadier Wilson (Brigadier Sir [Mathew John] Anthony Wilson, Bt, OBE MC, 1935–2019), ordered a line of advance to Fitzroy and Bluff Cove. As an alternative, we offered him a high-speed 'coup de main' operation, which he endorsed. A Company, having discovered the settlers' single landline linking the settlements, B Company undertook an armed recce to Swan Inlet to ring both settlements to gather the enemy's intelligence. The Argentine forces had vacated both locations. I gave out rapid battalion orders to execute a two- sortie Chinook lift, accompanied by two armed Scout helicopters, to secure the two objectives, which we achieved.

I then handed over my temporary command to the newly arrived CO, Lieutenant Colonel Chaundler.

The Surrender Instrument at the Battle of Goose Green

1. That you surrender your force to us by leaving the township, forming up in a military manner, removing your helmets and laying down your weapons. You will give prior notice of this intention by returning the POWs under the White Flag with him, briefed to the formalities, no later than 08.30 hours local time.

---

27 Major General Jeremy Moore RM (KCB, OBE, MC and Bar, 1928–2007), Commander Land Forces in the Falklands campaign; he arrived on 30 May, the day after the Argentine surrender at Goose Green.

2. You refuse in the first case to surrender and take the inevitable consequences. You will give prior notice of this intention by returning the POW without his White Flag, although his neutrality will be respected, no later than 08.30 local time.

3. In any event, and in accordance with the terms of the Geneva Conventions and the laws of war, you will be held responsible for the fate of any civilians in Goose Green and we, in accordance with the laws, do give you prior notice of our intentions to bombard Goose Green.

Chris Keeble
Acting Commanding Officer,
Second Battalion, The Parachute Regiment.
28 May 1982

Corporal Douglas McCready, 1 Section commander, Machine Gun Platoon, 2 Para

Along with OC Support Company, 2 Para and his interpreter, I was literally the first into Goose Green. When the Argies surrendered, we were all up at the gorse line and the next morning before first light we moved forward into the positions that we had some hours earlier, which were the two trenches on the gorse side of the estuary, near the schoolhouse and the dairy in a fucking open field.

When the surrender ceremony was taking place, the Machine Guns were ordered forward into Goose Green along the track, and I went in with my section leading, with the rest of the Machine Guns and Support Company HQ behind. Then the Argies came out, and there were hundreds and hundreds of them, and we passed each other on the track. We were so close I could touch them; it was very weird, very disturbing! They had eyes like a bulldog's bollocks.

To be perfectly honest, we were all fucking terrified, because we were now all well aware of the white flag incident, when the Argies pulled out their guns on our guys and shot them all dead! So, we still had that fucking with our minds, and I said to the guys, because we were ordered to make safe at this stage, 'Just fucking waste 'em if anything happens.' So, we're still tabbing towards Goose Green along the track, and when we got to the open space between the houses where the community centre was, all the civilians came running out. It was their Liberation Day. Three weeks cooped up like caged animals.

Lance Corporal Bill 'Basha' Bentley MM, Combat Medical Team 2 Para

The enemy came marching out, hundreds and hundreds of them, more than a thousand! They gave up their weapons and so the fighting was over. As soon as we could, we rushed down the hill to watch the continuing surrender. While the fighting soldiers of 2 Para still had their stags to do, for them the fighting was over, for now. We medics under Doc Hughes set up something that more resembled a regimental aid post than a handful of medics with rucksacks.

This was yet another long day for us, as quite a few lads who had been only slightly wounded came forward for treatment. One sergeant had a wound on his leg from shrapnel, which he had received during the first contact, but only came forward for treatment after his platoon were dug-in and ready to fend off any possible counterattack, almost three days later!

Lance Corporal Jimmy Goodall, Assault Engineers 2 Para

After the surrender, I was one of the first into Goose Green and I saw this young lady standing outside with a tiny baby, who I know now as Matthew McMullen. His mother had been hiding him under the floorboards of the community centre, as that's where the Argies put all the civilians. Matthew was about four months old. He was the youngest Argy prisoner. Of course, after the battle you see all the devastation, with bodies everywhere and bits of bodies too, and you think to yourself, *what the fuck is this all about?*

So, the young lady hands me this baby! Now, I'm stinking, and I'm in rag order, I haven't had a wash for two weeks. One of the lads took a photo and I looked at this baby and then things fell into place; I understood what I was doing there, what it was all about – freedom! And after that I was absolutely fine. Matthew still lives in the Falkland Islands and owns the farm overlooking Blue Beach, the beach where we, 2 Para, landed.

When a group of us veterans went back to the islands years later, Mal Simpson passed an order that I had to recreate that photograph of me holding baby Matthew, and I can tell you, it's the only order of Mal Simpson's I've ever refused, because I couldn't carry it out; I couldn't lift Matthew, he's huge now, ha-ha.

Sergeant John 'Taff' Meredith DCM, 12 Platoon D Company 2 Para

I wasn't keen on the surrender, I'd have rather shot 'em all up and I think we could have done it at first light, we could have annihilated then quite easily, because we now had all those extra GPMGs, and if you look at where Goose Green is located and laid out, once you've taken the airfield, there's nowhere for the Argies to go apart from the sea. They either surrendered or got shot up.

Anyway, after the surrender we were put into the garages in Goose Green near the airfield, so we had the job of looking after all the weapons the hundreds of Argies had laid down in that field during the surrender, and some of the locals would come up and ask, 'Any chance of a souvenir?'

'Very sorry, you're not allowed,' I'd say.

'But I've got a bottle of rum,' they'd say.

'Uhmm, yes, Okay then, help yourself.' Then another would come up with some beers or a bottle of whisky.

Later, I managed to move my blokes into the plumber's shed, where there was a furnace and peat so you could make a fire and get warm. So, when the blokes came back in from stag or a standing patrol, I'd give each of them a tot before they got their heads down in the warm, first time in a couple of weeks.

One time I was heading back to the plumber's shed, it was just turning dark, and I saw a Navy chopper land in a nearby field then kick out a load of these big bin bags. I wondered what was in them. I ripped open one, and it was BREAD, you know, the big loaves they bake onboard ship. They'd been flown in for the civilians, they weren't for us, but I helped myself to a couple. I went back to the blokes and we had been issued these ten-man ration packs that contained jam, so we all had jam and toast that evening – sheer luxury.

The following day, they started bringing in chocolate and cigarettes – Twix, Mars Bars, Benson & Hedges – so I had to tell them how many smokers and non-smokers I had in the platoon. I had seven non-smokers including me, but actually I had more than that, I had eleven non-smokers but some had decided to take it up; so I had seven bars of chocolate given to me, six Twix and surprisingly, one Yorkie bar, no Mars. So, all the non-smokers are looking at the Yorkie bar because everybody wanted it.

What I did was, I broke it up and gave each one a piece, and one Twix each, and then the next thing there's an argument going on; somebody had eaten somebody else's bit of Yorkie bar and it was SLRs at five paces. I said, 'Come on, lads, it was my Yorkie bar anyway.'

David Norris, general news reporter Daily Mail, *attached 2 Para*

On the day of the surrender, I remember waiting outside Goose Green for quite a long time while the senior Argy officer had to contact Buenos Aires to agree their surrender, then eventually we marched in with the Paras. I went into one of the houses and that's when I saw all the defecation the Argies had done inside this particular settler's house. Then I found out the Argies had shit in every house; it was sickening, but honestly, the Paras went into each house and cleaned all the shit up.

I mean, I couldn't believe it, these lads had just fought a massive battle and won, and now they were on cleaning duties, so that when the people were released from the community centre, they got back into a relatively clean house. They even shit in a baby's cot, yet the toilets were perfectly working flushing toilets; but they did it just to piss us off and get their own back because they lost. It was a terrible state of affairs.

Corporal 'Ginge' Dawes, clothing storeman, 2 Para

When we heard about the surrender, our main focus was getting the guys' kit forward, so we packed under slings full of sleeping bags and other kit. For some reason I ended up laying on top of one of these loads, virtually squashing me, while I was hooking up three cargo nets to a Sea King ready to fly them forward.

We almost had to beg for helicopters up until Goose Green, but really, those Fleet Air Arm guys were tops. Again, they were fantastic.

Captain Paul Farrar, OC Patrols Platoon 2 Para

When we arrived in Goose Green, we were completely knackered, we hadn't slept for at least three nights and hadn't eaten properly for about four, because we had been on the ambush and bouncing around. Of course, the good thing about that was, once we marched into the settlement it was like, 'Hallelujah!' We were back as reserve company. We had the rifle companies out holding the ground and we were just resting up in this bunkhouse complex, which was used for sheep shearers [previously occupied by Pucara pilots]. Two-man rooms, no mattresses, one bath, but still luxury, yet we still hadn't eaten. The rations hadn't quite caught up with us, then Bob Morgan found a trade-size tin of Argentine ravioli, so he and I sort of scuttled off somewhere and ate it between us two.

So, we had this enormous tin of ravioli and then fourteen hours' sleep.

I can honestly say it was a standing joke in my patrol, because I had an arctic sleeping bag, one of the extra-padded ones which I'd had from Norway some years before, and this was much envied amongst the patrol. My 2IC, Mick Mc, whom I'd known since he was seventeen, had said earlier, 'Well, boss, if you get fragged, can I have your sleeping bag?'

To which I replied, 'Yeah, of course you can, but the first time you climb into it, Mick, just remember; when you pull that zip, there'll be a light popping noise as the white phosphorus grenade wired to the zip goes off!'

Private David Minnock, GPMG gunner, 12 Platoon D Company 2 Para

Come daylight, I was still alive and the surrender had happened, but we weren't involved in any of that as we still had to secure the perimeter of Goose Green. So, Jim Barry's 2IC, a fellow called Page, Jacko Page, now General Page [Lieutenant General Jonathan 'Jacko' Page CB, OBE], comes and shows us where to dig in. You see, we had to dig trenches, because that's what we do, we secure the flanks and dig in.

Anyway, Jacko comes and sights me and me mate Smithy [Private Steve Smith, 12 Platoon, D Company] our trench position. Right, so we starts digging in, because I had to dig the gun in, and we'd only got down a foot and hit proper hard rock, and I thought, *for fuck's sake!* Anyway, this farmer comes along and says, 'What you doing, lads?'

'We're digging in,' I said, 'and I'm sorry about the state of your field and everything, but it's just one of those things.' I mean, his field was full of bomb holes and war shite anyway. He still tells us we can't dig there, so I says, 'Look, mate, I've just told you.'

So he comes back with, 'You go down another foot and you'll hit proper hard rock.'

I tell him our officer has told us to dig here and we've gotta dig it, and I'm there with a pick still digging. 'After what you lads have been through, I can't believe it!' he says.

Anyway, he walks away in disgust and he's back ten minutes later on his tractor pulling a big orange Ingersoll compressor unit and a bloody big jackhammer. He shows us how to operate it, but says to make sure you have a good grip on it, so me and Smithy are there proper digging in, then a bloke from my section comes over and sees us and takes the piss, saying, 'Good Airborne skills, that.'

'Wanker,' I says back, and then he tells us we're being relieved by the Gurkhas, so these two boys, Gurkha lads, come over. We showed them how to use the jackhammer, but they didn't appear to speak English, so we'd got down a few feet and the trench was looking good as trenches go. So, Smithy's in the trench showing one, and I'm telling the other about not to let the compressor drop below a certain point on this gauge, and then to knock it off to let the pressure build back up again, and if it stops, this is how you start it again, sort of thing! And I know I'm just not getting through to them at all.

Smithy's telling the other lad to grip it well, so the young lad grabs hold of the jackhammer and it's obvious he's never seen anything like it before; he pulls the trigger and it jumps way up and out of his hands. Now, this Gurkha is straight out the trench and legging it. He didn't even pick up his rifle or his webbing. I looks at his mate and he does the same and legs it as well. He just legs it! I says to Smithy, 'Jesus Christ!'

Smithy looked at me with a fag in his mouth and says, 'Fucking mercenaries, I've shit 'em!'

Jacko Page comes back and asks what had we done to the two Gurkhas. I tell him we haven't done anything. 'Look,' I point, 'their kit's still here and their rifles!' Anyway, Taff comes over a bit later and says, 'Never mind that shit, get your stuff and let's go.'

Lance Corporal Denzil Connick, Anti-Tank Platoon 3 Para

When I first heard about Goose Green, we were making our way to Estancia on our mammoth seventy-odd mile tab. I remember this, because I ran out of fags on the way, well before Longdon. That's mainly because the non-smokers were so full of nerves and stress, they took the free daily ration of a pack of twenty Bensons & Hedges over ONE Mars Bar. Even the anti-smokers of the day, you know, the ones who let you know they really hated it, puffed happily away on twenty B&H.

We were all told by word of mouth what our brothers in 2 Para were going to be doing, which was fine; and then, of course, slowly but surely the casualty figures came drifting back to us. Most of us could not imagine how or what 2 Para had been through, none of us in 3 Para could have. I'd had experience being on the two-way-range on an ambush in Northern Ireland, but nonetheless, I really didn't understand or have a grasp on the gravity of what we were doing – full-on infantry bloody warfare – and neither did anybody else. Not even the Special Forces amongst us like the SAS did. In fact, I would hesitate to say the SAS were out of their depth on some occasions.

When the battle for Goose Green was over, it was a massive victory against all the odds, which we didn't know about and nor did you guys in 2 Para; you didn't realise what you were opposing. When we found out, there was lots of, 'Oh yes, come on!' And of course, that was the bar set for us guys of 3 Para. It made us realise, more than anything in the world, that we were good enough for the job – more than good enough, as failure was never in our vocabulary. That victory at Goose Green was a victory for everyone who loves the Union Flag and freedom.

Acting Sub Lieutenant Mark Stollery, HMS Fearless, *Royal Navy*

On the day of the surrender, everything happened very quickly. As soon as the Argentines surrendered, we needed someone who spoke Spanish to find intelligence such as documents and plans, and debrief key Argentine prisoners. I arrived by Wessex helicopter straight after the surrender, together with the ship's doctor, a weapons engineer, and an RAF bomb disposal officer. We flew scarily low, because enemy air attacks were still very much going on.

I remember looking out of the helicopter's open door on the starboard side, seeing a continuous blur of green and the occasional flash of white as we zoomed over sheep, and lurching every so often as we had to go over a fence or hedge. We landed at the end of the village green away from the sheep-shearing sheds. I took off my badges of rank, basically because it was tactically useful not to advertise how junior I was!

It was the immediate aftermath of the battle, yet there was no tension. People were just milling around, lots of Paras and some POWs, as well as villagers trying to sort themselves out as they returned to their looted houses, after being locked up in the village hall for a month. Most of the Argentines POWs were in the sheep-shearing sheds to keep them dry and, of course, out of the way. It felt a bit like the morning after a heavy party, people quietly wandering about. There were a few Argentine officers who had not been put into the sheds, including one rather smarmy and arrogant young guy in a bright green beret (Special Forces?), who spoke English and was breezing about as though he owned the place.

I went into one of the houses belonging to the MacLeod family, I think, which had been used a billet for Argentine officers. I was looking for any useful documents they might have left. As I went through the back door into the kitchen, the first person I saw was Mrs MacLeod, who greeted me with, 'Would you like a cup of tea?' I vividly remember that she gave me a door-stop jam sandwich, and tea in a mug that had the Falkland Islands crest on one side and a commemorative design for the 1981 Prince and Princess of Wales royal wedding on the other. I was struck by how beautifully that encapsulated the spirit of the Falklands!

It was about lunchtime and I was at a loose end, so I decided to find a quiet place to eat my packed lunch from the ship. I plonked myself down on a wooden framework structure near the sheep-shearing sheds and got my lunch bag out. The wooden structure was filled with large metal containers, and as I munched and idly looked around, I noted that the writing on one container read 'Napalm' in Spanish. I dimly remembered something about napalm and Vietnam, but I certainly didn't know it was used in the Falklands [in fact, it had been dropped on 2 Para during the battle]. I alerted the RAF bomb disposal officer, who came over and swiftly dealt with it, or at least I assume he did, as I left him to it and put some distance between me and the napalm!

GOOSE GREEN

Private Phil Williams, Mortar Platoon 2 Para

When we got into Goose Green, I saw lots of napalm pods, all leaking the shit out of them.

Private Ian Winnard, 4 Platoon B Company 2 Para

I recall the ground was so up and down and difficult to fight across and if you turned an ankle, that would be it for you. But the worse thing for me during the whole battle wasn't the Argies, or the air strikes, mortars, or those 30mm Oerlikons that ripped up our positions and pinned us down for hours, no, it was the weather for me. I was absolutely freezing. I was wet from day one and then freezing thereafter and when we took the surrender at Goose Green, I was so happy, because my company was sent into one of the sheds out of the cold.

That's when I could take my boots off for a rest, but that was a big mistake, because as soon I took me boots off, me feet started swelling and really hurting. I had to keep them elevated to drain the blood out of 'em, but the Doc told me to put me feet into a bowl of cold water, and as soon as I did that, the pain stopped and I got me boots back on.

Private Mark Sleap, Patrols Platoon Company 2 Para

The morning after the surrender, int came in that there were a load of Argies at a farm between us and Bluff Cover, a settlement over to the west, so B Company were tasked to sort it out. But before they left, Johnny Crosland, OC B Company, was given the telephone number of that farm and he rung it. He was told there was no Argies there, but me and JY [Private JY, Patrols Platoon, 2 Para] got put in a Scout helicopter to lay an LS [landing site] and the pilot flew this thing real low on the skin of his arse, and basically, we found a suitable place for B Company to land their Chinook.

Anyway, we landed as it was just getting dark and I had a strobe light so they could identify it was us. It was deathly silence. Me and JY were alone and we see this vehicle, it was a Land Rover bouncing across the countryside with its headlight shining straight towards us, so we opened up a 66 and made it ready. Then at about fifty yards it stops and this big fat bloke in overalls and a big ruddy face, obviously a farmer, comes running up and he goes, 'Thank God the Marines are here.'

So JY goes, 'We're fucking Paratroopers, knobhead.'

Sergeant Major Colin Price, A Company 2 Para

A Company went firm on Darwin Hill while the rest of the battalion went forward towards Goose Green. I was still sorting out our wounded, ammo resup, and prisoners. We were held in reserve, and anyway I spoke to the new CO, Major Chris Keeble, and said we still haven't taken A Company's objective yet, which was Darwin, so please let us take Darwin. So he moved us into Darwin, and that was after the surrender of Goose Green.

I mean, we had to hold it, and that's why A Company never went into Goose Green; we held our objective, Darwin. And after the battle for Goose Green, we never went into Goose Green either. Then Colonel Chaundler came out to take over command from Keeble, and I met him with Farrar-Hockley. I didn't speak to the Colonel, but Farrar-Hockley came to me afterwards and said, 'Oh, we're going in reserve for 5 Infantry Brigade.'

'Reserve?' I questioned. I didn't believe the battalion should be going into reserve. I didn't believe we should be licking our wounds, because if you spend too long worrying about what you've done and what's happened to your mates, you fall apart a bit, it's doing something which keeps the men together.

I said to Farrar-Hockley, 'This battalion should be the first battalion into Port Stanley,' but when he briefed the platoon commanders and platoon sergeants that night, he told them we were going into reserve.

'The sergeant major disagrees, don't you?'

I replied, 'Yes, I do.' And who was the first company into Port Stanley? A Company 2 Para, and we raised the A Company flag up at Stanley Racecourse.

Captain Paul Farrar, OC Patrols Platoon 2 Para

We'd been in Goose Green barely twenty-four hours, and part of the intelligence prior had been that there were six LVTP-7 amphibious vehicles in the Goose Green area, but they weren't there when Goose Green surrendered. Chris Keeble had this idea that they had gone off with troops inside them, slid into the sea and gone off. Because we had Scout helicopters, we were then given a mission where he wanted us to fly off around the coast line looking for tracks where these things had come out the water and gone inland, probably to a harbour area somewhere. Then once we'd located them, we were to land and to keep eyes on them. I think it was D Company who were going to be flown in to then capture these LVTP-7s.

Chris was concerned that this element of Argentine forces was still around. We all thought, yeah, sounds good, just like an Eagle patrol in Northern Ireland, where you'd swoop in and set up a SVCP [snap vehicle checkpoint]. Anyway, it never came off.

Lance Corporal Geoff 'Johnno' Johnson , HQ Company 2 Para, attached to D Company 2 Para

There was this big booby-trap explosion by the shearing sheds that housed all the prisoners. Well, I was on that; it was all kicking off, I mean the rounds were cooking off all over, so RSM Mal Simpson says to me, 'Get around the back to the pumping station and get out the way.' Then I saw this Argy in a grey coat with his hood over his head and he's lying on his face. I don't know what it was really, but I jumped over this hedge and went to grab him, then suddenly from out of nowhere this bloke from the Brigade medics appeared, so we took an arm each and we dragged him away to safety.

There was this Land Rover that turned up and it had Doc Hughes in it, so I shouted to Doc Hughes, 'What the fuck are you doin' here?' Because I was so surprised to see him, and he just says, 'What have you got there?'

I says, 'It's a bloke,' but I didn't know what the fuck was really going on, and I didn't know what it was I had been dragging. I'd felt superhuman, strong like, when I grabbed him, and he didn't half fucking move with us. It wasn't until we got him on the Land Rover, I found out he had lost his legs, and all he had was his femur and kneecaps left. Doc Hughes said to me, 'You get in the fucking wagon.' So, I got in the wagon and they shoved him in and his head lay on my lap and he just kept looking at me with his big round brown eyes, and to this day it's one on my nightmares.

Doc Hughes cut his sleeves, inserted cannulas in both his arms and he gave us some IV fluids. The lines ran about two yards long, but when you're squashed up in the back of a Land Rover, it was a hard top Land Rover that belonged to one of the kelpers [Falkland Islanders], it was difficult. So Doc said, 'Never mind what I told you on board ship, just fucking squeeze it, and get it into him.'

This guy had the look of an Aztec about him, so was used to a much warmer climate, he shouldn't have been here, in this cold. Anyway, we got him off the Landy and moved him to our RAP and I can remember Hank [Lance Corporal Steve Hood, 2 Para Combat Medical Team] being there. Hank said in a professional way, 'What you got there?' and he looked at this guy and said, 'Bring him in.' So we brought him in, and there was a trestle table just on the left-hand side of the door as you go in. Hank then said, 'Put him on there.' It was really strange, because his legs didn't come over the table, and then a couple of the other medics came up and one said, 'We'll take over from here,' and they carried on.

The thing that upset me for such a long time after that, was the next day Hank and I crossed paths and I asked Hank about the man with no legs. and he said, 'Oh, he's dead,' as if it was just nothing. The experience of war had definitely hardened everybody. We had become less humane, and my reaction to Hank's reply was, 'Ah! alright then,' as if you'd just lost a bag of spuds somewhere. Sadly, the lad died on the helicopter flying out to the field hospital at Ajax Bay. You become very detached from everything, and I think it's because this self-preservation thing kicks in.

Private Greg Cox, light machine gunner, Patrols Platoon 2 Para

I was on guard up at the sheep sheds when the booby trap went off and the medic took John G's rifle and shot dead the Argy who was burning.

WOII Del Amos, Acting Technical Quartermaster Sergeant, B Echelon 2 Para

After the battle I was sitting with my mates in one of the sheep sheds having some scoff and a brew when all of a sudden, there was a massive explosion, which shook the place. We didn't know what it was (probably a Blowpipe misfire!). After the explosion, it wasn't like, 'Is everyone okay?' rather 'Who the fuck knocked my brew over?'

Later that day another explosion rocked Goose Green. I ran to the source of the explosion to find the RSM standing over a charred torso. I didn't know if the casualty was one of ours or an Argy. It turned out to be an Argy, who had tripped one of their own booby traps. We did what we could for the lad, but it was a pointless exercise.

I returned to my basha in the sheep sheds and immediately washed my hands, because they were sticky with the victim's plasma and stank of roast pork. Shortly afterwards, one of the lads came over and said he'd been approached by an Argy officer, who had asked him to pass his 'thanks to the man with the big moustache,' for being 'attentive' at the scene of the explosion. That memory remains constant.

19

GOOSE GREEN RE-ORG

Lance Corporal Bill 'Basha' Bentley MM, Combat Medical Team 2 Para

Helicopters started to arrive now that it was safe! Reporters and staff officers suddenly appeared all over the place. We were busy packing medical kit, whatever was still useable. I became aware that Doc Hughes was agitated, as some reporters were starting to unpack our dead to take photographs. Doc shouted to me, 'Stop them, Basha, stop them!'

I trotted down the hill and screamed, 'HEY!' I had their attention. 'If you make one more fucking move or touch one more body, you will be laying there dead next to them in one second.' They looked at me and were obviously convinced that I was not joking, and suddenly finding something else of interest, they buggered off very quickly. For this reason, there were never any pictures of our dead on this battlefield.

Bob Cole was wandering around in a daze, still with his bayonet fixed ready for action. A sergeant major called over, 'Corporal Cole, that bayonet looks bloody dangerous!'

'You're fuckin' right it is,' Bob answered, so the sergeant major decided there must be something more important to do and left promptly.

As darkness fell it was snowing heavily and I was able to take a break. I had become aware that yet another good friend of mine had fallen. Tam Mechan had been a really funny little man and had been the source of great amusement for our group over the past couple of years. I dearly wanted to see him one more time, and so I began my search. As far as I could gather, he was still out on the battlefield; over there. I went out through our lines and stumbled around, but the snow was getting ever deeper, I could not know if the ground had been mined, and I might even have walked over him and not known it; so I had to give up my search.

On arrival back in the lines, somebody told me that the Padre had gathered all of the bodies together behind a building; over there. I found a row of bodies wrapped in ponchos and opened them one after the other, but in the darkness and with their wounds I could not even identify my little friend. I gave each of them a kiss and a hug, wrapped them up again and went off to find a place to sleep.

Lance Corporal 'Duke' Allen, Defence Platoon 2 Para

Mostly it was me and Radar who basically loaded all our dead onto the only one flying Chinook,[28] but we couldn't load Tam Mechan on, as he was laid outside in the back garden of one of the houses that had been taken over by Tac HQ. The only reason Tam was here fighting in the Falklands was because he had signed on for an extra six months for the extra money LOA [living overseas allowance] he would earn, as we were supposed to go to Belize. But unfortunately for Tam, he didn't make it.

28 The four other Chinooks had been lost when *Atlantic Conveyor* was sunk by Exocets on 25 May.

He was about the last of our blokes to be killed, and we had to put a stag on his body to stop the dogs eating him. I did from midnight till two in the morning, or from two till four, or something like that, I can't remember. It was horrible making sure the dogs didn't get to Tam. I mean, the locals' dogs had been locked up for six weeks until we arrived and were obviously fucking starving to death! They'd already started eating the Argies, before we put a stop to that. The Argies didn't feed them, but they did in the end – bloody ironic or what!

Chief Petty Officer Rich Edwards, Special Communications Unit (SCU) Royal Navy

A day after the surrender, I flew back to Goose Green with members of the media to confirm the use of napalm. I and many others had felt there had been some contention over whether the Argentinians really used napalm at Goose Green. No! Surely they didn't! It was still not believed by many, but my claim to fame was – well, here you go – I'd just found a folded A4 piece of paper in-between a pile of these bombs the day before, which had *SECRETO* stamped across it. There's TV footage of me holding it in front of a BBC camera or some network as the evidence.

This piece of paper was the operating instructions for the napalm bombs, and then some air engineer commander whipped it off me pretty smartish. I should have insisted, and said, 'No, sir, I'm the Intel guy here and that's intelligence.' I will always remember: *SECRETO. Fabrica Armament de Argentina. Bomba Napalm. 220 kilograms.*

Corporal 'Ginge' Dawes, clothing storeman, 2 Para

It was all hands-on stuff. Colour Sergeant Frankie Pye commandeered a Land Rover and started moving kit forward. Real sad for the guys who got killed and wounded, but really happy to see the guys who had made it.

One of my tasks at Goose Green was to go through the kit of our dead. Sort out any personal stuff like photographs, driving licences and personal stuff. It all had to be done properly; written down, logged and then bagged up and put in a box ready to get repatriated back to the families. We would then redistribute their issued kit out to the guys. It's just one of those things that has to be done. You have to be non-committal, because you still have the colourmen coming in saying, 'I've got a bloke who needs a pair of denims. Have you got a spare pair?' Or a smock, or boots, or whatever, but it had to be one size fits all, if you know what I mean. We were still at war.

The boots were a big thing, those DMS boots were falling apart. Also, all the dead's clothing gets written off too, but in all honesty, as soon as the first shot gets fired, you start writing kit off.

Did we make them sign for the kit? Of course, we didn't make them sign for it as you would do in peacetime! We're not bastards in the stores, you know, ha-ha!

Private Bob Morgan, Patrols Platoon 2 Para

Paul Farrar was, and still is, a great guy. So, after Goose Green, we were totally bolloxed. Me and him had been together throughout the war, I mean I was his signaller, so we had to stay close to each other. But the only time he ever went off on his own was for O groups or on one occasion, a one-man-recce, which he only ever did the once! Well, this time he'd gone to an O group and when he came back, and I had just made a brew, he came up to me and said, 'Bob, we've gotta do it again!'

We had orders to attack a big, heavily defended mountain with thousands of Argies on it, the rock feature that overlooked Stanley,

Wireless Ridge.[29] He was looking at me rather intensely, so I just handed him my brew in one of those plastic water-bottle mugs, and we both sat in deep thought. Nothing needed to be said, and I tried to look cool, but inside, I was shitting myself, because it's like your first parachute jump, you know, you just jump out and do it – it's exhilarating.

Well, on your second one, you know what's going to happen and you think, *No! What am I doing this for?* You know just how fucking terrified you're going to be. You ain't going to be so gung-ho. And that's what gets me about folks who do the tandem parachute jump, say for charity; they've done the one and they think they've arrived! Well, okay then! Get up and do it again, solo, then see how brave you are. I was in the Parachute Regiment for twenty-two years and I hated jumping.

Lance Corporal Geoff 'Johnno' Johnson, HQ Company 2 Para, attached to D Company 2 Para

Post the battle I was tasked with looking after the prisoners, so a couple of days after the surrender, this Scout fell out of the sky and when it landed this officer got out and he was pristine. He had creases down the front of his trousers, and everything like his smock was just, well, so clean and pristine, and his boots were sparkling – and accompanying him were some Gurkhas carrying their kukris. We had a POW working party, because we had built up a rapport with them; so we used to go to the sheep-shearing sheds, where we'd put them once they surrendered, and get a working party together. Then we'd take 'em out to clean up all their shit they'd made, or get them repairing all the damage they'd caused around the settlement.

---

29   It must be noted, 2 Para were the only battalion to fight and win two battles during the war. They were also the first to 'hit the beach,' first to win a battle, and first into the capital, Port Stanley.

Anyway, when this working party saw the Gurkhas, their reaction was absolutely electric. They all started going off at each other in Spanish, and you knew straight away there was something going on here, and they were all pointing; and suddenly some of 'em spoke better English than they had been letting on! I mean we [2 Para] knew at some point we were going to move forward towards Stanley and the Gurkhas were going to take over from us. So one of 'em says, 'What are these doing here?' meaning the little men with big knives. They had heard about the Gurkhas and were shit scared of them.

'Oh, they're coming to take over from us,' I replied cheerfully, which of course they were, they were our relief.

'Oh no, no! We are YOUR prisoners!' They were really shit scared, because they had been fed stories that the Gurkhas would cut them all up and all this nonsense. They were really shit scared and thought they [the Gurkhas] should not be fighting this war because they were not British, that's what these Argies thought. The Argies hated them.

Colour Sergeant Frank Pye, Support Company 2 Para

One time I sent a group of Argy prisoners to go pick up their dead and to put them on an old farm trailer, so anyway, a Royal Marine Spanish speaker, Captain Bell, said to me, 'How are the prisoners getting fed?'

'It's all been sorted,' I said. The prisoners were being escorted in groups, down to where their rations were, getting rationed up and bringing them back to the sheep-shearing sheds and feeding themselves.

So Bell says to me, 'What about those prisoners out on the battlefield picking up their dead?'

I looked at him and thought, *What the fuck is he on about?*

'Well, we got people still out there who need to be fed,' he said.

I mean, I really thought he was taking the piss, but no, he was dead serious.

'What do you want me to do, sir, put fucking late meals on for 'em?' OC Support Company, Major Hugh Jenner was close by and spoke up, 'Calm down, Colour, calm down.'

Basically, he wanted me to put late meals on for the fucking prisoners. I mean, I couldn't believe it, but basically, the prisoners were very happy.

Sergeant Pilot Dick Kilinski, F Flight 656 Squadron Army Air Corps

Whilst at Goose Green my taskings weren't just military. One time I was tasked to take the *Daily Telegraph* journalist Max Hastings up to Brigade Headquarters. After a short flight, I landed and watched him enter the tentage HQ, then all of a sudden, two fast jet aircraft, Super Etendards, came screaming in from the left, and as they flew over, they dropped these little white things.

I later found out they were the parachutes on the back of retard bombs. Because they flew so low and if they were to drop their ordnance, the aircraft would pick up some of the blast, the British designed and supplied these little parachutes on the back of these retard bombs. These things came down towards us and there was a low stone wall off to one side. The bombs landed into the soft peat and, thank God, didn't go off except one, which landed the other side of this stone wall, and as it exploded it lifted up rocks and debris that then came raining down on my rotors, which were still turning.

I quickly closed down and tried to pull the rotor brake on, but you had to wait until the rotors had slowed down to a certain speed, otherwise you'd burn the brake out; and I daren't vacate the aircraft until the blades had stopped turning, because of the blade droop. Then we dashed out into cover, just in time to see the Super

Etendards coming back around, but luckily, they flew over and didn't drop anything else.

I could smell something acrid, then realised we'd taken cover in the bomb hole by the wall. Apparently, bombs don't land in the same hole twice! As I climbed out, I saw with utter astonishment that the debris hadn't damaged the blades at all, although there were loads of rocks in the back seat and the Perspex roof was smashed. I had the aircraft recovered, but was told we could have flown it away because of little damage. Quite amazing.

Acting Sub Lieutenant Mark Stollery, HMS Fearless, *Royal Navy*

On my second day, the POWs wanted to show me the grave of the RN [Royal Navy] Harrier pilot Lieutenant Nick Taylor, whom they had shot down several days before. So, along with a Royal Navy padre, a couple of islanders and two Argentine officers, we walked up the track towards Darwin and saw the grave. It was simply, but neatly done. The Argentines were touchingly concerned whether it was okay that they had given him a Catholic burial. I said that I was sure the family would understand, and thanked them for their kindness. I was about to take a photo of the grave to send to Nick Taylor's family, but coincidentally the RN padre knew them personally, so he took the photo on his own camera.

Chief Petty Officer Rich Edwards, Special Communications Unit (SCU) Royal Navy

The captured rapid-fire anti-aircraft guns the Argentinians had at Goose Green, well, it was our guys on *Fearless* who got one of the guns working and test fired it over the sea, and this was the gun that took down Nick Taylor's Harrier. Nick's body was still in his Martin Baker ejector seat when he was recovered by the residents of

Goose Green, and he was buried under Argentine supervision with full military honours, very close to where he landed.

That was near where the Pucaras took off from, and many of them had been damaged when they came in to land. The Argentinians had propped them up on fifty-gallon oil drums to make out they were still serviceable, but they weren't; they were there to act as decoys, so that when the Harriers flew over, they would come in and try and destroy these aircraft, leaving the Argentine ground troops alone.

Corporal Stu Russell, B Company Signals Detachment commander 2 Para

I was John Crosland's radio operator on the battalion net and that gave me an almost unique position on the battlefield in terms of situation awareness, because John Crosland's leadership style was very much right up at the coalface, up front coordinating the platoons and the company, yet at the same time I had a good picture of what was going on on the rest of the battlefield with the other companies because I was on the battalion net and I was listening to everything that was going on.

There were a number of sets of brothers in 2 Para fighting that day (I can recall at least fourteen plus four of the Camp brothers) and my brother Jim who's three years older than me and who was also a corporal. He was a section commander in 1 Platoon, A Company, and Jim was wounded at Darwin Hill. I recall looking across and seeing all the red and green tracer over at A Company's battle and had this strange feeling wondering if my brother was okay and if any of that tracer was ripping through his chest! I know it sounds a bit macabre but that was the thought going through my head at the time. Soon after it was my time to stand up and advance towards the enemy then my thoughts quickly turned to me and my job and my own frailty and mortality. The battle lasted over fourteen hours and on the second evening we got a resupply of ammo and radio batteries bought over by the MTO [Motor Transport Officer] Lieutenant Alex Ward, he somehow managed to get hold of a vehicle he'd commandeered from the Marines. He saw me and came over because he knew I used to be in A Company and he knew me and my brother very well and he said to me, 'I've seen your brother Jim and he's okay.' He didn't say he'd been wounded, just that he was okay, so I thought, *ah, that's one less thing I have to worry about!* Great Jim's okay, so I assumed he was unscathed and come through the battle fine. Now, after the surrender the next day, elements of the battalion moved into Goose Green but B Company didn't. We stayed another cold miserable night on a hill feature just to the south of Goose Green to counter any movement from the Argentine helicopter reinforcements who had flown in late on the day of the battle before the surrender. We actually got into Goose Green a whole twenty-four hours after the surrender. As I was walking through the settlement I bumped in to Dave 'Pig' Abols, A Company, and he laughed at me and in typical squaddie humour said, 'Ah, I see Jim got a Blighty one then! He'll be back home in time for the World Cup.' That shocked me dead because I was told he was okay!

'Yeah, he'll live, he'll survive, but he got wounded and he's been evacuated.' And that was the first I knew my brother had been wounded. He took a blast of Argy mortar to the back.

Acting Sub Lieutenant Mark Stollery, HMS Fearless, *Royal Navy*

We received intelligence suggesting that more troops were being brought to the area in an Argentine 'hospital ship' the *Bahia Paraiso*, in contravention of the Geneva Convention. I was therefore detailed off to board and inspect the ship, along with the ship's doctor and a technician to look for any cryptographic equipment, also banned under the Convention. I drew a sidearm, but then made it unreachable behind the enormous zip of a protective dry suit for the flight to the ship; but then, as any Royal Marine will tell you, there are few things more dangerous than a sailor with a gun! We were accompanied by some SBS operators in our helicopter, with more troops in a second helicopter, in case things turned nasty and we had to fight our way off.

On landing on the ship, all I could see were a few men in uniform by the hangar door. But they seemed curious rather than alert, and there was no sign of weapons. So I climbed out and indicated to the pilot to shut down engines. The boarding party was then escorted to the bridge, where we met the captain and explained our purpose. He was relaxed and let us wander all over the ship, where we looked for signs of military intent or equipment. We found none. When we returned to the bridge, he offered us a glass of whisky – a nice gesture but an awkward moment. We declined, as it seemed improper to accept.

As we left, I told the captain that he might want to get ready to take up to 1500 troops back to Argentina, as we had just captured them at Goose Green. He was taken aback, and clearly unaware what had happened ashore.

Chief Petty Officer Rich Edwards, Special Communications Unit (SCU) Royal Navy

I too was despatched in a stripped-out Wessex to fly to the Argentine converted ice-breaker *Bahia Paraiso*. The ship was being declared under the Geneva Convention as a hospital ship. My task was to ascertain if the ship had been secretly fitted with online crypto. Not an easy task in a large ship in a short time. The captain told me, that not long before, he had been on a course at HMS *Dryad* [School of Maritime Operations (Southwick House) UK]. This is close to where I live. He asked me how the war was going, to which my reply was, they [Argentina] were coming second. We left on amiable terms, which made the whole episode quite sad.

Lance Corporal Jimmy Goodall, Assault Engineers 2 Para

After the battle we got time for some well-needed recuperation, so we rested up for a few hours, then it was back to work. One of my tasks was prisoner detail. One time I was tasked to take out a party of prisoners, stiff-collecting, like! Obviously, we wouldn't let them touch our blokes, but only to collect theirs. As I took this particular bunch of prisoners out, we walked past this load of already collected bodies all laid in a row, Argies. Suddenly one of the Argy prisoners starts crying, then another prisoner who spoke English says, 'Excuse me, sir, he's just seen his brother. Can he go and see him please?'

So I tell him, 'Yes, okay then.' So we stop and I let this Argy approach this body and he picked this body up and he kissed it and indicated if he could take the rosary beads from around this body's head, so I says, 'Yes, that's okay.'

He was having a right old job trying to get the beads off him, because this body was in a contorted position and as stiff as a board too. He eventually succeeded and held them up to show me, it was his brother! Then we must have only walked two or three yards and the same Argy saw another familiar body and he indicated again if he could do the same. I said yes, again, but as he picked this body up, the head just fell off!

So I called out, 'You're not going to get his beads, are yer!' I mean it was quite gruesome. The fallen Argy was a relative of the guy, but not another brother.

The following day I was tasked to take another prisoner detail of about six or eight back up to Darwin Hill for some more stiff collecting. So, as we were making our way from Goose Green, this one prisoner starts acting funny, like he was shitting himself. I'm thinking, he thinks we're marching them out to get shot, like, and we're his firing squad. I thought, *I'll keep an eye on the twat.*

The next thing, someone shouts, 'MINEFIELD!' I stopped suddenly. Well, we'd walked into this fuckin' minefield and I looked down at me feet and saw two AP [anti-personnel] mines, one to the left and one to the right with trip wires. I just thought, *oh fuck, they're all linked up!* And that's why I'm guessing this Argy was shitting himself, he thought we were walking them through the minefield to clear it using them as mine detonators. What a dozy fuck.

Anyway, we carefully retraced our steps back out, but what must have been going through this Argy's mind. Who knows? Probably thinking, maybe I should have said something to the British a bit earlier. But honestly, the look in his face for a few minutes was priceless, ha-ha!

20

FOR YOU, THE WAR IS OVER

Private John Bolland. Recce Platoon 2 Para

I was flown to Ajax Bay Field Hospital. At one time I saw this wee Marine lying opposite me. He looked like he'd been cut in half, and you know what he did? He gave me the thumbs up and called out, 'Magic, pal.'

I woke up in the middle of the night and I could still see him. His mate was next to him crying, holding his hand, and next to him was this squeeze-box thing, which was helping him breathe. I came-to a bit later on and his mate was still there, but on his knees this time, crying his eyes out.

Private Steve Tuffen, 2 Platoon A Company 2 Para

From Ajax Bay I was flown to the hospital ship *Uganda*. I have no memory of being at Ajax Bay, nor any real memories of being on the *Uganda*. I only remember the odd fragment, as I was totally blind at this time. My first proper memory came whilst on the ambulance ship HMS *Hydra*. From there I was flown home, spent a night at RAF Hospital Wroughton, and then on to Queen Elizabeth Military Hospital, Woolwich, where I had more operations, one of which was to remove bits of bone and foreign bodies from my brain.

After the operation, the little eyesight I had became a bit clearer, whereas before then it was blurry as though looking through tears all the time. A year later I had a plate put in my skull to cover the hole in it, which was roughly the size of a clenched fist.

Corporal Marty Margerison, 6 Platoon B Company 2 Para

Ajax Bay. I woke up some time later and they'd stitched my face up, stitched my shoulder up. I had been put in a blue cotton prisoner-type, two-piece suit, then got flown on to the hospital ship *Uganda*. Now, there's a rule under the Geneva Convention that states, once you get to a hospital and you are treated, you are not allowed to go back to war. The *Uganda* was a hospital ship, but there was one lad who'd got shrapnel in his hands, got treated, and somehow managed to jump on a helicopter and return back to B Company.

You were meant to be disarmed completely before you were allowed onboard, but there was all sorts of shit the lads brought on board with them, like grenades and shit, which was stashed away in the air vents.

They took out what bits of teeth they could, sewed up the gums, and sewed up the left-hand side of my face. Sewed the top and bottom lip too, but what they had done was put a zig-zag in my mouth going from the left for about an inch to stop it splitting. Now, I only realised this when I was woken up at feeding time and I couldn't get a spoon in it. They couldn't do anything with my shoulder and I had this wound on my leg, which was probably a slight bullet wound too.

So, the *Uganda* would sail out of the danger zone first light and sail back in at night to receive helicopters full of wounded, and the staff on board there were amazing; Army, Navy, RAF, and I think civilian. And the crew were doing their bit too with the hearts and minds, you know.

One time I woke up in bed and I saw all the IV drip stands had berets on top of them, so then you could see who was Para Reg and who were the hats, ha-ha. There was this fella in the next bed to my left, he was an Argy! I'm trying to focus, trying to get my bearings, and this guy is on the edge of his bed combing his long black hair, and his hair is being blown across me and I've gone, 'Fucking hell, what the fuck!'

So, I'm having a paddy now and I get a bollocking off the nurse, then I notice on another bed there was Tony Tighe, who'd got shot in the arm at Goose Green. I gets this bollocking because it's the Hippocratic Oath – everybody gets looked after the same, and it's only when you get older, you realise that's the way war is. After a few days of going back and forth into San Carlos Bay, only then did the Argies get put into a different ward. I then got transferred again, onto another ship.

There were three Navy survey ships down south and they'd all become hospital ships, the *Herald*, the *Hydra* and the *Hecla*, and what they were doing was picking up the wounded being flown off the *Uganda* and taking them to Montevideo, Uruguay, and then flown on to the UK.

[*During my interview with Marty, he openly and continually contemplated his fate lying in bed on the* Uganda.]

The aftermath of all this is, why did I go over the top? Why didn't I stick to my guns and stay down until we got to the bottom, then we'll call you forward? Why didn't Chip say that? Why didn't JC say that? We were so exposed, as the light came so fucking quick, and everything [Argy fire] seemed to be concentrated on D Company and A Company. Possibly we thought we'd got away with our advance, because you could hear what was going on over the company and battalion net, so we didn't understand that command and control aspect at that time.

But in later years I really beat myself up, because I was the man who in four years had done all my courses, all A Grade confidential, and I was a flyer. There was no problem with me being an RSM now, and then an officer; my career was made out. So I should have said, 'Hold on now, we're going into bad territory here,' and I have to live with the fact. If I was such a good soldier, why did I put my lads in such danger? And now I'm no longer there to look after them. That's what you do, they are your subordinates, you look after 'em! I've gotta live with that fact.

Private John Bolland, Recce Platoon 2 Para

Now on the *Uganda*, I woke up once and there was an Argy in the bed next to me; I was gonna burn the cunt. Everything on the *Uganda* was geared up towards the Roman Catholics and the Argies. The priest gave 'em new rosary beads and everything. The International Red Cross came on board too, with a load of priests and boxes of fucking rosary beads.

I've got this big sealed dressing on, and once when I opened my eyes, there's this cunt with the *cloth* on, so I says, 'What you doing, yer cunt?' It was one of the priests who was starting to give me the last rites. 'Fuck off, I'm a Protestant,' I tell him.

Still on the *Uganda*, and I'm hobbling about with a colostomy bag, so I'm watching Straza and looking at his Meccano set they'd built, because he'd been shot in the ankle and leg. Jimmy got his nickname because he married a German girl; *straße*, pronounced 'strarzer', means street in German. They took me and Straza from the *Uganda* to the *Hydra*, one of those weather ships,[30] which was now

---

30   In fact, a *Hecla*-class ocean survey ship.

carrying more wounded to Montevideo. Then they flew us to RAF Lyneham, and then in a two-man ambulance to the Cambridge [the military hospital at Aldershot].

So, me and Straza got a bottle of peach brandy in the back of the ambulance and Straza still had his Meccano-set thing in his leg and I had one lung. When we got back, we both knew it was all over for us, our lives in the regiment would be no more. So Straza tells the driver to pull over and leave us be, and fair play, he and his mate let us be, and we drank.

The Cambridge Hospital. They put all us wounded Paras in one ward, the psychiatric ward, Ward 6, during the nurses' strike, and they stuck two military policemen on the door with sidearms. It was the first time I'd known Scouse Madge so quiet, because he'd got his jaw shot off.

About a month later and still in the Cambridge, I was taken down to the Parachute Regiment Officers' Mess at Browning Barracks at two in the morning, to get debriefed by Sir Anthony Farrar-Hockley, 'Farrar the Para' – he was God.[31] Two guys came and got me. I was sent for!

Farrar the Para was sat there with this ivory cigarette holder with a gold tip between his lips, and he says to me, 'Are you happy with your treatment on the hospital ship and was everything alright?'

I told him, 'No, my treatment wasn't alright, because me, a Marine from 42 Commando, and three other guys were put under armed guard on the *Uganda* by a wee bandsman with a 9 mm [a Browning pistol], because we objected to the Argies being put on the same ward as us.'

He then says, 'I'm going to ask you that question again.'

There was a tape recorder on, so that tape might still be around!

---

31   General Sir Anthony Farrar-Hockley, GBE, KCB, DSO and Bar, MC (1924–2006), Colonel Commandant of the Parachute Regiment 1977–83, and a former CO of 3 Para. He was the father of the OC A Company.

I'll always remember he held his cigarette holder up right in his left hand as he pulled it away from his mouth, like a Noël Coward pose. He was very interested in our treatment. So I says it all again and elaborate and I tell him I was taken out of the intensive care unit on the *Uganda* with this Marine, who had been on the islands when the Argies invaded, and a couple of others. We were put in a separate area near where the anchor was, at least I think it was, because when I came out of anaesthetic there was this cunt [an Argy] lying next to me, who could have killed Tam Mechan, rest in peace [Pte, D Company].

You know where I'm going with this! On my mother's life, they put us under armed guard on the *Uganda*, and this early hours interview was to get me at my lowest ebb purely to suss out the truth and to put a tick in the box to say 'This patient was a danger to other patients on an international hospital ship' – because I created fuck when waking up from anaesthetic then seeing an Argy in the next bed! How the fuck would you feel? That's all that meeting was about! But why wasn't I asked if I'd come across any American mercenaries down south? Because we had.

I felt, and still do feel, we were treated like shit in the *Uganda*; the loyalties were given to the Argies because the Red Cross was on board. I had a catheter put in, I was not numbed or fuck all. It was in for three days and the nurse came and pulled it out and the pus hit the ceiling. They had to put me back on a drip, because I couldn't drink and I was terrified to piss. It left a scar. They took my stitches out right across my chest; no anaesthetic, fuck all, just cut 'em and pulled 'em out. The fucking pain. Metal Mickey was with me at the time and he stuck a beret on me head to stop me from screaming as they pulled on them and all the pus spewed out.

We had all our berets up on our drip stands, and one time this guy says, 'Get those berets down,' and we all tell him to fuck off.

Then he puts his beret on, and he's a fucking cabbage hat, and all us Paras burst out laughing and start slagging him off.

One day everybody was issued Royal Air Force blue pyjamas, because the Queen was coming to pay a visit. Even the amputees were forced to wear them. I had this bad chest injury and I had to put them on too, and as soon as the Queen left, they were taken off us and we were ordered to get back into our usual wear: open field dressings and shorts.

Anyway, she was moving down the line, having a chat with the wounded. Straza was in the bed to the right of me and there was a boy on my left, I forget his name now, but a Para who was shot through the arse. He was told, if asked 'Where?', he was to say, 'In the posterior, Ma'am.' So, the Queen comes around and we're all in our beds on the ward and she comes to this Para, and the Queen asks, 'Where were you injured?'

'I got a bullet straight through the arse, Ma'am.'

Fair play, she never batted an eyelid, and I just knew what was coming with Straza, what with his leg slung up in the air still with this Meccano set stuff all attached, so the Queen says to Straza, 'And where were you injured?'

'Are ye blind, woman, are ye blind? Can I get a sub, cause I'm skint?' She never batted an eyelid at that one either.

21

PREPARE FOR
BATTLE AGAIN

Private Tom Crusham, Signals Platoon, attached HQ Company 2 Para

When the battle for Goose Green had finished, we were still with 3 Commando Brigade, but now 2 Para was being switched over to 5 Infantry Brigade, so I was detailed to go back to Blue Beach, San Carlos Water, where all the main headquarters were. I had to find out where the main CP was, because 2 Para were switching brigades, so we needed to get all the radio codes like SLIDEX [a manual code system] changed over. I had to try and get a lift, because it was miles and miles away.

There was this helicopter, a Scout, parked up on the green at Goose Green and there was this guy standing next to it wearing a Denison smock [the old camouflage paratroopers smock taken out of use in 1977] sporting a 1 Para DZ flash. So I goes up to him and he sees I'm 2 Para and I ask if he could take me to Blue Beach, because I've all these codes to change over. He says, 'Yes, but you'll have to wait a bit, I may have taskings coming up.' So I waited.

About an hour later I gets this shout from the pilot, who I now know to be Dick Kilinski, and we take off. So, I'm sitting in the back and we've been flying hard for about fifteen minutes when we eventually arrive at Blue Beach, San Carlos, and Dick says, 'I'm not sure I can take you back. I might get a call.'

So I says, 'No problems.'

We put down on Blue Beach, and it was like something out of World War Two; blokes dug-in all over the place in trenches, scoffing and brewing-up. Landing craft were coming ashore offloading stores, it was a real busy place. Anyway, I ask this Marine in a trench where the main CP was and he points over to some place, so I make my way through all these clean-looking Marines and arrive at this big dug-out with overhead protection. I go down the ladder for about ten feet; it had obviously been dug by a machine. I had me maroon beret on, because I was in Marine territory and I knew it would piss them off. There were about ten Marines in there. I tell this bloke my name and one of 'em says, 'Have you come for the codes?'

I tell him I have, 'Yeah!' Then this bloke tells me to sit next to him and I can remember these Marines kept looking at me, giving me the eye. I'm thinking, something ain't right here. Then one of 'em says, 'God, it smells in here.'

'What!' I says, knowing he's taking the piss, probably a Marine thing.

'When did you last have a wash?' he says.

Cheeky fuck, I thought.

'When I got off the fucking *Norland* about two fucking weeks ago, doing your job of storming the beach, you knobbers,' and that sort of cleared the air!

Anyway, we were swapping all these codes, which took a couple of hours and we had to double-check everything, SLIDEX and all that stuff, and there was comings and goings on the net, and then this Marine says to me, 'Are you happy with everything?'

Well, I did get a cup of tea, so I says, 'Yes, thanks very much.' He asked me how I was getting back, so I told him I'd scrounge a lift back, and started to leave; but as I was going back up the ladder there was an air raid warning going on, so I started back down the ladder. The next thing, a load of blokes starts piling down the ladder too, and I was pushed into a corner, and I just sat there and waited.

One of the Marines who had come down the ladder was the big cheese, General Jeremy Moore. I still had me beret on, but he obviously didn't see me, and then he turns to his entourage and says, 'This is not looking good for us. Bloody Paras, they were first ashore and now they've just done Goose Green, they're completely running the fucking show and if we don't get back into this war, we're going to look bloody stupid, because the Paras are ruling the roost.'

Of course, I'm thinking this is brilliant and the next thing was the air raid warning all clear, so I stood up out of the shadows, made sure all the codes were safely tucked down in my smock, adjusted me beret and looked at the General. Then everything went dead quiet, because the Marines who were already in the bunker had completely forgot about me being there, because their *God* had come down the ladder. I saluted the General, all the time smiling my head off and wearing the biggest cheesy grin ever, and I couldn't help myself from laughing. I mean, the whole bunker was in total silence. As I was going back up the ladder, I heard the General grumble, 'Where the fucking hell did that bloody Para just come from?'

I managed to get a helicopter back to Goose Green and I passed all the codes over to the Sigs Officer. I relayed this story to him and he didn't seem that bothered, but the other blokes loved it, and that was my war story. After that, I was ordered back to my old rifle company, A Company Sigs Det. When I got there, the OC, Major Farrar-Hockley, says to me, 'It's good to have you back. I've got the old team back together.'

I don't know the reason why they sent me back to A Company,

because they had a full sigs det! Anyway, I was with them on the next battle, the battle for Wireless Ridge.

Private Phil Williams, Mortar Platoon 2 Para

So, we're in Goose Green getting all our kit sorted out, then one of the companies got tasked to go to a place called Fitzroy Heights, and our mortar detachment was to go with this rifle company. Right, we're all in a line waiting for the choppers to pick us up – me, George Smith, and a bloke called Knocker Hughes [all Privates, Mortar Platoon] – and there was this big long line of Argy stiffs, which had been collected up and laid along this hedge.

So anyway, Pip [one of the mortar platoon sergeants] had been his usual self; fucking shouting at everybody and pissing the blokes off. You know something? There was three NDs [negligent discharge of a live round] near Pip during the war, he was liked that much! I'm not saying any names, but you get my meaning! So Pip disappears somewhere to go get his final orders and he leaves his bergen with us.

There's this poor Pucara pilot, and when he'd crashed, he'd gotten a bit bashed-up and his leg was by the side of him; it was clearly *his* leg, because one of them was missing. I'll tell you something about the stiffs at Goose Green, it was the only place where the snow stayed and didn't melt; weird as fuck, like, all the snow would melt, but wouldn't on those Argy stiffs.

Anyway, Knocker starts laughing.

'What the fuck's wrong with you, like?' I ask

'You see that Pucara pilot, he's got his leg off,' he says.

'Yeah?'

'Well, I'm gonna put that leg in Pip's bergen.'

So we all start laughing. Knocker goes over and picks up this leg, while me and George open Pip's bergen and then puts this leg under the top flap of his bergen, tie it all up and put it back down. We're all giggling away like schoolkids and Pip comes back and we're still laughing and he says, 'What the fuck you laughing about?' We all kept quiet. Nothing more was said about it and then the choppers came in, loaded up, flew off and we got dropped off on top of Fitzroy Heights.

Anyway, we start getting onto the mortar line and sorting ourselves out, and as we get there the Argies starting shelling us from Stanley with the 155's [long range artillery], so we pull back on to the reverse side of this feature and set up the mortar line there. The Argy shells were going over the top or hitting the top; it was scary, but they weren't doing us no harm. Not nice, because that 155 makes one hell of a sound!

We're there getting our kit sorted out and then everyone stops and watches Pip pick up his bergen and put it on this big old rock. We're all watching, like, and as he's undoing the straps, he flips open the top flap and this fucking leg falls out. He went, 'Arhhhhhhhrr!' and every one of us on the mortar line was dying and pissing ourselves laughing. Actually, fair play to Pip, he saw the funny side of it and started laughing too. He'd guessed it was me, George and Knocker who were the culprits.

We stayed on top of Fitzroy Heights for maybe two or three days and the weather was that bad the blokes started going down with the cold weather. In the end, we tabbed off Fitzroy Heights to the bay and got on a landing craft. When we got off, we managed to get into a sheep-shearing shed, but it was bitterly cold and many were suffering from frostnip or frostbite and trench foot. I actually saw guys jabbing themselves up with their morphine syrettes, which we had to keep on the inside of our helmets.

The helmet liner was made out of polystyrene and you had to cut a slot out and put your morphine in it and masking tape over it. It was the standard place to keep it, so if you got hit, then the blokes would know where to go for your morphine [never use *your* morphine on anyone because *you* may need it]. Yeah, guys were using it because their fingers and toes were that bad. Some were that close to death!

Sergeant Pilot Dick Kilinski, F Flight 656 Squadron Army Air Corps

When we got into Goose Green, the locals gave us rooms in their houses. This one particular family kindly gave us an empty room upstairs, so we all got our green maggots out [Army-issue sleeping bag] and we were packed in there like sardines. There was no furniture in this room either, so we just laid down side by side. It was the first night we were in this house and I had just got my head down and was drifting off to sleep, when the flight commander came in and said, 'Kilinski, there's a night job on. We need you to fly a recce team up to Mount Pleasant to do a night recce.'

The guy who we were going to take was a Royal Signals major called Mike Forge [205 Signal Squadron], who was also, and just by chance, an old skydiving buddy of mine. We were going to take him and his party up there.

'Oh boss, come on, please. I've been flying all bloody day and I'm absolutely knackered.'

'You're right,' he replied, 'the Gazelles haven't done much, you get yourself back to sleep. Staff Griffin [Staff Sergeant Chris Griffin, 656 Army Air Squadron] can do this job.' So, they picked on a Gazelle to do this job instead of a Scout and Chris Griffin and his crewman Simon Cockton [L/Cpl, 656 Army Air Squadron], who had just got married the day before leaving for the Falklands, were tasked.

They flew off and never came back. Early morning, we hunted for them and we found them just after first light. HMS *Cardiff* had shot them down. They had seen them on the radar and without asking or confirming anything, they shot them down. I found the remains of the Gazelle, Chris and Simon, Mike and Joe [respectively, Major Michael Forge, OC 205 Signal Squadron, and Staff Sergeant Joe Baker, 205 Signal Squadron]. For me, the war was all about lucky escapes.

Corporal Steve Long, Crewman, Gazelle Flight 656 Squadron Army Air Corps

My squadron headquarters was set up at the settlement of Goose Green, and from there my Gazelle flight continued to conduct numerous liaison and forward reconnaissance. One time, Jim Sutherland [Sergeant Pilot] and I were tasked to fly 5 Infantry Brigade commander Brigadier Tony Wilson to attend the temporary burial ceremony of the 2 Para dead at Ajax Bay. This was a poignant visit for us, as we had lost two squadron members two days previously, Chris Griffin and Simon Cockton, after HMS *Cardiff* had shot them down in a friendly fire incident. Chris and Simon were also to be interned at the ceremony.

A day earlier, we had the privilege to be tasked to deliver a very large, hardwood cross and brass plaque to the burial site to mark the temporary grave for the men of 2 Para. Up until then we had been flying across to West Falkland on several reconnaissance tasks to search after a member of an observation patrol, who had disappeared a few days previously near Port Howard. Suddenly we were re-tasked to go to the small barn complex on the top of Green Beach, on the opposite side of San Carlos overlooking Ajax Bay, to get briefed by the quartermaster (QM) of 2 Para and more details would follow.

We arrived soon after 14:00 hours, landed and were briefed. The QM had engaged the services of a local Falkland Islander to produce a cross and a large brass plaque. It was of a very high quality and stained to survive the elements. I can remember Jim and

I looking at each other, and me quietly saying, 'We're gonna need a bigger helicopter!'

Trying to work out how we could ferry this across Falklands Sound in one piece was a game. After a lot of discussion, we were able to squeeze it in with the head of the cross protruding out through both sliding windows by at least several feet. It was a very tight fit and I can remember Jim just managing to reach the flight controls with it laying across our chests and all that. A few minutes later, we were airborne heading across the open stretch of water, but we came close to never making it.

Unbeknown to us, whilst we were debating how to fly this cross, we had missed the latest air raid red warning, which was broadcast across all radio channels each time an Argentinian air attack was imminent. This stretch of water we were now flying across was only a short stretch of sea, but was always swarming with Argy fast jet activity since day one. It was nicknamed Bomb Alley for a reason, and my God, HMS *Ardent* and *Antelope* had already succumbed to Argy destructive power.

So, we were mid-channel at 300 to 400 feet and we met two Argentinian Dagger aircraft,[32] also low level. When Jim spotted both aircraft across our right side and closing fast, he threw the helicopter into a very tight evasive manoeuvre to starboard; a move designed to break a potential gun solution, as we presented ourselves as a slow crossing target and easy prey for these Peruvian veterans, who were still very much in the fight.

Then two things happened, first, and lucky for us, they were on re-heat [afterburner] and I guess too fast to get a gun solution on us and the Navy had them under intense pressure with small-arms fire. Then second, because of our evasive action, unfortunately the cross shifted

32 The Dagger was a hybrid variant of the French Mirage 5 produced under licence by the Israeli defence industry. Several had been sold to the Argentinian Air Force and many were being flown by Peruvian pilots.

just a little and it had braced itself against our chests making both our movement very limited, but Jim was still able to keep control of the aircraft. We landed beside the Ajax Bay factory complex intact a few awkward minutes afterwards, albeit sticky with adrenalin.

Jim and I were both very honoured to be given this mission. We got the cross delivered to 2 Para's RQMS in time to be set in place for the following day's grave marking ceremony. Our meeting with the Daggers was what happens in war. We were very lucky. Mission accomplished.

Private Steve Taylor, 3 Platoon A Company 2 Para

We didn't have it easy in Goose Green, because we always had to stag-on. Sleep, eat and stag-on, but it gave me a chance to take my boots and socks off.

It was the first time I'd had the chance to inspect my feet in days. It's instilled in you for day one training, don't take your boots off! In hindsight, that was wrong. There's lots of things you do in training that you wouldn't do in war; conversely, there's lots of things you do in war you wouldn't do in training, like when we were tabbing on that long one to Goose Green, and blokes were putting their weapons in sleeves (weapon sleeves) to protect 'em. You wouldn't get away with that on an exercise, would you? A massive non-tactical thing like that!

When we were on Sussex Mountains, there was this stupid practice whereby you had to carry your webbing on you at all times, so if the enemy were watching, they wouldn't think you were in a defensive position. Ridiculous, utterly ridiculous – the premise being, never give anything away to the enemy as they may exploit the intelligence – but it was so obvious we were in a defensive position, as three thousand men had just landed on the beaches below and were building sangars and trying to dig trenches.

Sometimes the webbing could weigh sixty pounds, and to walk say, from here to there, a few feet out of your trench, you had to put it on; so in the end we just binned it and walked about with our rifles and pockets full of ammunition and a water bottle.

Private Mark Sleap, Patrols Platoon 2 Para

It was shortly after Goose Green when we was going out on a recce and we got stopped, I think it might have been around D Company lines, as there was some more information to give us before we moved on. Anyway, it was pitch black and we were just standing around talking and a single 155 came in and landed, you know, like twenty metres away. I felt that compression on the chest and we all went down, and fucking hell, when we got up, I went, 'Kev, [Lance Corporal Sissons, Patrols Platoon] your 66 is smoking!' He had a 66 on his back and a piece of shrapnel had gone through the rocket motor and it was smoking, so he went and put it in the smoking hole the 155 had just made.

Then Mad Dog Warren had one of those issued Ho Chi Minh suits under his windproof and all that fluff filling was coming out of one of his sleeves, because the blast had penetrated his skinny arms and the filling was spilling out. Kev also had a piece of shrapnel that had gone into his mag pouch, hit his mag and set off one of the rounds, which then fired out through the front of his mag. That round made a perfect round hole in the side of the mag.

Lance Corporal 'Duke' Allen, Defence Platoon 2 Para

There was a TV crew who looked like they were going to film me and Radar picking up the dead, but it was the Argy dead we were picking up, so I told them to fuck off, because our dead were there also. The dead are the dead and they all needed to be treated with respect. Then some time later I was shown footage of me and Radar on the TV, so this crew must have filmed us before I told them to fuck off, or sneaked away and carried on filming.

Corporal 'Ginge' Dawes, clothing storeman, 2 Para

Tied up alongside the jetty at Goose Green there was a small, green British coastal freighter the *Monsunen*, previously an Argentinian supply vessel before *we* captured her, and one of my jobs was go and clean it up, because the Argies had defecated all over it. So I rounded up half a dozen prisoners and a couple of our guys and went on board. One of the Argies could speak really good English. He was a carpenter from Buenos Aires and his family roots were back in Wales. At the same time, we had to get an engineer from 59 Commando, a diver, because the Argies had purposely wrapped a heavy rope around the propeller and started the engine up.

So this diver turned up in all his full kit, holding a big hacksaw that he'd borrowed from the local butcher at Goose Green, and started hacking through the rope. Also, as he was swimming around the dock, he was picking weapons off the bottom that the Argies had thrown in, and every now and then, he'd appear and toss rifles and pistols up onto the jetty.

Later, when the vessel was cleared, we received orders to sail it around to Fitzroy, so me and about a dozen of us set sail at night with a Navy crew and a local guide, who was like a pilot for the Navy lads, because he knew the safest way round the islands to get us to Fitzroy. I remember getting into Fitzroy, it was still dark, and I could see these two big ships anchored there, which were the *Galahad* and the *Tristram*. One of the Navy guys says, 'Oh, why don't you sleep onboard the *Galahad*, where it's nice and warm and watch a video?'

'No, thank you very much, I'd sooner get me feet on wet

land,' I said. We disembarked, then got our heads down in some sheep sheds.

I woke up first thing in the morning to go through some kit, when I heard someone scream, 'Air red!' – it had been shortened to that by now, instead of air raid warning red. I ran out and as I did, and I don't know why, I looked to my right and there was this guy with a Blowpipe missile launcher on his shoulder and he fired it off. I mean, I was probably about fifty metres away from him, but it didn't go up in the air as it should have, instead the missile very slowly corkscrewed, turned and came for me. I took cover and it went into the sea. I don't think it exploded either! He was firing it at the Skyhawks who were attacking the *Galahad* and *Tristram*. We all rushed to the shoreline saving blokes.

I remember this one guy in one of those orange survival suits, but he hadn't got it zipped right up. He'd been in the water when one of the rescue helicopters picked him up on the winch and kinda dumped him on the beach right by me. So, me and Gordon Fawcet [Cpl QM's Department] got him, I mean this guy's suit was full of water, so I got a knife and cut the suit at the ankles and all the water just gushed out. He was a sergeant major medic from Mytchett Camp just outside Aldershot. I think he said he was in charge of environmental health, but I couldn't imagine what he was doing on board the *Sir Galahad*.

Funny, I met him years later in The Trafalgar pub in Aldershot, and he cries out, 'I remember you, you're the guy who saved my life!' I found it all a bit embarrassing, especially being in front of the lads and all that.

22

CONSEQUENCES

You blink, and where's forty years gone?
But for some veterans, it's still crystal clear.

Private Andy Hutchins, 5 Platoon 2 Para, posted to IDB Warminster UK

When our dead came home, I was detailed to go on the 2 Para firing party for the burials all around the UK; to the towns where the families wanted their boys to be buried.[33] We tried to make a joke about it, like we were a rock band on tour, because it was so depressing, and a lot of people forget about that. I reckon I was put on the firing party because I wasn't there, but to make me feel a part of it. There was about twenty of us, all Paras, and we toured for about two weeks. Didn't fire live rounds, only blanks.

I came through Depot Para with Tam Mechan and Sully, who was killed over the white flag incident. And here's a strange thing, when I passed out of Depot Para, all us recruits were given a choice of what battalion we wanted to go to, which was quite unusual at that time – 1, 2 or 3 Para – so I chose 2 Para, because Sully was my

---

33   In a break with tradition, many of the dead from the Falklands campaign were, at the request of their families, brought back to the UK and interred here. Previously, Britain's war dead had been buried close to the place of their death, in graves tended by the Commonwealth War Graves Commission.

corporal in Depot and was a great soldier. I learned so much from Sully and I wanted to be like him. Top man was Sully.

Private Tom Caughey, Rear Party, Mortar Platoon 2 Para

After passing-out I was posted to A Company 2 Para, who were posted to Berlin. When we came back, the battalion was posted to NI for two years, and it was early in that tour when I got injured. I was in the back of a 4-tonner on our way to relieve B Company at the Bessbrook location, when we got hit at Warrenpoint. I was blasted out the back of the 4-tonner and received 35 per cent burns and multiple fractures, which I'm still suffering from to this day; weeping, pus-y legs and all that. I was lucky to survive, because apart from Paul Burns, RIP [Pte, A Company 2 Para], we were the only two to survive out of the 4-tonner from the first bomb. Corporal Johnny Giles, Lance Corporal Chris Ireland, Privates Gary Barnes, Michael Wood, Jeff Jones, and Dylan Vaughan-Jones did not. RIP all.

After months and months of hospital I was keen to get back to the battalion, but I was never fully fit, never recovered; well, you wouldn't with my injuries. When you guys were still in NI, I spent some time on the Recruiting Team and when you came back, I was posted to Support Company, mortars, as their storeman, because I still couldn't do too much.

Mortars had an intake of young lads who didn't particularly know me, and one of them thought I was a crow, then one day he called me Paddy. So I says to him, 'Listen, you call me Tom or you call me Caughey, not Paddy.' I mean, all the guys told him to wind his neck in and had told him what had happened to me, but he didn't shut up and kept on winding me up and calling me Paddy. So I said to him, 'You call me fucking Paddy again, I'm gonna fill you in,' which I did, and the fucker bubbled me.

I goes on Orders in front of Colonel Jones, but before I do the RSM, Mal Simpson, says to me, 'Go in and keep your mouth shut.' So I goes in, not marched in in double-time as you do, because I couldn't walk properly, obviously, and Jones reads out the charge of assault, Section 69, and that sort of thing.

'Why did you hit him?' Jones asks.

'Because he's a wanker, sir.' I replied, and I could see from the corner of my eye, the RSM bracing up.

'Oh,' he says, 'do you hit everyone who's a wanker?'

'Well, sir, it's in my training sir, but you probably wouldn't know that being a Devon and Dorset.' I had no idea where that came from, or why I said it, it just spilled out.

Then Jones went ballistic, he went absolutely fucking mad and screamed, 'Get him out, get him out, get that man in jail!' I mean, he was screaming like a madman. I've never seen anything like it before or since!

Then Mal Simpson says, 'Sir, he's not fit for jail.'

'I don't care. Get him in jail and let him sit there for twenty-eight days.'

So, I gets twenty-eight days on the day before the battalion goes on pre-Belize leave, and when I come out, the battalion's already left for war down south. So I didn't get a chance to see the guys before they left. I felt totally useless, and, of course, my head is still fucked from Warrenpoint and all that, but I mean, I could have helped out on the ship, or worked in one of the echelons, done something useful.

Anyway, I get put on Rear Party and designated OC Rear Party, Major 'Squeak' Holborn's driver. During the day I would wait for the reports to come in and see how you guys were doing, and in the evening, I'd go down town on the piss. In the morning I would pick up Squeak and carry on through the day. When Goose Green happened, the names of the fallen started coming in, Stevie Prior,

Chuck Hardman, Tam Mechan, and I was like *shit*, but the names just kept on coming: Jones, Captain Dent, Captain Wood.

The casualty list, well, it just went on and on and I knew most of the blokes, and then I would have to drive Squeak around in my Land Rover to deliver the message to the widows and families. I would sit in the Land Rover while Squeak broke the devastating news. Then a couple of days after Goose Green something clicked inside and I said to Squeak, Major Holborn, 'Sir, I want out.' Then two days later I was out of 2 Para, and out of the Army. I drove from Aldershot back across to my home in Newtownards [NI] while all you guys were still fighting, and it was the biggest mistake of my life. I was immensely proud of what you guys were achieving and that made it harder for me, as I wanted to be a part of that, to make up for Warrenpoint. Goose Green was that trigger for me.

Corporal Douglas McCready, 1 Section commander, Machine Gun Platoon 2 Para

We initially covered D Company as they were assaulting the airfield above C Company heads, and then we moved forward with all the SF and took over some Argy trenches, but they were more like shell scrapes. Then there were reports we was shooting you up! But I can't remember none of that, definitely not. I mean Bob Cole rants on that we, Machine Guns, were shooting you boys up in C Company, but I don't know who spread that rumour. We were firing at the Argy fuckers, not you fuckers!

Private John Bolland, Recce Platoon 2 Para

When I was fit enough to go back to battalion, I was put in the Int Section, out the road. The IO [Intelligence Officer] Captain

Coulson, a lovely bloke and a Jock too, said, 'You're fucked, John, they're having you out.'

They didn't like us injured back then; bad for morale. How many wounded did they keep in? The only one I can remember was Metal Mickey, RIP, they put him up at PCAU [Parachute Course Administration Unit] Brize Norton, in the stores right out the way. They got rid of every one apart from Metal Mickey, as far as I know.

Captain Paul Farrar, OC Patrols Platoon 2 Para

Some people will say H Jones was not shy of sacking people. Pete Adams [the previous OC Patrols 2 Para Captain], is a case in point, and I don't know what happened, but whatever happened between H and Pete, it was irrecoverable. Had H Jones not died, then there were several people in our battalion in fairly key positions who would have been given their marching orders after the battle for Darwin and Goose Green, for perceived professional weakness, and/or failure. H Jones would have had none of it. The fact that he died meant that sackings never happened, but it would have been interesting. You were either in with H Jones or you weren't. There are several who would have not survived contact if he had lived.

Captain John Greenhalgh DFC, Scout Flight 656 Squadron Army Air Corps

During the war, small helicopters (Scouts and Gazelles) picked up over 300 battlefield casualties including many Argentinians. Doc Steve Hughes pleaded with me to take out the badly wounded Argentinians above our less wounded Paras, which I did.

Colour Sergeant Pete Vale, HQ Company 2 Para

Colonel Jones. He had a very, very short fuse, and by contrast, Chris Keeble had that quality where he could bring him down and they were a good team. They complemented each other. Keeble could take Jones aside and was probably one of the only guys who could.

Corporal Marty Margerison. 6 Platoon B Company 2 Para

I didn't particularly like H Jones and I'll explain. In 1981 we had the battalion Skill at Arms week down at Hythe and Lydd Ranges and I was an Army shot as a junior soldier. My weapon skills were that good on the SLR I could hit a target at 600 yards, and because I was so good with the SLR, I got put into the Junior Army Shooting Team, and that is what they call an Army shot.

So, during the battalion's yearly Skill at Arms week, I'd got through to the final stage, and who am I up against? Well, Bonzo Head. Bonzo was a full-screw in C Company and also part of the CO's Rover Group, his bodyguards; all the battalion shooting team, you know, Taff Evans, all of them, if ever we deployed, they'd become the CO's bodyguards. Well, that was the idea.

Now, I'm firing against Jones's best man and it comes down to one last round and I've gone, 'Shit, Bonzo's fucked up here!' because he's hit *my* target by mistake, a falling plate target, and his is still up! He's got no rounds left, but I have one, so I've won. I am now the battalion champion. We came off the firing point and Jones came over and he was iffing and ahhing and he made us have a re-shoot, because his boy didn't win. We had a re-shoot and I beat Bonzo again; I knocked all the targets down before he did, and completed it.

I am now the winner – undisputable, ha-ha, but when I went to receive my cup, and you know the procedure – you march up, you salute, he gives you the cup, you take the cup in your left hand and say 'Thank you very much, sir,' you salute again, and off you go. Anyway, so I goes up, salutes, and he doesn't salute me, he doesn't repay my salute; he didn't say thank you, kiss my arse, or fuck all, and I thought, *you twat!* Subsequently from that day on, and I wouldn't say he knobbed me off for any reason after that, but he wasn't respectful to what I achieved as one of his corporals, and that's how I felt every time I bumped into him.

It always seemed to be about him. I mean, of course I respected him for what he did, but that shooting incident always stuck in my head and I felt he was quite selfish if things didn't go his own way. Look, he was my CO, and loyalty, integrity and honesty for the best part was how I played my career, and I was never asked if I wanted to go into the battalion shooting team. Not that I fucking ever wanted to!

On the trip down we used to get daily updates and then the lads started to ask, what's going right and what's going wrong! And it was all about us landing. If you kept information back from your Toms, they'd question things – they're not dickheads. Private soldiers aren't stupid and they would question stuff like, 'Why are we breaking in ski march boots when we are crossing the equator?' I didn't have a clue about why! How *they* didn't recognise what kit we were supposed to have. We had Marines garrisoned down there for years, and I can't remember any cold weather clothing being issued; okay we had the arctic tops and bottoms underwear, but most of the lads wore their jungle issue kit.

Private Steve Taylor, 3 Platoon A Company 2 Para

I recall Captain Chris Dent sitting down with me and the blokes sharing a KitKat and I had this feeling he was going to die down there. I had a similar feeling about Stevie Prior, too! I dunno what

351

it is, but every time I get a similar feeling, I tell them now, even if it spooks them or they think I'm an idiot.

Private David Minnock, GPMG gunner, 12 Platoon D Company 2 Para

After the war, I served a bit in the TA [Territorial Army] and they tried to get me drunk so they could get me to tell them stuff about Goose Green, and I only remember certain bits, but those bits are embedded in me for life; other bits, forget it, it's like a complete memory block.

A 22 SAS call sign

I got married to the missus in 1970, and we're in 1982 now, been married twelve years, and I've been away on operations all over the place, and the only time I've seen her get upset was when all the fleet came back from war. I think it was the *Hermes*, it had docked in Portsmouth and the Queen had come down to meet it, and they're all giving it the waves and all the rest of it, you know, the pomp. She was upset, she said, 'How come there was no flags or banners and nobody welcomed *you* back?'

'Luv, nobody ever welcomes us back. We go out there, we do it, the business, and we come back, you should know that by now, luv.'

'Look what they are doing for everybody else! And you went down there first.' And that's what really upset her, and I never knew she felt like that until very recently.

Private Mick Crockford, Recce Platoon 2 Para

My dad and my stepmum came and picked me up at Brize Norton and they gave me, Bernie Bolt and Drew [2 Para] a lift to Aldershot.

I didn't want to talk to them, I couldn't. I just wanted to get back to Aldershot and get on the piss.

Lance Corporal Pete 'Stubbo' Stubbs, MT Platoon 2 Para, attached to the Red Devils Parachute Display Team

Well, Duke's mum and dad came all the way down from Turriff, Scotland, which is further north than Aberdeen, it's way up there, and his parents came all the way to see Duke and he said hello to them and just shot off and left them at Brize.

I had this sign pinned up on my bunk door which read, *Fuck off You War Heroes. I'm sick to death of it. I'm sick of it all. Leave me alone.* I was really feeling it, because I'd spent years with Duke and Radar and all the others in MT and the rest of the battalion, and to see them on TV picking up the dead one time, well, I thought I should have been there too, but that's just something I had to live with and still do.

Well, the blokes did come into my bunk and they were completely bonkers. I mean, I was really gobsmacked at just how mad the guys were. They were fuckin' fizzing. The blokes were getting minging [drunk] and you weren't giving a flying fuck. Discipline had gone out the window, and you guys had gone mad! No doubt about it.

Lance Corporal 'Duke' Allen, Defence Platoon 2 Para

When we all came back, Stubbo was still in the Red Freds. I went to see him over in Arnhem Barracks and he had put a notice on his door saying something like, *Fuck off, I don't want to hear any war stories* . . . like a big piss-take, you know, but I actually said to him, 'Stubbo, you dozy fucker, if you would have been down there, well, you would have dragged me in to some sort of trouble and we'd have been dead!' After I'd said that, he felt a lot happier about things, you know about missing the war.

Sergeant Major Colin Price, A Company 2 Para

After the battle for Darwin Hill, I recall Ted Barrett came down to see me and I still had this little Argy by my side, who was actually behaving himself, he was a good lad. Ted asked if Stevie Prior was dead.

'Yes,' I answered, and I was aware Stevie was Ted's best mate and he took his bayonet out.

'I'm gonna kill this little Argy,'

'Through me, Ted, through me.' I told him very firmly. Ted looked at me with that stare he had; Ted was a big man but we were mates.

'And please put your bayonet away,' I ordered.

Private Steve Taylor, 3 Platoon A Company 2 Para

General Jeremy Moore was a bitter man, he is quoted as saying, 'Goose Green should have been left to wither on the vine. We will save all our shells for Stanley. Goose Green was a sideshow.'

Tony Smith, Falkland Islander

On 29th of May our hopes and prayers were answered when the Paras defeated the heavily garrisoned settlement of Goose Green and took the surrender from the Argentine forces. It was then I knew the tide was turning and it wouldn't be long before our beautiful Falkland Islands were British once again! It was a day I will never be forget. The victory, the battle for Goose Green is now part of our history.

CONSEQUENCES

Roy 'Wendy' Gibson, steward and ship's pianist, MV Norland

When the Paras came back on board you could tell they were traumatised and were so tired. They were offered another ship to get home quicker, but they said no, they wanted to return home on the *Norland*, and they were glad to get back on the *Norland*, and a couple of the Paras said to me, 'Oh, well done, Wendy.'

'Why?' I said, 'I've done nothing.'

'You got a Mention in Despatches,'

'Well, I never.' I mean, I didn't know what despatches was! I thought, *what's this Mentioned in Despatches? What is it?*

'It's like a pat on the back.'

'Well I never, I don't bloody know!'

I was like an agony aunt on the way home. I must have had a dozen or so lads come to my cabin, crying and stuff. I used to say, 'Come on in,' and the crew always had beers in our cabins you know, we had these little fridges, so they'd have a beer and some were on Valium and they were upset about Colonel Jones and about all the other lads who didn't come back.

Regimental Sergeant Major Mal Simpson, 2 Para

The day I joined 2 Para as the Regimental Sergeant Major, RSM, Murray Smith – the chap who I was taking over from – was getting wheeled out in a wheelchair, because he'd damaged his back. There was no handover as such. The CO, Colonel Jones, was not in barracks, he was away sailing, so I thought, *good, nobody around*. I met the Mess members and gave them my way of doing things, which I think at first they found difficult to accept but that's the way of life; I was the Chief and they were the Indians.

Everything settled, I decided to go and do some sport parachuting. I love my sport parachuting, but unfortunately, I was playing around a bit too much under the canopy and hooked it on landing. I broke my arm, smashed my shoulder and kidneys, and all this while the CO was still away sailing. So when the CO comes back from sailing, he's still got no RSM, because I'm walking round with a bloody great big plaster on my arm, and that's when the relationship between myself and Colonel Jones turned out – badly!

A 22 SAS call sign

Recently, I was at a reunion and the subject of Goose Green came up – again. Colin Price, Sergeant Major, A Company 2 Para, pulled me and said, 'You never told us anything.'

'Hang on a second, mate,' and I pulled him to one side and told him, 'I've been getting this shit for years!' We gave *them* all the int and I told the people who were debriefing us I would go over to 2 Para and brief them up personally, but I couldn't just jump on a helicopter. I mean, I would have, even though my body was in bits from weeks out in the cuds [behind enemy lines], and within an hour of landing on ship, we were getting debriefed. We had a dhobi, had something to drink, no food apart from toast, then we were whipped into the briefing room and got debriefed. After the debrief, only then did we go for food. And that's the way it happened.

Colin was very, very upset, so I said, 'Let's have a drink on it,' just to calm things. Then the Sergeant Major B Company, 2 Para down south, Pete Richens, who was also standing with us, mentioned one time he was at a school down in Somerset, about to give a talk about the Falklands War. As he was about to start, one of the organisers says, 'Oh by the way, before you start, Pete, see that guy in the front row? Well, that's General Sir Michael Rose and he was CO 22 SAS at the time.'

'Well, no pressure then,' Pete said! So, after the talk, Pete told me he ushered the General to a quiet spot and brought up the subject of the lack of int for Goose Green. The General told Pete that H Jones had all the int we had, 22 SAS passed it all over, and that included *my* complete reinforcement assessment. What H did with that int, Pete said, the General couldn't say. But he was adamant that every piece of information 22 SAS patrols gained was sent straight away across to 2 Para.

Corporal Tom Harley MM, section commander, 10 Platoon D Company 2 Para

There was a company of mercenaries at Goose Green and on the features around Stanley, too. They were from all nationalities, Americans, two Brits, Dutch, Germans; there were about a couple of hundred of them mercenaries in all. I couldn't believe how many there were and they were good, they put up a ton of resistance. I would say there were at least fifty of 'em at Goose Green. I reckon there were a couple of hundred all together and [they] were put in different locations. I remember some of my boys talking to them in Stanley, but I didn't. I didn't want to.

Captain Paul Farrar, OC Patrols Platoon 2 Para

I spoke later to Colin Connor MC, who I'd seen come through Depot, and of course, seen come through P Company, and as you know, we were platoon commanders and we were working in bubbles during the battle. He came up to me the day after the battle and apologised for not supporting the Patrols Platoon when we attacked the schoolhouse area. I said, 'There wasn't enough room for any more people.'

'No, no, there was so much fire coming down, we just couldn't follow you,' he replied. I thought, well thanks, Colin! I didn't really know much about Recce's war and I think with hindsight, after the battle for Goose Green and maybe after Wireless Ridge too, we should have sat down with people and said, 'Right, John, what was your take on this or that?' or 'Pete, what did you see?' We should have done an after-action review. It was something we weren't particularly good at, at the time. We are better at it now.

After the Falklands I don't think I ever saw Colin Connor again. I think he went to the Depot and I stayed for three years in Patrol Company and left in early 1985.

Look, it wasn't the thing you did, you didn't sit down and say, how was it for you? Only with hindsight do you realise that everyone's got their own little frailties and how hard it is to be brave. Sometimes you know you've been a bit this, or, well I should have been a bit that, or maybe, I was a bit too much the other! Sometimes you don't always share that with people.

I've always had this theory, and I served thirty-six years regular service, from a seventeen-year-old recruit in the Light Infantry to a fifty-five-year-old retiree, but the Falklands for me remains the most formative period of my service and most enjoyable, and the whole period around there. If I'd missed that in my career, I'd have been just distraught.

Contemporaries of mine who didn't go to the Falklands, who happened to be in 1 Para or instructors at the Depot or Sandhurst; I mean, to miss the Falklands, well! And it's always refreshing to hear from the many men I served with who went up to Hereford and did all the stuff they did in the SAS: Western Iraq, Afghanistan, and other missions. For them, it is still the Falklands which is their defining experience and that makes me quite proud to say I was a part of it.

23

SCARS OF WAR

Private John Bolland, Recce Platoon 2 Para

I was sectioned[34] because of PTSD with Dave 'Charlie' Brown and another Para lad who I'll call Harry, not his real name, down at an old house that used to be owned by the sugar people, Tate & Lyle, Ty Gwyn in Llandudno in Wales. A beautiful place overlooking the bay and all that.

There was this woman, a specialist like, who had decided she was going to have a group session and she told us not to smoke. I thought, *here we fucking go.*

'You are not to smoke in here.'

So I says, 'I don't give a shit, I'm smoking.' So, we just sat there, then bang on cue, two Tornados comes screaming across from Llandudno Bay and all three of us hit the deck and she sat there and says, 'Have you got a problem?'

Then Dave fires into her big style. The other lad, Harry, had been on the *Galahad* pulling bodies out of that burning ship. And with

---

34 Detained in a mental hospital for treatment under Section 4 of the Mental Health Act.

that she says, 'I'll tell you what we'll do, we'll all go to Manchester airport tomorrow, to the viewing deck, to watch the planes take off.' She lasted ten fucking minutes. She asked if any of us wanted a coffee and then disappeared. I never seen her again ever! She never came back.

The day before, she gave Harry a teddy bear smelling of lavender, and told him, if he was having a nightmare, to wake up and smell the teddy. So the next morning the teddy was found nailed through the neck on the door of her office.

Private Dave 'Charlie' Brown, HQ C (Bruneval) Company 2 Para

At the time, there was about thirty of us in this Tate & Lyle house, all crap hats (apart from the Paras) from NI or Gulf War One. On day one, we were asked if we had any dietary needs. 'Only whisky,' says John.

In the afternoons the chef used to make sandwiches, and one day he made two trays of corned beef.[35] Well, Harry, me and John thought the chef was taking the piss, so Harry scoops up both trays and throws them in the bin and that's when all the hats started to complain about us.

Private David Minnock, GPMG gunner, 12 Platoon D Company 2 Para

Nigel 'Mino' Smith KIA, RIP. Years later I was visiting the Military Cemetery in Aldershot, and I was at Mino's graveside paying my respects when this young lady comes up to me and says, 'Did you know him?'

'Yeah,' I says, 'I put him in there!' She then bursts into tears.

'I'm his sister,' and then I did too. I've never done that before

35 Still to this day, most Falklands War veterans will always opt for Brazilian corned beef over Argentinian.

at anyone's grave. She went on to tell me she wanted to be by the graveside as her brother was being lowered down, but she was not allowed. She had to stand back. She was only a little girl back then, about six or seven.

Corporal Douglas McCready, 1 Section commander, Machine Gun Platoon 2 Para

Goose Green was a crazy battle. The Argies could have killed us from miles away. If they had stood their ground, we wouldn't have had a hope in fucking hell, and if they'd sorted their mortars out. It was the peat that saved us, those mortar rounds just bedded right into the peat bogs. And the noise on the battlefield, it was just so fucking loud and it lasted for hours.

Private Dave 'Charlie' Brown, HQ C (Bruneval) Company 2 Para

Eleven wounded and sadly one killed out of fifty-five brave men. Never forget Mark Holman-Smith KIA, RIP mate. So many years on and I always remembered that time with pride. But yet, I still feel I wasn't there [in the battle] because, out of the whole of C Company Headquarters, I didn't have a scratch on me. Even to this day I still feel that.

Reg Kemp, night steward, MV Norland

The 2 Para lads were not only our passengers, but our boys too. I was into fitness, so when I finished at early o'clock, I would usually see all the lads doing a bit of training and I liked to keep in shape a little bit myself. I was doing a bit of jogging around the decks when it was warm, but as we sailed further south the weather turned cold, and I got talking to this guy, a nice fella, and never give it more thought than that really. Then one night one of the lads said to me I'd been hobnobbing it with one of the officers, and I says, 'Who's that then?'

'Captain Dent,' he replies. Well, he was just another one of the guys, you know. I mean, I only ever saw him in training kit, no rank like. So, as the time went on, we swapped a few stories, and I remember him saying he was married with a couple of children, and he was just a really nice fella. As we sailed further south of the equator, he did say he'd not be around so much because of operational stuff and that kind of thing, and that's the last time I ever saw him.

Shortly after the Goose Green battle, one of the crew members told me about Chris, and when I heard, I were very sad, very sad. I was told about the other lads too, and I thought *fucking hell!* I didn't think it could be Chris somehow. I just thought he seemed a guy who would survive. And then later on, when we went back to the Falklands after dumping off those Argy prisoners, it was explained to us exactly how he'd lost his life.

H Jones said something like, 'Look, you go there and you fuckin' get on with it,' and he did it, and he lost his life, and he's got a little fuckin' pile of stones where he fell, and H Jones has got a big pile, you know! It don't seem right somehow, and I've been back there myself and seen where H Jones's pile is, and where Chris's is too; behind and over to the side. A big pile for a life and a small pile for a life. It really don't seem right, but there you are!

Corporal Tom Harley MM, section commander, 10 Platoon D Company 2 Para

As far as the Military Medal's concerned, mine was for the whole of the battle, no specific thing, and I've never read the other two citations Gaz and Baz [Privates Carter and Grayling D Company] received, but it's like anything else, these things are just a lottery anyway. Lots of names get put forward, but only ten per cent get picked up, and I think it is more luck than achievement. So we got three MMs in my section and that's just the way it worked out. When I found out Major Neame got a MID, I just fucking threw a track![36] And Chaundler [the new CO 2 Para] said, 'Tom, Tom, I understand what you're saying.'

'It stinks,' I replied, 'it's Army politics.'

Phil Neame's father was awarded the Victoria Cross in the Second World War and I reckon that's what it was; there must have been a bit of friction between him and Jones and that just carried through!

I love Major Phil Neame. I think, for me, he was the unsung hero, because at the end of the day, there are two battle honours on our flag, which are Goose Green and Wireless Ridge, and D Company was at the forefront of both of them. And I know all the rest of the company commanders and the battalion know that Neame was sold short. Bloody Army politics. His men loved him too, because from what I've seen and read, he was the only OC up there doing the fighting with his men. The other OCs were of course there doing their role managing their company, but we were fractured; the plan had gone out of the window very early on, and it was all ad lib.

It was a section commander's war and they took command and Neame knew the importance of this piece of land we'd just cleared of Argies, probably half a dozen trenches, because when we then got up on the brow of this hill, we could see right across Darwin Hill and our objective, the airfield and Goose Green.

Corporal Marty Margerison, 6 Platoon B Company 2 Para

We all wanted to go to war and we all wanted to get a medal – all of us. It's nice to be rewarded with something you can put on your chest. I had issues which played on my mind about getting wounded

---

36 Army slang. When a tank throws a track, it can't move, which is very annoying and can take a long time to repair.

and not being there for my blokes, some of whom got trench foot, and this is part of my diagnosis of PTSD, because I beat myself up about that. I consider myself a good soldier and I got shot. I got caught out, but what also happened was we killed the scarecrow sentry, then we did this little left flanking and cleared those trenches, we were now advancing forward and then I got shot.

Unlike Crossmaglen or Forkhill in Northern Ireland, none of that ever frightened me, I was never frightened going into a contact; never afraid of getting into a car except for once when we all had Army haircuts. I was never frightened of anything, but what I never experienced was having been in a contact, withdrawing, re-grouping, battle prepping and doing it again, whereas all my boys did; and up until that point, no one in the British Army in recent times had done that. All my boys did, 3 Para did, but not me.

So, this is it, would I have had the bollocks to do that? And I know what my answer is to you, and I know what other people say, but knowing Stevie Illingsworth had been killed and Jimmy Street shot through the leg and to go and re-org and to do it all again, well!

I've been in the looney hole and I've seen 'em fucking turn up and tell you they've got PTSD, and they're fucking liars, I've seen 'em scam. I've seen 'em say to counsellors, and I've trained as a counsellor, 'Ohhh, fuckin' hell. Bonfire night! Oh, I'm under the table.' Then next they're sitting in the telly room watching World War One and World War Two films. Now, up until four years ago, I couldn't watch any film of the Great War it was so shocking, but it's part of that process where you have to bury your demons. It's how your head tries to find answers for a situation that has happened.

Take divorce. In the majority of divorces, when it happens and the initial breakdown starts, you try to find an answer, yet sometimes there isn't an answer. Sometimes you just fall out of love, or you're not compatible and you want different things out of life, but soldiers are structured, that's how we're moulded; all my shirts are still hung up all neat and tidy, it's like a form of OCD. But when it's the middle of the night and somebody's shooting at you and you run out of bullets (if you're talking to civvies, rounds if soldiers), you've only got a second or two to go to the right place to get those bullets [*sic*] or the right piece of equipment; there's no time to get your torch out and start fucking about. It's embedded in you! I personally thought I was a good soldier, so why didn't I stop at the top of the hill?

Private John Bolland, Recce Platoon 2 Para

I'm lying in the hospital ship *Uganda* and our boys have been killed and I'm lying between clean sheets. Do you have any idea how that feels? The boys have been killed and I'm lying between clean sheets. The guilt [of surviving]. I can't go to reunions, because I can't face 'em.

Corporal 'Ginge' Dawes, clothing storeman, 2 Para

When I came back, I bumped into Pop Turvey [2 Para], who was a good old boy and was on Rear Party. He said someone had sent him some white feathers when we were down south, and he'd found it rather upsetting. I consoled him by saying it was an order, Rear Party was your duty, you had to stay. I'm not sure who sent the white feathers, it could have been one of the wives! I couldn't see it being any of the lads.

Captain Paul Farrar, OC Patrols Platoon 2 Para

Let's not forget, Northern Ireland was fairly gritty in its day, but some people who went to the Falklands, well, they sort of measured themselves against their own personal template and thought, yes, I'm okay at this, I can live with this. Others went there, came back and thought, *Thank goodness I survived that. I didn't embarrass myself, I did the job, but you know what? I'm gonna leave.*

There were quite a few officers that left who were on the career path, who said, 'Well, I've had my war and I'm going.' I did wonder if that was genuine, or is it that you've just measured yourself and you're not entirely sure you like what you see? I've always felt that from the Falklands War.

Private John Bolland, Recce Platoon 2 Para

Going back to the dairy. I didn't know this, but the lad who was holding my hand in the dairy that day was an Argy. All these years I thought it was one of our own, but in that sentence, I'll give him my total forgiveness.

Corporal Tom Harley MM, section commander, 10 Platoon D Company 2 Para

There was one thing I carry with me; I was never a bully. I was cruel but fair you could say, and all of my section to a man, they thanked me after for getting them through it all, and that makes me so proud. I had a young eighteen-year-old in my section and we are still in regular contact to this day. It was the most traumatic experience of their lives and of mine too. I never slept in my own basha, I'd spend every night in a different one in the section, talking to the lads and keeping the faith up, and that's the way I gained their respect and friendship.

Corporal Marty Margerison, 6 Platoon B Company 2 Para

As we were getting near the Falklands, I got into a bit of scuffle with Baz Barsley MM, RIP, and he'd loosened one of my teeth, so I had to fly over to HMS *Fearless* to see the dentist. While I was there, I bumped into an SAS lad I knew, Paul Bunker – he and Davey 'Chuck' Hardman and me were on Senior Brecon together – so we had a bit of a chat and he told me he was waiting to cross-deck on to another ship then fly on to the island. I didn't know Paul had gone down in that SAS chopper which was cross-decking until after Goose Green. So that was Davey RIP and Paul RIP, gone! This was later to play a part in my PTSD.

The Falklands war was the last conventional war the British ever fought with the tactics we employed, and I remember going down to Brecon, the British Army Infantry Battle School and the Jungle Warfare Instructors' Course and just to talk to some of the DS [directing staff], and it was a common thought: we are not going to change our tactics just because you fucking lot [the Parachute Regiment] won against all the odds. That was the mentality.

After the battle for Goose Green, the 66 was not simply a medium anti-tank weapon, but was used to take out trenches and bunkers too, and all sections now carried 66s in the Parachute Regiment. Yet all these hats refused to change their tactics, because it wasn't them!

Less than three years before, 2 Para and the Welsh Guards were stationed together on the Berlin tour and shared the same NAAFI. The veterans of the Welsh Guards are quite bitter for several reasons, a very proud regiment, and you gotta remember, in Berlin we had a big fight with the Welsh Guards in the NAAFI, but then we all became friends.

Now this is my opinion, the Welsh Guards weren't prepared for the Falklands War. They weren't fit, their tactics were poor, and I believe to this day that's the reason why they went on the *Galahad* and *Tristram*, because they would not have been able to tab across the ground as we did. They were *not* poor soldiers, but some of their commanders were, and I tell them that. I don't pull any punches, and it's not slagging the *guys* off, they are great blokes. I get a muted reaction for most of it; sometimes they don't know how to reply.

On a recent trip back down to the Falklands, the first person I met at Liberty Lodge was the old CO of the Welsh Guards of 1982, a retired brigadier now, and the CO and his Quartermaster of the existing Welsh Guards. When we're introduced, the old CO shakes my hand, and the first thing he says is: 'What did you think of H Jones?'

'Really! Is that a question you want to ask me?' I threw at him, 'Thirty-six years later, you want me to say . . .'

'Oh, I was just posing a question,' he says.

I thought, *no he's not, he's still trying to find fault, still trying to justify their poor fucking planning skills*, and I found that disgraceful.

The Guards ran the British Army; there was no way they were not sending a contingent to war. Some hated all things Parachute Regiment, yet we had the most fantastic company in the Parachute Brigade, the No 1 (Guards) Independent Parachute Company; if not the most professional organisation in the world, on a par, if not as good as the SAS – and weren't the Welsh Guards taken off public duties and given a crash course in Brecon before they set sail?

When you look at a soldier you look at his persona, you look at how he's dressed, how he or she holds themselves. For example, when I passed out of Depot, I was standing by the square watching this company of 2 Para, who had recently returned from a tour in Malaya and I looked and thought, *fuckin' hell, I'm now one of them!* I could smell the testosterone on these blokes. These are fucking soldiers and I'm now part of this; am I going to be able to reach their level? Then you look at the Welsh Guards, and I'm not saying most are not soldiers; they almost certainly are, they're peacekeepers, they guard the Queen – very pretty, sergeant major, but can they fight?

When I did my Skill at Arms course down in Warminster as an instructor, this major from the Trials and Development Unit turns up and we're all sitting in the lecture hall and me being the gobshite that I am, I always questioned the kit we got issued. So anyway, I'm sitting there and he's telling us about the new webbing coming in and all this bollocks, and I inadvertently asked him, 'Can you tell me, sir, why do all these other regiments want to have a Parachute Regiment helmet and a set of webbing, which is all water bottles and ammo pouches?'

I'm sitting in this lecture hall full of soldiers from other regiments and we're all mates. Well, the major just fucking lost it, he absolutely lost it. 'Who do you think you are? Just because you're in the Paras. We design this equipment for the remainder of the Army, not just you!'

'Oh, sorry, sir, I'm asking this question because of the ground troops, the soldiers on the ground. I'm special, because I can choose my own pouch selection and not these two big useless fuck-off kidney pouches on the back, in which we're meant to carry all sorts of equipment like boot-cleaning kit. Yet all these soldiers here want *my* webbing.' He lost it again.

Now, you look at today's webbing, it's the same configuration of pouches to what 2 and 3 Para had in the Falklands, albeit made from the latest technical material. So I like to think my big bollocking down at Warminster that day went some way to changing the mindset of the powers-that-be.

That was the way of thinking back then, but I will say, what the Parachute Regiment did at Goose Green was phenomenal, because we were on the brink of losing it all. We'd run out of ammo, we didn't get resupplied or just couldn't get those supplies down to the troops, and we were lucky being in the Parachute Regiment, which understood keeping the momentum going; and if we lost momentum, we were going to lose the war. Putting all my kit on and being able to do a ten-miler in one hour forty-five max, when the Army standard was eight miles in one hour fifty, honestly made all the difference in combat.

To this day, I still stand by the fact that being exceptionally fit was one of the two big reasons that I and Steve Tufnell, who got shot in the head, survived. First, we had fantastic medics; second, our level of fitness. Now, Hank Hood, RIP, told this story, and it's common knowledge among certain Goose Green vets. When Hank got to Steve, he couldn't see an injury, but when he took Steve's helmet off, his skull came off too.

Hank used to tell how he saw Steve's brains and went, 'Oh fuck!' and gently put his helmet back on. Then he put his hand in Steve's hand and said, 'Squeeze my hand,' and he didn't. Hank said it again, 'Squeeze my hand,' and he didn't. 'If you don't squeeze my hand, Steve, I'm gonna give you another syrette of morphine.' Steve already had two syrettes because of this injury and one more would have OD'd [overdosed] him, as the man was dying; his brains were hanging out.

Then Steve squeezed Hank's hand. Now, timewise, Steve was shot before me and he was casevaced after me, because they couldn't get him in a helicopter. Steve was lucky, he was only eighteen and had recently come out of Depot, so his level of fitness was top.

The Parachute Regiment has an *esprit de corps* second to none. Yes, we are infantrymen on the ground, but in practice we were mass murderers; you weren't going to kill my friends without reaping some form of retribution! And that was our mentality.

In my time, I don't ever remember saying to any of my blokes who were in the sections, 'The sergeant major says this needs doing.' I'd just say, 'This needs doing,' and 99 per cent of the time it was done with no mention of the sergeant major. Maybe that was just respect for me, because I'd *been there*. We've all mopped up, done dixies, cleaned the bogs out, and done shit stuff we didn't want to do. I've done twenty-eight days in jail, I've been reduced to the ranks twice, so I knew what it was like to be a fucking Tom. So if I had to say to one of my blokes, 'Get up there because we can't locate the enemy,' he'd do it. Gain the respect of your men and lead from the front.

I always looked after my blokes, and I recall saying to a mother of a recruit when I was an instructor down at Depot Para after the Falklands War, when she commented on how strict everything was, and some form of bullying was mentioned. I told her, 'There's no need for us to bully in the Depot. If I need to punish somebody, I say, "Get your gear on, get your helmet on, get your rifle, and let's go do the assault course," because the end result would be, the fitter your boy is, the more chance he has of passing P Company, the more chance he has of becoming a paratrooper, and the more chance he has of surviving on the battlefield.'

I think my words hit home. Then I said, 'Because I don't want to knock on your door. The last thing I want to do is knock on your door telling you your son is dead because my training standards were poor.'

24

REFLECTIONS

Padre David Cooper, 2 Para

Steve Hughes, our exceptional medical officer. 2 Para was his first posting to a regular unit and he had showed himself to be a dedicated and committed doctor who always put the needs of his patients before anything else, and was to all intents and purposes fearless when it came to personal risk whilst doing his job. It was clear that his ethic had carried through to his medical aid team, whose work with that of Steve, ensured that every casualty that reached his aid post subsequently survived, and that included some very seriously injured soldiers.

He was cited for a Military Cross and his subsequent award of a Mention in Despatches never really signified the recognition that his work, courage and impact on the battalion fully deserved. He had broken a bone in his ankle shortly after landing, but had continued to soldier on, without making mention to anyone until shortly before we reached Wireless Ridge when it had proved too much of an injury to tolerate. We were fortunate in being able to ferry him forward in a passing Gazelle, to meet up with him again on the Ridge itself, overlooking the road into Stanley, when he was able to limp, with some help, into Stanley.

Sergeant Major Colin Price, A Company 2 Para

As a company sergeant major in a rifle company, you take up so many different roles, you actually don't realise how many you're doing. Initially I was in charge of discipline, welfare and admin for the guys, but when you're on active service it will also include casevac, casualty treatment, resup of ammunition, and resupply of food once the colour sergeant has got it to you; it's then up to me to dish it out to the different locations.

If you're in a defensive position, for instance, you've got three platoons separated, so you've gotta make sure they get their scoff and ammunition, and make sure they're powdering their feet and drying their socks; this is the sort of minuscule stuff that you have to do, which you don't realise you're doing until you're doing it.

Every morning when you're walking round the defensive position, you're constantly telling the lads, 'Make sure you're taking your socks off, dry your feet and powder 'em up, and try to dry your socks off any way you can: under your armpits,' – that sort of conversation. I guess, in a way, you have to be a bit like a daddy.

I was very lucky because in my twenty-two years' service I only ever threw one guy in jail. It was a guy who'd gone absent, AWOL, whilst we were on exercise on a cold February in Thetford. Two of 'em went absent actually and I can't remember either of their names, but one of 'em came back after two weeks, so he got his two weeks in nick and carried on soldiering. The other one stayed away until he heard we were going to the Falklands, and he turned up. He was in Northern Ireland, in A Company when he went AWOL. So he turned up and I said, 'What are you doing here, son?'

He says, 'I've come back to go to war with the battalion.'

So, I says, 'You didn't soldier with me in peacetime, you're not soldiering with me in wartime, so get your arse in fucking jail.' He was later discharged.

After the war, about a year later, 2 Para continued their six-month tour of Belize and I was on a spot of R&R, a night out, in a bar in Punta Gorda. This kid from Support Company 2 Para comes over, and I couldn't tell you his name, only a little lad, and he says, 'Hello, sergeant major.'

I replied, 'Hello, son, how you doing?'

He says, 'Alright, and hey, do you remember when we were at Wireless Ridge?'

I says, 'Yeah, go on then.'

He says, 'Remember, when we got all the wounded guys together?'

'Yes,' I replied, because Support Company had been hit by those Argy 155s and a few of them got blast wounds, but I couldn't remember this lad.

So, he goes on, 'And remember you came and had a chat with us?'

'Yes, because I was doing my sergeant major keeping-up-morale chat.' I found out they'd all been treated medically, so I just had a chat and assured them they'd all get casevaced out soon, and not to worry. They mainly had broken legs, blast injuries, hands and stuff like that. So this little lad carries on, 'When you left us, one of the wounded says to me, "Who was that you were talking to?"'

'What do you mean *who* was that?' I says.

He says, 'That bloke standing talking while all that artillery fire was going off?'

I say, 'Of course, he was chatting to us, he's the fucking sergeant major, in't he!'

You see, my point is, even though I was scared of the 155s

coming in all around, he respected the rank – the rank of sergeant major – and that was such a nice thing to say to me. I'm sure he didn't realise what he said in that bar all those years ago, but it still brings a tear to me today.

It was a crazy time. I was thirty-seven at Goose Green, married, and it was the one chance I had to do my job properly – for real, and I'm grateful for that chance as a rifle company sergeant major to be given the opportunity. I shared a cabin on the *Norland* with Sergeant Major 'Nobby' Clarke and as we were getting close to San Carlos Water, we lay on our bunks contemplating the coming fight, and Nobby says to me, 'What you thinking, Col?'

'I just hope I do what my soldiers expect me to do,' and I think I did. Because your soldiers expect that, and that's all I can say, apart from when I fired a 66 and missed!

Colour Sergeant Frank Pye, Support Company 2 Para

You know what, I don't think I ever heard any of the blokes' moan during and after the battle for Goose Green. Not even the wounded, and as you know, many were badly wounded; take Big Scouse Connell, he had to get in the Land Rover because he couldn't even walk, he'd got hit in the chest.

Corporal Ken Raynor, patrol commander, Recce Platoon 2 Para

When we got back to the UK, I was posted to Lympstone for two years on the bootneck [Royal Marine] equivalent of the Brecon Command Course. A lot of staff had massive chips on their shoulders, and this is where Doc Jolly [every casualty who made it to his field hospital survived, Brit and Argy], the Surgeon Commander, CTCRM [Commando Training Centre Royal Marines], was stationed. I used to sit with him for coffee probably two or three times a week when he was writing his book *The Red and Green Life Machine*, and lots of bits in his book came from my gob. He once asked me, 'What was the worst or scariest part of the war?'

'Not knowing when endex, end of exercise, was going to be called.' You see, you always had to keep back that pair of dry socks or that bar of Tiffin, or that bag of rolled oats, not to mention ammo or the last ten minutes in the battery to get that last message out, or to play that last track from Jon and Vangelis, 'The Friends of Mr Cairo'. Doc Jolly was a great guy, for a sailor.

Lance Corporal Graham Eve, GPMG commander, 4 Platoon B Company 2 Para

After we took Goose Green, we moved into the sheep-shearing sheds to rest up. So, we're all lying down and in came a few lads from 42 Commando, long after the battle was over, but anyway, one of them sat down next to me and started chatting. I said, 'Yous have to carry any mortar rounds when yous landed?'

'Fuck that,' he says, 'I threw mine over the side of a hill.'

That stuck in my memory to this day, and because of that incident I've had a different perspective of the Marines, as we always had a wee bit of banter with them, give and take, but it never went through my head that any of us in the Airborne would do such a thing. They were Marines and no matter what *we* thought, you did have some respect as they were actually good soldiers, but the mortar round story didn't sit with me at all.

I didn't reply to him. Those two rounds could have saved lives or taken enemy lives, and we actually ran out of mortar rounds attacking Goose Green! But having said all that, I attended the twenty-fifth anniversary of the Falklands War [in London in 2007] and as we, 2 Para, were marching back from the Mall, the Royal Marines were in front of us. Then they broke ranks and formed up both sides of the Mall and clapped us, 2 Para and 3 Para, as we marched through them, and I do take my hat off to them. To me, that was a show of respect for what 2 Para and 3 Para achieved in the war, a recognition, and well done the Paras.

Private John Bolland, Recce Platoon 2 Para

The proudest time of these sixty-six years on this planet was to serve with the 2nd Battalion the Parachute Regiment, and you know there isn't a day goes by when I don't think of the boys who didn't make it back. Hank, wee Chuck Hardman, Steve Prior, Sully, Tam . . . all of 'em.

Private Bob Morgan, Patrols Platoon 2 Para

Some years later I was posted as a full screw [corporal] to Catterick Holding Company, where my old OC in Patrols during the war, Major Roger Jenner, was the Officer Commanding Holding Company. The set-up was half Guards and half Parachute Regiment, so we had a Guards RSM and a Para CO. The CO was overall in charge of the Training Battalion, and as a new posted-in NCO I had to introduce myself to the OC. So I walked into Holding Company lines where I met with the WO2 Guards sergeant major, which was the normal practice, a Grenadier Guard, very smart and rigid, and he marched me into Major Jenner's office.

I really didn't know what to expect, but as protocol dictates, I had to introduce myself in the correct military fashion to the OC, while the Guards sergeant major was standing rigid to attention, watching my every move. That was a throwback to the old Army days, when it wasn't unheard of for some lower ranks to attack their officers, so the WO2 was there to act as the OC's bodyguard.

Well, as I came to attention in front of Roger and saluted, he cried out 'Roberto, Roberto!' and he came forward and embraced me in a big bear hug. This sergeant major, well, he didn't know where to look, and the thing is, he's probably thinking now, how do I deal with this soldier? How do I deal with this corporal who gets on so well with the OC?

I mean I really wasn't expecting Roger's embrace, but I guess it was a sort of friendship forged in combat.

Regimental Sergeant Major Mal Simpson, 2 Para

Before we left for war, I gave a talk to the mess members, as there were some who had left their wives in not too good a place financially, so I said to those who were married to make sure everything was in order. The rear party will look after any difficulties as far as any finances are concerned. There will be get-togethers for your wives and your children, and I ended my talk by saying, 'Whatever happens, you'll all becoming home again.' I didn't say dead or alive, but I meant you will all be coming back.

Because, you should remember, prior to the Falklands War we'd never returned fallen soldiers back to the UK, they have always been buried in the country they fell. I made that promise and I kept to that promise. The Adjutant, Captain David Wood, was killed and it would have been his job, but now I had the responsibility of getting our guys back.

I met Surgeon Commander Rick Jolly, Royal Navy, at Blue Beach along with a CPO [chief petty officer] to identify our dead. Our guys were naked and I had to observe what was going on, because Rick Jolly was making notes of entry and exit wounds and cause of death, and all that sort of stuff, so it had to be accurate. There was nowhere we could adequately keep them, so the decision was made, not by me, that we would temporarily bury them and reinter them later.

I remember asking Rick, 'Please make sure they don't dig the hole too deep.'

'Why?'

'Because they ain't staying here,' I replied, 'I'll make sure they go back, even if I have to come back here with a gang and dig them up and put them on board the boat. They ain't staying here.'

However, when we got into Stanley and victory, I went to see General Moore and I expressed my concerns and then the decision was made. Navy guys were buried at sea, but we would repatriate those whose families who would like their boys repatriated. For those families who wanted their boys to remain, we would make sure there was a suitable place to lay them to rest; a military cemetery that would be looked after by the Commonwealth War Graves Commission. If there is only one promise I can hold my hand up to, it was this one.

Colour Sergeant Frank Pye, Support Company 2 Para

RSM Mal Simpson did a good job on the battlefield. He was where he was supposed to be, doing what he was supposed to be doing, calm and cool. I mean, Colonel Jones hated him, it all really started on the Kenya trip a few months earlier, and normally the RSM is with the CO in battle; so Mal was very lucky, because he could have been with Captains Dave Wood and Chris Dent!

Lance Corporal Jimmy Goodall, Assault Engineers 2 Para

I thought 2 Para RSM Mal Simpson was a bloody hero. He was the right bloke in the position at the right time, was Mal Simpson, and he was great for morale. Certainly great for me, because when I'd got blown up by that artillery round, me boots got burnt, and he actually found me a pair of Argy boots which were so much better than ours. Don't know where he got them from and I didn't ask, ha-ha! I took it some poor Argentinian chap didn't require them any more.

Some weeks later on the way back home, I got into an argument with my sergeant and Mal came to see me and says, 'Corporal Goodall, you're going to jail.'

'Yes, sir,' I says.

Then he says, 'Do you want to be on my side of the counter or the business side of the counter?' And me being a big brave bastard pleaded to be with him on *his* side of the counter. I ended up doing penance on the Provost Staff for two years after that.

Lance Corporal Paul Bishop, 3 Platoon B Company 2 Para

As a young lance corporal in 2 Para, it was a pleasure and honour to serve with what I think was the best rifle company in the British Army, B Company 2nd Battalion the Parachute Regiment; and Major John Crosland was the finest company commander and leader I have served alongside during my eighteen years in the Parachute Regiment. The men of B Company would have followed him all the way to Buenos Aires if we were ordered to.

Private Mark Sleap, Patrols Platoon 2 Para

Captain Pete Adams, (OC Patrols, 2 Para before Colonel Jones sacked him from Patrols shortly before we went down south) was the most professional officer I have ever served with. Mind you, Pete did push it a bit far, though, what with his unpolished jungle boots around camp, ha-ha.

GOOSE GREEN

Sergeant Pilot Dick Kilinski, F Flight 656 Squadron Army Air Corps

Shortly after the battle for Goose Green, we parked our Scouts on the green of Goose Green and the kids there would come running out, and there was one lad called John M, about fourteen, who came over and gazed at the aircraft in total amazement. So I waved him over and said to jump in the pilot's seat and to put my helmet on, then I took a photograph of him.

Then I said, 'I tell you what, you jump in the back seat and I'll take you for a little flight,' so I did. We circled around Goose Green and landed again. This lad was so made up and afterwards I took out my soldier's notebook and wrote in it, 'To John M, I hope you enjoyed your flight from the crew of X-ray Zulu Six Five Six,' my aircraft call sign. Then I ripped it out and gave it to him.

In 2012, the Falklands thirtieth anniversary, I went back down there, and this lad is now the chief engineer for Bristow Helicopters in Stanley and when we met, he opened up his wallet and pulled out the same piece of paper I wrote to him thirty years before.

Colour Sergeant Pete Vale, HQ Company 2 Para

I was a thirty-two-year-old colour sergeant when I went down the Falklands and that was quite old. I was a Tom for five years, yet I should have been a corporal in two, but early on in my soldiering career I unfortunately started my regimental conduct sheet. The first entry was dated 13 June 1966. The charge read: *Striking his superior officer contrary to Section 33 1a at Paradise Camp Sabah, Borneo when on active service.*

You see, we had a bully in the ranks and he'd already been warned a couple of times, but he kept on, so I dealt with it. When the CO sentenced me, he said he couldn't let me off, and awarded me seven days' field punishment. I lost those days' wages too and I'd

382

just come back from Malaya where I'd done the Lead Scouts course, so they couldn't afford to lose me.

In those days us Toms, or Nicks as we used to be called, were never encouraged to map read. I was lucky because this SAS guy, Sandy Powell, who was finishing his time, took me and a lad called Jimmy Rag under his wing; and we were always fit, always out running. He used to take us up in the mountains and taught us navigation in the jungle: pacing, time and distance, river flows, and all that: if you make a thousand yards in a day you'll be doing really well. All that extra knowledge I gained, I'm sure it made me make better decisions than bad ones during the battle for Goose Green.

Brian Lavender, radio officer, MV Norland

I found it really interesting working with the Royal Navy, the Army and all the rest of 'em, because it was a big eye-opener for us crew. I'd sailed up the Dong Nai River while working for Shell during the Vietnam War. Well, the Americans flew the Phantom and the Skyhawk in that war, and when the Vietnam War was over, the Americans sold all their Skyhawks to Argentina.

So I was left wondering, as I was taking cover on the decks of the *Norland* when Argentinian Skyhawks missiles came in, showering the ships with shrapnel and almost knocking out the aft end of my ship, whether any of them ever flew in Vietnam. One time I'm being protected by them and the next, being bombed by them! I often think about that.

Private Ian Winnard, 4 Platoon B Company 2 Para

Looking back at it now, and I've always found this strange, although we were B Company and I were in 4 Platoon, in one of three sections, we were completely different families; three sections to a platoon and three platoons to a company, and you wouldn't really know any others from outside your own platoon. You certainly wouldn't know any blokes from A, C, or D Companies, unless you came through Depot with them or had attended the same course somewhere. That's weird, but that's the way it works out.

I've got friends on Facebook who were in 466 Platoon, the platoon I came through Depot with, and one of them keeps putting up photos of old faces saying, 'Remember this one, or this one?' but I've not got a clue. I don't know who they are, but when they turn up to the reunions, the memory all starts coming back.

Sergeant John 'Taff' Meredith DCM, 12 Platoon D Company 2 Para

During the white flag incident, one of my lads, Private Carter, had this skid mark made by a bullet right across the back of his helmet like nobody's business, So I asked how he's got it, and he replied, 'I wasn't running away, honestly. I just turned around to see if you were still with us, then BANG, something hit me.'

Private John Bolland, Recce Platoon 2 Para

Jock the Waff [Pte, Rear Party 2 Para] was caught getting free drinks up at 9 Squadron bar in Aldershot, telling everyone how he won the Falklands; the bastard was never there, but he's still one of us.

Staff Sergeant Pete Harburn, PT Corps 2 Para's Physical Training Instructor

You know what? I've had thirty-seven years of this, right! I go to the PT Corps conventions, and I get the piss taken out of me all the time, saying, 'Some bodyguard you are!' Colonel H Jones and all that, or, 'Hey, it's Staff Harburn, Colonel H Jones's bodyguard.'

And I say in my defence, 'I was Chris Keeble's bodyguard, and *he's* still alive and kicking.' British Army humour can wear a bit thin after thirty-seven years!

Lance Corporal Graham Eve, 4 GPMG commander Platoon B Company 2 Para

The history books say that 600 paratroopers attacked Goose Green, but you want to know something? As a fighting man on the ground, only two and a half companies actually went forward. That's about 250 Paras, albeit supported by the rest of the battalion, and that's before you start to add up the body count and wounded.

Captain Paul Farrar, OC Patrols Platoon 2 Para

I was delighted to be in 2 Para and it was a great job. Although I'd asked to go to 3 Para for a variety of reasons, 2 Para certainly came up trumps, but even if I'd stayed in 3 Para, I'd have gone with them to the Falklands. However, I would have been like a spare officer looking after the press, or assistant ops officer or something, so actually I was glad in a personal way to be back into a front-line role. A complete twist of fate, and to this day those three years I served in Patrols, C (Bruneval) Company, 2 Para, first as Patrols commander and then as the OC, were amongst the best three years of my regimental service.

Roy 'Wendy' Gibson, steward and ship's pianist, MV Norland

After the war I went down to Aldershot by train. P&O paid for me ticket, they paid for me hotel too, for a reunion at the Paras' Browning Barracks. They got a beautiful piano for me to play. I met the comedian Jim Davidson and I got presented to Margaret

Thatcher. I shook hands with her and I said, 'Pleased to meet you, Mrs Thatcher. I'm Merchant Navy, MV *Norland* crew in the Falklands.'

'Yes, I know, I've heard so much about you.' I shook hands, and with her husband too, the man with the glasses, Denis. The buffet was in a big marquee, but it pissed down with rain so it all got transferred into the Mess, and of a night time I played the piano and I met Denzil Connick from 3 Para too, he had his leg blown off in the Falklands War.

Corporal Lonnie Donoghue, 10 Field Workshop REME (Parachute Detachment)

I joined the Army on 6 August 1974 and ten days later I got on a train at Birmingham and sat opposite a bloke and asked him, 'Where you going, mate?'

'I'm off to Aldershot to join the Paras.'

'So am I,' I says. So, we went through Depot with 408 Platoon and I joined 1 Platoon A Company 2 Para, and my first army pal joined 3 Platoon. In 1977 I transferred out to the REME (Royal Electrical Mechanical Engineers) hoping to come back into 16 Independent Airborne Brigade, but that didn't happen because 16 Independent Airborne Brigade got disbanded. So I did two years in Germany, then came back into the Airborne REME role under the newly formed 5 Airborne Brigade attached 3 Para – 3 Field Workshop Para Detachment.

On my birthday, the second of April was also the day the Falklands War started, and my unit's name was changed to 10 Field Workshop and we became the Parachute Workshop Detachment. Primarily I was FRT (Forward Repair Team) commander for 2 Para. That means when 2 Para deployed, I deployed with them as their second-line support, to do things like clear the DZ when a heavy drop came in, provide engineering support with welding facilities, heavy spares for vehicles, engines and gearboxes alike, and we would change them in the field. The armourer came under our role as well.

We were supposed to deploy with 2 Para, but there was a bit of a row going on with Brigadier Tony Wilson, the brigadier in charge of 5 Brigade. We had been with 2 Para and had deployed with them to Kenya just a few months earlier, so we were destined to go down south for sure, because, and this was just by chance, I bumped in to Colonel H outside Nanyuki Post Office, in Kenya.

He stopped me and Mal Reid, who was our welder and ex-1 Para, as we were walking across the grass. When he saw us, he came across and asked us all the questions; what were we doing and all that, and he was sort of fitting us mentally into his battalion orbat [order of battle], but from my OC, the story goes like this. When 2 Para got the Warning Order to sail, we were all ready to go, but Brigadier Wilson said, 'No! you are to stay back and form another brigade if necessary.' So, we ended up sailing down on the *QE2* (the *Queen Elizabeth 2* luxury cruise liner) under 5 Infantry Brigade.

I made it ashore two days after the battle for Goose Green on 31 May and immediately set up the radio workshop at San Carlos Bay and manned three radios: Brigade Maintenance Area Red Beach, Brigade Maintenance Area Blue Beach, and Brigade Administration Area; and we also monitored the FEBA (forward edge of the battle area/HMS *Fearless*) radio.

What does that mean? Well, one of our jobs was to get all the ammo forward. I'd get an ammo request, say for 105s or 762 or 762 link or whatever, then I would send that through to *Fearless*, who would dispatch a Sea King that would come in and pick up the ammo, and we'd then give the pilot a grid where to drop it off. So, all your ammunition came through us. Anyway, following the battle for Goose Green, naturally we were all a bit subdued. It was now 2nd June and being ex-2 Para, we still didn't know who were the Goose Green casualties. Our Workshop Company sergeant major, Jack 'Geordie' Smith, had been a sergeant in A Coy, 2 Para as well.

One time I was mauling about, having just finished an eight-hour radio stag, trying to get the white noise out of my head and chill, so I decided to go around to see the armourer for a brew and a chat. When I arrived, he was busy with stuff, and I says, 'What you doing there, Joe?'

'Oh,' he says, 'I'm making up the nameplates; plates for the Goose Green dead. Here, have a look, you might know some?'

They were small with the details of the fallen soldier. He handed me the plates and I went through them one by one, like I was checking through a pack of cards. Yeah, I know him! I know him, and then I instantly recognised the regimental number 24353770, because mine is 24353761 and I knew who it belonged to! It was Sully's, the boy who I'd met on the train at Birmingham all those years ago, my first ever army pal! But I didn't have to see his name to know it was Sully, only his number. He was just nine numbers behind me in joining up.

I had to sit down; that was a kick in the balls, to be honest. I'd last spoken to Sully in June 1981 at Depot Para. He was drilling some junior Paras on the parade square as I was passing on my way to Ash Ranges training for the South East District Skill at Arms competition, so I pulled over. He saw me and came over for a chat. We were both corporals now, and he said, 'I'm going back up to Battalion and then we're off to Kenya.' I told him I was going to Kenya too, so we'd arranged to grab a beer over there; but it didn't happen, because I was attached to mortars for the whole exercise and he was posted to D Company and time, well, it just ran out.

REFLECTIONS

Private Mark Sleap, Patrols Platoon 2 Para

I remember just before we set sail, me and Dennis [Private Wheatley, Patrols Platoon] were in the Gorge café, Aldershot, a place made out to look like a cave. I mean, the place was painted all over in grotty Tango orange, and they did this thick white toast with butter on, proper bread; and when we were down south, that's all we longed for, fucking thick toast from the Gorge café! And we had been issued these Ho Chi Minh suits, sort of quilted jacket and quilted trousers and we would have frozen to death if we didn't have them and those Yogi Bear hats.

Lance Corporal 'Duke' Allen, Defence Platoon 2 Para

I remember those stupid ski boots we were issued. I threw them away, and guess what I wore? Yep, my fucking Northern Ireland boots! But big, big mistake, because that evening on Darwin Hill, I hate having cold feet – I can't stand it – so I was standing in the burning gorse all the time. So what happened? The boots fucking melted, and I ended up with no fucking grip on me soles, and you know that flowery pattern under the tread which comes off the rubber? Well, I had that instead, so when it got icy, which it did, a few hours later after the surrender, I was on me arse more than me feet – terrible.

Chief Petty Officer Rich Edwards, Special Communications Unit (SCU) Royal Navy

I picked a stamp collection up out of an Argy trench. Obviously, the last inhabitant had stolen one of the Goose Green islander's stamp collection. Strangely, the new owner had written on the front of them, *Sellos* (Spanish for postage stamps). When I make my journey back to the Falkland Islands, I'd like to go and return this collection.

Roy 'Wendy' Gibson, steward and ship's pianist, MV Norland

I was twenty-seven at the time of Goose Green and when I got home, I was twenty-eight. On board it was self-service as you know, and I used to collect the food and the dirty plates and clear the tables. I used to talk to this lad and he was real nice to talk to, and his mates on a table of four, and he was one of the lads who didn't come back. I was upset about that.

Colour Sergeant Pete Vale, HQ Company 2 Para

On the *Norland* we were given a brief by this RAF Regiment guy who was a qualified Arctic and Mountain Warfare leader; like, by now, we didn't realise it was going to be cold, and he had the laser rangefinder, which was a dead new bit of kit back then. He was the expert on it, and his main job was to bring in the Harrier strikes. I was looking at him, because you know with the RAF, you can serve up to almost your retirement age, and this guy was fifty-odd, and I'm thinking, he's just not fit.

Anyway, we were tabbing up Sussex Mountains and he was in front of me and then I overtook him and he looked down and out, knackered, and that's when he had to be casevaced. I remember him saying, 'Don't take my laser, I signed for that. It's coming back with me!' The rangefinder was a G10 [officially issued] piece of kit and you could get court-martialled if you lost it, so he wasn't gonna give it up lightly, but he was persuaded to, ha-ha. That was the last I saw of him [probably casevac no. 3]. He never came back.

The one good piece of advice he did give us, though, was to put our gloves on strings and tie them through our sleeves. He said, 'You can't be without gloves in an extreme cold climate.' I mean, we didn't do it, yet when I look back now, I think, yeah, he had a point, because when we'd finished fighting, Goose Green was littered with single gloves. Not because we lost them, it was because we only took them off when they melted through when we warmed them over our Hexi fires. I reckon these issue gloves were about ten per cent cotton, ninety per cent nylon, ha-ha!

Lance Corporal Bill 'Basha' Bentley MM, Combat Medical Team 2 Para

Major Keeble's plan/bluff had worked. I don't care what others might say, but I can tell you, if it were not for Major Keeble the battle could so easily have been lost. God bless you, Chris, you have my undying respect. It was your plan and not that of the fallen Lieutenant Colonel Jones that saved the Parachute Regiment from its greatest disaster since Arnhem, and you turned it into a victory that will be hard to surpass. If a plan works, it was the right plan on the day.

Private Pete O'Hare, 480 Platoon Depot Para

I was a recruit in Depot Para when the very first TV documentary called *The Paras* was filmed back in 1982 and subsequently released in 1983.

I'd just passed P Company when the Falklands War kicked off. Then the next thing I saw was 3 Para sailing down south followed quickly by 2 Para, but as we were due to go to Brize Norton to get our wings up, there was a rumour going around saying my training platoon was going straight to the Falklands to jump in on the war as reinforcements. That way, we wouldn't have to do the mandatory eight jumps to qualify for our wings!

We all wanted to go – I mean, operational wings straight away would be something! That would have made our day, that, but it wasn't to be, so after Brize my platoon, 480 Platoon, those who'd passed out, ended up going straight to Fermanagh, Northern Ireland, on a rural tour of Bandit Country with 1 Para: fucking bored stiff.

It was a terrible tour, of course, what with reading in the papers everyday about 2 and 3 Para, about what you were all getting up to.

After you guys came back as war heroes, we were posted to our battalions. I was designated 2 Para. It's bad enough being a *crow* in Battalion, but imagine being a crow and being on the telly as well? It's ten times worse.

So, of course, I've joined 2 Para and you're all war heroes and the next thing I know I'm on the telly on *The Paras* programme, and I failed P Company the first time, so I had to do it again. If I'd have passed first time, I wouldn't have been on TV and that would have made my life a lot easier, ha-ha. The blokes in the battalion actually turned out to be great, you were just all on the piss all the time, understandably.

I was posted to A Company and I do remember my second or third night in the block, there was this little signaller, turned out to be a nice guy, but he'd been out on the piss and I'd been pressing me kit, as you do as a crow. I remember waking up when he came in and he started to walk round pissing everywhere, and my pressed kit was laid out very neatly on a chair and he's pissing all over my kit. Of course, I'm shit scared to say anything to him; he's a war hero and all that, but I thought, *fuck off, you cunt!*

He eventually got in his bed and fell asleep, then I went back to kip as well. Yes, it was an experience joining the battalion after you'd returned from war, but I will say, I've been watching the recent programme about P Company on YouTube and it seems to be just as hard as in our days, which is a good thing.

Corporal Douglas McCready, 1 Section commander, Machine Gun Platoon 2 Para

I don't remember seeing any Royal Marines in Goose Green, no! No fucking Royal Marines anywhere.

Colour Sergeant Frank Pye, Support Company 2 Para

Did you know, 2 Para was the only regiment to have fought in the Falklands War not to have been awarded a non-gallantry medal? We didn't get one BEM [British Empire Medal] or one MBE [Member of the British Empire]! 3 Para only got one MBE, but 2 Para didn't get a single thing. These types of medals are generally awarded to those in the echelons as a job well done, because without the ammo, medical supplies and stores getting through to the front-line troops as it did, there may not have been a victory at Goose Green.

I'm not sure what the real reason for that was, but I did hear they were all written up over one night in Stanley, and 2 Para put in for seventy-odd medals and only forty-odd were given. A lot of our MiDs [Mentions in Despatches – generally given for a job well done] were MMs [Military Medal, now replaced by the Military Cross], because the awards were dropped down a level, don't ask me why! But I suspect it was just a numbers game.

Private Irwin Eversley, GPMG gunner, 2 Platoon A Company 2 Para

Later on, I was told I didn't have to get off the *Norland* and didn't have to fight because I didn't have a passport, I wasn't a proper legal resident of the UK, but they wouldn't have stopped me getting off the boat and fighting with my mates. I wouldn't have missed what we achieved at Goose Green for anything.

Captain Paul Farrar, OC Patrols Platoon 2 Para

I had a soldier called Dennis in Patrols. Dennis was a strange guy. He was one of these guys, pre-Falklands, in that sort of phoney-war period, who had been on a charge for biting someone's ear off, and I was his Defending Officer at his court-martial. Now,

Dennis was quite a well-educated bloke; quite well-off parents, professional types, and he went to a good school; but he was the *big man*. He liked to play the hard man and had this persona that he was *the man*!

In truth, I don't think he was that brave, but in the Falklands, he had to live up to his persona when things got a bit gritty. I really didn't see that much of him because he was in a different patrol, other than when he came up to me in Goose Green just after the battle and said, 'Sir, you know if you conduct a parachute descent on operations against the enemy, then that entitles you to wear the parachute wings, yes?'

Which is true, if you are say, for example, some non-Para trained signaller on a mission gets thrown out of a plane conducting a parachute descent against the enemy, you're entitled to your wings. It's in Queen's Regulations. So, I says, 'Yes, I know that.'

Well, he says, 'Because we've done an assault beach landing, can we have a commando dagger?'

To which I answered, 'Why the fuck do you want a commando dagger?'

'No! No, hell no! I don't want one, I just want the opportunity to refuse one!' he replied.

EPILOGUE

Nigel Ely: During the two-year tour of Northern Ireland that 2 Para conducted prior to the Falklands War, I was jailed for twenty-eight days for fighting, so as a consequence I was taken off the Drill and Duties cadre to promote me to lance corporal by my OC, the now-retired General Sir Mike Jackson. And praise to him, because he stopped me from getting a court-martial.

The fact was, at that time in my life I was not mature enough to handle responsibility, or indeed lead soldiers into battle. I couldn't see the need for all this marching around; all this *drill* and *duty* bullshit. That is probably why, a year later, I passed the physically brutal cadre into the battalion's Pathfinders C (Bruneval) Company, where the hard old sweats and no-nonsense characters hung out. Basically, it was where we did our own thing under the protective eye of Colonel H Jones, because training, fitness and tactics were so much more important. Yet Goose Green taught me I could lead. Passing SAS Selection confirmed that.

I can still hear my grandfather saying he'll never buy a Japanese car because of the way they treated our POWs so cruelly, but then he went out and purchased a Volkswagen! And when people ask me what I think about the Argentinians, and do I forgive them and welcome reconciliation? My reply is quite simply, no, I am just not ready; but please do ask your question to the people of the Falkland Islands. Having said that, I did support Argentina against France in the recent finals of the Rugby World Cup. Maybe it's only a matter of time before the scars of war heal.

I recently returned to Goose Green. It has not changed much since 1982, but there is a café there now to welcome returning veterans and tourists. Many tourists, American and Japanese on cruise ships, stop off at the islands in vast numbers to enjoy the wildlife and, of course, the penguin colony. It is a great source of revenue for the Falkland Islanders. Many of these tourists also take in the Goose Green battlefield tour.

In the café, the walls are adorned with the memories of 28 and 29 May 1982, in particular, Parachute Regiment paraphernalia. The place was busy, not just with returning veteran paratroopers and tourists, but with veterans from across the armed forces – Army, Air Force, Navy and Merchant Navy – after all, it was an all-arms effort that won the battle for Goose Green, not just 2 Para.

Back home, living as I do in a rural community in deepest Herefordshire, I understand the privacy enjoyed by farming folk, so I was curious as to what the locals thought of this steady stream of visitors upsetting the daily running of their farms. I asked if they ever get tired of old Paras coming and disturbing their way of life?

The reply was, 'No! No! Not one bit. You will always be welcome, and when your children come, our children will look after them, and when their children come, ours will do the same.'

GLOSSARY

105 – 105mm field howitzer, or ammunition for it

2IC – Second-in-command

50 cal – .50-inch heavy machine gin

66 – Disposable, one shot only, shoulder-fired anti-tank rocket
  launcher

762 – 7.62mm ammunition (rifle and machine gun)

84 – Shoulder-fired anti-tank recoilless rifle, known as the Carl
  Gustaf

Atlantic Conveyor – A roll-on, roll-off Merchant Navy container ship

Basha – Makeshift shelter

Belgrano – The ARA *General Belgrano*; a light cruiser

Bergen – Large Army-issue rucksack

Bootneck – Slang for a Royal Marine

Blue-on-blue – Friendly forces accidentally attacking each other

Cabbage hat – Slang for a Royal Marine, also cabbage head, because
  of their green beret

Casevac – Evacuate a battlefield casualty

CO – Commanding officer

Colour – Parachute Regiment term for a staff sergeant; *also* colour man

CP – Command post

Cpl – Corporal

Crap hat – Para vernacular. A derogatory term for any soldier who does not wear the maroon beret; the SAS, who wear a sand-coloured beret, are termed 'hats light'

Crow – A new recruit or inexperienced soldier

DCM – Distinguished Conduct Medal. The oldest British gallantry award, awarded to other ranks and ranked second below the Victoria Cross; replaced by the Conspicuous Gallantry Cross

DF – Direct fire. A pre-plotted position. (Also direction-finding)

DFC – Distinguished Flying Cross

Dhobi – Slang for a wash

DMS – Direct moulded sole. The standard British Army-issue boot

DS – Directing Staff

DZ – Drop zone

Endex – End of exercise

Fragged – wounded, especially by shrapnel. Originally from fragmentation grenade

Full screw – Corporal

Gimpy – General purpose machine gun (see next)

GPMG – General purpose machine gun; belt-fed 7.62mm air-cooled machine gun

Hats – Para vernacular: a derogatory term for any soldier who does not wear the maroon beret

HE – High explosive

Illumes – Illuminating flares

Int – Intelligence/Intelligence Corps

IWS – individual weapon sight, an infrared night sight or image intensifier

JC – Major John Crosland, MC, OC B Company 2 Para

Kelper – informal term for a Falkland Islander, from the kelp that surrounds the islands

L/Cpl – Lance corporal

LCU – Landing craft, utility

Link – Belt of 7.62mm ammunition for the GPMG

LMG – Light machine gun; this was the updated L4 Bren gun

LVTP-7 – Assault amphibious vehicle. Tracked vehicle that can carry up to 18 troops and 3 crew

M79 – Single-shot, shoulder-fired grenade launcher

MC – Military Cross

MiD – Mentioned in Despatches

Milan – Wire-guided anti-tank missile

MM – Military Medal, gallantry award for other ranks, now replaced by the Military Cross, which was formerly only for commissioned ranks

MT – Motor transport

NATO – North Atlantic Treaty Organisation

NCO – Non-commissioned officer

NI – Northern Ireland

NVG – Night-vision goggles

O group – Formal orders brief

OC – Officer commanding

OP – Observation post

Pinky – SAS armed-up Land Rover, nicknamed the Pink Panther

Pte – Private soldier

PTI – Physical training instructor

PTSD – Post-traumatic stress disorder

QM – Quartermaster

RAP – Regimental aid post

REME – (Corps of) Royal Electrical and Mechanical Engineers

RFA – Royal Fleet Auxiliary

RIP – Rest in peace (from Latin *requiescat in pace*, 'May he or she rest in peace')

RQMS – Regimental quartermaster sergeant

RSM – Regimental sergeant major

RV – Rendezvous

SAS – Special Air Service Regiment

SBS – Special Boat Service, the maritime equivalent of the SAS

SF – Special Forces *or* sustained fire

Sheffield, HMS – A Type 42 guided-missile destroyer

Sgt – Sergeant

SLR – Self-loading rifle. Designated the L1A1 in the British Army, it was a semi-automatic version of the Argentine FN FAL rifle, which was fully automatic; both were 7.62mm calibre

SMG – Submachine gun

Snowcat – Volvo BV 202, a tracked all-terrain vehicle consisting of a forward cab and a linked trailer, capable of carrying up to eight fully equipped troops

SOP – Standard operating procedure

SPW – Spare parts wallet

Stag/stag-on – Guard duty *or* to guard

Stick – A line of paratroopers preparing to jump

Stinger – Shoulder-fired anti-aircraft missile launcher

TAB *or* tab – Tactical advance to battle *or* move fast with full kit

Tabbing – Para vernacular for moving fast with full kit

They – The powers-that-be, the head-sheds, the chiefs, the top brass

Tom – Regimental slang for a private soldier of the Parachute Regiment

Triple A – Anti-aircraft artillery

u/s – unserviceable

VC – Victoria Cross. The UK's highest award for gallantry 'in the presence of the enemy'

WOCS – War Office controlled stores

ACKNOWLEDGEMENTS

I am deeply indebted to such a large number of people: those 114 veterans who had to endure my interviewing techniques and the abrupt manner in which I may have carried them out. Sorry if my style came across a bit like a 'Resistance to Interrogation'.

To my daughter Morgan, for her unwavering patience, and for possessing such stellar drive and belief in *Goose Green* from conception to end. I thank her so much.

To Dave 'Charlie' Brown, my wingman as we travelled across this great nation of ours meeting the warfighters of Goose Green.

To my first and second mentors in the art of soldiering, Marty Margerison and Ken Raynor. Marty first, because so very early on in my military career he taught me to *'stay switched on'*, which undoubtedy saved my life through several decades of fighting and covering wars. And Ken, who taught me not to be so impatient to close with the enemy, and to laugh in the face of adversity – and get a brew on. Both have very different leadership styles, and both styles work, while both have been so inspirational, although they probably didn't know it back then.

Finally, I must say a massive thank you to the team at John Blake Publishing and Bonnier Books UK, and in particular Toby Buchan for his steadfast guidance, warm nudges of advice, and the charming manner in which he always gave it.

INDEX

403

INDEX

INDEX